Cool Characters

Cool Characters

Irony and American Fiction

LEE KONSTANTINOU

Harvard University Press

Cambridge, Massachusetts
London, England
2016

First printing

Library of Congress Cataloging-in-Publication Data
Konstantinou, Lee, author.
    Cool characters : irony and American fiction / Lee Konstantinou.
        pages cm
    Includes bibliographical references and index.
    ISBN 978-0-674-96788-5
1. Irony—Political aspects—United States—History.   2. Counterculture—
United States—History.   3. Irony in literature.   4. Politics and culture—United
States—History.   5. Postmodernism (Literature)   6. Irony.   I. Title.
    BH301.I7K66 2016
    813'.540918—dc23

                                                                    2015033860

Dedicated to Julie, and I mean it

Contents

Preface

I FIRST READ *Infinite Jest* (1996) in the Year of the Perdue Wonder-chicken while I was a graduate student in the English Department at Stanford University.[1] A partisan of difficult fiction, a fan of the encyclopedic tradition, I hoped that David Foster Wallace would give me more of the experimental fix I craved, but Wallace's wrist-straining novel did not deliver what I thought I wanted. Instead, it sought to cure me of my addiction to postmodern fiction. The novel valorized the "[i]rony-free zone" of Alcoholics Anonymous (*IJ* 369). Attacking "jaded irony" and "weary cynicism," Wallace seemed instead to celebrate "gooey sentiment" and "unsophisticated naïveté" (*IJ* 694). And in his essay "E Unibus Pluram: Television and U.S. Fiction," Wallace more broadly attacked the literary legacy of post-modernism. "The next real literary 'rebels' in this country," he wrote, "might well emerge as some weird bunch of anti-rebels, born oglers who dare somehow to back away from ironic watching, who have the childish gall actually to endorse and instantiate single-entendre principles."[2] In this frequently quoted passage, Wallace declares his hope for a better, postironic literary future, but he fails to describe this new world in any detail and does not suggest a means for getting there. Moreover, the antirebel who might have the power to tran-scend postmodern irony is here only thinly sketched. Wallace's diffi-culty in imagining what specific form an alternative to irony might take gives evidence of the wider failure of imagination that char-acterized his time. After all, the American 1990s was self-consciously a moment of historical stasis. At the end of the Cold War, Margaret Thatcher's dictum that "there is no alternative" to capitalism (the so-called TINA doctrine) threatened to become an ineluctable political fact. Postmodern consumerism, it seemed, might rule the globe forever. For some, it allegedly became "easier to imagine the end of the world than to imagine the end of capitalism."[3] Wallace did his level best to imagine a world beyond cynical postmodern consumerism. Nonetheless, *Infinite Jest* figures the end of capitalism as something very much like the end of the world. Market-cultivated cynical reason might, Wallace suggests, simply self-destruct, taking much of humanity with it. But something bothered me about *Infinite Jest*'s political prophecy beyond its apparent pessimism. Wallace's dystopian future was, I felt, astonishing, hilarious, and alarming, but also finally unconvincing. The near future of the novel looked rather different from the 2005 I inhabited. In Wallace's Year of the Perdue Wonderchicken, postmodern irony (imagined as the literal infinite jest of addictive entertainment) threatened to strangle the world. As I read *Infinite Jest* at 3 A.M. in Happy Donuts in Palo Alto, California, a few weeks after George W. Bush was sworn into office for his second term, I could not help but recall that postmodern irony was said to have died on or around September 11, 2001. Irony's end was "the one good thing" that might "come from this horror," according to Roger Rosenblatt in *Time* magazine.[4] Calling for an end to irony no longer seemed to voice hopes for a better future but instead threatened to participate in the project of arresting critical intelligence at a time of global crisis.

The gap between the fictive Year of the Perdue Wonderchicken and the 2005 I inhabited persuaded me, in a way that no critical analysis could, that the concept of postmodernism no longer adequately described the present. Postmodernism was being supplanted by something different, and Wallace, no less than Rosenblatt or Bush (or I), partook of that broader change. Perhaps the postirony that Wallace desired had not failed but was instead becoming dominant. A culture that celebrated Dave Eggers's *McSweeney's Quarterly Concern* did not, it seemed to me, live in an age of infinite jest but rather of *Infinite Jest*. Though the emerging contemporary era did not yet have a convincing name, its core characteristics were already becoming salient. Any account of our post-postmodern moment, I decided, would have to make sense of the increasingly troubled relationship many prominent artists, critics, and philosophers seemed to have with irony. I grew obsessed with irony and quickly discovered that impassioned analyses of irony are almost as old as the written record of philosophy itself. It is tempting to argue that little has changed since Plato had Alcibiades describe Socrates's life in the *Symposium* as "one big game—a game of irony."[5] Indeed, contemporary scholars often still feel the need to defend the tradition of Socratic irony. So the first problem faced by anyone who wants to write about irony is how to do justice to its centrifugal energy. I did not want to write yet another defense of irony (Socrates did it! You should too!). Nor did I want to join the effort to overturn irony's alleged hegemony. I was, instead, fascinated with *why* irony had become a flashpoint for recent cultural and political debates. Whether irony is an example of infinite jest or, as Søren Kierkegaard wrote, "infinite absolute negativity," it arouses surprising passions. We may bristle at bad metaphors, but few of us would claim to live in an age of metaphor or profess to hate metaphor as such. Likewise, no one is particularly eager to witness the death of zeugma. Of the four master tropes that Kenneth Burke enumerated—metaphor, metonymy, synecdoche, and irony—only irony draws blood.

This book argues that irony cuts to our core because it is more than a trope or a figure. Irony is also, as the dissident intellectual Randolph Bourne put it in a 1913 *Atlantic Monthly* essay, a life, a specific (often oppositional and critical) way of being in and interpreting the world. Scholars of ancient philosophy have, likewise, shown that irony was part of a regime of "spiritual exercises" (Pierre Hadot) or an "art of living" (Alexander Nehamas). At the most general level, the ethos of irony is a dialectical model of mental or moral character that invites us to seek disjunctions, contradictions, or mismatches within what we (or our interlocutors) most cherish. And though the attitude of irony does not have any necessary political content—it is not inherently liberal, radical, or conservative—it is inescapably connected to political life because it forms, dissolves, and governs communities and informs action. The pages that follow show that American political debates about irony, from Village Bohemianism to the Occupy movement, have invoked irony in specifically characterological terms. I therefore analyze recent defenses and critiques of irony through intensive case studies of character types that have significant relationships to irony: the hipster, the punk, the believer, the coolhunter, and the occupier. These characterological models are not uncontested systems for living. There is, as any good punk will tell you, no one correct way to be a punk. Nor are these types easily reducible to the lived practices of empirical subcultural communities. *The punk* is never simply identical to what self-professed punks do, though self-professed punks have engaged in critically sophisticated characterological self-theorizations. Rather, my chapters interpret historically prominent debates involving a range of actors who attempted to imagine normative models of individual and collective life that incorporate or reject irony. I show that fiction is one of the key sites for the articulation and consolidation of such characterological models. When taken together, these character studies also tell a larger story, demonstrating a shift in U.S. literature, politics, and culture from countercultural irony through postmodern irony to contemporary postirony.

The contest over the significance of these character types is ongoing. With his suicide on September 12, 2008, at the age of 46, Wallace's claims about irony have come under increasing scrutiny. No fewer than six anthologies dedicated to Wallace's writing (one of which I coedited) have seen print as of this writing. In the pages that follow, I try to contribute to this lively critical enterprise not only by analyzing Wallace's writing (and the writing of those he influenced) but also by rereading the literary tradition he loved and labored to overcome. What my analysis will show is that Wallace misread the political history of irony. First, he wrongly assumed, as many still do, that irony had an unambiguously critical mission at midcentury. Instead, I contend in my chapter on the hipster that irony offered a vision of political freedom troublingly imbricated with Cold War liberalism. Second, Wallace's account of irony's co-optation was based, I argue in my chapter on the punk, on a misunderstanding of the relationship between capitalism and oppositional subcultures. Third, in my chapters on the believer and the coolhunter, I suggest that Wallace failed to see how his desire to move beyond irony might inadvertently serve the political economic order that he sought, in other ways, to resist. In short, irony's significance has radically transformed over the last sixty years. Indeed, the political meaning of irony has sometimes seemed to shift even as I have been writing these pages. Nonetheless, the life of irony may, if properly understood, have more to offer today, at our postironic moment, than it did during the immediate post-WWII period. What may matter most, I conclude in my discussion of the Occupy movement and the figure of the occupier, is not whether we live lives of irony but rather where we target our irony and how our ironic attitudes inform a larger sense of political mission.

Cool Characters

Introduction

THE CHARACTER OF IRONY

In a 2007 essay published in two parts in *The Guardian*, Zadie Smith reflects wistfully on the plight of novelists "who came of age under postmodernity" and who have become "naturally sceptical of the concept of authenticity." This, she claims, is her own plight. Despite their ingrained skepticism, writers of Smith's generation supposedly find themselves confronting a hard truth, "the fact that when we account for our failings . . . the feeling that is strongest is a betrayal of one's deepest, authentic self." Such failings lay bare that "what appear to be bad aesthetic choices very often have an ethical dimension." On this view, the success or failure of literary style discloses something essential about the integrity of the novelist's character. Style is "a personal necessity," "the only possible expression of a particular human consciousness."[1] Fashionable academic and critical orthodoxies notwithstanding, "[s]tyle is a writer's way of telling the truth. Literary success or failure, by this measure, depends not only on the refinement of words on a page, but in the refinement of a consciousness, what Aristotle called the education of the emotions." Novelists have "only one duty": "to express accurately their way of being in the world." Smith contrasts her own supposedly "unfashionable" view that there is an ineluctable "connection between personality and prose" with those passages of "Tradition and the Individual Talent" (1919) where T. S. Eliot asserts that "[t]he progress of an artist is a continual self-sacrifice, a continual extinction of

1

personality."[2] She also criticizes unreflective readers who are "armed with the reading systems for which they paid good money in college," such as "the post-colonial, the gendered, the postmodern, the state-of-the-nation" systems of interpretation. Readers who rely on reading systems want novels to be a "view from nowhere," but the truth is that good novels "know" that life is always a "view from somewhere." She finally lambasts the narrow-minded figure of the "corrective critic"—she likely has James Wood in mind—who recasts his "own failure of imagination as a principle of aesthetics." Writer-critics should, instead, treat criticism as a "non-cynical truth-seeking exercise."

In this short, dense essay, Smith attacks a startling array of targets, grouping together very different critical concepts and intellectual projects. Modernist impersonality, postmodernist skepticism, postcolonial interpretative values, poststructuralist claims about the death of the author, and contemporary journalistic reviewing culture all come to seem like forms of cynicism. Her equation of these heterogeneous projects, and her advocacy of "unfashionable" alternatives such as authenticity, character, emotional education, ethics, and "non-cynical truth-seeking," invite symptomatic interpretation. Smith here seems to join the larger reaction against the alleged hegemony of theory.[3] This interpretation of her essay might be especially tempting after we read Smith's 2005 novel, *On Beauty*, which rewrites E. M. Forster's *Howards End* (1910) as an academic satire largely set in a fictional American university town. This novel meditates, in a barely allegorical fashion, on the question of who will inherit the estate of the liberal arts. At the start of the novel, Howard Belsey, an untenured poststructuralist Rembrandt scholar, is losing a war for his son's affections to the pompous neoconservative Rembrandt scholar and public intellectual Monty Kipps. Howard's son Jerome "had liked to listen to the exotic . . . chatter of business and money and practical politics; to hear that Equality was a myth, and Multiculturalism a fatuous dream; he thrilled at the suggestion that Art was a gift from God, blessing only a handful of masters, and most Literature merely a veil for poorly reasoned left-wing ideologies."[4] Smith clearly means to poke fun at Jerome's neoconservative conversion. And yet her satire is also uneasy. Monty is, after all, described as a character "on guard against any irony, attentive to its approach" (113). He will not allow himself "to be satirized retrospectively," as though he means to resist the genre within which Smith has attempted to emplot him (113). Behind Smith's satirical rhetoric, then, we would not be wrong to notice admiration for Monty, if not for his political views then at least for the confidence with which he is able to defend the eternal value of great art. Indeed, much of the plot of *On Beauty* revolves around how various characters negotiate the temptation that Monty poses. Howard's mistress, the avant-garde poet Claire Malcolm, admits that, against her better judgment, she "just adore[s]" the "dapperness" of Monty: "He's so compelling . . . It's probably entirely pheromonal, you know, like nasal . . . God I am so fascinated by him . . . See how he works the room? He's everywhere, somehow" (119). The secret love affair of the literary artist (Claire) with critical theory (Howard) has, Smith implies, become strained at just the same moment that newer, neoconservative suitors (Monty) pheromonally ply their thrilling wares.

However tempting this allegorical reading might be, it would be a mistake to describe Smith as a literary-critical reactionary. Her formally innovative novels, such as *The Autograph Man* (2002) and *NW* (2012), as well as her advocacy for literary experimentalists, give substantial evidence of the importance of the avant-garde, modernism, and postmodernism to her aesthetic commitments.[5] Smith does not wish to roll back the critical traditions that her *Guardian* essay groups together under the label *postmodernity*, but she is also broadly uneasy with this inheritance. What may be most striking about Smith's uneasiness is the seemingly simple point that she can claim to have "come of age under postmodernity" in the first place. If nothing else, Smith's comments signal that the term *postmodernism* and its cognates have, at some unspecified time, achieved a newly historical status. Whatever it once was, *postmodernism* no longer designates anything like the cutting edge of ambitious aesthetic and theoretical production. At a moment when the jacket flap of a major literary novel (David Mitchell's 2004 *Cloud Atlas*) can preemptively describe its author as a "postmodern visionary," postmodernism may be said to have become little more than a marketing category or, as we shall see, the official ideology of marketing as a practice. My book tells the story of how postmodernism became historical by examining the turnover of literary generations in the United States after World War II, showing how the textbook postmodernism of writers such as Thomas Pynchon and Kathy Acker gave way, starting in the late 1980s, to serious reconsideration of literary postmodernism and postmodernity as a critical concept. Recent writers such as David Foster Wallace, Colson Whitehead, Jennifer Egan, Jeffrey Eugenides, Jonathan Lethem, Salvador Plascencia, Sheila Heti, Mark Z. Danielewski, and Tao Lin, as well as writers associated with the literary enterprises of Dave Eggers, have, like Smith, understood themselves as coming of age under postmodernity. Members of this cohort are able to conceive of themselves in this way precisely because postmodernism has become an intermediary figure, a reified image fairly or not associated with a range of aesthetic, critical, and philosophical propositions as well as with the equally protean term *theory*.[6] The former critical battles over postmodernism—celebrations of its subversive political powers, acrobatic efforts to explain how it defies definition, fears about its pernicious effects on young minds—today seem dated. Postmodernism has been translated into a handful of durable critical slogans, theoretical claims, literary techniques, anthology selections, and course catalog descriptions.[7]

The fate of postmodernism is, as *On Beauty* shows, difficult to extricate from the academic humanities and social sciences as well as the recent history of institutions of higher education more generally. Smith's novel playfully implies that only those who inhabit social worlds centered on the American-style university can have ever seen postmodernism either as a vibrant intellectual project or as some sort of indomitable foe in the first place.[8] In making this observation, Smith joins a group of writers who belong to what Nicholas Dames has called the "Theory Generation." Dames's analysis offers another way of understanding what the writers I enumerated above have in common. The Theory Generation, Dames argues, "studied the liberal arts in an American college anytime after 1980," were educated in critical theory, and have subsequently attempted to confront its troubling implications—for many novelists, through their fiction.[9] Dames's description of the Theory Generation exposes a serious literary-historical gap in the otherwise compelling story of the meteoric rise of creative writing programs that Mark McGurl tells in *The Program Era*. Though he calls his own book "an assemblage of what used to be called 'influence studies,'" McGurl does not discuss the influence of what once was called "postmodern theory" on university-sponsored writers.[10] His account focuses instead on how New Critical categories affected workshop pedagogy, making it seem as if there was (and is) an impervious firewall separating academic humanists and their creative writing colleagues. Judith Ryan's *The Novel after Theory* does something to correct this lacuna by investigating a range of novels that since the 1970s have incorporated concepts drawn from critical and literary theory. Ryan argues that novelists who engage with theory largely "attempt to correct the erroneous impression that theory consists in a facile manipulation of unfamiliar terms," and have "put flesh on the bones of" theory's abstractions.[11] Ryan's study supports the view that American novelists fully participated in the "creative misunderstanding between French texts and American readers" that François Cusset documents in *French Theory*.[12] However, as Dames notes, Ryan's account might be criticized for assuming that "novelists and critical theorists would march hand in hand, each new theoretical vista finding its narrative mate, while syllabi virtually constructed themselves."[13] Instead, novelists and theorists have had a far more disputative relationship. Smith's own ambivalence—her claim elsewhere that "ideological inconsistency is, for me, practically an article of faith"—partly arises from this conflict.[14] It is a byproduct of her aspiration to become a major writer-critic. To become a genuine writer-critic, she must reconcile New Critical (creative) and poststructuralist (critical) assumptions that, though by no means isolated from one another, nonetheless arise from sociologically distinct disciplinary positions within the university.

David Foster Wallace, who attended Amherst in the early 1980s, betrays a similar ambivalence, an expression of conflicting intellectual imperatives, often visible in his writing at the level of the individual sentence. For Wallace, postmodernism constituted "a certain set of aesthetic values and beliefs, and maybe a set of formal techniques that might—just might—help the writer to chase his own click."[15] By Wallace's influential account, postmodern "values and beliefs" had disseminated into the broader culture and had, in so doing, exhausted their critical function. Wallace claimed in a widely cited interview with Larry McCaffery that "what's been passed down from the postmodern heyday is sarcasm, cynicism, a manic ennui, suspicion of all authority, suspicion of all constraints on conduct and a terrible penchant for ironic diagnosis of unpleasantness instead of an ambition not just to diagnose and ridicule but to redeem. You've got to understand that this stuff has permeated the culture. It's become our language; we're so in it we don't even see that it's one perspective, one among many possible ways of seeing. Postmodern irony's become our environment."[16] A full analysis of Wallace's influential interpretation of postmodernism will have to wait. For now, there are three points worth making about the literary tendency Wallace, Smith, and other members of the so-called Theory Generation represent. First, ambitious American writers have, like the rest of the U.S. population since the end of World War II, increasingly come under the university's sphere of influence, and they have concomitantly adopted terms of self-reflection cultivated within the academy. When they engage in what McGurl calls the "autopoetic process"—the form of reflexivity most characteristic of the program era—they are therefore compelled to become writer-critics.[17] By taking account of dominant academic discourses on literary art, these writers participate, often reluctantly, in the recent history of what Mark Greif calls (borrowing a phrase from James Wood) the "big, ambitious novel," where "ambition" requires some minimal effort by the writer to think critically about the nature and purpose of literary art.[18] Second, the aspiring post-postmodernist writer does not typically take a straightforwardly anti-postmodernist stance. She does not think she can turn back the clock or simply dismantle the "environment" of postmodernism. Postmodernism as a literary style, set of theoretical claims, or socioeconomic phenomenon cannot simply be evaded, sidestepped, or wished away. Third, and most importantly, the project of moving beyond postmodernism has for many theoretically attuned writers found a concomitant strategy: transcending irony.

Over the past thirty years, irony has become a major flashpoint for contemporary cultural and critical debate. Numerous pundits have told us that we live in an age of irony, cynicism, and snark.[19] Following the September 11, 2001, terrorist attacks, *Vanity Fair* editor Graydon Carter echoed the sentiments of many mainstream commentators when he predicted that the attack would mark "the end of the age of irony."[20] Edward Rothstein claimed that the terrorist attacks might help settle disputes over postmodernism when he wrote in the *New York Times* that the "Attacks on U.S. Challenge Postmodern True Believers." "[T]he relativism of pomo," he argued, requires "a form of guilty passivity in the face of ruthless and unyielding opposition," a passivity hard to maintain after the September 11 attacks, an event whose enormity inaugurated something like a return of the real for our culture.[21] Such declarations are nothing new, long preceding 9/11. Carter himself was concerned about the menace of irony as early as 1989, while serving as an editor at the satirical *Spy* magazine. An essay in that magazine claimed that America was suffering from an "Irony Epidemic."[22] There has also been a more serious critical and philosophical counterpart to the popular turn against irony. Franco Moretti, for example, has argued that "a century of Modernism teaches us" that "irony, extraordinary cultural achievement though it is, has to recover some kind of problematic relationship with responsibility and decision—or else, it will have to surrender history altogether."[23] Peter Sloterdijk claims that "[w]ith incessant irony, modern philosophizing . . . shrinks to a circuslike rationalism that, in its efforts to train the praxis tiger, proves itself to be embarrassingly helpless."[24] Irony has allegedly devolved, by his account, into cynical reason. We ought instead to return to the "pantomimic materialism" of the Greek cynic (Diogenes of Sinope, sleeping in his tub, is the key figure here), who "discovers the animal body in the human and its gestures as arguments."[25] Slavoj Žižek has likewise described cynical reason as a "paradox of an enlightened false consciousness" in which "one is well aware of a particular interest hidden behind an ideological universality, but still one does not renounce it."[26] Whereas irony once had a critical function, "in contemporary societies, democratic or totalitarian, . . . cynical distance, laughter, irony, are, so to speak, part of the game."[27] Eve Sedgwick, meanwhile, has suggested that Sloterdijk's concept of "enlightened false consciousness" "is, specifically, paranoid in structure."[28] When it becomes dominant, "subversive and demystifying parody" threaten to "impoverish the gene pool of literary-critical perspectives and skills," rendering critics less capable of responding to changing political conditions.[29] Literary critics have, for this and other reasons, been losing faith in "deconstruction, ideology critique, and the hermeneutics of suspicion," suspecting that "demystifying protocols [have become] superfluous."[30] Many have proffered slogans meant to summon forth a new interpretive ethic, slogans such as reparative reading (Sedgwick), surface reading (Stephen Best and Sharon Marcus), generous reading (Timothy Bewes), uncritical reading (Michael Warner), postpositivist realism (Satya P. Mohantay; Paula Moya), the phenomenology of enchantment (Rita Felski), the hermeneutics of situation (Chris Nealon; Jeffrey T. Nealon), and so on.[31] This critical tendency, I would argue, arises from pressures similar to those that produced the literary and popular backlash against postmodern irony.

I call the project that these creative writers, critics, and philosophers are collectively engaged in *postirony*. These postironists are, to be sure, a diverse lot. Their responses to postmodernism, however conceived, have been as heterogeneous as postmodernism itself. Nonetheless, postironic writers have largely told the story of irony in a similar way, as a dialectical movement of resistance and incorporation. Irony begins as a critical mode of the avant-garde or the counterculture but then gets absorbed into mainstream media and popular culture, thereby losing its cutting edge. Unlike anti-ironists, then, postironists want to move beyond postmodern irony partly because irony has lost its critical power or because irony's mode of critique no longer adequately addresses contemporary reality. They seek to imagine what shape a postironic, rather than an uncritically earnest or naïvely nostalgic literary practice, might take. They agree that one cannot simply will oneself back into a preironic state of being. Indeed, they often view irony as a necessary phase of critical or artistic practice whose lessons must never be forgotten. One must, it seems, pass through irony's negativity en route to some troublingly unspecified postironic paradise. Many postironists would not want to regress to a moment before the dominance of irony even if they could. After all, irony's détente with decision and responsibility and sincerity and ethics and enchantment and commitment seems, in Moretti's formulation, fated to be "problematic."

In a different sort of critical study, I might have tried to develop a descriptive poetics of the full range of contemporary postironic art, accounting for multiple postironic genres, media, and national traditions.[32] However, this project pursues a different strategy. To make sense of the significance of the turn against irony, I undertake two related tasks in these pages. First, I reconsider the literary, critical, and political history of postmodern irony that has aroused so much opprobrium. Second, I analyze how the desire for postirony has influenced recent literary production, mostly among well-known American writer-critics working in the genre of prose fiction. I adopt a historical, reflexive, and critical perspective on the problem of irony in the post-1945 U.S. literary field. My approach is historical in that it sees the concept of irony as a moving target. That is, the form and significance of irony have changed across the twentieth century, especially after World War II, in tandem with larger transformations in American political, economic, and educational institutions. I am reflexive in that I assume that it is unwise (and perhaps impossible) to study irony's conflicted history without necessarily reflecting on how irony is complexly enmeshed in one's own critical practice. The critic too should engage in a ruthless autopoetic process. Finally, I aim to be critical in that I wish to be evaluative—to assess both past articulations of political irony and to take issue with how postironists, both literary and critical, tell the story of irony's dominance. We must not only take seriously the aspirations of those seeking postirony, but also expose the intellectual and aesthetic errors of the postironic enterprise as it has been articulated. The pages that follow are therefore unabashedly normative.

Four Types of Political Irony

Assessing the political significance of irony is a difficult task.[33] Those who extravagantly defend or attack irony in general and postmodern irony in particular often do not seem to share a common definition or underlying model of irony. It might be tempting to conclude that irony is usually a vague or poorly chosen stand-in for other targets of political approbation or contempt. When Americans become politically credulous, cultural critics prescribe a reparative dose of irony. When the reproduction of capitalism seems to depend on the adoption of particular models of rationality, we hope that irony might liberate us. When we feel U.S. public discourse is insufficiently serious, irony can suddenly become a worthy target for assassination. Every use of the term threatens to spawn new, only semistable meanings, irreconcilable with prior uses, frustrating efforts to make sense of the thing itself. Indeed, to attempt to speak of irony can sometimes arrest the capacity to speak altogether, a failure that is itself taken as one of irony's core characteristics. In this section, I will rehearse three dominant models of political irony (which I will label *the cognitive, the antifoundational,* and *the historicist*) before outlining a fourth approach *(the characterological)* that incorporates and, in my view, surpasses the others.

The cognitive understanding of irony sees its political power as arising from its status as a speech act. Analyses that depend on this understanding begin from H. W. Fowler's insight that irony always constructs a "double audience," "consisting of one party that hearing shall hear & shall not understand & another party that, when more is meant than meets the ear, is aware both of that more & of the outsiders' incomprehension."[34] Formalizing Fowler's definition, contemporary analysts of irony working in linguistic pragmatics have described it as "echoic mention," as "pretense," and as a "viewpoint phenomenon."[35] For such analysts, an ironic Speaker S echoes the utterance of (or pretends to be, or adopts the viewpoint of) an ironized Speaker S' addressing a complexly constituted audience— only some of whom understand the ironist's polysemous speech act. Under these models, both speakers and audiences can be real, imagined, or some mixture of the two. The political implications of this cognitive model are unclear. Some argue that irony is a "weapon of the weak," to use the phrase of the anarchist political scientist and anthropologist James C. Scott. Scott discovers "in ridicule, in truculence, in irony, in petty acts of noncompliance, in foot dragging, in dissimulation, in resistant mutuality, in the disbelief in elite homilies, in the steady grinding effort to hold one's own against overwhelming odds" what he calls "a spirit and practice that prevents the worst and promises something better."[36] Irony would, on this view, politicize everyday life. Hidden meanings create secret zones of human freedom. Alternately, one might argue that irony is the natural weapon of an elite. In *The City and Man* (1978), the political philosopher Leo

Strauss describes irony as the "noble dissimulation of one's worth" or the "humanity peculiar to the superior man," who "spares the feelings of his inferiors by not displaying his superiority."[37] The use of irony follows from "the fact that there is a natural order of rank among men."[38] Irony might then be the meeting ground for superior dissimulators. Such disparate statements lead Linda Hutcheon to argue, quite sensibly, that "irony can and does function tactically in the service of a wide range of political positions, legitimating or undercutting a wide variety of interests."[39] Nevertheless, whether they investigate what Wayne C. Booth calls "stable irony" or wade into the "bogs of unstable irony," these theorists all unavoidably invoke some notion of communicative rationality.[40] This is equally true of Bakhtinian terms such as "dialogism," "heteroglossia," and "polyphony," which many literary critics understand to be forms of irony.[41] Such ironies all posit a relatively unified subject (whether speaker or listener) capable of recognizing the disjunction between what is said and what is meant, between the typical workings of this or that system of tropes and the manipulation of the system, between one frame of reference and another, between direct and indirect communication.

But perhaps the politics of irony does not finally reside in some subject's awareness of the disjunction between different levels of meaning. The tradition of irony that has followed from German Romanticism suggests a different model of the political significance of irony, one not easily assimilated to contemporary cognitive approaches.[42] Perhaps the politics of irony inheres not in its epistemological complexity, or even in our inability to settle on a final interpretation of unstable ironies, but rather in irony's power to disrupt our capacity to parse statements. Irony exhausts, blocks, or undermines the reasoning mind, breaking down the process through which subject formation and the subject's effort to apprehend the world happen in the first place. Irony defeats our capacity to make sense of our environment because it is, as Friedrich Schlegel famously put it, "a permanent parabasis."[43] Parabasis was the moment in Attic Comedy when the chorus interrupted the play's action to insult the audience. In another fragment, Schlegel calls irony "the clear consciousness of eternal agility, of an infinitely teeming chaos."[44] Irony as "permanent parabasis" or "eternal agility" promises to intermit all philosophical, critical, aesthetic, and political foundations. Hegel complained that Romantic irony made the subject all powerful, giving subjectivity a "God-like geniality," but others have associated Schlegel's "permanent parabasis" with "unrelenting antifoundationalist skepticism."[45] In the view of some contemporary critics, antifoundational irony becomes political precisely because it "severs the continuity essential to the very logic of making sense."[46] It is, Lee Edelman suggests, "the queerest of rhetorical devices."[47] In their strong form, such claims about the politics of irony seem to me to be no more tenable than cognitive models. As Christian Thorne explains in *The Dialectic of Counter-Enlightenment*, the thesis that one's views on the foundations of knowledge have any necessary political implications is "an *epistemological determinism* fully as egregious as the economic or technological determinisms that have preceded it."[48] Thorne demonstrates that "anti-foundationalism is *not* everywhere the same," mounting his persuasive brief via a number of case studies in the long history of anti-Enlightenment thought.[49] Much the same objection could be leveled against arguments that take irony's alleged antifoundationalism as politically determinative. The problem is not, as Hegel argues, that "[t]he ironical . . . consists in the self-annihilation of what is noble, great, and excellent."[50] Instead, the problem is that antifoundationalism arrives on the scene with no political guarantees; its power is, at best, tactical and contingent.

Nevertheless, though irony's politics are never determined in advance, we cannot simply transform irony's political importance by changing our individual opinions or attitudes toward this or that ironic speech act (or to irony as such). Irony might once have had a progressive or critical function but because of changes in social, economic, and political life may no longer perform that function. That is, irony's political importance might be historical. Søren Kierkegaard proffered an early version of this thesis. In *On the Concept of Irony with Continual Reference to Socrates* (1841), which builds on Hegel's critique of Romantic irony, Kierkegaard argues that Socratic irony was world-historically justified because it smashed the icons of the Sophists and of Athenian state power, paving the way for a new historical moment. Socrates's irony anticipated a similar negation of Mosaic Law by Christ's crucifixion. Romantic irony was, by contrast, "not in the service of the world spirit," and therefore "Hegel's hostile behavior toward [Romantic irony] is entirely in order."[51] Contemporary critics often deploy similar historicist rhetoric to discuss postmodern irony. In her excellent survey, *Irony*, Claire Colebrook rehearses the claim that "our very historical context is ironic because today nothing really means what it says. We live in a world of quotation, pastiche, simulation and cynicism: a general and all-encompassing irony."[52] A proposition such as this one is common but should be regarded as strange. Taken literally, it cannot possibly be true. The critic who makes this claim, for one, must mean what she says. Second, and more to the point, how can a third-person-singular neuter pronoun "say" anything, let alone *not mean* what "it" says? And what about our "historical context" gives rise to the dominance of irony? Stronger versions of the historicist perspective might with various degrees of rigor invoke concepts such as Zeitgeist, episteme, paradigm, habitus, or structure of feeling to explain how irony can become historically "all-encompassing."[53] Weaker versions of the historicist thesis draw on the concept of what Roman Jakobson called "the dominant," the "focusing component of a work of art," which "rules, determines, and transforms its remaining components."[54] Literary and cultural critics have extended Jakobson's notion of "the dominant" from the individual text to account for the "cultural logic" of whole epochs or periods.[55] Irony would, by these models, become the cultural dominant of postmodernism.[56]

For Paul Fussell, irony became the dominant of Western societies after World War I. The Great War, Fussell writes, "was more ironic than any before or since."[57] It was "a hideous embarrassment to the prevailing Meliorist myth which had dominated the public consciousness for a century."[58] Though the Great War was in Fussell's view more ironic than wars that followed it, it could not help but infect the meaning of all subsequent wars. "The irony which memory associates with the events, little as well as great, of the First World War has become an inseparable element of the general vision of war in our time."[59] Moreover, by this account, irony reaches beyond our memory and attitudes toward war. Irony may originate from "the application of mind and memory to the events of the Great War," but it becomes the "one dominant form of modern understanding."[60] Modern thought as such is "essentially ironic."[61] Irony would, on this view, be politically important not for its specific hidden meanings, not because it has unavoidable consequences regarding the foundations of knowledge, but because it dominates specific historical communities. To say that we live in an "age of irony" means, on Fussell's view, that irony has undermined our faith in the possibility of communicative rationality, communal action, authority, perhaps political life as such. The so-called public sphere has collapsed into myriad counterpublics, each of which deploys incompatible standards of value. For some, irony may challenge not only the existence but also the desirability of the concept of the public. This is one reason Lyotard's definition of postmodernism as "incredulity toward metanarratives" could seem politically liberating or threatening.[62] It is the danger that Richard Rorty wishes to guard against when he insists that he cannot envision "a culture whose public rhetoric is *ironist*," why he wishes to persuade us that irony ought to remain "a private matter."[63]

Such worries, though more persuasive than other efforts to account for irony's politics, seem overwrought to me. For even if it were possible to overcome communicative rationality as a foundation for political life (an open question), it would not follow that we were living in an age of irony. Indeed, it is almost certainly the case that we do not live and have never lived in an age of irony in Fussell's sense. At best, we might say that within certain social and cultural worlds, at particular historical moments, irony has achieved a prestigious status. Using irony or debating its powers has had a tactical value under historically specific circumstances. Some elite cultural producers obsess over irony, and use their discursive power to promulgate their obsessions far and wide. Worrying about irony can, today, win you column inches in America's paper of record.[64] Those tormented by anaphora are not so fortunate. In making this claim, I do not mean to dismiss political debates about irony. Nor do I wish to deny that irony can be a vital weapon against power, though those in a position to have their ironic speech acts widely heard (say, Stephen Colbert at the 2006 White House Correspondents' Dinner) have often already attained a certain level of renown. On the contrary, I am hoping to describe how irony has actually functioned in those zones of American life intellectually centered on the university. However, localizing irony, describing the specific ways that highly educated metropolitan writers have obsessed over it, does not solve irony's mystery. After all, if they are not arguing about the spirit of the age, and if there is no necessary politics to irony, and if the claim that irony has undermined the possibility of public discourse is wildly overstated, what are these artists, critics, and philosophers fighting about? What idea of irony, if any, do they share? When those advocating antifoundationalist views butt heads with those who, with Jürgen Habermas, regard modernity as "an incomplete project," what are they talking about?[65]

This discourse of irony, I contend, is ultimately characterological. Whether they are concerned with irony's cognitive, epistemic, or historical dimensions, those who argue about irony use a rich language of character, attitude, sensibility, disposition, and ethos. This characterological rhetoric is the common language with which artists, critics, and philosophers have debated the value of irony. There is, of course, a long tradition of discussing irony in characterological terms. Aristophanes used *eirōneia* in his plays *Birds* and *Wasps* as a term of abuse, to mean something like "deception." Characters in Plato's dialogues (Callicles, Thrasymachus, and Alcibiades) likewise use the term *eirōneia* to interrogate Socrates's character.[66] It is not clear whether *eirōneia* in Plato should be translated as *irony* in anything like our modern sense. Gregory Vlastos has influentially argued for such a translation, suggesting that Socrates inaugurates a new form of "complex irony" in which "what is said both is and isn't what is meant."[67] *Pace* Vlastos, Melissa Lane argues that "[m]any translators and scholars of Plato have imported an Aristotelian framework into their understanding of *eirōneia* in Plato."[68] Such translators mistake the eirōn (a liar or deceiver), whose purpose is to "conceal what is not said," for the ironist, whose purpose is to "*convey* what is not said."[69] Lane translates *eirōneia* as "conceal by feigning" both in Aristophanes and in Plato. It is, she argues, only Aristotle's effort to "stabilize the meaning of *eirōneia* to suit a technical purpose of rhetoric" that shifts the term from its Aristophanic-Platonic origins to something like our contemporary sense of the term.[70] Whether we find Vlastos or Lane more convincing, the eirōn nonetheless remains a particular kind of person whose value is under debate. This remains true in Aristotle. In his *Nicomachean Ethics*, Aristotle redefines stock characters drawn from Greek comedy (the self-effacing eirōn and his opponent, the braggart alazōn) into rhetorical and ethical stances. On the one hand, the "boastful person" or alazōn, he writes, "seems to be the sort to lay claim to esteemed qualities that he either does not have or has to a lesser degree than he claims"; the "self-deprecating person [*eirōnes*]," on the other hand, "seems to disclaim those [qualities] he has or to play them down."[71] Aristotle views both as ethically defective types, but prefers the eirōn to the alazōn. Unlike the boastful person, those who are self-deprecating "speak, not for gain, but in order to avoid pomposity. And it is especially qualities held in esteem that they disclaim, as Socrates used to do."[72] Cicero picks up Aristotle's characterological definition of Socratic irony, describing *ironia* (the Latin transcription of *eirōneia*) as "being mock-serious in your whole manner of speaking."[73] The first-century Roman rhetorician Quintilian further argued that irony could be not only a rhetorical "trope" but also a "figure." Whereas irony as a trope "says something different" from a literal meaning, irony as a figure "pretend[s] something different," conveying "a whole meaning," which means "a whole life may be held to illustrate Irony, as was thought of Socrates."[74] These remarks spawned a long tradition of treating Socratic irony as a global outlook or life, which of course informed the post-Romantic and modern traditions of irony I have already briefly rehearsed.

This reading of Socrates also clearly informs Randolph Bourne's important essay, "The Life of Irony" (1913), which argues that "irony is a life rather than a method."[75] Irony is, he writes, a stance that "colors every idea and every feeling of the man who is so happy as to be endowed with it."[76] Bourne wants to insist that "[t]he ironist is born and not made," a proposal that others reject—and that I also will reject.[77] Nonetheless, and notwithstanding his gendered assumptions about the person of the ironist, irony cannot be casually adopted or easily discarded. Irony is not a method or a tone or an affect or merely a property of language or a feature of communicative action.

It is an ethos that consumes the whole person, a whole life, and, in the view of some critics, threatens the integrity of the person. Amanda Anderson reaches a similar conclusion about irony and critical distance in her valuable study of contemporary cultures of theory, *The Way We Argue Now*. In one of the essays in this volume, Anderson outlines the way in which "temperament and character, with *manner* broadly construed, is a fundamental, ongoing, and relatively distinctive feature of pragmatist thought," focusing on how various pragmatist figures (Rorty, Barbara Herrnstein Smith, and Stanley Fish) rely on characterologically rich styles of persuasion.[78] Such pragmatist appeals "move toward a descriptive thickness that evokes the literary, and often they can be situated with regard to generic literary modes such as irony or comedy."[79] These thick descriptions, in Herrnstein Smith, for example, give a sense of the "attitude, stance, or temperament that marks the postmodern skeptic."[80] In Rorty's *Irony, Contingency, and Solidarity*, the active project of sketching normative types is on full display, the "liberal ironist" being his most beloved type. Rorty is less interested in mounting an argument than in moving the reader to live a certain way. Pragmatist philosophers happen to be more open than most in using characterological rhetoric, but we can find such language everywhere in debates about postmodernism. Even for Lyotard, postmodernism was defined fundamentally as an attitude (incredulity). Michel Foucault, meanwhile, approvingly described *Anti-Oedipus* as "a book of ethics," which proffers an "art of living," that might help us "ferret out the fascism that is ingrained in our behavior."[81]

Drawing on Foucault's work on the "care of the self," the political scientist Stephen K. White has noted that the concept of ethos has in recent years gained increasing prominence in political theory, philosophy, and literary analysis.[82] The growing popularity of this concept might arouse our suspicions. The term ethos—and the characterological account of irony—may seem to be irredeemably tainted by a shallow liberal individualism that is balefully quietist. Indeed, when critics argue that Foucault's later work marks a dramatic break with his earlier intellectual concerns, they often mean to criticize him for "abandon[ing] his research on the social canalizations of power and becom[ing] cozy with a kind of liberal individualism."[83]

Others, such as the intellectual historian Richard Wolin, celebrate the radical left's turn to "cultural politics," which reconceives of politics as "self-transformation and the search for personal authenticity."[84] It is certainly true that certain intellectuals, such as Rorty, have reimagined radical critiques in individualistic terms easily assimilated to contemporary liberalism. For such liberal individualists, cultivating personal irony might, at best, allow us to shelter ourselves from the nastier depredations of capitalist modernity without having to do the hard work of engaging in political action or transforming dominant institutions. However, ethos transcends such local or tactical developments of the concept. It is a much richer concept than it is sometimes assumed to be. It is, along with pathos and logos, one of the three artistic persuasive modes *(entekhnos pistis)* in Aristotle's *On Rhetoric,* a form of rhetoric that "is spoken in such a way as to make the speaker worthy of credence."[85] Aristotle's idea of ethos is not easily assimilated to the speaker's personality, beliefs, or history, or to other biographical facts about her. Crucially, ethos as pistis does not refer to "a previous opinion that the speaker is a certain kind of person"; it is not, as in Cicero's version of the concept, a function of received opinion, but rather the construction of credibility in the speech act itself.[86] Aristotle's exclusion of prior authority is sometimes taken as a defect of his *Rhetoric,* but this exclusion has the virtue of emphasizing the performative, collective, and ineradicably discursive dimensions of this notion of character.[87] To the degree that critical, philosophical, and political arguments depend for their efficacy on ethos, they are also unavoidably artistic or literary performances. The empirical rhetorician who employs the appeal of ethos; who crafts her credibility through writing, speech, and other forms of art; who thereby responds to and changes community norms, cannot help but also be a literary artist.[88] And those who recommend that we adopt an ethos of irony are recommending that we adopt a specifically literary art of living. If ethos is a performative aesthetic relation, specific deployments of ethos (as well as normative models of ethos) therefore require not only philosophical and political analysis but also literary criticism.

This concept of ethos should not be mistaken for Pierre Bourdieu's concept of habitus (derived from Aristotle's notion of *hexis* or

disposition). Though part of the same intellectual history of character analysis, habitus imagines individual actions to be constrained
by prior socialization. Bourdieu's concept was devised as a way of
bridging the gulf between collective and individual models of
sociology, as a way of resolving the apparent contradiction between
systems-level and agent-based determination, but ultimately considers the individual to be conditioned.[89] Habitus, he writes, "contains
the solution to the paradoxes of objective meaning without subjective
intention," encoding as disposition "primary conditioning."[90] I would
not deny the usefulness of a concept of habitus for describing how
actors exercise creative agency within acquired social frameworks.
Bourdieu's concept, at root, seeks to explain processes of social
reproduction and must be judged in these terms.[91] The discourse of
irony I will investigate here, however, would describe habitus as a
version of social character. Nonetheless, the concept of social character has an important dialectical relationship to the concept of
ethos.[92] The tradition that I am analyzing often explicitly opposes
the social determination that Bourdieu describes. Advocates of the
ethos of irony (or postirony) imagine themselves as able, to some
degree, to determine their own characterological fate, as able to
retool or dissolve the ossified bonds of habitus wherever they find
them. Indeed, we will find a general discursive pattern that puts
ethos in opposition to habitus. The countercultural characterological tradition arguably always constructs its opponent as suffering
from some form of social conditioning. Whereas the ironist, for
example, is thought to have an ethos, the nonironist stands accused
of merely having a socially conditioned habitus. When irony becomes
merely a form of embodied cultural capital, postironists get nervous.
Every striving Bohemian overman is, perhaps necessarily, rhetorically chained to an indolent last man.

The effort to overcome social character, to artistically construct
one's own character, invokes and continues the philosophical tradition of *askesis* (spiritual exercise). Pierre Hadot, whose writing on
ancient philosophy influenced Foucault, uses the term "spiritual"
warily, but argues that the term best conveys the aspirations of the
tradition he is reconstructing. By means of such exercises, the individual "re-places himself within the perspective of the Whole."[93]

Ancient philosophy was, Hadot argues, a "mode of existing-in-the-world, which had to be practiced at each instant, and the goal of which was to transform the whole of the individual's life."[94] It was "an exercise of the thought, will, and the totality of one's being, the goal of which was to achieve a state practically inaccessible to mankind: wisdom." Ancient philosophy promised "peace of mind (*ataraxia*), inner freedom (*autarkeia*), and a cosmic consciousness."[95] Though specific human beings adopt these exercises, we should not assume that askesis is necessarily individualistic. It would be more accurate to say that such philosophical exercises try, in a dialectical fashion, to yoke the individual into a definite relationship with some hypothetical cosmos, putting the person into confrontation with an external order. The philosopher "never ceases to have the whole constantly present to mind. He thinks and acts within a cosmic perspective. He has the feeling of belonging to a whole which goes beyond the limits of his individuality."[96] Cosmic consciousness, unlike scientific knowledge, "consisted in becoming aware of the place of one's individual existence within the great current of the cosmos and the perspective of the whole."[97] Askesis is never straightforwardly social, ethical, or moral. Discourses concerning ethics, affect, tone, and sociality become, on this view, components of a cosmologic characterological discourse. Such characterological philosophies can as easily endorse as attack ethical discourse. They can be, as we will see in the case of punk, as easily social as antisocial. They can speak as easily to one's relation to other people as to things. So irony is *characterological* in two senses that are conceptually distinct but are in practice difficult to disentangle.[98] When described as an ethos, irony is the name for a credibility-building rhetorical appeal. When described as askesis, irony promises to set right the individual's relationship to some cosmic order with which she is not properly aligned. The ironist thus has a relationship not only toward other persons but also toward a cosmos, adopting an art of living that is ineluctably normative, aesthetic, and political.[99] Recalling the key terms of Kenneth Burke's *A Grammar of Motives*, we might say that characterological irony tries to answer all five of the "metalinguistic" questions that organize his dramatistic pentad. The ironist puts herself—or is put—into a relation with her environment, furnishes reasons for action, and articulates preparatory exercises meant to condition the person for activity. Advocates of postirony, meanwhile, create, circulate, and enact alternative characterological models, producing competing prototypes of the art of living.

Fiction is well suited to participate in such characterological debates. Some novels, such as Sheila Heti's *How Should a Person Be?* (2012), straightforwardly represent specific characters who attempt to live in particular ways or critically assess various philosophical propositions on how best to live. More frequently, however, fictions engage in these debates through stylistic or formal means. As Joshua Landy has suggested, fictions might be viewed not only as containers of meaning but also as instruments of self-formation and cultivation.[100] Certain fictions, what Landy calls "formative fictions," can "present themselves as spiritual exercises . . . , spaces for prolonged and active encounters that serve, over time, to hone our abilities and thus, in the end, to help us become who we are."[101] Such fictions are tools, just as much as philosophy or a well-furnished gym, for partaking in what Peter Sloterdijk has called "anthropotechnics." Developing the claim that humans partly create their own conditions of existence, Sloterdijk defines *anthropotechnics* as "human self-production," not to be confused with "'spirituality,' 'piety,' 'morality,' 'ethics' and 'aestheticism'" (which are for him subsets of the broader project of human self-creation).[102] The concept of the exercise is central to Sloterdijk's account of anthropotechnics. He argues that this concept may become the dominant theme of twenty-first-century philosophy. That is, ancient discourses of the spiritual exercise, both Western and non-Western, are increasingly coming to be incorporated into genealogies of contemporary thought. It might, as I have already suggested, be tempting to read this emergence symptomatically, as a willful forgetting or betrayal of the scientific aspirations of semiotics and materialist cultural analysis, and Sloterdijk's political conservatism might leave us uneasy with the concept. However, anthropotechnics can also plausibly be described as a natural consequence of the linguistic turn. After all, at the end of *Metahistory*, sounding a little bit like David Foster Wallace, Hayden White expresses his existential faith that "the recognition of this Ironic perspective [of historiography] provides the grounds for a transcendence of it. If it can be shown that Irony is only one of a *number* of possible perspectives on history, each of which has its own good reasons for existence on a poetic and moral level of awareness, the Ironic attitude will have begun to be deprived of its status as the *necessary* perspective from which to view the historical process."[103] Moral and aesthetic criteria, White hopes, will come to shape the practice of historiography. Likewise, Jameson figures his notion of cognitive mapping as a science fictional imperative for the human person to "grow new organs, to expand our sensorium," in response to postmodernism.[104] What else is White or Jameson calling for, then, but an anthropotechnics of history? White may place excessive faith in the power of recognition, but as should be clear, anthropo-technic schemas need not assume that embracing or transcending irony is an easy task. On the contrary, it is more often claimed that being an ironist or overcoming irony will require strenuous effort applied over time. We may, as Jameson playfully suggests, need to grow ourselves new organs. Nor, for that matter, is there any guar-antee that recognizing the contingency of irony will lead one to value it in a certain way. What is missing from White's concluding flourish is an aesthetic or ethical argument for preferring one or another relationship to irony (these come later). Landy's account, too, makes a convincing case that fiction *can* become an instrument in projects of self-transformation, but offers no grounds for joining one literary gymnasium over another. American cultural debates about irony, we will see, have addressed precisely these questions, investigating not only how to value irony but also what character-ological form might best serve the goal of living or transcending the life of irony. Though ancient in origin, this is a living debate, nowhere near settled, and is a major part of the history of American cultural (and countercultural) politics.

Birth of the American Cool

For over a century, debates about irony in the United States have occasioned searching reflections about the relationship between cul-ture and democratic politics. Such debates have gained force as irony has moved from the margins of American official culture into the mainstream, from Bohemia to network television and the Internet.

Until recently, it was primarily through analyses of the Bohemian ideal that American writers found the resources to criticize and live the life of irony.[105] Irony has been a central characterological feature of the Bohemian from its earliest formalizations. In the "unheard-of idiom" of the Bohemian, Henri Murger wrote in the 1850 preface to his collection of vignettes *Scènes de la vie de bohème*, one discovered that "irony has the intensity of the strongest of acids and the skill of those marksmen who can hit the bull's-eye blindfolded."[106] The Bohemian is "a slang intelligent, though unintelligible to those who have not its key, and the audacity of which surpasses that of the freest tongues."[107] It would, of course, be wrong to take too seriously Murger's claim that "Bohemia only exists and is only possible in Paris," though Bohemia manifested itself differently in the United States, where the Bohemian's political opponent, the bourgeois, was constituted differently than in France.[108] In *Bohemia in America, 1858–1920*, Joanna Levin documents Bohemia's American history from antebellum New York to the west and back again to Greenwich Village in the 1920s. The founding figure in her account is, as in most accounts of American Bohemia, Henry Clapp Jr., the "king of Bohemia," who returned to the United States from Paris in 1850 and organized a lively artistic scene centered at Pfaff's beer cellar on Broadway.[109] Clapp edited *The Saturday Press*, a countercultural newspaper that extensively covered New York's Bohemian communities, which championed writers such as Walt Whitman, Fitz-James O'Brien, Ada Clare, and John Brougham.[110] Part of the initial appeal of the Bohemian ideal, Levin argues, was its foreign origin. Bohemia was "part literary trope, part cultural nexus, and part socioeconomic landscape."[111] It "promised to connect (and at times disconnect) the regional and the national, the national and the cosmopolitan, the modern and the traditional."[112] It moreover, from its beginnings, connected experiments in living to experiments in literary style. William Dean Howells described the New York Bohemians as a "sickly colony, transplanted from the mother asphalt of Paris," whose prose style was "shredded" "into very fine paragraphs of a sentence each, or of a very few words, or even of one word."[113] Clapp, he wrote, was possessed of an "open and avowed cynicism" and "sardonic power."[114] His *Saturday Press* was, meanwhile, "clever, and full of the wit that tries its teeth upon everything."[115] Bohemia proffered an ethos through which to withdraw from stultifying bourgeois respectability, Boston-based genteel culture, and middle-class moralism, to imagine life "outside the constraints of the American liberal consensus."[116] It both rejected the nation and claimed to better speak for the nation's democratic ideals. Irony, satire, and parody provided the characterological means to achieve these ends. Whether this form of characterological self-cultivation constitutes serious opposition to power has long been the subject of debate. As Malcolm Cowley acidly observed in *Exile's Return* (1934), "bohemia attracts its citizens from all economic classes: there are not a few bohemian millionaires . . . Bohemia is Grub Street romanticized, doctrinalized and rendered self-conscious; it is Grub Street on parade."[117]

At the beginning of the twentieth century, modernist writers who emerged from such self-exiled circles came to see a more public-minded political mission for irony. In *The Politics of Irony in American Modernism*, Matthew Stratton links American political irony to the popular reception of Friedrich Nietzsche in the 1910s. Nietzsche's antidemocratic thought, among other fads and movements, magnetized American intellectuals who sought not only to resist bourgeois values but also to articulate a form of life that might serve American democracy. Stratton persuasively argues that many American modernist writers "figure irony as an aesthetic politics that actively democratizes the unsayable . . . as a means of encouraging the transvaluation of values that have become habitual and thus invisible."[118] They proposed the paradoxical view that true democracy should consider "antidemocratic rhetoric as its interlocutor rather than its monstrous other."[119] Among this smart set, irony was associated with core features of Nietzschean perspectivism, the claim that the world is always "interpretable otherwise."[120] Perspectivism is not merely an epistemological thesis, not just a way of noting that all truth claims arise from situated beings who inhabit specific lifeworlds. Nor is it just a way of raising doubts about the universal validity of particular claims made by such situated beings. It is also a recommendation for how to regard the fact of our own entrapment within perspectives. Randolph Bourne was one of the writers who translated these ideas for an American audience. Irony, Bourne explains, is a way of "letting things speak for themselves and hang themselves by their own rope," a way of merely repeating "words after the speaker, and adjust[ing] the rope."[121] Whether or not this victory in ironic rhetorical combat actually changes the world, the ironist benefits immeasurably from the life he leads: "Life, not fixed in predestined formulas or measurable by fixed, immutable standards, is fluid, rich and exciting" for the ironist.[122] A term such as *perspectivism* brings with it the weight and the temptation of visual metaphor, and is perhaps too easily associated with theorizations of narrative point of view. Nonetheless, the visual metaphor was, as Stratton shows, indeed a major bequest of Nietzsche's thought in the United States, which can be traced across a range of discourses, from pragmatist philosophy to literary experiments with perspective.

However, we should also note that Bourne's ironist not only understands that different people have different points of view but also emphasizes that there are other ways of *linguistically* slicing up the world. For Bourne, our awareness that words often do not conform to reality—that reality departs from our avowed ideals—can bring us closer to the truth. By exposing such contradictions, the ironist helps democratize knowledge production. Though his focus is on language, Bourne retains a sense that irony has something to do with our distance from an objective world. The same assumption governs Adorno's description of irony in *Minima Moralia* as "the difference between ideology and reality."[123] Adorno concludes that irony (or rather satire) is no longer possible in a world where ideologies justify themselves in terms of their realism. What interests me here is not whether Adorno is correct in his assessment about the impossibility of satire, but rather the theoretical model of irony that he assumes. Using language almost identical to Bourne's, Adorno suggests that irony "convicts its object by presenting it as what it purports to be; and without passing judgment, as if leaving a blank for the observing subject, measures it against its being-in-itself."[124] Such language takes for granted the existence of a substantive nonlinguistic reality in relation to which the observing subject stands in a definite relation of judgment. Adorno has a different assessment of the politics of irony, regarding it as a largely conservative force for most of its history, in that it makes use of a prior common understanding of the good in service of attacking change. Nonetheless, whether we regard irony as conservative or radical, the modernist account of irony's politics is vague about the precise mechanism by which one's ironic disposition might have political significance. Or rather, it presumes that critical knowledge leads to definite action without feeling much need to explain the mechanism by which it might do so. Indeed, in these accounts, it is never clear what ought to come after irony, or how individual ironic awareness vouchsafes one action or another. Such accounts of irony's power do not yet feature a fully articulated theory of cultural, symbolic, or spectacular politics.

A veteran of the Bohemian Village scene in the 1920s, Kenneth Burke was among the first American critics to tie the therapeutic powers of irony to a systematic theory of symbolic or cultural politics. Burke referred to himself at various points as an "agro-bohemian" and a "Marxoid," terms that indicate the scope of his intellectual ambitions.[125] In *Language as Symbolic Action*, Burke stipulates that *"[m]an is the symbol-using animal."*[126] From this stipulation, it follows that our attempt to apprehend reality is necessarily tropological in nature, filtered through various "terministic screens." Burke writes, "We *must* use terministic screens, since we can't say anything without the use of terms; whatever terms we use, they necessarily constitute a corresponding kind of screen; and any such screen necessarily directs the attention to one field rather than another."[127] Moreover, "much that we take as observations about 'reality' may be but the spinning out of possibilities implicit in our particular choice of terms."[128] This is one reason, for Burke, that tropes have an inescapable role in "the discovery and description of 'the truth.'"[129] (Note the scare quotes around both "reality" and "the truth.") Irony numbers among Burke's "four master tropes," the trope he most associates with dialectic. In effect, Burke reimagines the politics of irony not only as a matter of perspective, not only as a matter of the world being "interpretable otherwise," but also as the whole person's involvement with language and history. Within his idiosyncratic body of writing, the term "attitude" (his translation of *quo modo*) came to "designate the point of *personal mediation* between the realms of nonsymbolic motion and symbolic action."[130] Burke drew attention to the problem of mediation between the realm of the "symbolic" (associated with the term "action") and the realm of the "nonsymbolic" (associated with the term "motion"). Humans never merely encounter the world, but encounter a world filtered through screens of symbolization. Our political task is not to overcome screening but rather to develop better screens. Burke's unique socio-literary criticism had a bracing effect, influencing a wide range of intellectuals and writers, including Ralph Ellison and Susan Sontag. Even Fredric Jameson—who regrets "that Burke finally did not want to teach us history"—advocates "prolong[ing] [Burke's] symbolic inference until it intersects with history itself," thereby extending Burke's project.[131] The emphasis across Burke's writing is less on the observer's distance from some presumed "reality" or "the truth," but rather on a thorough interrogation of the terministic screens and mediating attitudes that we cannot live or be political without. Burke's theories joined other ambitious efforts to systematically link cultural and political life, to conceptualize a politics of culture, after World War II. A wide range of intellectuals from across the political spectrum came to agree that culture was becoming newly political. As early as 1948, Lionel Trilling could be taken seriously when he described the American "middlebrow" as enacting "a cultural Stalinism, independent of any political belief."[132]

Debates about cultural politics were often openly characterological, as in David Riesman's *The Lonely Crowd* (1950). In this bestselling study, Riesman distinguishes personality from character, defining character as "those components of personality that also play the principal role in the maintenance of social forms—those that are *learned* in the lifelong process of socialization."[133] He focuses on shared characteristics, which he dubs "social character." These forms of social character serve "not only to limit choice but also to channel action by foreclosing some of the otherwise limitless behavior choices of human beings."[134] Social character mediates between individuals and governing social structures; the changing construction of social character, what he calls "historical characterology," is therefore at once cultural and political.[135] Riesman's study aroused fears that the inner-directed type's "psychological gyroscope" was giving way to social "radar," characteristic of other-directed types employed in white-collar workplaces.[136] For other-directed types, "relations with the outer world and with oneself are mediated by the flow of mass communication."[137] Politics is "experienced through *a screen of words*."[138] Though Riesman attributes the rise of "other-directed types" to the slowing rate of population growth, at stake in his analysis was the process of socialization, education, and acculturation that reproduces social forms. Riesman celebrates the "autonomous" person over against "adjusted" types or "anomic" dropouts from American life, attempting to distinguish the ethos of autonomy from the habitus of adjustment. It was Riesman's "screen of words"—a form of mediation at once technological, institutional, and characterological—that came under increasing political scrutiny at mid-century. Such medial politics was widely associated with the rise of image culture, what the historian and media critic Daniel J. Boorstin called in 1961 "the Graphic Revolution," our enhanced "ability to make, preserve, transmit, and disseminate precise images."[139] Anticipating better-known analyses by Marshall McLuhan, Guy Debord, and Jean Baudrillard, Boorstin argued that visual media had taken on new political powers starting at the end of the nineteenth century and with increasing force with the rapid spread of television in the United States.[140] The Graphic Revolution facilitated the rise of what he called the "pseudo-event," a sort of event that "comes about because someone has planned, planted, or incited it," and that therefore has an "ambiguous" relationship to an "underlying reality."[141] Under the reign of pseudo-events, reality becomes harder to distinguish from sham. The Graphic Revolution casts "klieg lights on face and figure, mak[ing] the images of different men more distinctive."[142] It degrades the "great simple virtues" of the hero's character (ethos), enthroning instead the "trivia" of the celebrity's personality (habitus).[143]

C. Wright Mills similarly saw an epochal change in the relationship between American culture and politics. In 1959, he labeled this shift "the post-modern period" or the "Fourth Epoch."[144] The Fourth Epoch was marked by the realization that "increased rationality may not be assumed to make for increased freedom."[145] The gap between rationality and freedom arose from the individual's inability to reason effectively about her position within the gargantuan bureaucracies and organizations that increasingly governed life. "Caught in the limited milieu of their everyday lives, ordinary men often cannot reason about the great structures—rational and irrational—of which their milieu are subordinate parts."[146] Consequently, Mills emphasizes that "men live in second-hand worlds" comprised of "stereotyped meanings and shaped by ready-made interpretations."[147] Humans are not only, per Burke, symbol-using animals. In addition, residents of what Mills called the overdeveloped world found themselves to be symbol-using animals enmeshed within a symbol-producing "cultural apparatus," defined as "all the organizations and milieu in which artistic, intellectual, and scientific work goes on, and by which entertainment and information are produced and distributed."[148] Like Boorstin, Mills is worried that in the new epoch "culture is produced and distributed—and even consumed—to order."[149] The political task, as Mills saw it, was for intellectuals to "repossess our cultural apparatus, and use it for our own purposes."[150] Intellectuals must formulate "radical critiques, and audacious programmes," "from the standpoint of explicitly utopian ideals, if need be," proffering "alternative *definitions* of reality."[151] Political action for the intellectual becomes nothing other than to "define and re-define reality."[152] Mills figures this form of refusal in characterological terms. To ignore his call to refusal, Mills tells us, would be to adopt "a *mannerism* of the irresponsible."[153] To adopt Mills's refusal of the cultural apparatus might then be regarded as a mannerism of the responsible, a way to affirm oneself as a "moral center of responsible decision."[154]

If a ruthlessly sincere cultural Stalinism demanded obedience, conformity, and credulity, then perhaps irony could stand as a direct challenge to the hegemony of the other-directed type, the Image, or the cultural apparatus. Irony could be an emblem of democratic freedom, a way to rescue critical thought in an era determined to eliminate the spontaneous event—to replace events with pseudo-events, to crush human autonomy. Irony was thought to be symbolically potent because it offered aspiring rebels a life through which they could separate themselves from the stupid, conformist, Stalinoid squares living next door to them in the suburbs. One manifestation of this rebellion was the tradition of liberal satire, including the influential art of *MAD*, the Second City, and Mort Sahl. As Stephen E.

Kercher shows in *Revel with a Cause*, liberal satirists saw humor as a "momentary flight from the *unreality* of postwar American life," hoping that satire might "destroy the suffocating, banality, artifice, and hypocrisy infiltrating American life and culture."[155] One sees a similar concern in Richard Yates's satirical novel *Revolutionary Road* (1961). Frank Wheeler, the protagonist of the novel, concludes that "[i]ntelligent, thinking people could take ... the larger absurdities of deadly dull jobs in the city and deadly dull homes in the suburbs [in stride]. Economic circumstance might force you to live in this environment, but the important thing was to keep from being contaminated. The important thing, always, was to remember who you were."[156] Ironic distance from economic necessity became one strategy for helping "remember who you were." The problem here is not that submitting to economic necessity is bad in itself but that doing so destroys one's authenticity and autonomy.[157]

Revolutionary Road makes clear that one's cultivated character isn't only a path toward self-transformation but also a socially potent—and fraught—strategy through which one can make distinctions between those who know and those who don't, through which we allocate prestige. Over the past fifty years, American ironists have created communities by separating community insiders from real or imagined outsiders.[158] This form of discrimination oscillates between two poles, a reflection of two ways cultural style can divide insiders from outsiders. On the one hand, style can separate a waning or aspiring aristocracy from the tastes of the bourgeoisie (here Bohemia's affinity with the history of dandyism can be discerned).[159] On the other hand, style can be the road by which we join an intellectual elite. This form of distinction relies, as Mark McGurl has argued, on mastering aesthetic difficulty.[160] In the first sense, the taste for certain unpopular or offbeat art forms marks one's superiority from the mainstream. In the second sense, the hard work one undertakes to be able to appreciate (or produce) difficult art performs essentially the same function. After World War II, the American ironist combined these two distinct forms of characterological self-differentiation. The ironist knows in two senses: he knows what he is supposed to find aesthetically disgusting—at different times, the kitschy, the middlebrow, the lowbrow, the pop, hippies—and he knows when a text is winking at him. The ironist thus simultaneously adopts a disposition toward taste and toward understanding, which he uses to affirm his status as part of an elect minority, a master of the cultural or symbolic field. That said, the point of joining such in-groups was not only to accumulate countercultural capital (to cash in one's cool habitus), but also to attack powerful institutions that were thought to consolidate their power through cultural means. Cultivating irony was also a means of promulgating the "relentless self-criticism" that Morris Dickstein argues was "the real key to postwar culture."[161] Within the sphere of influence of the literary humanities—where taste formation and aesthetic self-cultivation came to be seen as intimately related to ideology critique and to the production of knowledge—irony took on a similar definition and function. If irony could be defined in terms of the polysemy latent in the heart of language (as the New Critics claimed), and if language comprised our only access to reality (as various structuralists and poststructuralists would later insist), then the ironist has a special power. The ironist has the capacity to unravel power by systematically exposing the infinite web of connotation behind every hegemonic denotation. For critics worried about "semiotic totalitarianism"—defined as the "assumption that everything has a meaning relating to the seamless whole, a meaning one could discover if one only had a code"—irony promised a great deal indeed.[162] In a milieu where one's "antirealist epistemology" could be viewed as "a requisite for any progressive politics," and where "realism, foundationalism, or universalism" stands with "all that is regressive in our society," the ironist rules.[163] The ironist debunks rigid ideologies, unweaves foundationalist "master narratives," and deconstructs every conceptual or philosophical description of the world through the close investigation of language. To be an ironist is to have the power and inclination to reveal the gaps and holes in hegemonic conceptions that pass themselves off as common sense. Within this political landscape, the necessary lack of fit between our descriptions of the world and the phenomena these descriptions are supposed to map becomes especially apparent when words or phrases—the foundational terms through which we allegedly apprehend reality—are revealed to have different denotations in different contexts.

Poststructuralists did not necessarily agree on *how* irony attains its power. Though neopragmatism and deconstruction are sometimes thought to have a "shared provenance," Anthony Reynolds convincingly shows, these traditions differ on how they describe the nature and power of irony.[164] For Paul de Man, Friedrich Schlegel upset the foundation of dialectics by revealing that Johann Gottlieb Fichte's comprehensive tropological system (in his 1794 *Science of Knowledge*) was susceptible to "permanent parabasis." In his lecture "The Concept of Irony" (1977), de Man locates Schlegel's key disruptive move in *Lucinde*, in a chapter that initially seems to be a long philosophical discourse but turns out to be a coded description of sexual intercourse. This moment of allegorical "double-voicedness" leads de Man to conclude: "Words have a way of saying things which are not at all what you want them to say . . . There is a machine there, a text machine, an implacable determination and a total arbitrariness . . . which inhabits words on the level of the play of the signifier, which undoes the reflexive and the dialectical model, both of which are, as you know, the basis of any narration. There is no narration without reflection, no narrative without dialectic, and what irony disrupts . . . is precisely that dialectic and that reflexivity, the tropes."[165] Proliferating linguistic connotations do not only upset denotative certainty but call into question the foundational categories that vouchsafe our ability to make meaning in the first place. Rorty, meanwhile, offers a more cheerful view of the ironist. For Rorty, an ironist is someone who has "radical doubts about the final vocabulary she uses" and doubts that "her vocabulary is closer to reality than others."[166] The ironist is aware that she is trapped within the contingent assumptions of her own final vocabulary, and that her own deepest commitments have no foundation. She therefore "takes the unit of persuasion [in an argument] to be a vocabulary rather than a proposition," and believes that "there is *nothing beyond vocabularies*," that "persons and cultures are . . . incarnated vocabularies."[167] Whatever their differences, de Man and Rorty agree on the power and primacy of language, on the foundationally linguistic and tropological nature of understanding. Their disagreement regards whether irony operates within our tropological understanding or breaks down such an understanding. Nowhere here do we find, as in Bourne or Adorno, a discussion of the ironist's distance or relation to some conception of extralinguistic reality. For both de Man and Rorty, Reynolds argues, irony "facilitates" nothing less than our "passage into a materiality beyond the reach of metaphysics."[168]

Such theories have come under critical attack by a range of writers who associate theories of symbolic, cultural, and linguistic politics with American counterculture and the New Left. These critics are suspicious of countercultural discourses, suspecting that they conceal pernicious libertarian assumptions. They worry that projects of ethical self-transformation might encourage political quietism. Why bother transforming social institutions, after all, when you can enjoy the pleasures of ironic autonomy? In *The Conquest of Cool* (1996), Thomas Frank goes beyond the charge that the counterculture promoted quietism, showing that business "welcomed the youth-led cultural revolution not because they were secretly planning to subvert it . . . but because they perceived in it a comrade in their own struggles to revitalize American business and the consumer order generally."[169] He attacks countercultural rhetoric as an adjunct to capitalist exploitation, suggesting that would-be rebels have much more in common with advertisers and entrepreneurs than they would care to admit. Other writers criticize counterculture in the same breath as identity politics and multiculturalism, imagining themselves to write from the perspective of something like a revived Old Left. Sean McCann and Michael Szalay have attacked the political priorities of the New Left, which eroded the distinction between the "symbolic" and the "real," and enthroned "a new political vision built in large part on the appeal of the spontaneous, the symbolic, and ultimately, the magical."[170] Liberals and leftists who write in this mode argue that the conflation of "symbolic" and "real" politics has neutered the efficacy of reformist and revolutionary political projects. Practitioners of symbolic revolt are, they say, at best ineffective at achieving their aims and at worst secretly complicit with the oppressive systems they claim to oppose. On the whole, revisionists argue against the academic left's commitment to antirationalism, mysticism, identity politics, blanket antistatism, anti-instrumental thought, and antinormativity, and they call instead for a reinvestment of progressive energies into collective projects of social transformation.

However, in their antipathy to the symbolic, these critics risk reproducing the error they accuse their symbol-loving opponents of. Yes, many literary texts are organized around a symbolic political logic and depict fictive magical resolutions to intractable socioeconomic problems. And yes, some critical theorists may have an inflated sense of their individual power to effect social change through cultural analysis. But culture takes on a mystifying—and arguably mystified—power to block "real" politics in these polemics. When Walter Benn Michaels argues that "[c]ulture has become a primary technology for disarticulating difference from disagreement" and "disarticulating difference from inequality," culture is not shown to be irrelevant, but turns out to have tremendous power.[171] Culture must be powerful indeed if it is the "primary technology" through which neoliberals cloud the political judgment of those who otherwise claim to be liberals or leftists. The family resemblance between fictive plots and libertarian rhetoric can be enough to convict academic humanists and novelists. Leslie Marmon Silko's *Almanac of the Dead* (1991) features the execution of a Cuban Marxist for "crimes against history."[172] Silko therefore, Michaels claims, promotes the idea that a supernaturally empowered "history" rather than "liberal capitalism" causes all indigenous oppression.[173] The popularity of Reagan-era films such as *Ghostbusters* and *Caddyshack*, Frank suggests, partly explains "why liberals will probably never be able to come to grips with what they winningly call 'inequality.'"[174] "One small reason for the big *economic* change," we learn, "is the confusion engendered by the *cultural* change" (emphasis in original). It is almost as if the implementation of neoliberal policies was not, as David Harvey has memorably put it, part of a ruthless "project to restore class power to the top elites" after the 1970s.[175] In a discourse that sometimes seems to hope to dispense with culture in the name of politics, culture can take on a ghostly power. McCann and Szalay are right to take issue with the view that "analysis of [symbolic] forms *itself* constitutes significant political action, or, equally, that the ability to affect culture is, *independent of other means*, also therefore politically efficacious."[176] But when Michaels writes, "[I]f you hold, say, Judith Butler's views on resignification, you will also be required to hold, say, George W. Bush's views on terrorism," one cannot help but wonder how such a requirement arises.[177]

Michaels's use of the second person clarifies what is at stake in this argument. What Michaels proffers is, at heart, another character-ological analysis. He is invested in "describing what people ought, if they were consistent, to believe and to want."[178] Michaels claims to care very little about *who we are* and to care very much about *what we believe*, based on the assumption that those who care about difference are poorly equipped to battle political economic structures that per-petuate inequality. And yet, to prefer disagreement over difference is to be (or become) a certain kind of person (we could call this nor-mative type the disagreer). It turns out, especially from the perspec-tive of someone Michaels might be trying to persuade, that *who we are* matters at least to the degree that it shapes whether we value difference or disagreement. Michaels's disagreer is, I would argue, just as much an example of a postironic characterological form as those offered by literary writers or critics who aspire to move beyond skeptical reading.[179] That is, these post-countercultural critics do not eliminate the technology of culture in favor of "real" politics but construct an alternative political technology of culture that aspires ultimately to transcend the limitations of poststructuralism and var-ious post-Marxist traditions. To care more about redistributing income than celebrating difference, to interpret *Ghostbusters* as a political parable celebrating Reaganism rather than a touching nar-rative of the human triumph over the (Stay Puft Marshmallow) Man, is nonetheless to be a type of person, to adopt a certain stance regarding the cultural basis for effective political action. We should, in my view, remain critical of anyone who would pursue symbolic political projects at the expense of organizing efforts and coordi-nated activism, while also recognizing that there is no simple way to blithely differentiate between the real and symbolic (or, as Burke put it, the realm of motion and the realm of action). If it is true that that liberals might be better equipped to combat inequality if Harold Ramis had been nicer to the EPA, cultural production is a powerful political weapon. Whatever else we might prefer, we must admit that symbolic analysis is important in many politically charged contexts, including the context of the university, and that as a practical matter we cannot easily "disentangle the concern over questions of social justice from the countercultural critique—and to jettison the latter, while continuing to pursue the former."[180] If we could easily disentangle these concerns, we would already have a good model of how cultural life impacts political life more broadly. We would have already accomplished the political tasks we deem important. We would already understand how irony influences political life. This book hopes to contribute to building such models. A detailed account of cultural and symbolic political action must be central to any literary history seeking to understand the legacy of postmodernism as a cultural mode and the political lessons counterculture teaches. It is my contention that these discourses, both countercultural discourses that celebrate irony and post-countercultural discourses that hope to move beyond irony, have been grounded in characterological forms of analysis. How these discourses affect larger changes in the world is a question of another order.

Canons of Character

Postironists do not condemn irony as such but rather condemn the ironist and the postmodern skeptic as mental attitudes or character types, which they hope to supplant with better attitudes or types. *Cool Characters* therefore studies the transition from irony to postirony in the United States after World War II as a procession of important characterological types that have interesting relationships to irony. These ironic and postironic models of character ramify through various cultural forms and practices. They are not, it is important to emphasize, identical to subcultures or other sociological groups.[181] They are rather conceptual models—what we could call canons of character—that simultaneously require sociological, philosophical, and literary analysis.[182] I tell the story of the transition from irony to postirony in characterological terms, because doing so highlights the assumptions that both groups of writers, contrary to their own claims, have in common, and because the category of ethos articulates a specific, perspicuous relationship between cultural politics and other registers of political action. The main

distinction between the postironists and the postmodernists is not—
as Zadie Smith suggests—that the postironist accepts more easily
than her predecessors a communicative and ethical role for literature. In the revisionist account of postmodernism that these pages
develop, I will show that postmodernist fiction and theory were
never devoid of character. Postmodernist thought in its broadest
sense proffered the life of irony in art and philosophy that was peo-
pled with characters, laden with moral propositions, thick with affect,
and obsessed with history. The real conflict between ironists and
postironists was about how irony might fit into a salubrious anthropotechnic stance.

I also offer the term *postirony* as a contribution to the critical
project of naming what comes after postmodernism. This enterprise
is at an early stage of development, though it has already spawned
numerous books and special issues of journals.[183] Nonetheless, certain critical patterns in this debate are already apparent. There are
three broad views on our post-postmodern moment. Some see the
present as a hyperextension or intensification of postmodernism.[184]
Others regard post-postmodernism as an effort to return to a
moment before postmodernism (realism, modernism).[185] Still others
claim that contemporary writers have moved toward new areas of
artistic and cultural concern—that post-postmodernism constitutes
a genuine break with the prior cultural dominant. Critics have developed a variety of terms to name the alleged new dominant, including
post-postmodernism, late postmodernism, cosmodernism, altermodernism, metamodernism, digimodernism, hypermodernism, performatism, and contemporaneity.[186] These terms discuss a variety of
successors to postmodernism, and affect as many domains as postmodernism itself was once thought to affect. What they have in
common is that critics who invoke these terms often self-consciously
engage with postmodernism as a critical object, regard postmodernism as somehow past, and seek to articulate the logic of a new cultural, theoretical, or socioeconomic / historical dominant. Jeffrey T.
Nealon offers one of the more ambitious efforts to name the new
moment, trying to do for post-postmodernism what Fredric Jameson
did for postmodernism. That is, he tries to link contemporary
culture and arts to new developments in capitalism, regarding

post-postmodernism as an "intensification" of postmodernism. Nealon's efforts are not entirely successful, partly because we still do not have a systematic picture of contemporary artistic, literary, and cultural production. By contrast, Jameson captured an already rich scholarly debate on postmodernism, and when he wrote his influential essays, *postmodernism* had already largely defeated competing terms such as *surfiction, black humor, irrealism, absurdist literature, fabulation, the antinovel,* and so on.[187] The debate about postmodernism's successors is only at a preliminary state, and our sense of the cultural present is unsettled. I do not propose postirony as a new cultural dominant that exhausts the contemporary scene. Nonetheless, debates about irony stand at the intersection of theory, politics, and aesthetics, and will therefore shed light on this larger project of naming the present.

The term closest in spirit to postirony is New Sincerity. Art Spiegelman has described "neosincerity" as "sincerity built on a thorough grounding in irony, but that allows one to actually make a statement about what one believes in."[188] Adam Kelly discusses New Sincerity as a cultural mode that is, on the one hand, obsessed with intersubjectivity while, on the other hand, afraid that sincere communication is not possible. Extending the schema developed by Brian McHale in *Postmodernist Fiction,* Kelly argues that fiction working in the mode of New Sincerity takes on an "ethical" dominant, and performs "the confusions that divide the writer's own self and that complicate the old notions of inner truth and wholeness which underlie both sincerity and authenticity."[189] New Sincerity writers suggest that "meaning requires the futurity of the reader to provide a dialogic engagement that is not simply codifiable as a decidable ethics."[190] Though New Sincerity discourses address themselves to many of the same themes and concerns that postirony does, their focus on sincerity too narrowly maps the contemporary literary field. Analyses of New Sincerity seem to imagine sincerity as the opposite term to irony, but the precise relation between sincerity and irony remains unclear. Why, after all, would sincerity be the aspired state one might want to attain if one was concerned about irony? Why not commitment, or passion, or emotion, or decision? More importantly, Kelly's focus on the "ethical" accounts for only a narrow sector of contemporary efforts to move beyond the postmodern. The characterological or anthropotechnic perspective adopted here toward the literary history of irony is meant to address not only questions of traditional ethical or moral concern but also a broader universe of mental training, including political life, of which the ethical aspiration to sincerity is indeed one important dimension.

My first chapter analyzes the ironic figure of the postwar hipster. I reconstruct the ethos of the hipster through discussions of Norman Mailer's "The White Negro" (1957), Ralph Ellison's *Invisible Man* (1952), Thomas Pynchon's early fiction, and the cultural politics of the CIA-funded Congress for Cultural Freedom. Dominant critical accounts describe the hipster as an oppositional figure, a smasher of middle-class conformity, reviled by the establishment. Against these claims, I show how easily the hipster was accepted by the liberal establishment of the early Cold War, an establishment that adopted an adulterated version of modernist irony as its official style. I demonstrate that *Invisible Man* deploys a New Critical conception of irony, filtered through Kenneth Burke's theory of symbolic action, to dramatize the transformation that the invisible man undergoes near the end of the novel. It is the figure of the hipster, made visible by the mysterious character B. P. Rinehart, that ultimately teaches the invisible man how to master the irony of postwar modernism and to overcome the ideological limitations of the Brotherhood. A decade later, Pynchon invokes a post-Beat version of the hipster as a means of finding a middle ground between postwar modernism and newer registers of value associated with the emerging counterculture. Drawing on original research conducted in the Thomas Pynchon archive at the Harry Ransom Center, University of Texas at Austin, I demonstrate how Pynchon's attempt to compromise between both sources of cultural legitimacy inflected his early fiction, including his unpublished musical comedy, "Minstrel Island" (coauthored with Kirkpatrick Sale). In the context of the Cold War, irony was understood by intellectuals to stand against "totalitarian aesthetics," where this term could be enlarged to include "Stalinist" middlebrow mass tastes. To be an ironist along the model of the hipster provided Ellison, Pynchon, and Cold War intellectuals with a way of confronting their own society, especially on questions of racial injustice,

in a safely anticommunist way, to criticize both the monological
rigidity of the Cominform and the mindless conformity of postwar
American life. In *V.* (1963), and especially in his rendition of the
African American free jazz saxophonist, McClintic Sphere, Pynchon
transitions from this Cold War liberal understanding of the political
power of irony to an emerging posthumanist vision that imagines
identity and culture to be configurations of information.

In my second chapter, I examine the figure of the punk as it was
formulated in the 1970s. I argue that punk intensified the oppositional ethos of hipness. For the hipster, irony was a tool for evading
the political trap of semiotic totalitarianism. Knowing the difference
between what was said and what was meant, and skillfully manipulating that difference, promised a special form of human freedom. By
contrast, punk irony was from its inception less invested in knowingness. Punks were, instead, types of person who thought irony could
break down the linguistic and cultural foundation of political power.
Emplotting themselves in a narrative genre I call "positive dystopia"
(an anit-Utopian genre that has informed certain debates within
queer theory), the punk sought to constitute a form of life that moved
beyond language and sociality. On this view, social life itself oppressed
subjects by means of centralized, concentrated, and hierarchical systems of meaning. Punk proffered a semiotic anarchy, a technology
for opposing linguistically constituted forms of power, and is therefore much more profoundly a literary phenomenon than has been
commonly recognized. I reconstruct punk's radical irony through
the study of William S. Burroughs and Kathy Acker, two writers
associated with the New York punk scene (and punk in general).
Their literary experiments—their use of irony, negation, and
cut-up—informed and were inspired by punk aesthetic priorities.
Burroughs's *The Wild Boys: A Book of the Dead* (1971) and Acker's
Pussy, King of the Pirates (1995) suggest that the politics of punk has
been largely misapprehended. Punk irony is often taken as inherently anticapitalist in orientation, on the assumption that capitalism
depends on rationality as such for its survival. Critics who make such
claims, I show, misrepresent both punk and capitalism. It is true that
the punk aspired to oppose authority, to challenge patriarchy, racism,
traditional religious discourses, and the state. But punk's professed

anarchism and antistatism stand in considerable tension with its claims about capitalism (including claims made by Burroughs and Acker). I argue that it is better to understand punk as an ethos that participated in the transition from one moment in the history of capitalism to another. Punk was a characterological way station from midcentury Keynesianism to neoliberalism. It was therefore never defeated or co-opted, as is commonly supposed. Rather, the ingenious antisocial attitudes constructed by Burroughs and Acker, which I defend as a good representation of the ethos of punk, were wildly successful. The punk is a figure whose D.I.Y. ethic has found fulfillment in popular neoliberal discourses of entrepreneurialism and creative labor.

My third chapter transitions from ironic to postironic figures. It studies a character type I call "the believer" in David Foster Wallace's writing, David and Diana Wilson's Museum of Jurassic Technology in Los Angeles, and Dave Eggers's various enterprises (*Timothy McSweeney's Quarterly Concern, The Believer,* 826 National). A contemporary secular ethos constructed by all of these authors, publications, and organizations, the believer was formulated against dominant accounts of postmodernism and in response to the End of History triumphalism that marked the end of the Cold War. In his essays and fiction, Wallace casts the believer as a tragic victim of postmodernity, someone who desperately seeks grounds for belief while fearing that no such grounds exist. Hoping to transcend irony, Wallace reconfigures metafiction, constructing a postironic genre I call "credulous metafiction," to foster the reader's capacity to believe. The content of this postironic belief is, we will see, less important than the capacity to believe as such. In *Infinite Jest*, Wallace imagines how a genuinely successful avant-garde artwork, one that transcends the separation of life and art, might affect these mental capacities. Eggers and his associates extend Wallace's project, figuring the believer as a type of person who hopes to create worldly reenchantment through an aesthetic practice of quirky juxtaposition. I analyze the popular aesthetic category of the quirky through an extended discussion of the Museum of Jurassic Technology, and argue that Eggers's various publishing enterprises, though they are the product of collective effort, can be fruitfully viewed as extended paratexts of his memoir, *A Heartbreaking Work of Staggering Genius* (2000). Eggers's paratextual institutions construct an image of a figure I call the "Mean Reader," the snarky opponent of the believer. These writers and artists all describe irony as a toxic by-product of postmodernity, and they are especially focused on how popular media generates and then co-opts irony and cynicism. All, finally, join a larger effort to put the capacity to believe at the center of a postironic ethos that might help one endure or overcome the negative effects of contemporary irony.

My fourth chapter studies the coolhunter (also called the trendspotter). The coolhunter is a contemporary culture worker who promises to help large corporations identify and commoditize cool. In literary and journalistic accounts, the coolhunter is a job description as well as an ethos, an aspirational way of living (often coded as a woman) within global capitalism. This figure, I argue, has come to be regarded as a postironic form of neoliberal life. I defend this claim through analyses of Alex Shakar's *The Savage Girl* (2001), William Gibson's *Pattern Recognition* (2003), and Jennifer Egan's *A Visit from the Goon Squad* (2010). These novelists compose socioeconomic science fictions that invoke contemporary branding theory, and self-consciously reflect on how the novelist has increasingly been forced to brand herself. *The Savage Girl* imagines a world where all values, including oppositional values, have been commodified by what might well be called the counterculture industry. Shakar's characters work at a hip boutique trendspotting firm and forecast the next big "megatrend," the rise of what they call "postirony," a backlash against postmodern irony. The competition among Shakar's characters to define the word *postirony* reproduces, at the level of content, the formal problem readers face in deciding whether *The Savage Girl* is itself a satire or a farsighted marketing guidebook. Gibson's *Pattern Recognition* confronts postmodern irony less directly. Gibson's protagonist, the coolhunter Cayce Pollard, is a model of how one might endure the ironic world of neoliberal consumerism, a world in which the cultural economy often offers greater opportunities for corporate profit than the so-called real economy. Gibson uses a brand-name-laden style to create cognitive maps of economic globalization. The ability to construct such cognitive maps is, for

Gibson, the core capacity of a postironic hermeneutic disposition. Those who adopt this coolhunting disposition see the international division of labor and global supply chains as nothing other than the true meaning of the brand. For Gibson, the coolhunter thus balances a detached (ironic) understanding of economic globalization with a nonironic appreciation of brand meanings. Jennifer Egan's *A Visit from the Goon Squad*, finally, explores a similar dialectic between irony and engagement by imagining a postironic future in which charges of commodification and reification have lost their scandalous force. Egan means to show, in the final chapters of her popular novel, that reified forms (such as PowerPoint) allow for genuine artistic expression and emotional involvement for her characters, and, by allegorical extension, for the contemporary novelist, who finds herself caught within a multinational corporate publishing industry that requires the freelancer-novelist to engage in a continual process of what I call autoreification. In destabilizing the line between production and consumption, the coolhunter offers a unique window on the dynamics of cultural work in the present. The work of the coolhunter is, Chapter 4 shows, an almost-textbook example of how affective, immaterial, and creative labor regimes have "feminized" work and of how neoliberal management gurus have reimagined workers as independent owner-managers of their own human capital.

I end by studying Rachel Kushner's *The Flamethrowers* (2013) and Jonathan Lethem's *Dissident Gardens* (2013), two novels that invoke the international Occupy movement. These novels illuminate and participate in imagining the characterological dimensions of the Occupy protests, speaking eloquently to fears that Occupy might become co-opted or devolve into little more than a political brand name. I argue that such commonly expressed fears are misguided. The possibility of branding the Occupy movement, I show, is a consequence of its core political concept: the notion of "the 99%" as the agent of political action. Not exactly a statistical category, nor the designation of a class, the 99% is best described as an ethos, and specifically a postironic ethos, that must negotiate all of the paradoxes of action my previous chapters outline. I label this paradoxical figure as "the occupier." The occupier, as distinct from the empirical

99%, adopts a "prefigurative" disposition. *The Flamethrowers* and *Dissident Gardens* imagine this disposition as requiring a passage from sincerity through irony toward renewed postironic commitment and political engagement. Both employ a genre that I describe as the postironic Bildungsroman, which sees irony as a necessary way station through which individual characters must move before becoming occupiers. The figure of the occupier is emplotted within a conversion narrative whose dynamics have much in common with the concept of figuration that Hayden White derives from Erich Auerbach. The occupier occupies space and institutions in anticipation of or preparation for a vaguely specified postcapitalist future (a future in which the nominal 99% becomes an empirical 99%). The challenge the occupier faces is how to move from postironic prefiguration to fulfillment through action.

Whether ironic or postironic, all of these figures—the hipster, the punk, the believer, the coolhunter, and the occupier—have pursued political ends through the transformation of the individual person's disposition toward the world. They can, and often do, appear as representative characters within fictive worlds. The works I discuss feature hipsters, punks, and coolhunters, among other figures. But they do more than showcase different models of ethos in imagined worlds. They also conceive of literary style as a vehicle through which to transform the reader's orientation toward the world. To read literary texts a certain way (or to read the world as a special class of literary text) is, they assume, the prerequisite for becoming a certain kind of person. The named figures I study are therefore, it is important to reiterate, not meant to refer to empirical persons or specific subcultural communities or even to fictive character types. Rather, these figures are aspirational, speculative, and political literary dispositions. Each of my chapters discusses these characterological types in relation to their historical, sociological, and political contexts. Doing so helps us understand why each project was appealing to certain communities at certain moments—why one might have wanted to become a hipster at midcentury, why postmodernism could seem to be a fearful opponent at the end of the Cold War. I also analyze the strengths and limitations of each vision, hoping to aid the political project of constructing better alternatives. What I offer is a genealogy of the effort to live the life of irony in the United States after World War II, and the subsequent efforts to move beyond that life toward some better world whose contours have yet to take their final shape. Neither threat nor palliative, irony is best understood as a canonical form of life through which many of us have tried to understand, criticize, and transform political reality.

PART I:

Irony

1

The Hipster as Critic

IN HIS 1957 *Dissent* essay "The White Negro: Superficial Reflections on the Hipster," Norman Mailer paints a grim portrait of "the psychic havoc of the concentration camps and the atom bomb upon the unconscious mind." The postwar world, Mailer argues, confronted Americans with an existentially novel situation, the prospect that they might die "as a cipher in some vast statistical operation in which our teeth would be counted, and our hair would be saved, but our death itself would be unknown, unhonored, and unremarked, a death which could not follow with dignity as a possible consequence to serious actions we had chosen, but rather a death by deus ex machina in a gas chamber or a radioactive city."[1] Perhaps unsurprisingly for a novelist of his titanic egotism, Mailer cared less that he faced a greater chance of death than that he might die among a crowd, "unknown, unhonored, and unremarked," separated from the machinery of social recognition. Mass death exceeds its empirical effects for Mailer, threatening to extinguish not only life but also honor and dignity. And yet, in this essay, Mailer celebrates not himself and his own worthy achievements but rather the cultural hero perhaps most capable of matching, if not exceeding, his apocalyptic self-regard. For the "American existentialist," the type best able to navigate this "bleak scene," is not the novelist but instead "the hipster, the man who knows that if our collective condition is to live with instant death by atomic war . . . then the only life-giving answer is to accept the terms of death, to live with death as immediate danger, to divorce oneself from society, to exist without roots, to set out on that uncharted journey into the rebellious imperative of the self."[2]

Over fifty years later, Mailer's grandiose claims about the hipster appear more quaint than revolutionary. His invocation of black experience and claimed insight into the psychic effects of racism are themselves troublingly racist in how they characterize black male sexuality. And his celebration of the political power of the male orgasm, the supposed solution to the problem of totalitarian terror, evinces Mailer's infamous sexism. Finally, the "rebellious imperative of the self" he here extols can today seem like little more than a juvenile pose motivated by the desire to achieve distinction as well as a marketable image that advertisers hope will motivate teen-aged consumers to buy sneakers, music players, and carbonated sugar water. Malcolm Cowley had already in 1934 trenchantly diagnosed the Bohemian lifestyle of Greenwich Village as, at root, a "*consumption* ethic," observing that "self-expression and paganism encouraged a demand for all sorts of products—modern furniture, beach pajamas, cosmetics, colored bathrooms with toilet paper to match," that "[l]iving for the moment meant buying an automobile, radio or house, using it now and paying for it tomorrow."[3] Andrew Hoberek is thus correct to locate the ultimate legacy of Mailer's essay in "the tendency of cultural studies to celebrate 'transgressive' politics of style, thereby romanticizing those excluded from power rather than seeking to open power up" for the powerless.[4] Writing about a more recent pedigree of Bohemian rebel, the contemporary gentrifiers of Wicker Park in Chicago, who are also called "hipsters," the sociologist Richard Lloyd has made a similar point about the fundamental compatibility of consumerism and counterculture. Neo-Bohemian "resistance to the terms of bureaucratized, 'corporate' labor-force participation," it turns out, "now contributes to the ready acceptance by educated intellectuals of manual-labor jobs in the post-Fordist entertainment industry."[5] In other words, twenty-somethings with college degrees, determined to escape the corporate "machine," often celebrate low-paying jobs (as waiters and bartenders) as signs of rebellious freedom and personal fulfillment, rather than seeing their new jobs as signs of downward social mobility. Skeptical readings of the hipster emphasize, quite accurately, that the postwar consumer economy had special use for a countercultural population of "white negroes," workers forced to embrace a Protestant ethic in the office on pain of unemployment who (frustrated by disempowered work lives) lived in a state of perpetual Bohemian carnival while off the clock.[6] Rebellious imperative of the self, indeed.

Whatever criticisms we might justly make of the countercultural romance of the margins, we should not so easily dismiss the hipster, for he is also a figure with a significant literary history, one which exceeds Mailer's misguided celebration of him. By studying the hipster, the Ur-ironist of postwar life—a character type many artists and intellectuals thought was best adapted to the age of abundance—we can reconstruct the foundations of our contemporary picture of irony and, in doing so, revise many deeply ingrained assumptions about its subversive power. The hipster was a negative type, an ambiguously racialized figure that aimed for pure negation, often in the name of liberation, defined more by what he disavowed or stood against than by what he fought for. Despite the doubt some have expressed about the viability of consumerist rebellion, many critics have continued to see the hipster's political significance in his mastery of codes of consumption. In his classic *No Respect: Intellectuals and Popular Culture*, Andrew Ross gives one version of this argument, writing that the hipster "stands in a similar, structural relationship to cultural capital as does the intellectual."[7] Hip is "a mobile taste formation that closely registers shifts in respect / disrespect towards popular taste"[8] Part of what makes it "mobile" for Ross is that hip functions differently for lower-class and middle-class hipsters. Whereas lower-class hipsters are overinformed about popular tastes, middle-class hipsters pretend to be underinformed, to engage directly with popular life. What may be surprising to those who adopt Ross's view, however, is the degree to which those writing in the midcentury's highbrow cultural forums (*Partisan Review, Dissent, Commentary, The Noble Savage*) saw hipness not only as a "taste formation" or attitude toward consumption, but also as a specimen of political awareness, a critical tool whose use went well beyond "advanced knowledge about the illegitimate."[9] Armed with hip knowingness, critics hoped to oppose what Dwight Macdonald called "midcult" or what Theodore Roszak called "technocratic society."[10] Hipness promised nothing less than, as Scott Saul has put it, "a new way of living," a way to chart the limits of American freedom.[11] All hipsters, of whatever class position, saw power as a function of knowledge, curated taste, and strategic consumption. Hip was a theory of power.

In studying the history of this hip ethos, we should heed the musicologist Phil Ford's warning that contemporary critics have tended to discuss hipness in terms of "the most extreme and marginal figures . . . rather than the less exotic (but more commonplace) kinds of people for whom hipness was less the point of existence than a happenstance of it."[12] Even the most extreme individual hipsters, those whose lives might serve as case studies for students of hip subculture, never embodied hipness in some pure way, but instead stood in relation to a contested public image of the hipster as a figure, a midcentury racial fantasy jointly constructed by a range of intellectuals and artists. It is this public image of the hipster, and the fight to fix the meaning of this image, that I take as my object of study. Michael Szalay has argued that hipness served the Democratic Party as an important ideological component of a political-literary strategy for reconciling white professionals with African Americans. The concept of hipness helped white liberals imagine that they could inhabit black bodies, taking on a "second skin."[13] It created an acceptable way to "appeal to blacks without alienating racist whites."[14] Drawing heavily on Mailer, and Mailer's claim that John F. Kennedy was "the Hipster as Presidential Candidate," Szalay gives a persuasive account of one facet of the hipster's cultural history. But the hipster's political significance goes well beyond Democratic electoral strategy.

The hipster indeed facilitated a racial fantasy wherein white bodies might rebrand themselves as black, thus (it was imagined) frustrating a white mass society. But the hipster did more. He symbolically resisted the dominant culture using attitudinal strategies that intellectuals and critics increasingly prized. Irony—so hard to detect in the intensity of Mailer's overheated prose—was the hipster's primary attitudinal weapon in his war against mainstream conformity and square life. The hipster's irony, his mastery of symbolic manipulation, harmonized with emerging white-collar fantasies of professional labor at midcentury. At a moment when writers came to see themselves as "cultural educators and national therapists" who worked in a world where "social reality is determined by ideas and values disseminated by intellectuals within the rapidly expanding new class," the hipster's expert use of irony as a political weapon was nearly irresistible.[15] Irony was especially important for a specific subset of professionals—that is, intellectuals and critics—who thought they did a unique kind of knowledge work, who imagined themselves as manipulators not of information but of meaning.[16] These assumptions inform Cleanth Brooks's essay "Irony as a Principle of Structure," a classic New Critical statement that identifies the "compelling reasons" that "modern poetry" emphasizes irony, which he defines as "the acknowledgement of the pressures of context" on poetic meaning.[17] Among these compelling reasons are "the breakdown of common symbolism; . . . the general skepticism as to universals; . . . the depletion and corruption of the very language itself, by advertising and by the mass-produced arts of radio, the moving picture, and pulp fiction."[18] Irony, in this programmatic New Critical argument, is not just a structural principle that constitutes all poetry but also a weapon in a war of taste waged against "a public corrupted by Hollywood and the Book of the Month club, . . . a public sophisticated by commercial art."[19] Brooks's argument depends on a crucial, undefended conflation of fact and value. For the New Critic, irony is simultaneously the objective, structural property of *all* poems, even those that seem nonironic (like lyric poetry); what the professional critic must learn how to discover in these poems (through the practice of close reading); and the poet's preferred strategy for dealing with the depravities of modern culture, what every good poet ought to want to do. Because it guarantees that no poem is ever identical to its own denotative information, irony renders paraphrase not only heretical but also impossible.[20] At the same time, once it is encoded in an object, irony must replicate itself in the cognitive faculty of the discerning critic, who will need to cultivate the capacity to read doubly. Without the critic's taking up the normative mantle of ironic reading, irony will in some sense perish on the page. Irony's survival and efficacy crucially depend on the critic's willingness to hone a particular ethos, a characteristic way of being in the world, defined by one's manner of interpreting that world. Pursuing this cultural program, the postwar modernist poet-critic and the hipster stand together—*ironic, knowing, witting*—against technocratic society, mass consumerism, and white-collar (not to mention *white*) conformity. The postwar hipster thus fused a specific social ontology (society as the arena of symbolic struggle), a hermeneutic strategy (close reading), and a normative attitude (irony).

The startling similarity of the postwar modernist poet-critic and the hipster—their common sense of superiority, justified in terms of *knowingness*, the convergence of highbrow intellectual culture and counterculture at midcentury—is starkly visible in Ralph Ellison's *Invisible Man* (1952) and Thomas Pynchon's *V.* (1963). Like Mailer and other midcentury intellectuals, Ellison and Pynchon looked to African American vernacular and popular culture for the resources with which they might devise strategies to survive middlebrow society. For both authors, becoming an intellectual hipster or hipster intellectual was a way to achieve an aesthetic détente between the modernist establishment and emerging countercultural values. Capable of supping from very different founts of prestige, the hipster promised to liberate language and undermine society, all while retaining literary and political credibility. Because he wrote *Invisible Man* at a time when the New Criticism was still relatively dynamic and ideologically in flux, Ellison adopted the title of critic with less trepidation than did Pynchon, who came of age amidst a more entrenched New Critical establishment at Cornell in the late fifties, during the Age of Criticism. Despite the significant differences in their biographies—Ellison and Pynchon are rarely read together—each places critical irony and a version of the hipster at the center of his artistic vision, sharing more than literary historians have recognized.

In *Invisible Man*, B. P. Rinehart—Ellison's "name for the personification of chaos"—is the most obvious hipster-like figure, but there is a sense in which the invisible man himself becomes, by the end of the novel, a sort of hipster, a critical ironist, if not a personification, then a manipulator of chaos.[21] I will argue for this claim by juxtaposing the ironic invisible man with the allegedly sincere protagonists of Richard Wright's fiction and by considering the invisible man's journey toward self-perception in light of Kenneth Burke's theory of symbolic action. Pynchon brings the hipster and the critic together in different ways: first, in his rendition of the free-jazz saxophonist McClintic Sphere, a character modeled on Ornette Coleman, whom Pynchon watched at the Five Spot Café in the Bowery during the late fifties, and second, by structuring *V.* around the opposition between postwar modernism (Herbert Stencil) and the hip (Benny Profane), a bifurcated form he first experimented with in "Entropy" (1960), a Beat short story provocatively published in the traditional *Kenyon Review* at a time when it was edited by the former CIA agent Robie Macauley. Ellison and Pynchon turned hip irony into a principle of literary design that continues to cast a shadow over contemporary debates about irony.

Jive Criticism

The origins of hipness are obscure. John Leland writes that the word *hip* derives from the West African language of Wolof, from *hepi* ("to see") or *hipi* ("to open one's eyes"), a claim repeated in several histories of hip counterculture.[22] Efforts to link "hip" and its cognates to Wolof are empirically thin, but the etymology, whether or not true, already participates in a hip critical practice. The stakes in finding the true origin of hipness are ultimately less philological than political, more about lavishing the prestige of an ancient (read: authentic) pedigree on a particular contemporary subculture than about uncovering historical truths. The earliest recorded uses of the term *hip* and its cognates can be found in popular explications of jazz subcultures. *Cab Calloway's Hepsters Dictionary* was one of the earliest discussions of jive language.[23] First published in 1938, it went through six editions over the subsequent six years. Jack Smiley's *Hash House Lingo*, a 1941 dictionary of slang defines a *hipster* as "a know-it-all" and *hep* as "aware."[24] In his *Hepcats Jive Talk Dictionary* (1945), Lou Shelley maintained that jive slang was an "incomprehensible dialect to all save those who [are] hep."[25] Dan Burley's *Harlem Handbook of Jive*

(1941; republished in 1944 as *Dan Burley's Original Handbook of Harlem Jive*), meanwhile, combined a serious desire to "educate readers about the origins, history, and social context of jive" with more playful conceits, such as jive parodies of classics, an anticipation of the comedian Lord Buckley's later rendering of literary classics into the idiom of the "beatnik."[26] In all cases, hipness encompasses both knowing jive slang and a broader knowingness. In-group style here becomes not only a form of countercultural capital but also a means of attaining what Phil Ford calls "asymmetrical consciousness . . . The hipster sees through the square but not *vice versa*."[27] At the same time, these writers paradoxically use dictionaries and guidebooks, instruments of mass education, to argue that hipness is distinct from mass culture. However, by insisting that jive slang requires expert explication, these dictionaries may have done more to reinforce than dispel the mystique of the hipster.

These early discussions already hint at the terms that will be most important to fuller analyses of hip's power, but Anatole Broyard offered the first sustained analysis of the hipster in his brilliant 1948 *Partisan Review* essay, "A Portrait of the Hipster." The hipster, Broyard reports, is essentially "nowhere" and longs to be "somewhere," but because he finds himself thwarted in "his inevitable quest for self-definition" by "those who owned the machinery of recognition," he is "forced to *formalize* his resentment and express it symbolically," and thus "harmonized or reconciled himself with his society" by accepting society's monopoly on symbolic power.[28] Hip slang ("physiognomic talk," "jive talk"), Broyard theorizes, becomes the means by which the hipster represents and through representation relieves his anxiety; the hipster allays his anxiety "by disarticulating himself," by embracing parody and irony. At the same time, this inarticulate, semiverbal urban "primitive," this hip sexual aggressor whose "use of the sexual metaphor was also a form of irony," is treated as a powerful cultural producer. The hipster's "dichotomously" absolute and sexualized vocabulary allows him to show that he "knows the score"; he uses "metonymy and metonymous gestures" in order to "connote[] prior understanding" to signal to fellow initiates that, more than anything, he "digs" his situation.[29] He is a kind of aspiring strong poet whose medium is social life, and whose willful misprision seeks (but fails) to wrestle cultural power to the ground. The hipster is "separate, critical, and defining" and makes use of a type of critical irony that Broyard calls "second-removism," a knowingness that "established the hipster as keeper of enigmas, ironical pedagogue, a self-appointed exegete," a level above those "who still tilted with the windmills of one-level meaning."[30] In this striking description, the hipster seems like nothing less than *an intellectual*, almost New Critical in his acumen, all seeing, someone whose ultimate weapon is his ability to manipulate meaning and confront the symbolic logic of social life. While celebrating the hipster's insurgency, Broyard takes care to declare his exciting, dangerous energies all but consumed, a common trope in postwar discourses on hip. Popular success and the lavish attention of "intellectual *manqués*" ("the desperate barometers of society") destroy the hipster—"once an unregenerate individualist, an underground poet, a guerrilla."[31]

Postwar approaches to hipness might, with some justice, be considered an updated version of modernist primitivism, extended now to black popular culture. In his memoir of life in Greenwich Village, Broyard gives evidence for this view. He wrote his hipster essay on assignment for Delmore Schwartz, whom he knew through Milton Klonsky. Soon after writing the essay, he ran into Schwartz, Clement Greenberg, and Dwight Macdonald having a conversation about primitivism in the San Remo bar in Greenwich Village. Enticing them with stories of hipster violence, Broyard took them to the Park Plaza, a dance club in Spanish Harlem. Though he wished himself to be an intellectual, Broyard believed that Village intellectuals had "lost the world itself," having "no room for the raw data of actuality."[32] They had "very little sense of rhythm," both on the dance floor and on the page, and were usually "standing outside of culture looking in."[33] By describing "intellectuals *manqués*" interested in the hipster as "desperate barometers of society," and framing the hipster himself as a sort of authentic "street-corner" intellectual, Broyard is poking fun at *Partisan* on its own pages, proffering the hipster as a more authentic intellectual than the intellectuals who studied and fetishized him. At the same time, Broyard seems genuinely committed to imagining the hipster as a vernacular intellectual, informed by experiences of racial isolation and symbolic violence. In his essay, Broyard calls the hipster a "critic," a "pedagogue," an "exegete," and a "poet," albeit the underground variety of each. Whether or not his editors detected any mockery directed at them, Broyard forged his early career from this act of bridging the hip and the square worlds, "passing" as an intellectual and as a hipster, a performance that prefaced his later life of racial passing as a book reviewer for the *New York Times*. Acting as a consultant for New Directions, Schwartz would only a few years later notoriously insist that Chandler Brossard alter his novel *Who Walk in Darkness* by removing fictionalized references to Broyard's life of racial passing.[34] Schwartz, at the very least, must have been hip to Broyard, if no one else.[35]

Ralph Ellison disliked "A Portrait of the Hipster" and intended *Invisible Man* to challenge Broyard's conception of the hipster.[36] He was also no fan of Mailer's later account of the hipster. "These characters are all trying to reduce the world to sex, man, they have strange problems in bed," Ellison wrote to Albert Murray in 1958. "That's what's behind Mailer's belief in the hipster and the 'white Negro' as the new culture hero—he thinks all hipsters are cocksmen possessed of great euphoric orgasms and are out to fuck the world into peace, prosperity and creativity. The same old primitivism crap in a new package."[37] Despite these protests, Ellison's analysis of the hipster strongly resembles that of Broyard and Mailer. Ellison saw the hipster's power in his second-removism, his ability to understand his social situation and thereby manipulate that situation. In 1946, as he was beginning to compose *Invisible Man*, Ellison wrote to Richard Wright that black Americans were able to derive from experience what the French existentialists only theorized—the insight that "existence precedes essence."[38] For Ellison, who late in the war tried to escape the draft board, the hipster came to seem a poignant figure of resistance. Moreover, whatever Mailer's other substantial limitations as a critical thinker, we should not understand the psychopathic dynamism of the hipster solely as "the same old primitivism crap," as Ellison contends, or what Sianne Ngai would call the "affective ideologeme of animatedness," an ugly feeling that "harnesses . . . liveliness, effusiveness, spontaneity, and zeal to a disturbing racial epistemology."[39] Mailer's essay in fact attempts to disassociate affect (or, more precisely, attitude) from race. The very possibility of a "white negro" depends on the prior distinction between race and attitude: in this curious slogan, the adjective names a race, the noun an attitude. Hip, for Mailer, is primarily an attitudinal strategy for coping with an existential situation, albeit one grounded on the life-giving promise of "apocalyptic orgasm." The racial provenance of hipness turns out to be an accident of history, a by-product of the fact that oppression, first in the form of slavery and then via the Jim Crow system, confronted African Americans with instantaneous destruction at the hand of a totalitarian society before concentration camps and the atomic bomb supposedly generalized that condition.[40] Broyard, despite the primitivist impulses of his sponsors at *Partisan*, likewise regarded hipness not as the expression of a racial essence but as the symbolically formalized response to frustration and oppression, a kind of jive sublimation. These accounts in fact strongly resemble Henry Louis Gates's description of "Signifyin(g)" as "the black rhetorical difference that negotiates the language user through several orders of meaning."[41] Indeed, it is striking that Gates develops his theory of Signifyin(g) by drawing from Ellison in his capacity both as a novelist and as a critic, and that Gates looks to vernacular culture as embodying or encoding a *critical* tradition, a deconstructive mode *avant la lettre*. Whether analyzed in popular dictionaries, analytical essays, or literary representations, the hipster not only became raw material for critical theory but also was imagined to actively construct cutting-edge critical theory. The hipster could be more critical than the critics.

A No to Something

Ralph Ellison claimed that he first conceived of *Invisible Man* in 1945 after he spontaneously wrote the famous first line of the novel in a notebook. A "taunting, disembodied voice" intruded upon the composition of another attempted novel, a more conventional war fiction.[42] "I was most annoyed to have my efforts interrupted by an ironic, down-home voice," Ellison complained (xv). The voice teased him "with allusions to that pseudoscientific sociological concept which held that most Afro-American difficulties sprung from our 'high visibility,'" which he considered "a startling idea, yet the voice was so persuasive with echoes of blues-toned laughter" (xvi). From the outset, then, *Invisible Man* was an extended meditation on the figure of invisibility as it related to African American life in the era of Jim Crow, an attempt to confront commonplace sociological fallacies, a protest against conditions of oppression and discrimination. But it was also, perhaps more importantly, an effort to understand *what sort of voice* would be best suited to undertake such a meditation. Ellison strongly wished to avoid "writing what might turn out to be nothing more than another novel of racial protest instead of the dramatic study of comparative humanity," and so might have preferred to avoid his protest-inflected theme altogether, however compelling it was as a political critique (xviii). And yet "as I listened to its taunting laughter and speculated as to what kind of individual would speak in such accents, I decided that it would be one who had been forged in the underground of American experience and yet managed to emerge *less angry than ironic*" (xviii, my emphasis). Protest became an acceptable theme for Ellison because the protester was an ironist, someone who adopted an attitude of ridicule rather than anger toward oppression.

Focusing on the ironic character of the speaker rather than on the pseudosociology of race or on the angry militancy oppression supposedly engendered in all black Americans promised to rescue Ellison's emerging novel from falling into what he took to be a common trap: that "most protagonists of Afro-American fiction (not to mention the black characters in fiction written by whites) were without intellectual depth" (xix). Ellison shared this conviction with James Baldwin, whose "Everybody's Protest Novel," published in 1949 in *Partisan Review*, had trumpeted a generational insurrection of African American writers against Richard Wright, the metonymic embodiment of the so-called protest novelist. As he was completing *Invisible Man*, Ellison also read Richard Gibson's forgotten essay, "A No to Nothing," published in 1951 in *The Kenyon Review*, which lamented that "[t]he young Negro writer discovers to his bitter amazement that he is nearly trapped by the Problem."[43] Ambitious young African American writers faced two oppressors, neither of which would "allow a Negro the right to be human, to become a man and walk with his own strength his own way."[44] The first was, of course, the Jim Crow system, whose malevolent effects were widely documented. The second was the menace of the "Professional Liberal," who "[f]or the sake of *his* sanity" decides that "the Negro must bear the Problem, must be kept his pet, to be protected at the end of a leash" and who therefore categorically refuses to provide publishing contracts to black writers who might want to treat of any theme other than the "Negro Problem," since black writers supposedly "cannot possibly know anything else but Jim Crow, sharecropping, slum-ghettoes, Georgia crackers, and the sting of his humiliation, his unending ordeal, his blackness."[45] The black writer who gave the Professional Liberal what he wanted was something akin, in Gibson's scheme, to a collaborator in this more subtle form of racial oppression. Gibson concludes that Wright is "a doubtless *sincere* but defective thinker," and that unfortunately "there is not as yet a single work of literature by an American Negro which, when judged without bias, stands out as a masterpiece."[46] More damningly, Wright's novels "even fail as legitimate works of protest through their inhumanity, their frenzy, their unconscious acceptance of the stereotype. A simple tract urging one to contribute to the NAACP or the Urban League is much more rewarding reading."[47]

Though he resented the prominent—in his view, unearned—honor *Kenyon* had given Gibson, Ellison agreed with the basic argument of "A No to Nothing," though he reserved cautious praise for Wright, whom he had earlier championed as a genius, and who had helped him launch his own literary career. In "Richard Wright's Blues," Ellison initially defends Wright's *Black Boy* by claiming that Wright is "groping for individual values, in a black community whose values were what the young Negro critic Edward Bland has defined as 'pre-individual.' "[48] Ellison would later, in his famous disagreement with Irving Howe, reverse this position entirely, characterizing *Black Boy* as "a work of art shaped by a writer bent upon making an ideological point" and lamenting "that Wright found the facile answers of Marxism before he learned to use literature as a means for discovering the forms of American Negro humanity."[49] Ellison's most damning critique is that, far from working to articulate a convincing vision of African American individuality through his art (Ellison's original claim), Wright "could not for ideological reasons depict a Negro as intelligent, as creative or as dedicated as himself."[50] The essential problem, as Ellison came to see it, was not that Wright was protesting injustice but rather the degraded manner in which he conducted his protest. After all, Ellison was willing to address similar themes. Wright's Dostoyevskian story (a fragment of an unpublished novel), "The Man Who Lived Underground," first published in *Accent* in 1942, clearly influenced Ellison's initial conception of *Invisible Man*.[51] Very much like the invisible man, who ends up living in a basement, Fred Daniels, the protagonist of Wright's story, is driven underground by a system of brutal white supremacy in which he sees, in the words of Michel Fabre, "not reality in reverse . . . but the reverse of reality; he is still within the world, but because he is a spectator freed from himself and invisible, he is now omnipotent."[52] Houston A. Baker considers Daniels "[w]ily and resourceful, like the trickster of black folklore . . . the unseen seer, the tabula rasa . . . for an illicitly gained and radically revisionist comprehension of aboveground existence."[53] Whereas Baker, in my view, overestimates the wiliness of Daniels and the overall irony of the story, which uses relatively conventional narrative strategies, Baldwin and Gibson and Ellison all for their part underestimated Wright's irony, tarring him as a debased social realist and crassly ideological protest novelist in much the same way that Lionel Trilling excoriates Theodore Dreiser in "Reality in America."[54] In the case of both Dreiser and Wright, the most damning charge is that their aesthetic productions are born of commitments to an undialectical Marxism and to a vulgar socioeconomic determinism. In its meticulous documentation of the process through which Daniels builds his underground cave, Wright's "The Man Who Lived Underground" might indeed be seen as a realist counterpart to the surrealist tableau in the prologue and epilogue of *Invisible Man*, but the story is hard to dismiss as propaganda or as the dramatic rendering of some dogmatic Marxism. Nonetheless, comparing "The Man Who Lived Underground" to *Invisible Man*, we can see that Ellison much more completely than Wright adopts the ironic, essayistic style of Dostoyevsky's *Notes from Underground*, and seems determined to be seen as part of a European modernist heritage.

Ellison wanted to explore the same themes as Wright and to

absorb the ingenious elements of Wright's artistry, but also to distinguish himself from Wright. For Ellison, I would argue, the opposition between a humanizing cool irony and a dehumanizing angry sincerity became the significant axis of distinction between valid and invalid, artistic and nonartistic, forms of African American protest in fiction, between his own efforts and Wright's. Going even farther than Gibson in a sense, Ellison claimed that "if [complex and fully human African American characters] did not exist it would be necessary both in the interest of fictional expressiveness and as examples of human possibility, to invent them" (*Invisible Man* xix). It was the duty of the novelist dedicated to the project of "fictional expressiveness" to impose meaning "upon our disparate American experience" and "to create forms in which acts, scenes and characters speak for more than their immediate selves, and in this enterprise the very nature of language is on his side. For by a trick of fate (and our racial problems notwithstanding) the human imagination is integrative" (xx). Ellison thus saw the ironic narrator of *Invisible Man* not necessarily as an accurate reflection of the complexities of African American experience but rather, crucially, as a speculative means through which he might confer humanity upon even those who had had their dignity stripped from them, those who were rendered "invisible" as much by their own limiting beliefs as by the society that, seeing them as subhumans, overtly oppressed them. Riding the nonsegregated buses of Harlem in the thirties, Ellison came to recognize "a certain degree of freedom that had always existed in my group's state of unfreedom" and wondered "to what extent [he had] overlooked ... opportunities for self-discovery while accepting a definition of possibility laid down by those who would deny [him] freedom."[55] The form and content of *Invisible Man*, both of which pivot on the hinge of cool irony, answer this question. If *Invisible Man* became the African American literary masterpiece Gibson claimed did not yet exist—as Ellison hoped it would—it would both successfully represent hitherto unrepresented zones of black life and, more importantly, expand the range of aesthetic potential associated with black artists, symbolically redeeming his "group," and surpassing the hobbled genius of Wright. The novel itself would become something like an empirical proof of the universal humanity of

African Americans and the individual integrity of Ellison himself, a proof that he could harness "the very nature of language" to attain aesthetic heights the critical establishment increasingly associated with the emerging postwar canons of modernism (over against the corrupted forms of protest fiction).

Invisible Man is thus a Bildungsroman that simultaneously confronts its protagonist and author with the task of becoming a fully realized individual person. Each episode in the invisible man's development can be viewed, through this lens, as a battle with what Ellison saw as the destructive, dehumanizing power that ideologies of social and economic determination have over the person, ideological determinisms that resemble what Robert Chodat has called the "roles" that the invisible man encounters and performs.[56] At the end of the novel, Ellison's protagonist sees "Jack and Norton and Emerson merge into one single white figure. They were very much the same, each attempting to force his picture of reality upon me and neither giving a hoot in hell for how things looked to me ... I now recognized my invisibility" (508). These "roles" or "pictures of reality" have the perverse power to enact the dehumanization—the imposition of invisibility—that they theorize. If you accept yourself as subhuman, you risk making yourself just that.[57] The invisible man confronts a series of homologous pictures of reality, each of which by design constructs blacks as subhuman. Some of these pictures are structurally embedded in black practices, institutions, and ideologies—including the black college the invisible man attends and the violent nationalist ideology of Ras the Destroyer (né Exhorter)—while others, such as the ideology of the Brotherhood, manipulate genuine hopes for racial justice for other purposes. Rinehart and, more generally, the hipster become the first models of (almost) fully realized humanity that the invisible man encounters, the first person and type of person who do not merely passively accept prefigured roles and rigid ideologies but who instead author their own identities, in however imperfect a fashion. Astonishingly, relatively little critical attention has been paid to the pivotal role Rinehart occupies in Ellison's narrative and symbolic schema. Most critics attribute the invisible man's final epiphany to the death of Tod Clifton, failing to note that almost immediately after he witnesses

Clifton's death he begins for the first time to notice Harlem's hipsters—"men outside of historical time" (440)—who stand in for those areas of black life "invisible" to the ideology of the Brotherhood. Most critics either take the invisible man at his word when he claims to reject Rinehart or they characterize Rinehart as a kind anticipation or prefiguring of postmodernist themes (a selfless, self-deconstructing trickster figure, a dangerously decentered subject, or an amoral huckster / confidence man).[58]

Robert Genter, combining both claims, categorizes Ellison as a philosophical pragmatist who "was deliberately attempting to overcome the depoliticized character of postwar modernism without falling into the trap of social realism" in an effort to counteract the charge that Ellison is a "follower of a reactionary modernist aesthetic."[59] Genter claims that Ellison uses Rinehart as a means of defending his pragmatist commitments, while also recognizing "the dangers of detaching subjectivity from its transcendental foundations."[60] This argument errs on several fronts. However he categorized himself, Ellison's art embodies many core features of postwar modernist aesthetics. Moreover, Rinehart is not a warning of what could go wrong should you give up on having a self, but is rather a genuinely seductive figure, one whose (apparently) ironic self-conception is crucial to the invisible man's development, facilitating in him an "ironic leap of consciousness that was like looking around a corner" (500). If the invisible man eventually rejects Rinehart or "Rinehartism," it is more on ethical than on metaphysical grounds. Finally, to claim that postwar modernism was "depoliticized" is to ignore the political character of the era's literary culture. Whether we consider him to be a reactionary or not, Ellison conceived of the hipster as a powerful political figure.

Far from dismissing Rinehart-like figures, Ellison was, as Arnold Rampersad notes, "fascinated by characters who create and exploit chaos."[61] Unlocking the mystery of the hipster was, Ellison thought, a crucial task for black leaders. In an "Editorial Comment" for the *Negro Quarterly*, Ellison wrote that "[m]uch in Negro life remains a mystery; perhaps the zoot suit conceals profound political meaning; perhaps the symmetrical frenzy of the Lindy-hop conceals clues to a great potential power—if only Negro leaders would solve this riddle."[62] Compare Ellison's assertion that black leaders needed to understand the political significance of the "mysterious" symbolic forms (zoot suits, the Lindy-hop, etc.) of black urban popular culture with his later description of the invisible man as "young, powerless (reflecting the difficulties of Negro leaders of the period) and ambitious for a role of leadership" (*Invisible Man* xix). It is no coincidence that the invisible man's awakening to the power of symbolic action fully flowers while he is impersonating Rinehart. Lawrence Jackson writes, "Ellison thought the hipsters' leisure-based rebellions were important, calling to mind Kenneth Burke's *Counterstatement* [*sic*], which had proposed the bohemian as an antidote to the capitalist bourgeoisie, and named the 'aesthetic' approach as being *more capable than economic forces of solving the problem of fairness in a democracy*."[63] Ellison's lament that Wright failed to recognize how "the arts of music or speech or symbolic gesture" can "create within us moments of high consciousness" is a complaint about Wright's failure as a black leader.[64] Because he could at times be "too passionate"—an interesting comment when juxtaposed with Ellison's reputation as "cool"—Wright failed to recognize the symbolic significance of black popular culture.[65] The invisible man must avoid Wright's limitations; when he begins to understand the symbolic power Rinehart wields, he comes closest to achieving his ambition to lead. At this moment, the scales fall from his eyes, and he begins to fully see the inadequacy of the Brotherhood's account of history.

The Groove of History

After witnessing the murder of Tod Clifton, the invisible man struggles to understand how Clifton could possibly "give up his voice and leave the only organization [the Brotherhood] offering him a chance to 'define' himself" (438). Riding the subway, he inadvertently finds an answer to his question, becoming aware of boys who "sat as formally as they walked," wearing hats, tight-fitting suits, "communicating ironically with their eyes" (442). It is unsurprising that Clifton's death inspires the invisible man to notice these hipsters; he had earlier observed that "this Brother Tod Clifton, the young leader, looked somehow like a hipster, a zoot suiter, a sharpie—except his head of Persian lamb's wool had never known a straightener" (366).

Clifton's potential to become a hipster stands athwart his role as a leader, and his transformation into a street-corner peddler of Sambo paper dolls might be understood also as a transition from leader to hipster. At first, the invisible man laments that these hipster boys, like Clifton, have no access to the historical agency that the Brotherhood might offer them. But he eventually wonders whether they might indeed be "bearers of something precious" (441). Questioning his allegiance to the Brotherhood, the invisible man wonders, "What if history was a gambler, instead of a force in a lab-oratory experiment, and the boys his ace in the hole? What if history was not a reasonable citizen, but a madman full of paranoid guile and these boys his agents, his big surprise! His own revenge?" (441). Emerging onto 125th Street, the narrator becomes increasingly con-vinced of the failures of the Brotherhood, and he encounters, as if on cue, "other men dressed like the boys, and girls in dark exotic-colored stockings, their costumes surreal variations of downtown styles. *They'd been there all along, but somehow I'd missed them* . . . They were outside the groove of history, and it was my job to get them in, all of them" (443, my emphasis). In these passages, hipsters become metonymies for a population unrepresented on the Brotherhood's narrow map of black life. At the same time, the narrator evinces a conflicted under-standing of his relationship to the hipsters. A phrase such as the "groove of history" simultaneously evokes the Brotherhood's mech-anistic vision of history (history as "reasonable citizen," linearly fol-lowing a furrow or rut) and—contrarily—the notion that history itself might *groove* or *have a groove* (history as "madman full of para-noid guile").

The invisible man describes history's groove in the second sense at Clifton's funeral. The funeral draws "young zoot-suiters, hep cats, and men in overalls and poolhall gamblers," a possible, if ambiguous, sign that the whole community is genuinely interested in Clifton's death (451). An old man, singing "There's Many a Thousand Gone," touches "upon something deeper than protest, or religion . . . it was as though he'd changed the emotion beneath the words while yet the old longing, resigned, transcendent emotion still sounded above, now deepened by *that something for which the theory of the Brotherhood had given me no name*" (452, 453, my emphasis). When the Brotherhood's committee finally chastises the invisible man for organizing Clifton's funeral, Brother Jack explains, "you were not hired to think. Had you forgotten that? If so, listen to me: You were not hired to think" (469). This is the baldest confirmation yet of the Brotherhood's racism, a racism isomorphic with all the previous instances the invisible man has encountered, one that sees the black community as "raw materials to be shaped to [the Brotherhood's] program" (472). But the Brotherhood's problem is not only its racism, Ellison insists, but also its theory of history, which overlooks "the gin mills and the barber shops and the juke joints and the churches . . . the beauty parlors on Saturday when they're frying hair" (471). It fails to harness the black community to its side in part because it cannot recognize the power of vernacular culture (for which the hipster is an emblem) or take stock of the community's "whole unrecorded history" (471).

The invisible man's suspicions are confirmed in one of the novel's final, great set pieces. When he puts on dark green-black sunglasses and a wide-brimmed white hat to hide from Ras's men (482), who are using Clifton's death to rouse the community's anger against the Brotherhood, he discovers that he can impersonate B. P. Rinehart, a "Spiritual Technologist" (495). Women and hipsters address him as Rinehart. "They see the hat, not me," the invisible man thinks. "There is magic in it. It hides me right in front of their eyes" (485). The magic of the disguise induces a violent encounter with Brother Maceo, and the narrator realizes: "Here I'd set out to test a disguise on a friend and now I was ready to beat him to his knees—not because I wanted to but because of place and circumstance" (489). The invisible man's revelation turns out to be something like the discovery of the performativity of identity: "It was as though by dressing and walking in a certain way I had enlisted in a fraternity in which I was recognized at a glance—not by features, but by clothes, by uniform, by gait" (485). What had seemed at first to be a paradox, that Clifton could be both hipster and leader, melts away under the heat of a new insight: "I was not a zoot suiter, but a kind of politician. Or was I?" (485). Rinehart teaches the invisible man a new way of being in the world—a new *spiritual technology*—making finally visible a sector of reality invisible to those who wear the Brotherhood's ideological spectacles. Rinehart has "been around all the while . . . but I had looked past him"; his green-black glasses become "a political instrument," a prop that opens up "a new section of reality" (499). When he understands the hipster, he comes closest to becoming a genuine politician, a true leader. The invisible man's "discovery of Rinehart" shows him how, through irony, to recognize the symbolic machinery of real oppression and, in doing so, to become more fully human (501).

By suggesting that Rinehart (if not "Rinehartism") offers a better perspective on black life than the Brotherhood, Ellison entered headlong into the arena of Cold War cultural politics (504). Ellison saw the anticommunism born of the Truman Doctrine, the liberal, CIA-funded Congress for Cultural Freedom, and the House Un-American Activities Committee threaten artists and intellectuals everywhere around him, including his friend Langston Hughes and the critic F. O. Matthiesen. Even Wright, who wrote an essay for Richard H. Crossman's *The God That Failed* (1949), discovered that his anticommunism was insufficiently repentant, and eventually moved to France to work on literary projects related to African decolonization.[66] In this anticommunist climate, many intellectuals either renounced controversial political views altogether, becoming part of the mainstream liberal political establishment, or embraced the supposedly apolitical New Criticism.[67] Under these pressures, often with state sanction, black intellectual life shifted away from Hughes and Wright toward figures such as Baldwin and Gibson. "Everybody's Protest Novel" and "A No to Nothing" were, in fact, both selected for republication in *Perspectives U.S.A.*, a short-lived anticommunist publication, one of the first magazines the Ford Foundation created in what Frances Stonor Saunders has aptly called the "cultural Cold War."

A front for CIA money, the Foundation gave James Laughlin, an avid supporter of modernist art, half a million dollars with which to launch a magazine "targeted at the Non-Communist Left in France, England, Italy and Germany (and published in all those languages)" whose "aim . . . was not so much to 'defeat the leftist intellectuals in dialectical combat as to lure them away from their positions by aesthetic and rational persuasion.'"[68] Moreover, *Perspectives U.S.A.*

sought to demonstrate the advanced nature of American culture to European audiences, to "promote peace by increasing respect for America's non-materialistic achievements among intellectuals abroad."[69] Greg Barnhisel concludes that *Perspectives U.S.A.*, under Laughlin's direction, sought to redefine "the oppositional, even revolutionary impulses that underpinned so much modernist art . . . as being aimed not against bourgeois society, capitalism and liberal individualism but against middlebrowism, mass culture, and Stalinoid instrumentality."[70] At the end of the forties and at the beginning of the fifties, the punishment for deviating from the agenda of this modernism-armed coalition, even for avowed anticommunists such as Wright, could be devastating. Given this context, it is notable that Ellison excised from his final draft of *Invisible Man* early references to anticolonial struggles (which he had discussed extensively with Wright) and any references to the Brotherhood (a thinly veiled version of the Communist Party USA) that might be construed as too supportive of the left. Barbara Foley has documented what she calls the "anticommunistization" of *Invisible Man* across its multiple early drafts prior to its 1952 publication, and argues that the symbolic patternings and ironies that have made the novel so successful as a New Critical object of close analysis came at the expense of a more—though not entirely—sympathetic portrayal of the Brotherhood.[71] Seeking to dissociate himself from the left, and his own early leftist writings, Ellison removed many positive references to the Brotherhood and deleted all references to the journal of a black merchant marine, Leroy, whose political radicalization had originally been central to the invisible man's final political epiphany. Leroy's journal entries, stripped of language with any Marxist connotations, became instead the basis for the more generic epiphanies and celebrations of unlimited possibility of the novel's epilogue. In a sense, Rinehart displaces Leroy, becoming the new catalyst of the invisible man's transformation toward full (ironic) personhood. Even if we grant that Ellison freely and for purely aesthetic reasons systematically deradicalized *Invisible Man*, the final version of his novel became as a result more harmonious with vital center liberalism. Whether or not we consider the final version of *Invisible Man* superior, Foley is right to suggest that, in the political climate of the early fifties, the novel would probably not have won the National Book Award if its Marxist language remained unrevised, nor would it have been canonized so quickly.

Invisible Man was thus very much an "occasional novel," as Kenneth W. Warren argues.[72] Ellison's response to the cultural Cold War unambiguously conditions the irony of *Invisible Man:* this irony is consonant with the structural irony of the New Critics, the second-removism of Broyard, and the anticommunist ironic modernism of the New York intellectuals (and the CIA). Ellison's evolving literary commitments, broader changes in critical judgment, and Cold War politics were bound together. Foley's research is a major contribution to our understanding of the evolution of *Invisible Man,* but she fails to note that Ellison did not merely reject his former leftism for an "apolitical" New Critical idea of pattern and irony, but rather the New Criticism Ellison embraced imagined itself to be a rejection of and alternative to communism.[73] More specifically, Ellison rejected communism in favor of Kenneth Burke's theory of symbolic action, which emerged from Burke's engagement with Marx but by midcentury had come to resemble a version of the New Criticism.[74]

Ellison first encountered Burke in 1939 with Wright. Together, they attended Burke's seminar "The Rhetoric of Hitler's 'Battle,'" at the League of American Writers' Third American Writers' Congress in New York.[75] In this lecture (which would be published in *The Southern Review*), Burke argues that the symbolic economy of *Mein Kampf* deserves serious critical attention, so that one might better understand the foundations of Nazism, if only to "forestall the concocting of similar medicine in America."[76] Burke argues that the Nazis successfully displaced anxiety borne of real economic woe onto Jews, turning them into scapegoats whose total elimination could symbolically substitute for the real amelioration of economic problems. Ellison saw that this argument could be extended to help explain antiblack violence as the product of a similar dynamic of scapegoating. Burke's account became increasingly persuasive to Ellison, and he would eventually claim that the "one stable thing I have in this sea of uncertainty is the raft of [Burke's] concepts on which I lie as I paddle my way toward shore."[77] If Burke's account was true, the novelist could engage in a form of symbolic warfare, undermining stereotypes, disrupting fixed categories, unveiling the dynamic of symbolic action in the form of fiction. Building on Burke, Ellison claimed that "fictive Negroes are not, as sometimes interpreted, simple racial clichés introduced into society by a ruling class to control political and economic realities," but rather that "the Negro stereotype . . . is also a key figure in a magic rite by which the white American seeks to resolve the dilemma arising between his democratic beliefs and certain antidemocratic practices."[78] Many critics have previously noted that Burke's theories deeply inform *Invisible Man*. Donald E. Pease suggests, correctly in my view, that "Burke's theory of symbolic action supplied Ellison with the linguistic resources with which to differentiate his project from Wright's."[79] In "The Philosophy of Literary Form," Burke "proposed three terms as capable of defining the scope of dramatic action in art: purpose, passion, and perception."[80] In the Ellison archive at the Library of Congress, one finds these three terms—purpose, passion, and perception—written everywhere on drafts and stray sheets of paper, almost like an incantation. Assimilating these categories into his project, Ellison had his protagonist move from purpose (as a student) to passion (working for the Brotherhood) to perception (rejecting the Brotherhood, discovering his invisibility, witnessing the Harlem riot).[81] Rinehart, appearing near the end of *Invisible Man*, is a figure that embodies the possibilities of Burkean "perception," the catalyst for the invisible man's final (literal) enlightenment.

It is important to reiterate that the New Criticism and Burke's theory of symbolic action were not merely non-Marxist intellectual projects, but were also theoretical stances that for Ellison explicitly *contradicted* and *surpassed* Marxist political interpretations of socioeconomic order.[82] Whereas the New Critics found novel ways of analyzing literature without resorting to supposedly vulgar political analysis, Burke's Bohemian post-Marxism turned this innovation on its head, mapping the procedures of close reading to the analysis of symbolic communication—that is to say, all human communication and culture. Like the poem for Cleanth Brooks (who located the essence of poetry in its structure), symbolic forms are for Burke not pretty containers, arbitrary or decorative forms, within which content is to be found—the symbolic power of scapegoating is not the epiphenomenal manifestation of a socioeconomically determining base—but rather form and content are inseparable.[83] This convergence of vocabularies was possible, I think, because Burke shared with many New Critics a commitment to the distinctness and autonomous power of the symbolic sphere (which is what allows a phrase like "symbolic action" to be something other than redundant). Burke grapples with Brooks and Tate, among others, in his discussion of "master tropes" in *A Grammar of Motives*, although he makes sure to point out that his interest lies "not with their purely figurative usage, but with their rôle in the discovery and description of 'the truth.'"[84] Burke maps these tropes onto their "literal" or "realistic" equivalents: metaphor onto perspective, metonymy onto reduction, synecdoche onto representation, and irony onto dialectic. The stakes in equating irony with dialectic become clear soon enough. If we do not view history ironically, we risk taking too simple a view toward the ontology of historical development. Literal-minded Marxists will see the proletariat as "represent[ing] the *end* or *logic* of the development [of history] as a whole," Burke explains, whereas more ironically oriented critics will join Engels in noting that "[w]ithout the slavery of antiquity" there would be "no modern socialism."[85] Previous forms of oppression ironically create the productive preconditions that ultimately underwrite liberation, according to this view.

Understanding Ellison's relationship to Burke allows us to see that, far from condemning Rinehart, as many critics claim, Ellison reserves his most exuberant, ebullient, and theoretically sophisticated language for him—and for the mysteries of the hipster. This language is infused with a Burkean commitment to irony as dialectic:

Can it be, I thought, can it actually be? And I knew that it was. I had heard of it before but I'd never come so close. Still, could he be all of them: Rine the runner and Rine the gambler and Rine the briber and Rine the lover and Rinehart the Reverend? Could he himself be both rind and heart? What is real anyway? But how could I doubt it? He was a broad man, a man of parts who got around. Rinehart the rounder. It was true as I was true.

His world was possibility and he knew it. He was years ahead of
me and I was a fool. I must have been crazy and blind. The
world in which we lived was without boundaries. A vast seething,
hot world of fluidity, and Rine the rascal was at home. Perhaps
only Rine the rascal was at home in it. It was unbelievable, but
perhaps only the unbelievable could be believed. Perhaps the
truth was always a lie. (498)

In this crucial passage, the invisible man's discontent with the
Brotherhood leads him spontaneously to discover a specific, fully
formed theoretical alternative to their ideology: symbolic action,
paradox, contradiction, and irony as the definition of the "real." The
hipster helps him see a model of reality his previous commitment to
the Brotherhood's brand of historical materialism had blinded him
to. Only the "unbelievable could be believed." The "truth" turns out
to be a "lie"—indeed, the truth is perhaps *always* a lie. Only someone
like "Rine the rascal" can "be both rind and heart"; that is to say, only
Rinehart can master the symbolic forms (the "rind") that turn out to
be his content (his "heart"). Rinehart is "ahead of" the invisible man
in terms of his understanding both of the nature of reality and the
shape black leadership needs to take. He can see what Ellison's protagonist is "blind" to: the secret power of hip. Rinehart is, in short,
what the invisible man needs to become—a critical ironist, a dialectical man, someone who sees the (paradoxically) symbolic foundations of reality. Here, more than anywhere else in *Invisible Man*, hipness, New Critical irony, and Burkean symbolic action fuse into a
single ethos.

If the invisible man ultimately criticizes Rinehart, it is not on the
basis of his dialectical mastery of chaos. In fact, the invisible man
considers Rinehart possibly to be "a principle of hope for which [the
black community] gladly paid" and ultimately decides "I'd accept it,
I'd explore it, rine and heart" (506, 509). However, the invisible man
rejects "Rinehartism" because Rinehart uses his mastery of chaos
amorally and cynically to further his own narrow self-interest, apart
from the needs of the community and democracy (504). Rinehart has
taken his secret knowledge of the logic of symbolic action and has,
like Mailer's hipsters, chosen to use it merely in the service of

achieving apocalyptic orgasms. Nonetheless, Rinehart's powerful spiritual technology might be pressed into different ends. The guarded optimism of *Invisible Man*'s epilogue depends on the efficacy of this retooling of Rinehart's power. In his final close reading of his grandfather's advice, first presented in the prologue, the invisible man discovers in the structure of the injunction to "[a]gree 'em to death and destruction" what we can only characterize as a New Critical irony and paradox. For black Americans to say "yes" to white Americans means to "affirm the principle" behind American democracy "in whose name we had been brutalized and sacrificed" (574). At the same time that he discovers paradox and irony, the invisible man rejects "the freedom of a Rinehart" but continues to wonder, uncertainly, "what *is* the next phase?" (575, 576). The next phase remains ambiguous, but "my world has become one of infinite possibilities" (576). The definition of the world "is possibility. Step outside the narrow borders of what men call reality and you step into chaos—ask Rinehart, he's a master of it—or imagination" (576). Though the world remains much the same, as systematically racist as before, "now I better understand my relation to it and it to me" (576). In other words, though he is still oppressed—and though he has rejected efforts to organize against this oppression—the invisible man has discovered the nature of social ontology, its fundamentally ironic and semantically multivalent structure.

Ellison recommends critical irony—of which the ironic stance of the hipster is one variation—as the essential to achieving visibility. Adopting irony helps Ellison avoid, on one hand, racist stereotypes and, on the other hand, the "clenched militancy" of black nationalism. The racist stereotype and political nationalism, Ellison argued, both logically derive from an essentialist notion of "black culture" that ought to be rejected.[86] To the degree that irony offers something like a spiritual technology for the black artist of midcentury America, to the extent that merely writing ironically counts as a calling card of one's aesthetic powers and literary credibility, *Invisible Man* is an attempt by Ellison to justify his status as an individual and an intellectual. Ellison's achievement is, in my view, mixed. The aesthetic superiority of his novel over Wright's various fictions seems to me undeniable. But as a politically liberating or progressive figure, the hipster was—and remains—a dubious ideal. We need to give some credence to Irving Howe's claim in "Native Sons and Black Boys" that Ellison overestimates the power the invisible man achieved at the end of novel. It is certainly true, as Ellison notes in his reply, that to speak of "'infinite possibilities' while living in a hole in the ground" is deeply ironic, an irony of which he was undoubtedly aware.[87] What may be more ironic is that, following the publication of *Invisible Man*, Ellison did anything but live in a hole in the ground. His acceptance by the critical establishment was and remains nothing short of universal.[88] This acceptance might be well deserved, but it was also partly grounded, at least at first, upon a belief on the part of critics and intellectuals that being socially marginal but ironically aware is something like the very definition of freedom.[89]

The Hipster, the Critic, and the Industrial Business Machine

In 1958, while still an undergraduate at Cornell, Thomas Pynchon and the future environmentalist Kirkpatrick Sale began work on a dystopian musical satire called "Minstrel Island."[90] The incomplete musical—available at the Harry Ransom Center at the University of Texas at Austin—portrays an IBM-dominated future of 1998 in which artists and Bohemians "who have no place in the IBM world" have exiled themselves to the last countercultural harbor on earth, a remote island called Galilee.[91] "When you have an IBM machine that can produce whatever you want at a minimum of time, effort and expense you automatically have several million artists floating around without much to do," Pynchon and Sale's protagonist, named Hero, explains.[92] In the musical, IBM's corporate motto, "Think!" becomes a totalitarian slogan, and the corporation merges with the state. The plot of "Minstrel Island" revolves around a comic battle to control Galilee. A female character named Broad, a representative of IBM, announces that "the main computer at Poughkeepsie has decided this island is the ideal location for a computer, the Musical Unidirectional Force Field Equipped Tabulator ... Abbreviated MUFFET."[93] Broad is the sort of person who submits unthinkingly to "Big Mother Machine," who speaks "federally standardized English," and who "mak[es] love according to government pamphlet 1537-B."[94] In response to the invasion of his Bohemian enclave,

Hero uses the apparently ultimate weapon to subvert the IBMification of Galilee: "SEX." Hero tries to seduce Broad, to awaken her repressed sexuality, showing her ways of "making love" undreamed of in "pamphlet 1537-B," and in so doing to save the island from assimilation into the dominant socioeconomic order. For Pynchon and Sale, nascent countercultural politics finds its attendant genre in musical sex farce. They proffer what may seem to be a predictable thesis: that Bohemianism—in the form of willful inefficiency, sloth, Luddite pranks, and artful sexual play—might constitute effective resistance to the Industrial Business Mechanization of the world. Only *love*—"an archaic word referring to libidinous and almost always sexual stimuli occurring in the pre-civilized humans," which "[h]as no meaning, value or application in present society"—can save the day.[95] Like Broyard, Ellison, and Mailer, Pynchon and Sale saw hipsters as bearers of salacious political wisdom.

The unfinished collaboration is at too early a stage of development to make critical judgments about its hypothetical success. Characters, for example, have placeholder names such as Sailmaker, Bombmaker, Jazzman, and Whore. Nonetheless, as other critics have noted, many core themes that would come to define Pynchon's literary career are already visible in the collaboration. It is tempting to treat the musical as a "lascivious Luddite satire," to argue that it anticipates more serious warnings about "the pervasiveness of technology and society's deference to the machine," to use it as a sourcebook for Pynchon's mature work.[96] On this view, "Minstrel Island" gives evidence that Pynchon genuinely fears that people might become embodied IBM machines, humans turned automata, or that economic rationalization would destroy the art market. Such an interpretation would support the dominant tendency in Pynchon criticism. Emily Apter expresses the canonical take on these Pynchonian themes, suggesting that "[t]he writing of Pynchon . . . is as much a symptom of this postwar paranoid culture as its literary archive" and "imports into literature the mesh of cognitive modeling and conspiratorial globalism that gives rise to theories of paranoid planetarity."[97] Pynchon here becomes not only a symptom of socioeconomic change but also its most astute analyst, simultaneously a literary, cognitive, and critical resource. This sort of reading, which takes

Pynchon as a literary archive of paranoid culture, has endured for good reason. But this interpretation falters to the degree that it fails to recognize that Pynchon's ideas of "paranoid planetarity" derive from his historically specific engagement with postwar modernism and with the post-Beat subcultures and countercultural literary practices that sought to overcome that modernist tradition. If we fail to account for this point of origin, we risk continually rediscovering that our favorite critical methodologies (which often repose upon the same New Critical base) offer a suspiciously perfect means by which to explicate Pynchon's texts, without recognizing that Pynchon built his text with a sophisticated understanding of such methods.

Keeping this risk in mind, we might notice that "Minstrel Island," the creation of two Cornell undergraduates in the late 1950s, embeds another, less immediately obvious, understanding of the specific threat that IBM posed. The "federally standardized English" Pynchon feared he might be forced to speak, that he so passionately wanted to resist, was being spoken much closer to home, on campus. For Pynchon, as his occasional autobiographical writing makes clear, the local form of "federally standardized English" was nothing other than the language of literary criticism. References to IBM only thinly mask Pynchon's literary-critical fears. Indeed, in his influential 1952 essay, "The Age of Criticism," Randall Jarrell suggests that "a great deal" of criticism "might just as well have been written by a syndicate of encyclopedias for an audience of International Business Machines."[98] This bad criticism is "graceless, joyless, humorless, long-winded, niggling, blinkered, methodical, self-important, cliché-ridden, prestige-obsessed, almost-autonomous," and an "inexhaustible, unexceptional, indistinguishable" supply of it is available.[99] For Jarrell, critics had come to resemble "one of those robots you meet in science-fiction stories, with a microscope for one eye, a telescope for the other, and the mechanical brain at Harvard for a heart."[100] In this description, the critic resembles nothing other than V. herself (more human-shaped thing than person, a person who has swapped out her body for prostheses) or the test mannequins SHOCK (synthetic human object, casualty kinematics) and SHROUD (synthetic human, radiation output determined). Such criticism treated art as "data, raw material, the crude facts" to "explain or explain away."[101] If you fear becoming "like" SHOCK and SHROUD, as Benny Profane does in *V.*, one thing you might fear becoming is a robotic critic.[102] After all "Anthroresearch Associates" (the name of the firm that uses these mannequins) might as well be a synonym for the human sciences as such. In a fax interview with David Hajdu, Pynchon reminisces about the reputation of the critic among his set of English majors at Cornell: "In college one or another of us would come on like [a critic] every once in a while . . . and there would always be [Pynchon's friend] Dick [Fariña], pointing his finger, laughing, yelling, 'Critic!' 'Who,' you would say, 'me? Not me, man.' 'Eclectic,' he would yell back, 'academic, pedant. Ha!' He'd be right, of course. It helped keep you straight if that was something you worried about. He was like a conscience."[103]

In his 1983 introduction to Fariña's novel *Been Down So Long It Looks Like Up to Me* (1966), a book that is a kind of post-Beat book of cool philosophy and a *roman à clef* of undergraduate life at Cornell, Pynchon recalls his undergraduate days. "You have to appreciate the extent of sexual repression on that campus at the time," he writes. "Rock 'n' roll had been with us for a few years but the formulation Dope / Sex / Rock 'n' Roll hadn't yet been made by too many of us. At Cornell, all undergraduate women were supposed to be residing, part of the time under lock and key, either in dormitories or sorority houses . . . In these and other ways, the University believed it was doing its duty to act *in loco parentis*."[104] Students responded to the administration's social control by staging a protest, "like a preview of the '60s," on the lawn of the university president, a protest Fariña was involved in organizing.[105] For Pynchon, who feared he might become a sexless critic, perhaps aligned with university administration, Fariña embodied an alternative ethos. "Coeds I had lusted after across deep lecture halls were actually altering course, here, out in the daylight, to stop and talk to Fariña. He was inviting *them* to his party too. Oboy, I thought to myself, oboy."[106] Fariña wove fantastic stories about his adventures in Cuba and Ireland, and seemed like a latter-day Beat, a potent force of resistance. Pynchon describes Fariña's typical facial expression as "a half-ironic half-smile, as if he were monitoring his voice and not quite believing what he heard. He carried with him this protective field of self-awareness and instant feedback, and I never did see all the way through it."[107] Fariña, and the ironic hipster as a type, constituted a funhouse of the self: always monitoring himself; always watching others watch him; always adjusting his attitudes and behaviors, Rinehart-like, to remain one step ahead of the inquiring critic. Pynchon remembers, "[Fariña] was the crazy one, I was the rationalist—he was *engagé*, I was reserved— he was relaxed, I was stuffy."[108] Pynchon feared that he was Square, just another critic in a world full of them. When Pynchon writes that he could "never . . . see all the way through" Fariña's "protective field of self-awareness," we get an inkling that Fariña had somewhat pegged Pynchon. Pynchon *was*, critic-like, trying to "see though" Fariña, to read him like a text. What Pynchon learned instead from Fariña was that such readings could always be frustrated, because the object under critical examination was always slipping through the critic's fingers. The hipster could always remove himself from the scene or alter his behavior in ways designed to subvert interpretation, though such a defensive anticritical posture would logically require one to understand the protocols of the critic better than the critic understood them himself. If someone didn't get a story that he told, Fariña "would only half-smile, and shrug, as if to say, if you don't get it, you don't get it."[109]

Though he sometimes feared he might be nothing more than a critic, Pynchon did not simplemindedly embrace Fariña's hip irony. Instead, he seems to have felt ambivalently toward both criticism and hipness. On the one hand, becoming a hipster or a critic, mastering the practice of irony both figures prized, promised authority. On the other hand, both were losing their luster. Cleanth Brooks's assumption that irony might oppose middlebrow culture probably seemed less plausible than it had a decade earlier. And Beat-like attitudes, which had already garnered widespread publicity, also seemed exhausted. Like Oedipa Maas, herself an English major at Cornell, Pynchon was too young to be a Beat and too old to join newer youth movements. Moreover, though the critic and the hipster seemed like enemies to the young Pynchon, we have seen that the two figures were linked, that discourses of hipness were never straightforwardly antithetical to the establishment. As Morris Dickstein,

Andrew Hoberek, and others have shown, hatred of conformist organizations was nothing short of universal at the time when Pynchon was writing. Everyone feared IBMification. The dominant question was never whether to resist the vile power of conformity but rather how best to do so. In a sense, then, Hero's task in "Minstrel Island" is not to overthrow IBM, but to refurbish the paradigm of management it operates under, to find a way to make it more amenable to human flourishing. Hoping to transcend the limitations of the irony shared by the hipster and the critic, Pynchon sought a vantage point—a higher irony—from which to look down upon both figures. In pursuit of this new vantage point, Pynchon reconfigured in surprising ways the racial politics attending discourses of hipness. In his most famous short story, "Entropy," Pynchon's ironist continues to see the world as an object suffused with structural ironies, a connotation-infused textual object in need of critical interpretation. By the time he writes *V.*, Pynchon seems to decide that the most important political question facing midcentury Americans wasn't whether humans could resist becoming IBMified robots—we couldn't—but rather whether we might finally become robots capable of altering our own cultural programming.

The Education of Thomas Pynchon

The strangest fact about Thomas Pynchon's "Entropy"—"as close to a Beat story as anything I was writing then"[110]—is that it was published in *The Kenyon Review*, the little magazine most closely associated with the rise of the New Criticism. Allen Ginsberg once told Robie Macauley, who became editor of *Kenyon* in 1960, the year Pynchon's story was published, that he "would never submit anything to [*Kenyon*] . . . because they were so establishment."[111] *Kenyon* was published from 1939 to 1970, and though its circulation was low, its cultural importance, along with a host of other midcentury highbrow literary reviews, was considerable. Allen Tate argued that "[t]he ideal task of the critical quarterly is not to give the public what it wants, or what it thinks it wants but what—through the medium of its most intelligent members—it ought to have."[112] As Marian Janssen argues in her excellent history of *Kenyon*, such little reviews "shaped the literary sensibility of a generation," particularly by making literary criticism respectable. Publications like *Kenyon* "were manifestly and proudly highbrow and . . . published, first of all, serious, searching criticism, mainly of literature but also of the other arts. They also published poetry and fiction, which were usually selected according to the same criteria as the criticism and, consequently, complemented and highlighted it."[113] The principles of selection for *Kenyon*'s fiction were shaped by and meant to support its critical commitments, even under Macauley's less orthodox leadership. "Entropy" was therefore likely to be understood as compatible with *Kenyon*'s intellectual mandate, elevating the young Pynchon immediately to the sphere of the public's "most intelligent" members.[114]

But while *Kenyon* shaped its time, it was also unavoidably shaped in return. In the late fifties, faced with the success of new periodicals such as the *Evergreen Review*, which unashamedly advertised its Beat sensibility, *Kenyon* considered making itself more appealing to young intellectuals. In 1959, Eric Bentley wrote to Macauley suggesting to him that he should

> drag [*Kenyon*] down from its academic height . . . [A] sign of the victory of the critical approach in departments of literature is that even PMLA has become less arid. But as it moves toward KR, KR should back away fast! . . . As Chesterton said, nothing fails like success . . . Things have been quietly going to sleep recently, not just at KR but 'at' all such reviews. Evergreen Review has grabbed a new audience but not in a fashion I'd like to see you copy. But what to do?[115]

Although *Kenyon* had helped tip the balance in the academic war between scholarship and criticism in favor of criticism, Bentley understood that the intellectual situation had changed. New students of literature were coming into a university where criticism was no longer a revolutionary force. It was, instead, part of the literary establishment. Reacting against a domineering modernist tradition and the New Criticism tooled to explicate it, up-and-coming, Beat-influenced writers threatened to flee to new, hipper literary reviews. Pynchon was one of these writers.[116] Pynchon and *Kenyon* both found themselves caught between New Critical tradition and an emerging countercultural sensibility. When the narrator of "Entropy" describes "funny-looking cigarettes which contained not, as you might expect, tobacco, but an adulterated form of *cannabis sativa*," the contours of their shared dilemma become clearer.[117] This quote neatly exemplifies what a literary solution to their problem might look like. The implied reader of this sentence is meant, of course, to disidentify with the "you" who naïvely "expects" these cigarettes to contain "tobacco." (The empirical *Kenyon* reader might have needed Pynchon's helpful explanation, but might also have wished to pretend he did not.) At the same time, Pynchon adulterates countercultural pot humor with technical jargon. By describing marijuana as *"cannabis sativa,"* he invites the reader to distinguish between the story's standard-issue potheads and the implied author, who is sober enough to observe them with critical irony. A sentence like this shows how Pynchon and *Kenyon* could serve one another well, each helping the other inhabit a fantasy of transcending the critical-countercultural division. Publishing in *Kenyon* allowed Pynchon, as he put it, to "sophisticat[e] the Beat spirit with second-hand science," while simultaneously hanging on to some version of artistic seriousness, a feeling of literary refinement, and the prestige that came with publishing a short story in a highbrow magazine.[118] Publishing a story like "Entropy" allowed the editors of *Kenyon* to believe that they had countered the Beat menace without relinquishing their core values. All of this is visible at the sentence level, in the seemingly simple phrase "as you might expect."

The midcentury context I have reconstructed thus far is not only of interest as literary history. It also transforms how we might more generally interpret Pynchon's classic short story. "Entropy" practically allegorizes the conflict between counterculturalists and critics in the organization of its setting.[119] Callisto's vague Romantic / modernist musings in the upper-level apartment is to the New Criticism as Meatball Mulligan's raucous lease-breaking party in the lower apartment is to the Beat. Callisto's musings—his fear of entropy—combine various elements of the literary education Pynchon received at Cornell, most notably dramatizing the ideas of Henry Adams and linking Romantic weather metaphors to the

second law of thermodynamics. Callisto proffers the view that "warp-
ings in the atmosphere should be recapitulated in those who breathe
it," a sort of pathetic fallacy cosmically scaled up (83). In invoking
this recapitulation, as Joseph Tabbi notes, the story literalizes within
its fictive world categories found in M. H. Abrams's essay "The
Correspondent Breeze: A Romantic Metaphor," published in *The
Kenyon Review* in 1957.[120] In Romantic poetry, Abrams argues, metaphors of breeze—and the "symbolic equation" of breath and wind—
frequently mark the poet's "return to a sense of community after
isolation, the renewal of life and emotional vigor after apathy and
spiritual torpor, and an outburst of creative inspiration following a
period of sterility."[121] "Poetic man," by this view, turns out to be "an
instrument subject to outer impression," a picture of poetic production that relies on the "conceptual model" of the Aeolian harp.[122]
Thus the breeze becomes "the stimulus and outer correspondent to
a spring-like revival of the spirit after a frozen wintry season."[123]
Though breeze metaphors proved to be "peculiarly apposite to
some major preoccupations of the age," such Romantic figures are,
in Abrams's view, "reactionary" in the sense that they draw on (or
secularize) long-established poetic and religious analogies. Indeed,
Abrams notes, "[t]he Stoic concept of the World Soul—of the
Pneuma, or Spiritus Sacer, or Anima Mundi—originally involved, in
the literal sense of these names, the concept of a kind of breath, a
divine gas, infusing the material world and constituting also the individual human psyche."[124] Abrams here criticizes archetypal criticism's tendency to treat "loose analogy as though it were identity"
(he criticizes Marxist and Freudian literary criticism for the same
reason). Pynchon unabashedly appropriates the "material symbol"
Abrams documents, but transforms his "loose analogy" into an
"identity" within the fictive world of "Entropy."[125] "Entropy" aligns
cosmological thermodynamic conditions (rather than breeze) with
the plight of the individual personality. Somewhat misrepresenting
Abrams's argument, conflating the Romantics with their predecessors, Pynchon's narrator comments that "every good Romantic
knows . . . the soul (spiritus, ruach, pneuma) is nothing, substantially,
but air" (83). The thermodynamic concept of entropy provides
Pynchon's not only a figure but also a mechanism for coordinating
cosmic heat death and individual spiritual blockage.

Pynchon's entropy does not allow the poet to return to a sense of community, but rather dissipates both the community and the poet. Indeed, the entropic destruction of community is the theme of Callisto's autobiography (which he dictates to Aubade, in the third-person style of *The Education of Henry Adams*). In Callisto's mnemonic device for recalling the laws of thermodynamics—"you can't win, things are going to get worse before they get better, who says they're going to get better"—we already detect the broadness of Pynchon's vision of entropy (87). The term "things" in this sentence is significantly vague, allowing Callisto and Pynchon to discuss different levels of social, political, and cosmological organization in the same breath, suggesting an identity between these levels. Callisto says he realized "that the isolated system—galaxy, engine, human being, culture, whatever—must evolve spontaneously toward the Condition of the More Probable," a condition he takes not as a metaphor for social and cultural change but as a genuine law of social and historical development (87).

> He saw, for example, the younger generation responding to Madison Avenue with the same spleen his own had once reserved for Wall Street: and in American 'consumerism' discovered a similar tendency from the least to the most probable, from differentiation to sameness, from ordered individuality to a kind of chaos. He found himself, in short, restating Gibbs' prediction in social terms, and envisioned a heat-death for his culture in which ideas, like heat-energy, would no longer be transferred, since each point in it would ultimately have the same quantity as energy; and intellectual motion would, accordingly, cease. (88–89)

In his *Education*, Henry Adams imagines history as moving from unity to multiplicity. Callisto's gloomy thermodynamic narrative reimagines Adams, describing history as a movement toward social homogenization, mass and middlebrow culture (named here "consumerism"), and intellectual conformity. These are, of course, classic midcentury themes, but Pynchon has a more specific agenda. In expressing his fear that "intellectual motion" as such would cease, Pynchon reconciles tradition (Romanticism, modernism) as it was taught to him with the concerns of "the younger generation" (that is,

Pynchon's generation), refurbishing this tradition, building a bridge between social worlds and reading communities.

Though he seems to endorse Callisto's views of entropy, Pynchon opens up an important gap between Callisto and the story's implied author. This gap becomes most apparent in the climax to the upstairs narrative, when Callisto's lover Audabe, the only other person in the apartment, "as if seeing the single and unavoidable conclusion to all this," breaks the apartment's window with her hands and "turned to face the man on the bed and wait with him until the moment of equilibrium was reached, when 37 degrees Fahrenheit should prevail both outside and inside, and forever, and the hovering curious dominant of their separate lives should resolve into a tonic of darkness and the final absence of all motion" (98). Missing the point of Pynchon's undergraduate fatalism, claiming that Pynchon's story advocates meaningful action of some sort, literary critics often try to motivate Aubade's final violence. Victoria de Zwann, for instance, describes it as "a desperately nihilistic act and an attempt to introduce into this closed world a measure of new information."[126] If we try to discover Aubade's motive—even if this motive is to introduce "new information" into a closed system—we risk missing Pynchon's point. If it weren't Audabe smashing the window, disrupting the enclosed system of Callisto's apartment, something or someone else would do just the same. That is how entropy works in Pynchon's undergraduate gloss of the term: entropy, either at a personal or social level, is impossible to resist. However, there is at least one positive consequence of this view of entropy. The New Critical emphasis on autonomy or the intrinsic, Callisto's attempt to wall himself away from his environment, cannot be sustained. Pynchon figures the idea of autonomy (whether from other people or from nonpersonal forces) as a major intellectual error. Callisto's story can then be read as a critique of *Kenyon*, a loving satire of the views stereotypically associated with it.

This critique helps Pynchon justify the inclusion of the second strand of his story, the downstairs lease-breaking party. In this part of "Entropy," the most relevant Beat figures are Duke, Vincent, Krinkles, and Paco, the Duke di Angelis quartet, who at the beginning of the story sit "crouched over a 15-inch speaker which had been bolted into the top of a wastepaper basket" (81). The quartet "recorded for a local label called Tambú and had to their credit one 10" LP entitled *Songs of Outer Space*" (81). In his descriptions of the quartet, Pynchon repeatedly puns on the word "cool," associating it with thermodynamic "deep freeze." This association recalls a humorous essay on hipster parties Chandler Brossard published in *Neurotica* in 1950, which features a cast of hipsters "so cool they have frozen to death in this hip silence . . . Not a word has been spoken, not a gesture risked in hours."[127] The quest for cool has turned Brossard's partygoers into gestural ice cubes. They do not leave a trace, enacting a social heat death. Pynchon's Duke di Angelis quartet is an avant-garde jazz version of the cool partiers Brossard lampoons. The title of the group's first album, *Songs of Outerspace*, of course, invokes the "coolness" of deep space. So cool is this group that it ingeniously abstracts jazz to its seemingly ultimate limits. "In the middle of the room, the Duke di Angelis quartet were engaged in a historic moment. Vincent was seated and the others standing: they were going through the motions of a group having a session, only without instruments" (94). In a conversation with Meatball Mulligan, Duke explains his group's new musical discovery. Duke abstracts further from a jazz technique in which there are "no root chords. Nothing to listen to while you blow a horizontal line. What one does in such a case is, one *thinks* the roots." The next logical extension of this technique is "to think everything . . . Roots, line, everything." The quartet begins to "play," and Pynchon's narrator describes how, remaining silent and thinking their music, "off they went again into orbit, presumably somewhere around the asteroid belt" (95). By abstracting their music to the point where they no longer use instruments, the quartet has discovered another version of the "Condition of the More Probable" Callisto fears. This is satire, to be sure, and the word "presumably" in the previous quote signals Pynchon's ironic distance from the scene that he is imagining. At the same time, the quartet's music—which we might properly honor as a sort of minimalism—gives evidence of a crisis or division within the ethos of hipness itself, a crisis of irony.

We already see the origin of this characterological crisis in a 1959 article that Jack Kerouac wrote in *Playboy*. He wrote that "[b]y 1948 the hipsters, or beatsters, were divided into cool and hot." The cool beat, Kerouac claims, "is your bearded laconic sage, or schlerm, before a hardly touched beer in a beatnik dive, whose speech is low and unfriendly, whose girls say nothing and wear black." The hot, meanwhile, "is the crazy talkative shining eyed (often innocent and openhearted) nut who runs from bar to bar, pad to pad, looking for everybody, shouting, restless, lushy, trying to 'make it' with the subterranean beatniks who ignore him."[128] Kerouac describes himself as transitioning from a hot hipster to one cooled by the discipline of Buddhist meditation. Pynchon also aligned himself with the cool, or at least sees the cool as the more powerful historical tendency, and "Entropy" draws attention to two senses of the word, as we have seen. *Cool* both designates a social status associated with the nascent counterculture, synonymous with "hip," and describes "the eventual heat-death of the universe" (85). But if cool is merely the social manifestation of a more general thermodynamic heat death, then it is also dangerous. Those who proffered cool might find themselves devoured by its ruthless power. The "metonymous gestures" Broyard described as a form of resistance (which were already a response to powerlessness) become a fear of "gesture" itself, as recounted by Brossard. Critique risks passing into quiescence. This was the political problem Pynchon's "Entropy" discovers at the heart of cool. Aspiring hipsters may think that Fariña-like cool irony offers a way to resist the establishment, to slip through the cracks of power, but Pynchon's early invocation of entropy suggests that the hip ethos of Meatball Mulligan's apartment offers no better solution to the problem of cultural degradation than does Callisto's conservative, self-insulating response above. As its distance from "hot" varieties of hipness grows, such practices of irony may instead accelerate the heat death of social life (not to mention the universe). Against Mailer's uncritical praise of the hipster, Pynchon develops a critique of both the establishment and the Beat response to the establishment. He also tries, as we will see, to correct for the racism of accounts such as Mailer's. But he does not give up on irony itself as a potential political weapon. Pynchon wanted to develop a third ethos of political irony, a sort of irony most visible in his rendition of the character McClintic Sphere in *V.*

Sophisticating the Beat Spirit

The letter V appears everywhere in Thomas Pynchon's first novel. The book begins in Virginia, on East Main, a street whose mercury-vapor lamps recede "in an asymmetric V," and from there Vs and V names proliferate: Vheissu, Victoria Wren, and on and on (2). V-spotting critics often argue that Pynchon is building, at the level of plot, "a figural system in which V is the primary object of interpretation . . . a signifying centre which would be the 'spirit' informing modern history, giving it pattern, significance and direction."[129] Indeed, Vs are not only part of the book's fictive world, but the novel's narrative itself traces a V shape, with Stencil and Profane moving along independent trajectories toward their final intersecting point in Malta; this intersection itself is punctuated by the final period of the epilogue. The title of the novel is, then, homologous to its global plot structure, a structure that is also a formal allusion to James Joyce's *Ulysses* (with Profane as Stephen and Stencil as Bloom). The reader's search for V patterns at every narrative level, of course, mimics the paranoid reading strategies Herbert Stencil uses within the novel in his quest for the character V. Benny Profane, meanwhile, is most often taken as an antitype to Stencil, the aimless principle of disorder, chaos, and entropy, a figure for the possibility that Pynchon's V signifiers don't mean anything in particular. Pynchon is understood to be building toward one of two revelations, famously formulated in *Gravity's Rainbow* (1973): that either everything is connected (a view associated with Stencil) or nothing is (associated with Profane). We are invited to continually weigh these interpretations, to measure each against the other, since there seems to be no preponderance of evidence in the text for either stance.[130] Pynchon excites but then frustrates our desire to make meaning, challenges us to decide whether the novel's meticulous patterning means anything (or nothing). The novel's V references thus invite the reader to learn certain metahermeneutic skills—to cultivate a certain ethos. The stakes of the reader's newly forged critical consciousness remain, even today, poorly understood. Tony Tanner has argued that socio-technological transformations motivate Pynchon's recommendation of this new disposition, noting that his characters are trying to resist the subordination of the animate (the world of meaning) beneath the inanimate (the world of systems and technology).[131] Just as Stencil and Profane must respond to this crisis, so too must the reader.

My account of Pynchon's early career supports a different explanation for the significance of the novel's patterning. It is easy to see that the two narrative strands of *V.*, Stencil's quest and Profane's antiquest, also map onto the opposition between postwar modernism and the post-Beat counterculture, much as the upstairs-downstairs staging of "Entropy" does. This mapping is as much a matter of form (say, Pynchon's textbook parodies of modernist style) as content. *V.* might be said to project the bifurcated narrative structure of "Entropy" onto a world stage, oscillating between two supposedly irreconcilable domains of cultural value and prestige, in search of a superior irony over these two ossified stances. Yet it can be hard to discern what specific alternative model of irony Pynchon might be offering. I have, of course, claimed that the Bohemian ethos of hip irony, the Fariña-like distance from all definite positions, was far more compatible with the view of the New Critics and other postwar intellectuals than many (including Pynchon) would have liked to admit. As I have tried to show, the hipster-critic binary often dissolves upon careful scrutiny. Yet the opposition haunted Pynchon— or at least haunts his early fiction—and his attempt to imagine a third way continues to be a central concern in *V.* Pynchon's third way of irony finds its most compelling figure in McClintic Sphere, the free jazz saxophonist based on Ornette Coleman. In his portrayal of Sphere, Pynchon invents a characterological solution, which is also (as we will see) a formal solution, exemplifying how one might simultaneously transcend the Beats and the postwar modernism that establishment intellectuals advocated. This solution, Pynchon knows, is fraught with political danger. For in his rendition of this African American saxophonist, Pynchon faced the problem of racial appropriation or ventriloquism, risking charges of writing in literary blackface. He also risked, as Luc Herman and John M. Crafft charge, descending into a "youthful mixture of cautious liberalism and Beat cliché."[132] Based on a careful study of the typescript of *V.*, Herman and Crafft's critique—which also regards the published novel as "somewhat green" on matters of race—imagines Pynchon to be struggling with journeyman impulses, which he would later overcome. But Sphere, I will show, is more than just a youthful fantasy of liberal integration.[133]

Sphere's ethos—which I will equate with Pynchon's third way of irony—manifests itself not only in explicit descriptions of his character but also in the novel's elaborately staged, racially fraught focalization of his perspective. From its beginning, academic Pynchon criticism has argued that "Keep cool, but care" (393), Sphere's advice to himself after hearing Ruby / Paola's story, functions as "the novel's coda," a mantra that conjures an excluded middle beyond Stencil's and Profane's irreconcilable positions.[134] Some scholars criticize this anodyne interpretation of Sphere's mantra—and of *V.*—for mistakenly suggesting that Pynchon was something like a "cheerful humanist."[135] Despite such objections, critics today largely accept that Sphere's famous catch phrase might well indicate "how ethically responsible Pynchon wanted his main African American character [in *V.*] to be."[136] Though Sphere interprets his own aphorism to mean "[l]ove with your mouth shut, help without breaking your ass or publicizing it," the injunction to "care" also seems to respond to the fear we saw above, that hipness might logically entail political quietism (393). At the same time, perhaps fearful that his advice might seem sentimental or cloying, Pynchon attempts to "sophisticate" Sphere's viewpoint. This sophistication effort is already signaled in Sphere's name. Charles Hollander has argued that the character's name was inspired by the middle name of Thelonious Monk.[137] However, a 1962 letter from Pynchon to Kirkpatrick Sale refutes this plausible explanation: "[L]istening to the Juan Lopez Montezuma show," Pynchon writes to Sale, "I am informed that Thelonious Monk's middle name is Sphere. There is also a character in *V.* named Sphere, also a jazz musician, though he blows alto not piano, and his name was chosen because a sphere is a non-square in 3 dimensions."[138] Sphere is, to be sure, a minor character in *V.*, but we can already see two important binary oppositions that structure him, distinguishing him from other important minor characters in the novel (for example, Dudley Eigenvalue). First, Pynchon wants Sphere to be both caring and cool (both hot and cold, in Kerouac's sense). Second, as his account of the origin of the character's name signals, Pynchon wants Sphere to be both flat and (with apologies for the pun) round, at once a type (a characterological "non-square in 3 dimensions") and a moral singularity (whose wisdom instructs the reader). These characterological contradictions, I will suggest, transform the terms of the debate about the humanism or antihumanism of Pynchon's early fiction.

These characterological contradictions are fully visible in an early scene, when the Whole Sick Crew hangs out at the V-Note. Introducing Sphere, Pynchon writes:

> Inside McClintic Sphere was swinging his ass off. His skin was hard, as if it were part of the skull: every vein and whisker on that head stood out sharp and clear under the green baby spot: you could see the twin lines running down from either side of his lower lip, etched in by the force of his embouchure, looking like extensions of his mustache.
>
> He blew a hand-carved ivory alto saxophone with a 4½ reed and the sound was like nothing any of them had heard before. The usual divisions prevailed: collegians did not dig, and left after an average of one and a half sets. Personnel from other groups, either with a night off or taking a long break from somewhere crosstown or uptown, listened hard, trying to dig. "I am still thinking," they would say if you asked. People at the bar all looked as if they did dig in the sense of understand, approve of, empathize with: but this was probably only because people who prefer to stand at the bar have, universally, an inscrutable look. (55)

The key word in this passage is "you." What sort of relationship does the narrator have to "you," and how does this "you" relate to the denizens of the V-Note, or to Sphere for that matter? David Witzling takes Pynchon's focus on a white audience in the second paragraph to suggest that Sphere is "probably the focalizing character," but the narrator makes a point of approaching Sphere from outside, seeing him "under the green baby spot."[139] At the same time, this is not some neutral or purely impersonal camera-eye perspective. Roving throughout the bar, the disembodied narrator both lays claim to and disparages hipness, noticing the allocation of countercultural capital ("the usual divisions") among bebop aficionados, speaking "universally" about the bar-goers. It is in passages like these where content and form shake hands in *V*. For Pynchon's description of those who dig and those who do not, in their relative proportions, summons an autoreferential position outside hip's ironic knowingness that at the same time retains all the social, symbolic, and epistemic privilege of those who dig. This epistemic privilege, of course, evokes fraught midcentury debates about racial representation, which continue to this day. In the context of the saxophone performance, the description of Sphere's skin as "hard" indirectly raises a question about the character's race. What color are we supposed to imagine this "hard" skin to be? This question becomes especially pointed in light of Michael Szalay's claim that literary representations of hipness often served white liberal professionals as a cultural technology for "view[ing] themselves as simultaneously inside and cast out from the center of political power, as possessed of both white and black skin."[140] By Szalay's unsettling account, white professionals fantasized about imaginatively inhabiting black skins. In rendering Sphere, Pynchon risks participating in these fantasies, celebrating the structural marginality of African Americans as Mailer does in "The White Negro" and Jack Kerouac does in *On the Road*, when Sal Paradise infamously wishes "I were a Negro, feeling that the best the white world had offered was not enough ecstasy for me, not enough life, joy, kicks, darkness, music, not enough night."[141] Pynchon admired Kerouac, and there's evidence that he partially bought into the Beat romance of marginality. In a letter to Sale likely sent in 1962, casually referring to Ginsberg's *Howl*, Pynchon writes that he spent New Year's Eve "roaming the negro streets. specifically penn station and environs. us and the bums sleeping on the steps near the 31st. exit where it is warm."[142] In addition, Pynchon frequented the Five Spot with Richard Fariña, and together they saw Ornette Coleman—the model for Sphere—whom they viewed as "new, revolutionary, for some messianic."[143] Nonetheless, Pynchon's description of Sphere undermines white liberal fantasies that one might imaginatively don black skins. For, though highly mobile, roving around the V-Note with ease, the narrator cannot penetrate Sphere's "hard" surface. Sphere's ambiguously raced skin adheres too close to the bone, "as if it were part of the skull." Neither Pynchon's narrator nor "you" can easily don Sphere's skull-cleaving skin.

Sphere's impenetrable skin impedes Pynchon's narrator, but doesn't wholly debar reciprocal "digging" across racial lines. We can partially infer Pynchon's model of cross-racial understanding from his fascinating *New York Times Magazine* essay, "A Journey Into the Mind of Watts" (1966), written a year after the Watts Riots in Los Angeles. The headline promises an article that will explain—to the implicitly white reader—the mysteries of black ghetto life, figured here as Watts's "mind" (it's unclear whether Pynchon chose his own title). To a degree, Pynchon fulfills this expectation, invoking "realities like disease, like failure, violence and death, which the whites have mostly chosen—and can afford—to ignore."[144] Nonetheless, his journey into Watts's mind soon reaches a hard border. The reader encounters a familiar epistemic problem, the asymmetrical racial knowledge that birthed hipness in the first place. Pynchon writes, "A Watts kid knows more of what goes on inside white heads than possibly whites do themselves" (80). This assertion recalls James Baldwin's claim that "I think I know something about his [Norman Mailer's] journey from my black boy's point of view because my own journey is not really so very different, and also because I have spent most of my life, after all, watching white people and outwitting them, so that I might survive."[145] Not only are white people unable to see inside black heads, Pynchon contends, but they can't even see what's happening inside their own heads. Only black Americans, who are forced into double-consciousness, "always looking at one's self through the eyes of others, of measuring one's soul," can understand the shape of the white mind.[146] Pynchon updates W. E. B. Du Bois's formulation for the age of electronic media when he writes, "[w]hite values are displayed without let-up on black people's TV screens" (78). Pynchon's own vantage point here remains racially unmarked. In his interviews with Watts residents, he vanishes from view. Pynchon is not exactly adopting the norms of journalistic objectivity here, but seems instead to be trying to liquidate his own body, to rub out the first-person pronoun altogether, to speak of "white culture" and "white values" in the third person, without at the same time claiming the authority to speak from a "black boy's point of view." To efface his own whiteness, Pynchon must redefine race as essentially cultural. Throughout his essay, Pynchon describes the difference between Watts and Greater Los Angeles as a difference between "two very different cultures: one white and one black" (35). To be sure, these cultures have different relationships to something Pynchon wants to call "reality." Whereas Watts is in touch with "reality," the "Disneyfied landscape" of Greater Los Angeles ped- dles "unreality" (78). Nonetheless, Pynchon transforms the terms of racial oppression from Mailer's existentialism into an early ver- sion of culturalism, which is why Pynchon sees something omi- nous in white efforts to "cool" Watts with "a siege of persuasion," coaxing "the Negro poor into taking on certain white values," absorbing them into Greater LA's unreality (84). It is hard to imagine that anyone could "persuade" Mailer's "Negros" to ignore white supremacy.

Pynchon thus imagines racial identity along the lines of what Abigail Cheever calls "culturalist models of the self."[147] For Pynchon, race is a performance, detachable from specific bodies, though such detachment is never easy, reproducible as iterated codes or con- ventions, transmissible via television, subject to reconfiguration or erasure. By this account, African Americans do not master "white values" in order to "survive" (as for Baldwin) but as a by-product of watching unreal white culture on the tube. This culturalist model of race, already on display in *V.*, redefines the power of irony and reimagines the attitudinal conditions of white-black rapprochement. We can see how irony functions under Pynchon's culturalist view when, responding to a "Northern liberal" request that he play "Night Train," Sphere imagines saying, "Yes, bwana. Yazzuh, boss. Dis darkey, ol' Uncle McClintic, he play you de finest Night Train you evah did hear. An' aftah de set he gwine take dis ol' alto an' shove it up yo' white Ivy League ass" (298). Imitating a stereotypically black vernacular dialect, Sphere shows that he understands the cultural codes governing the condescending expectations of these white Ivy Leaguers better than they themselves do. Sphere's parodying speech is an example of what Susan Gubar calls "racechange": the "traversing of race boundaries, racial imitation or impersonation, cross-racial mimicry or mutability, white posing as black or black passing as white, pan-racial mutuality."[148] Sphere, of course, here imagines performing a cartoon version of his own blackness for a white audience. At the same time, Pynchon performs Sphere performing this caricatured blackness. If Sphere knows what white Ivy Leaguers do not know about themselves, then Pynchon and white readers might hope to gain self-knowledge by looking into the mirror of Sphere's rhetorical parody of white racist fantasies. Such racechanging performances can yield genuine understanding, can be more than a delusion or misguided invention, because—on Pynchon's protoculturalist view—there is no foundation or authentic ground to race in the first place. *V.*'s narrator cannot penetrate or wear Sphere's skin because, on this model of the racial self, the saxophonist (no less than the implicitly white narrator) is nothing but skin, all surface.[149] Were the narrator able somehow to penetrate Sphere's skull-hewing skin, he would likely uncover something resembling the "intricate understructure of silver openwork" that Fausto Maijstral imagines the Maltese children finding as they disassemble V. in her guise as the Bad Priest (370). Under such circumstances, the method by which one is able to "dig" changes. Whereas Mailer's hipsters believe they can absorb "the existentialist synapses of the Negro," Pynchon's higher ironist sees through (so to speak) such faulty depth models of hipness.[150] No longer a form of looking beneath surfaces (and even Ellison relied on metaphors of depth), Pynchon's irony becomes the successful analysis and mimicry of various linguistic or cultural codes. Racial reconciliation becomes a matter of reorganizing the socially asymmetric cultures that generate racial difference in the first place. What aspiring hipsters ought to seek is not experience but information.

And Pynchon strongly associates Sphere's musical practice with information theory, ensuring that Sphere himself comes to understand his art in precisely these terms. Talking to audio technicians, Sphere decides that he wants to learn about stochastic music and electricity because it "was helping him reach a bigger audience, some digging, some who would never dig, but all paying" (311). Sphere learns about "a two-triode circuit called a flip-flop, which when it was turned on could be one of two ways, depending on which tube was conducting and which was cut off: set or reset, flip or flop" (311). Flip or flop, "yes or no, or one or zero," turn out to be "the basic units, or specialized 'cells' in a big 'electronic brain'" (312). From this electronic education, Sphere concludes, "if a computer's brain could go flip and flop, why so could a musician's" (312). Sphere integrates this insight into the nonsensical lyrics he sings during his group's "signature" song, "Set / Reset" (311). Pynchon is, of course, alluding to Claude Shannon's "A Mathematical Theory of Communication" and the broader history of computation. Using the term "bit," short for binary digit, Shannon notes that "[a] device with two stable positions, such as a relay or a flip-flop circuit, can store one bit of information."[151] In this paper, Shannon also famously claimed that the "semantic aspects of communication are irrelevant to the engineering problem."[152] This founding declaration inspired numerous critiques both from within information theory and from humanists.[153] For his part, Pynchon is less interested in critiquing Shannon than in using the terms of information theory to describe social, historical, and individual problems of communication. If, as Sphere suggests, "a musician's" brain can also "flip and flop," it might be tempting to reimagine all human relations and action as a configuration of binary digits. "As long as you were flop, everything was cool," Sphere concludes, deciding that "a whole bunch of people flip at the same time and you've got a war" (312). Love itself—"that nasty four-letter word," as one character in "Entropy" describes it—is reimagined in *V.* as a sort of flipping ("Entropy" 90). By contrast, in "Entropy," love is associated with "Ambiguity. Redundance. Irrelevance, even. Leakage . . . noise" (90–91). It is easy to read "Entropy" as a New Critical defense of ambiguity against the rationalizing, ambiguity-killing force of communications theory. In *V.*, however, love occupies a significantly different place in Pynchon's appropriation of communication theory. No longer noise, love becomes a definite stance within an inescapable binary scheme. As Sphere notes, "Here in Harlem [after 1945] they flopped. Everything got cool—no love, no hate, no worries, no excitement" (312).

Considered in light of Sphere's revision of information theory, the slogan "Keep cool, but care" looks rather different than it did at the beginning of this section. Far from evincing a sentimental Beat celebration of black life, this aphorism constructs the person on the model of a digital computer, "BEset / With crazy and cool in the same molecule," as Sphere sings (312). Pynchon's point is no longer— as it was in the more sentimental "Minstrel Island"—that we need to protect the besieged human world of meaning from encroaching digital systems, but that the *human* digital system must not get stuck in an on or off position. To rephrase Sphere's apothegm, we should keep flip but retain the capacity to flop. Like Richard Rorty's ironist, who cultivates the ability to view her own "final vocabulary" as con- tingent, Pynchon's ironist seeks to avoid having her ethos become hardcoded. This view of hip irony bears little resemblance to feel- good liberal humanism. It would be better to call Sphere's slogan an antihumanist or posthumanist ethical injunction, an invitation to process information a certain way, to adopt a particular orientation toward one's own cultural programming. We should not, however, assume that Pynchon's nascent posthumanism automatically put him into conflict with established (presumably humanist) critical author- ities. To assume so would recapitulate, at a philosophical level, the inaccurate view (one Pynchon sometimes reproduces) that critics and members of the counterculture were irreconcilably in conflict. Even Pynchon's best critics have adopted this view. In her seminal early study of Pynchon, *Ideas of Order in the Novels of Thomas Pynchon*, Molly Hite is surprised to find that "Pynchon is frequently criticized for being the academic's academic, the writer whose books are intended to be taught, not read."[154] This is surprising to her because when she first read of the exploits of the Whole Sick Crew, she was "convinced she *knew* them, traveled in some of the same circles, and could recognize the rhythms of their speech in Pynchon's uncannily precise dialogue."[155] But as we have seen, even when he sometimes denigrated or mocked critics, Pynchon appealed both to academic audiences and to would-be countercultural rebels, cannily inte- grating numerous critical discourses into his fiction, so much so that his ideal reader might be viewed not as an academic's academic but as something like a hip academic. It should not then be a surprise to learn that, in 1965, Pynchon received a job offer to teach English at Bennington. The offer came from Stanley Hyman, who had praised

V. in the liberal anticommunist magazine *The New Leader,* home to many mainstays of the cultural Cold War (Irving Kristol, Daniel Bell, Rinehold Neibuhr). In 1948, Hyman published *The Armed Vision,* a clearinghouse of cutting-edge New Critical wisdom. He was a close friend of Ralph Ellison and an avid pupil of Kenneth Burke. Pynchon politely turned down the job offer but praised Hyman's review of *V.,* perhaps sincerely, as "criticism at its best."[156] One cannot help but suspect that Pynchon would have made a pretty cool member of the faculty.

Conclusion: Criticism Unlimited

By the end of the sixties, the hipster had already become an historical figure, an object of reflection and nostalgic tribute, a character type whose death had been declared many times over. In 1971, Milton Klonsky wrote that "the universal solvent of money on one side, and the adoption of a fashionable Hip style on the other, coming together, have blurred" the distinction between Greenwich Village and "the straight and squared-away world uptown," id and superego now mixed together.[157] For Klonsky, "the nonconformist and dissenting spirit of the Village, in art, literature, manners & morals, has by its success . . . resulted in the establishment of a new kind of disestablishmentarian Establishment."[158] This is, we should recall, almost exactly the same complaint that Broyard (who was one of Klonsky's best friends) made in his 1948 *Partisan Review* essay: mainstream success destroys the power of hip. As in Broyard's analysis, Klonsky links hipness to irony. *"Hip,"* Klonsky writes, *"is merely the local habitation and the name assumed by irony in our times."*[159] When everyone is in on the ironic joke, no one can be the victim of irony. The bourgeoisie, Klonsky laments, can no longer be scandalized by avant-garde pranks. The "dadaization of Dada into official culture" may be nothing less than what Kierkegaard calls "the secret trap door through which one is suddenly hurled downward . . . into the infinite nothingness of irony."[160] We have good reason to question Klonsky's account. Klonsky imagines that hip irony once upon a time posed a serious threat to "the straight and squared-away world," before being co-opted by power and money. We have seen, instead, that from its origin hipness strongly appealed to intellectuals and professionals.

The midcentury's dominant vision of hip irony fed into attempts to imagine a version of human freedom that overcame the problems of, on the one hand, consumer capitalism and, on the other, communism. Hip became part of Cold War liberal discourse, but transformed into a far less humanistic ethos by the time Thomas Pynchon published his first novel.

Klonsky is closer to the truth when he says that "The Village scene . . . was transplanted onto college campuses, among faculty as well as students."[161] Klonsky seems to be referring to the rise of protest culture on campus. But the truth is perhaps less comforting to those who would like to argue for an inherently critical or rebellious power to irony: the spirit of irony was warmly welcomed by just about everyone. When David Foster Wallace claims that "[i]rony and cynicism were just what the U.S. hypocrisy of the fifties and sixties called for," he assumes that irony had a now-exhausted historical mission to overturn hierarchies and expose hypocrisies.[162] We cannot, of course, rule out the possibility that irony might, under some historical circumstances, have had just such a liberating function. But in the two major cases studied here, the record does not support Wallace's (quite common) view. *Invisible Man* extends New Critical ideas of irony as structural connotation in language as well as Kenneth Burke's idea of irony as dialectic. Ellison put this view of irony in the service of a Cold War liberal vision of human freedom. Pynchon did not initially go far beyond Ellison, seeing in irony and ambiguity safe harbors for the human in an ocean of the inanimate. In the case of *V.*—which develops a view of hip irony as the capacity to do something like reconfigure one's own cultural programming— we should nonetheless hesitate to assume that Pynchon's third way of irony was radical. When his editor, Corlies Smith, wondered whether an early draft of *V.* might have some "Protest Novel" elements, Pynchon admitted that the Sphere-Winsome relationship "may read a little like a proletarian play or WPA post office mural and I will try to make it a little less doctrinaire liberal than it was actually meant to be."[163] Pynchon's *V.* is, of course, often described as a late modernist work rather than postmodern.[164] It remains to be seen how irony fared under unambiguously postmodern conditions. Telling this story is the task of the next chapter.

One might finally turn to Herbert Marcuse's *One-Dimensional Man* for another vocabulary to describe the problematic politics of mid-century irony. In Marcuse's Freudo-Marxist account, sublimation, the conversion of repressed libidinal energies into artistic productivity, was preferable to the postwar alternative of "repressive desublimation." Sublimation at least had the benefit of embodying a negative reaction to society as a whole. One was, though oppressed, aware of the Reality Principle at some level of consciousness. Desublimation, far from being desirable, does not eliminate the advanced industrial society's repressive apparatus. It only jettisons the negative defense mechanism meant to guard against oppression. One need not be a Freudo-Marxist to see the cutting accuracy of Marcuse's observation that the Beat and Bohemian posed little threat to the establishment: "[S]uch modes of protest and transcendence are no longer contradictory to the status quo and no longer negative" but are rather "the ceremonial part of practical behaviorism, its harmless negation, and are quickly digested by the status quo as part of its healthy diet."[165] But Marcuse's analysis also errs in two important ways: first, in assuming that previous forms of Bohemianism were authentically subversive and, second, more significantly, in thinking that the "status quo" opposed negative thought in the first place. Marcuse's passionate opposition to "positive thinking"—say in his descriptions of Bertrand Russell and the early Wittgenstein—betrays his affinity with other midcentury intellectual tendencies, which similarly denounced "sociology" and "science" and "positivism."[166] Institutionalized modernism, used by cultural cold warriors as a weapon against the dangers of international communism, in fact celebrated the critical spirit and flexibility of thought supposedly intrinsic to the liberal-capitalist order. When Marcuse says linguistic analysis must understand itself in the context of "gas chambers and concentration camps, of Hiroshima and Nagasaki, of American Cadillacs and German Mercedes, of the Pentagon and the Kremlin," he echoes Mailer's description of the contexts that inspire the hipster's critical quest for apocalyptic orgasms.[167] In 1963, Arthur M. Schlesinger Jr. could proudly write, with the election of John F. Kennedy to office, "Wit has become respectable; it is even presidential now. Satire has burst out of the basements of San Francisco and

Greenwich Village."[168] As I have tried to show, the quest for hip became a branch of a more general postwar quest for criticality as such, which was neither at odds with the liberal "status quo" nor just another form of positivism (in Marcuse's pejorative sense). Hipness became a characterological weapon in an intellectual conflict that pitted increasingly stale critical institutions against newer forms of knowingness, newer places outside of society that were, simultaneously, inside emerging subcultural groups or coteries that claimed to occupy advantageous epistemic vantage points on American life. We must conclude that the hipster—who signaled his exclusive knowledge through irony—lived in accord with the dominant spirit of the Age of Criticism.

2

Punk's Positive Dystopia

In 1977, while still a student at the Westminster City School in London, Gideon Sams wrote a 62-page novella called *The Punk*. Fourteen at the time, Sams composed his book for a school project and then discarded his typescript, marked with his teacher's corrections, into a rubbish bin.[1] His "over zealous mother" discovered the abandoned draft, "saw in it a chance for social redemption," and sought to have it published, with startling success.[2] Polytantric Press released *The Punk* as a limited edition paperback of 500 copies that featured a safety pin attached to the cover image of the Sex Pistols' Johnny Rotten. Corgi Books republished the book, printing over 50,000 copies. Sams briefly became a minor punk celebrity. Various television programs invited him to explain the folkways of the juvenile subculture that had scandalized the UK.[3] That anyone thought Sams could explain "The Filth and the Fury" of punk was, to be sure, quite strange, given that the young writer was "not a fan of the music," according to one friend.[4] Then again, he did avidly read the *New Musical Express*, the British music newspaper, which helped define punk's London scene. Despite his distance from the music, Sams's novella creates a powerful portrait of punk's significance in the late 1970s.

The Punk tells the story of forbidden love between a punk, Adolph, and a ted, Thelma. Sams's protagonist, Adolph Sphitz, has a safety pin in his nose and wears an earring featuring a "golden swastika surrounded by the star of David, painted in sky blue" (16).[5] With his punk friends, "Sid Sick, Bill Migraine, Johnny Vomit and Vince Violence," he visits the Roxy, where one of their "favorite pastimes" involves "insulting the straight people who walked past the queue" and "jeering at the rich and famous personalities" entering the night-club. Adolph despises "these people who seemed to him to be nothing more than a bunch of posers and 'plastic' people" and especially hates musicians who "talked about fighting the system and capitalism but always ended up as rich as millionaires" (9, 10). Later in the story, he moves into a flat owned by a punk named Tony, who is in prison for "beating up a National Front heavy" and who listens to Bob Marley—details meant to signal Tony's (and Adolph's) antiracism (29). All of the details here rehearse already-familiar punk clichés that were circulating in the British press. Indeed, the juxtaposition of the golden swastika and blue Star of David is a textbook example of the ironic punk resignification.[6] As Dick Hebdige describes this procedure in his classic 1979 study of British punk, *Subculture: The Meaning of Style*, punk's "ironic and impious uses" of "'sacred' artefacts" gives us "hints of disorder, of breakdown and category confusion: a desire not only to erode racial and gender boundaries but also to confuse chronological sequence by mixing up details from different periods."[7] By Greil Marcus's account in *Lipstick Traces*, the punk swastika was meant to show that "contemporary Britain was a welfare-state parody of fascism" and "that negation is the act that would make it self-evident to everyone that the world is not as it seems."[8]

In an early scene, set at his parents' flat, Adolph articulates a sense of his alienation that also invokes a perspectival sense of irony. Sams's narrator informs us that Adolph feels "he was looking down on reality," that he "was an observer, but not actually a part of the life of the flats" (15). In response to this sense of detachment from life, Sams's fictional punks use parody with oppositional force, meaning to undermine both capitalism and the British welfare state. The Dead Dogs, a fictional punk band in the novella, sing

> just gimme death
> or I'll kill your wife

had enough of the social security
had enough of life
(11–12)

These lyrics name the punk's enemy not as capitalism but as "the social security." Aldoph similarly reviles agents of the welfare state. After earning "an 'A' level in art," state employment authorities offer Adolph a job "label[ling] baked bean cans at Tesco's" (18, 19). Disgusted at the lack of work, or at least the lack of opportunities commensurate to his education ("I was looking for a slightly better job," he complains [18]), he takes a job working for a fishmonger instead.

Adolph's sneering irony, what Sams calls his "large smirk" (22), his refusal of what the Employment Exchange initially offers him, his complaint that he "can't even get a pair of good jeans" on "£19 a week," neatly evoke the political-economic situation that punk opposed (19). In the U.K., punk partly developed from life on the dole and has been associated with the slogan "No future," a line from the Sex Pistols second single, "God Save the Queen." Sams's novella shows that punks like Adolph have "no future" in a historically specific sense. Punk should be regarded as an attitude born from a trade deficit between educational achievement and available economic roles. The punk discovers that her art degree is terminal within the economy she inhabits, that she will not become the creative professional that she hoped she would become. The punk is thus a frustrated agent within the specific contradictions that marked the boundary between the midcentury welfare state (the U.K. had one of the most robust welfare states among advanced capitalist economies) and a still-inchoate (at least at the level of public policy) neoliberalism. The punk is, in short, the child of stagflation. In an economic sense, *stagflation* refers to a condition of low growth, high inflation, and high unemployment that afflicted various advanced capitalist economies during the 1970s.[9] One of the great legacies of this state was a loss of confidence in the technocratic authority that characterized the prior era. In the face of what seemed a "toothless" Keynesianism, stagflation "created an economic climate that brought the fundamental assumptions of politicians and experts alike into

question."[10] There seemed, of course, to be a technical question concerning how to fight inflation without raising unemployment, and
the broader mystery for policy planners of why growth was suddenly
so hard to sustain. Whatever else this situation portended, stagflation was partly a crisis of confidence in the future, especially among
the unemployed young. On the one hand, the emerging punk experienced firsthand the decline of an industrial base in her home
country, a welfare state in crisis, and newly manifesting constellations of labor (service labor, affective labor, immaterial labor). On
the other hand, she lived at a moment of countercultural decline,
when the Utopian hopes of the sixties seemed to be exhausted. Punk
was one means of addressing this situation.

For the punk, stagflation was not only an economic crisis but also
a spiritual condition. The punk's solution to her lack of an economic
future is complex, but can be identified with the second great punk
slogan, the idea that you should, with proper entrepreneurial verve,
"Do It Yourself," make your own culture, bypass official channels of
recognition, join what we might today call the creative class.[11] In
short, the punk came to see the solution to political-economic
dilemmas in her cultivation of a specific ethos. Making use of cut-up,
irony, and negation more generally, the punk sought to join the
sphere of cultural production on her own terms. I will reconstruct
punk's style of irony indirectly, through the study of the careers of
William S. Burroughs and Kathy Acker, both of whom worked in a
punk genre that I will call positive dystopia. Positive dystopia is an
ironic narrative mode that finds the conditions for survival in
destruction. It is a genre whose enactment constructs Bakhtin's
second world of carnival laughter but rejects the carnival's politics of
future regeneration. To imagine a positive dystopia, to sing, as Sams's
Dead Dogs do, "just gimme death," is not really to celebrate or ask
for death. Instead, the punk uses irony to gain access to an imagined
zone of autonomy outside of language and signification. Punk esca-
lates the critical irony of the hipster. Whereas the hipster used irony
to draw attention to the polysemy of language, to manipulate language in pursuit of what he saw as human freedom, the punk
uses linguistic polysemy in an effort to stop or arrest language itself.
Punk is thus at least as much a literary as a musical or subcultural

phenomenon.[12] Literary scholars have, of course, long associated punk with the Poetry Project at St. Mark's Church in-the-Bowery, and have studied the literary productions of figures such as Patti Smith, Richard Hell, and Jim Carroll.[13] Such accounts tend to focus on the effort of punk performers and poets to "overcome the distance between performer and audience" and to stand against Beat / hippie "passivity" and "pastoralism."[14] Even so, literary dimensions of punk are typically taken as ultimately secondary to the music.[15] Fanzines, meanwhile, are celebrated as of a piece with punk's attempt to democratize the means of cultural production, but the 'zines themselves were usually about the bands, the music, and specific punk scenes.[16] By contrast, I want to understand what it might mean for literary scholars to understand punk in characterological terms, as a self-figuring practice that responded to and helped shape the world of early neoliberalism.

Sams's *The Punk* is an appropriate place to start looking for a neo-liberal art of punk living because, as Miriam Rivett has argued, it is not just a novel about punk. Rather, "it *is* punk."[17] The Corgi edition and subsequent editions of the novel have made a similar claim, calling Sams's slim book "the first punk novel" or "*Romeo and Juliet* with Safety Pins" (cover flap). *The Punk* might be said to perform punk. Indeed—if I might be excused for crossing the Atlantic—I would suggest that at the level of the sentence, *The Punk* unwittingly bridges the supposed gap separating what Robert Siegle calls "downtown writing" from the mainstream literary genres known as "dirty realism" and "blank fiction."[18] Joel Rose and Catherine Texier, editors of the important literary magazine *Between C & D*, distinguished between downtown writing and dirty realism, but their description of downtown fiction as "sometimes shocking in its frank sexuality or violence, in its absence of sentimentality, in the deliberate sketchiness of the characters" would seem to apply as much to Dennis Cooper as to Bret Easton Ellis.[19] The description also aptly characterizes *The Punk*, which ends by depicting a crowd that "stood looking at Adolph and Thelma as they lay in a huge pool of blood" (62). What is less obvious is the degree to which *The Punk* is a pastiche or stitching together of journalistic accounts of punk, a litany of stereotypes drawn from sources such as *NME*. When we look into Sams's "huge pool of blood," we can almost glimpse the process of historical change itself. Just imagine it: a fourteen-year-old boy, an avid reader of *NME*, someone who was taken for a punk but who was more of a fan of the Stones, mining stereotypes drawn from journalistic accounts of a still-new musical subculture, hooking his appropriation from these sources firmly to a warmed-over love plot, a plot supposedly borrowed from Shakespeare (whom Sams never read), all as part of a school assignment, published at the urging of his mother, a boy subsequently invited onto television as an avatar of the subculture whose semiotic code he had mastered through precocious feats of media consumption. What must his teacher have thought?

The Art of Selling Out

From the mid-1970s through the 1980s, the visibility of punk communities, styles, and music was widely understood as a marker of urban blight, a sign of the dissolution of everyday life in the overdeveloped world. Zack Carlson and Bryan Connolly document this cultural association in their encyclopedic survey of punk on film, *Destroy All Movies!!!* (2010). They carefully catalog a "tried-and-true tradition of punk equaling decay, delinquency, and dystopia."[20] As Carlson and Connolly show, this view of punk was popular across the political spectrum. Whether in antipunk films such as Mark L. Lester's horrific *Class of 1984* (1982) or in films that use punk styles as a vehicle for political critique, such as Derek Jarman's delightful *Jubilee* (1978), the figure of the punk became a metonymy for the destruction of social life, either as cause or as visible symptom.[21] This association spawned both condemnations and celebrations. Slavoj Žižek claims, for example, that "punk imitating the 'sadomasochistic' power ritual is ... the negation implied in the positive act of imitation."[22] Likewise, Curtis White writes, "Punk argues, 'Look at us! We're ugly! You made us ugly! We're stupid and you made us stupid! We hate you for it!"[23] Punk is, by this view, a form of "popular resistance to administered life," a signal that "even at its most defeated, with the Reagan-Thatcher ghouls sunk in our collective neck, refusal is possible."[24] Punk refusal-through-self-abjection is, White complains, "the strategy of a Caliban, the strategy of a slave."[25] Having "no positive [political] content," punk "sets up its home in mutila-tion."[26] These canonical interpretations of punk refusal strikingly fail to account for punk's actual fate, which should force us to revise our view of its allegedly empty political content. For today, the associa-tion of punk and urban decay has either vanished or been trans-figured, giving way to neo-Bohemian urban enclaves populated by members of the so-called creative class. The sociologist Richard Lloyd writes, "In contrast to theories of the city as trending toward increased homogenization and sanitization . . . the definition of diversity typically proffered by local artists [in such neo-Bohemian enclaves] gives special value to the illicit and the bizarre . . . elements of urban experience that are usually considered to be an aesthetic blight become instead symbols of the desire to master an environ-ment characterized by marginality and social instability."[27] The suc-cess of this neo-Bohemian view is hard to dispute. One can today even go on an "Anarchy in the UK Punk Rock London Day Tour," which asks, "Wanna relive those years or understand the 'whys and wherefors' of punk history? See where the barricades were manned and the events of the period unfurled? Then this is the day for you."[28] Punk has shifted from urban blight to something more like heritage industry.

Punk's "shit-stirring anti-style" has become a productive force, transforming from a liability into an economic resource (or cultural capital in a more strictly accurate sense of the term).[29] The most amusing emblem of this change might be Richard Laermer and Mark Simmons's 2007 book, *Punk Marketing: Get Off Your Ass and Join the Revolution*, which calls on marketers to join the punk revolu-tion. They define *punk* as "an attitude of rebellion against tradition" and *punk marketing* as "a new form of marketing that rejects the status quo and recognizes the shift in power from corporations to consumers."[30] *Punk Marketing* proffers fifteen "articles" that "should be followed without fail for the revolution to carry you along with it and not leave you trampled underfoot," such as "Make Enemies" and "No More Marketing Bullshit."[31] In the office, punk involves "[i]ntroducing some managed chaos . . . to unshackle people's thinking," to "let your mind make creative connections to go at problems in a new way."[32] When the Sex Pistols were inducted into the Rock and

Roll Hall of Fame in 2006, Johnny Rotten sent a handwritten note politely declining the honor. The note explained that, "Next to the SEX-PISTOLS rock and roll and that hall of fame is a piss stain. Your museum. Urine and wine. Were not coming. Were not your monkey and so what?"[33] Laermer and Simmons argue that "the only true message that you will notice [in Rotten's note] as a marketer is that the band used a gimmick that worked! It's the same gimmick they've used since day one: be outrageous, get attention."[34] Though we may be tempted to reject *Punk Marketing* as an odious appropriation of a complex subcultural movement, it is hard not to credit Laermer and Simmons's interpretation of Rotten's letter. As James F. English writes, "the scandal of refusal [of a prize] has become a recognized device for raising visibility and leveraging success," so that "the refusal of a prize can no longer register as a refusal to *play*."[35]

How did punk refusal transform from a scandal into just another way of playing the game? One common view is that punk was either co-opted or sold out. Once upon a time, punks were committed to producing what Stacy Thompson calls "anti-commodities" or "punk commodities," specially tooled aesthetic products that might "overturn the commodity market" by encouraging use but discouraging exchange.[36] Today, however, punk has been largely integrated into ordinary commodity production. Jon Savage contends that punk's "sophisticated, ironic rhetoric" was "steam-roll[ed]" by the "mass market."[37] Thompson goes further than Savage, suggesting that punk was in some sense designed to be co-opted, to "highlight[], dialectically, both the continuing need for an aesthetics that escapes commodification and the impossibility of arriving at such an aesthetic realm within the constraints of capitalism."[38] Another explanation, which would be critical of the co-optation theory, suggests that counterculture and marketing culture have far more in common than is commonly recognized. By this view, punks were, just as much as other partisans of counterculture, dupes, victims of wrong-headed magical thinking, weavers of what Sean McCann and Michael Szalay describe as a "cherished and ultimately comforting folklore of the late capitalist economy" whose ultimately individualistic political commitments actually obscured questions of class and inequality.[39] By this account, the problem with punk is not internal to punk itself, but is just another manifestation of the problem of thinking that stylistic rebellion might substitute for political action, that subversive appropriation represents a serious threat to power. As Susan Sontag suggested, "the Sex Pistols and the other groups would be quite acceptable if they seemed more ironic to people . . . [T]hey're not perceived as ironic and once they are perhaps that will be their form of domestication."[40] On this view, punks are little more than confused spinners of capitalist folklore with a taste for safety pins. This second answer, though in some cases convincing, fails to explain punk's specific success. Punk would be just one of an array of ineffectual rebels. I will propose a third explanation for punk's success, one perhaps stranger still. I will argue that the ethos of punk—or at least one major historical variation of this ethos—can be understood as a form of management theory. The pursuit of *punk marketing* does not corrupt punk, or misapprehend its dialectical power, but propagates one of its core projects. Marketers such as Laermer and Simmons have not co-opted punk, but have instead been outclassed by more sophisticated punks, and are scrambling to catch up. Punk's reorganization of the postindustrial city was, on this view, an authentic prolepsis of a new mode of urbanism. Avatars of what the sociologists Luc Boltanski and Ève Chiapello call "the projective city," punk only looked like a form of decay from the perspective of those committed to the regime of justification of the prior "industrial city."[41]

In *The New Spirit of Capitalism*, Boltanski and Chiapello use the term *city* in an idiosyncratic way. Building on an account of justification Boltanski and Laurent Thévenot develop in *On Justification*— and Boltanski's "pragmatic sociology of critique"—*The New Spirit* is concerned with "a kind of very general convention directed toward a common good, and claiming universal validity," which necessarily undergirds all social arrangements, including under capitalism.[42] This set of conventions is "modeled on the concept of the *city*."[43] A city is a set of justifications linking everyday institutions, practices, and habits to capitalist accumulation processes. This city is less a physical space than a way of addressing "the question of justice."[44] Cities are normative regimes that serve as warrants for justification. We might thus view them as the ideological presuppositions that enable collective life to function at all. Boltanski and Chiapello identify various "logics of justification" (that is, cities) across a range of periods.[45] The authors admit that a variety of logics can coexist, but they are primarily interested in the transition from what they call the *industrial city* to the *projective city*. This transition comprises a major shift in the norms that legitimate and constrain capital accumulation. The dominance of the industrial city roughly corresponds to the period of "embedded liberalism," the post-WWII environment in which labor, capital, and the state worked more or less in tandem toward common ends (called in the United States the "golden age of capitalism," in France *Les Trente Glorieuses*). The rise of the projective city, meanwhile, corresponds to neoliberalism's rise. A great watchword of political debate in recent years, neoliberalism as an economic phenomenon is usually taken to refer to the historical disembedding of capitalism from other forms of social restriction and political control. Neoliberal policies deregulate previously controlled sectors of the economy, privatize public enterprises and state assets, remake surviving state enterprises so that they operate more like private firms, weaken labor unions and welfare programs, globalize manufacturing, eliminate or reduce capital controls, enthrone finance, increase economic inequality, and spread workplace precarity. Neoliberal thought leaders have reimagined the worker on the model of the intrinsically motivated artist; the artist herself, meanwhile, is figured as an entrepreneur, an owner and manager of her own creative capital.[46] But, as many critics have noted, neoliberal polities do not simply deregulate the economy. Instead, they deploy the power of the state to construct an idealized version of the free market, imposing their malign vision of market freedom, often by force, globally. This process might better be seen as a sort of "*re-regulation*, in which more regulations were introduced than in any comparable period of history . . . telling people what they could and could not do, and what they had to do to be beneficiaries of state policy," all of which was designed to "prevent collective interests from acting as barriers to competition."[47] When understood as "re-regulation," the aims of neoliberal policymaking look somewhat different from the standard story, often propagated by neoliberal thinkers themselves, which conflates neoliberalism's market statism with laissez-faire economics or libertarianism as such. David Harvey convincingly argues that such reregulation was a "project to restore class power," which concealed its aims behind rosy rhetoric celebrating individual freedom and consumer choice.[48] Far from defanging themselves, agents of the state have used their considerable "powers of persuasion, co-optation, bribery, and threat" to further this (upwardly) redistributionist agenda.[49] Such a narrative of reregulation from above, however empirically accurate, risks overlooking the popular reception of neoliberal ideas. When they do not simply use force to impose their will, neoliberal elites are said to secure popular support through deception or dissimulation, redefining freedom as market freedom, saying democracy but meaning general access to markets, without anyone noticing. As we might expect, political leaders such as Ronald Reagan, Margaret Thatcher, and Augusto Pinochet and intellectual networks, think tanks, and wealthy donors figure prominently in such accounts. By contrast, Boltanski and Chiapello salubriously throw light on the popular dimension of neoliberalism.[50] The neoliberal or projective regime of justification, by this view, was not only imposed from above but also evinces "the real but sometimes paradoxical impact of critique on capitalism."[51] The spirit of May 1968 posed a genuine challenge, and the agents of capital responded to that critique.

Punk played a role in this regime change, and punk negation very much had a positive political content or at the very least a historically important function. Punk facilitated the end of one city and blasted the way for another. Though other dimensions of punk demand attention, including important punk institutions such as 'zines, small record labels, and important performance venues, we will here investigate the varieties of irony most associated with the New York and London scenes of the mid-1970s. As we will see, punk came to view large, durable collective institutions (and arguably social life *as such*) as oppressive, and imagined that cutting up or negating hegemonic discourses could undermine power by transforming what we will for the moment call "individual" political consciousness. Today, debates about the power of antisocial irony continue in queer theory.[52] Some strands of queer theory have, like punk, argued for the political importance of cultivating an antisocial ethos.[53] Although he dismisses punk as "little more than Oedipal kitsch," Lee Edelman cannot help but evoke the history of punk and participate in punk's refusal of regenerative Utopian visions in a book entitled *No Future*.[54] In Edelman's account of what he calls the *sinthom*osexual ("he who refuses the Child"), Edelman retains a punk faith in irony as the "queerest of rhetorical devices," which is politically powerful because it "severs the continuity essential to the very logic of making sense," thus undermining hegemonic notions of reproductive futurity.[55] Shucking social life, escaping the totalitarian political logic of the Child, promises to give access to "a signifying formulation beyond analysis, a kernel of enjoyment immune to the efficacy of the symbolic" (one description of Jacques Lacan's concept of the sinthome).[56]

My insistence on treating punk's antisocial irony as an ethos might be regarded with suspicion, given the seeming dependence of the concept of ethos on some version of social life. Yet, as I will argue, punk is in practice anything but antinormative, and, in any case, normativity should not be equated with the social as such. One might also object to analyzing punk ideas apart from specific punk communities. Ben Watson, for instance, insists that taking the "recorded product" of punk too seriously is to be "obedient to the priorities and perspectives of the capitalist pop industry, allowing the commodity to dictate what constitutes musical culture."[57] Against this view, Watson valorizes "the tribunal of live performance" and punk's true "risk and violence," which contemporary critics hide behind "a genteel screen" and a "liberal language of justification."[58] Watson's account seems sentimental to me (you just had to *be there*, apparently), but his broader point is correct. Ideas or styles can never be separated from practice. The concept of ethos that I have been developing is meant to fuse ideas and practice, to argue for their inseparability or dialectical entanglement.[59] Punk's irony was never only an aesthetic category, and its antisocial imagination never escaped social life or normativity. Theory always becomes practice through the routing station of justification, and justification depends on the category of ethos, whether at the level of the individual, the community, or the institution. Nonetheless, this dialectical truth guarantees nothing about punk's politics.[60]

For punk's critique of administered life, which included a critique of the dole, effectively won the day, helping reorganize or reinvent the spirit of capitalism. Punk was an ethos that challenged the legitimacy of the residual industrial city and promoted the values of the emerging projective city. This new projective city valorizes the creative and free individual who, disembedded from mediating institutions (and arguably from social life as such), forms temporary project-oriented groups linked together into voluntary networks.[61] The marketing guidebook, the seeming paradox of the idea of *punk marketing*, is the perfect genre to facilitate this transformation. For punk aspires to be both uncompromisingly oppositional and accessible to everyone. It is uncompromisingly oppositional in the sense that the punk imagines herself to stand against all hegemonic systems of thought and culture. It seeks to be universally accessible in the sense that it commands you to Do It Yourself, and instructs you how. Punk aims to teach a mass audience how to overturn convention. The possibility of reading punk's project in this way—as a form of management theory—is already apparent in Julien Temple's fantastic 1980 mockumentary about the Sex Pistols, *The Great Rock 'n' Roll Swindle*. A punk response to films such as *A Hard Day's Night*, the film openly depicts itself as a marketing guide, a handbook explaining how to successfully manufacture controversy around a punk band. Malcolm McLaren, playing a character called The Embezzler, instructs: "Find yourself four kids. Make sure they hate each other. Make sure they can't play."[62] Later, he says: "cultivate hatred; it is your greatest asset. Here at home, create a tour that no one can turn up to. Throw the group's name away, and leave a question mark in its place. Create confusion. The Sex Pistols made sure that they failed to turn up at certain venues. Spreading false rumours wherever they could."

Critics have debated whether the film's naked cynicism accurately represents punk. The film is certainly, as David Huxley shows, "a carefully constructed piece of myth-making," and should not be mistaken for a factual account of the formation of the Sex Pistols.[63] The film might be said to allegorize the debate between the more radical Jamie Reid, the artist responsible for much iconic punk imagery, who did the film's art direction, and the self-styled Embezzler Malcolm

McLaren, whose libertarian views were sometimes hard to distinguish from those of the character he played in the film.[64] As Stewart
Home writes, McLaren formed the Six Pistols because he "wanted to
sell a lot of trousers!"[65] However, debates about the radicalism of the
Sex Pistols look quite different if we take the film to be a genuine
guidebook for the self-starting small businessperson who needs to
find a way to compete with the big labels. On this view, punk's enemy
was not capitalism as such but rather an older moment in the history
of capitalism. In light of this interpretation, the faith of one punk fan,
expressed in the New York–based 'zine *Punk*, seems misplaced: "In
the true sense of the word, it seems that the only punks are the SEX
PISTOLS . . . who else has destroyed not one but two recording
contracts?"[66] I do not mean to deny that many actual punks hated
capitalism or (as Craig O'Hara's *The Philosophy of Punk* argues)
thought of themselves as anarchists. Nor can one deny that punk has
inspired many to engage in anticapitalist activities. Nevertheless, by
analyzing the writing and thought of William S. Burroughs and
Kathy Acker, I hope to show that punk—at least when understood as
a characterological model—participated in a critique of a specific
moment in the history of capitalism. Far from have no future, punk
helped make the future.

Godfather of Punk

William S. Burroughs's connection to punk has been widely cited
but is only poorly understood. For more than thirty years, critics and
biographers have relied on a range of slogans to link the man to the
movement. Along with Iggy Pop and Lou Reed, Burroughs has frequently been called the "godfather of punk."[67] *Trouser Press* magazine
called him "The Greatgodfather of Punk."[68] Burroughs's biographer
Ted Morgan describes the Beat movement as "the granddaddy of
the . . . punk scene." Burroughs's former assistant, Victor Bockris,
meanwhile, has argued that "[t]here was a profound connection
between the punks and William Burroughs: They were his children."[69] Barry Miles makes a subtler argument, suggesting that
though he is largely associated with the Beat movement, Burroughs's
fame actually peaked in the 1970s: "Kerouac was the hard-drinking,
loudmouth fifties, Ginsberg the psychedelic, antiwar sixties, and now

Burroughs represented all that was cool about the seventies."[70] Though frequently repeated, none of these claims is entirely convincing. Burroughs himself resisted being associated with punk. "I am not punk," he said, "and don't know why anyone would consider me the godfather of punk."[71] Burroughs's literary successors, such as Kathy Acker and Stewart Home, both of whom made heavy use of cut-up, did identify themselves with punk. But the man himself denied the link, was not a fan of rock music, and even suggested that the "so-called punk movement is indeed a media creation."[72] In fact, the term *godfather* itself lexically equivocates, suggesting that Burroughs had a merely honorary or at best spiritual relationship to the movement.

There are, however, more promising points of contact. Burroughs did, of course, have some biographical connections to the New York punk scene in the late 1970s. He lived in the Bowery starting in 1974, in an apartment he called The Bunker. In 1978, the critic and theorist Sylvère Lotringer organized the Nova Convention, a three-day festival honoring Burroughs, celebrating him as a "philosopher of the future," someone uniquely able to make sense of "post-industrial society."[73] Burroughs became a celebrity in the downtown art and music scene in his mid-sixties.[74] Burroughs also sent a letter of support to the Sex Pistols after they released "God Save the Queen." In "Bugger the Queen," a short routine he read at the Nova Convention, and first published in 1979 in Dennis Cooper's punk / poetry magazine *Little Caesar,* Burroughs ties his support of the Sex Pistols to the lyrics of a song he wrote (with the same title), noting that it is "almost treason in England to say anything against what they call 'OUR Queen.' "[75] Burroughs's song instructs us to *"Pull the chain on Buckingham"* and "BUGGER THE QUEEN!" (77). After presenting the song's lyrics, Burroughs ends the routine with a narrative fantasy of an unspecified audience's reception of the song: "A vast crowd [marching] on Buckingham Palace screaming "BUGGER THE QUEEN!" (80). Burroughs concludes that, "It's like a remake of the Magna Carta. Owing to a power shortage the Queen signs her abdication by flickering torchlight...and good riddance to the Gombeen Woman" (Ibid.). The political power of this song is tied, in Burroughs's fantasy, to its willful violation of cultural taboos, the demolition of the Pavlovian conditioning of "that happy breed" who "grovel in front of the Queen" (79). In calling the queen "the Gombeen Woman," Burroughs conflates state power with the usurious economic power of the Gombeen. Simply by repeating the phrase "BUGGER THE QUEEN!" a revolutionary community can undermine this political-economic despot, causing a "power shortage" in two senses. As the chant spreads, "[a] vast dam is broken" (77). In an interview, Burroughs explained, "England doesn't stand a chance until you have 20,000 people saying 'Bugger the Queen,'" which was why he thought the Sex Pistols had offered a "constructive, necessary criticism of a country which is bankrupt."[76]

We can better understand the political significance of this fantasy—and what it might tell us about punk—by examining another piece Burroughs read at the Convention, a satirical routine called "Roosevelt after Inauguration," which he first sent to Allen Ginsberg in a 1953 letter, and which was published in LeRoi Jones's *Floating Bear #9* (1961). Admitting reluctantly that his art was making "very definite political statements," Burroughs said before his performance of this routine that "Roosevelt after Inauguration" "appears in retrospect as designed to devalue the whole image of the presidency, a devaluation which was consummated at Watergate."[77] The routine features FDR appearing "on the White House balcony dressed in the purple robes of a Roman Emperor" and shows Roosevelt's constituents "grunting and squealing like the hogs they were."[78] An "old queen" is made Joint Chiefs of Staff; a "transvestite Lizzie" becomes Congressional Librarian, bans "the male sex from the premises," and stages "Lesbian orgies" at the library; and other social misfits are given cabinet positions, displacing "men who had gone grey and toothless in the faithful service of their country" (42). When the Supreme Court resists "the legislation perpetuated by this vile rout," FDR forces the members of the court "to submit to intercourse with a purple-assed baboon" (Ibid.). The Court tries to carry on "with a screeching simian shitting and pissing and masturbating on the table" (Ibid.). In time, as simians replace murdered justices, "the Supreme Court came to consist of nine purple-assed baboons; and Roosevelt, claiming to be the only one able to interpret their decisions, thus gained control of the highest tribunal in the land" (43).

The mode of satire here, by Burroughs's own admission, is broad, meant to reformulate the reader's attitude toward American icons of power. Burroughs mobilizes a characteristically misogynistic aesthetic of disgust in an effort to undermine the reader's sympathetic identification with the person of the president. Yet in his 1978 comments, Burroughs either misremembers or misrepresents the specific context of his routine. For "Roosevelt after Inauguration" was not merely an attack against "the image of the presidency," but against a liberal New Deal vision of the strong executive inaugurated by FDR. In the late 1940s, hoping to become a gentleman farmer, Burroughs started a farm in Pharr, Texas, growing oranges, cotton, and marijuana. Struggling to make his farm profitable, Burroughs resented the Border Patrol, which deported his Mexican immigrant workers, and he came to hate the Department of Agriculture, which regulated what he could plant.[79] Even as he received a government support price for his cotton, he loathed the New Deal and what he described as the "octopus of bureaucratic socialism," fearing that the United States would become, "a Socialistic police state."[80] Big government liberalism was "a cancerous element that will stifle every vestige of free life in the U.S."[81] Also no fan of unions, Burroughs found himself agreeing with the rightwing columnist Westbrook Pengler ("the only columnist . . . who possesses a grain of integrity") and pined for "our glorious Frontier heritage of minding your own business."[82]

Burroughs was an avowed enemy of the liberal New Deal state. He feared that "[t]he Welfare State is on the way to be a Communist State, and that means a *bureaucratic police state*."[83] Burroughs held to a consistent view of American capitalism throughout his life. In a conversation with Bockris in the early 1980s, Burroughs recalls that the United States "looked like it was going to develop into a repressive police state, but then that didn't happen."[84] The "repressive police state" in question, associated for him with midcentury state capitalism, is what the New Deal threatened to become. In the same interview, Burroughs explains to Bockris that "[n]othing has come from the federal government except trouble and expense," celebrates that there are "so many groups and occupational differences," and seems to harbor free market fantasies, especially in drug manufacture and delivery.[85] At the very least, we must accept that Burroughs's satirical routine has no obvious or necessary anticapitalist politics. On the contrary, we might well argue that Burroughs saw the form of the routine as integral to his lifelong antistatism. Starting in the 1940s, he developed a specific theory of the routine as a mode of satire that extends an idea or narrative situation to its limit. Anticipating several core features of cut-up, the satirical routine was a literary solution to a political problem. "Routines are completely spontaneous and proceed from whatever fragmentary knowledge you have." A "good routine" promises "unmalicious, unstrained, pure laughter . . . that gives a moment's freedom from the cautious, nagging, aging, frightened flesh."[86] Some routines like "Roosevelt after Inauguration" seem to have specific political targets, but others, like the talking asshole routine in *Naked Lunch*, are self-justifying—their mode of irony bashes taboos in a more general way. Like the talking asshole itself, routines threaten or promise to destroy the human bodies through which they traverse. Moreover, these routines require "receivers." "If there is no one there to receive it, routine turns back on me ~~like homeless curse~~ and tears me apart, grows more and more insane (literal growth like cancer) and impossible, and fragmentary like berserk pin-ball machine and I scream 'Stop it! Stop it!' "[87] Like the cut-up, the routine is built from fragmentary discourses that pass through the mind of the transmitter; these routines then pass to a receiver. Satirical language becomes a weapon with which to break down the barriers separating persons from one another. Burroughs hoped routines might join his mind to that of another, a process he called "shlupping" (the telepathic union of souls). It would be a mistake to call schlupping a form of sociality or intersubjectivity. Instead, schlupping entails the utter destruction of the social, the subjective, and the personal. Burroughs repurposed what Stephen E. Kercher calls "liberal satire" for decidedly antiliberal ends.[88]

The political fantasy of "Bugger the Queen," it should now be clear, assumes a specific model of literary production and reception, one that also informed punk aesthetics. By this model, corporate-state political power depends centrally on linguistic control. Reverence for public icons such as the queen promotes mental servility that undermines human freedom. In a 1978 essay "The Limits of Control," Burroughs makes the linguistic mechanisms of control explicit: "words are still the principal instruments of control. Persuasions are words. Orders are words," and "any control machine" that uses only force will "soon encounter the limits of control."[89] Burroughs explains that "[c]ontrol needs time in which to exercise control," emphasizing that all models of control depend on a conceptual distinction between those who control and those who are controlled. After all, "You don't control a tape recorder—you use it."[90] The mass media are the main mechanism of control. As mass media become "more sophisticated they also become more vulnerable," which means that "[o]ne technical sergeant can fuck up the whole works."[91] Burroughs imagined his writing as participating in the project of dismantling control systems. He saw himself as a literary engineer, a "technical sergeant" who might gum up the works of control. Burroughs called the project of eliminating control "decontrol."[92] Punk's place in this scheme becomes clear in an interview with Patti Smith, who saw Burroughs as an intellectual and artistic mentor. In one of his more favorable assessments of punk, Burroughs suggests that "the whole punk generation, essentially . . . are antiheros. See, they're rejecting the old values, because having been woken up, they realize that all this nonsense they've been brought up on is nonsense. And all these standards. And they're rejecting those standards. So we could regard them, if you will, as something that you [Patti Smith] have been instrumental in creating."[93] Given's Smith's devotion to Burroughs, it would be fair to imagine that Burroughs saw himself as part of the lineage that produced punk. And Burroughs was received as such not only by Smith but also by a wide range of self-professed punks, including the Boston-based straightedge hardcore band Society System Decontrol, which draws explicitly on Burroughs's concept of decontrol.[94] Burroughs himself is not a punk but rather awakens a new style of antiheroic life that he names punk. Punk is not only a musical style but also an attitude toward power, an ethos that defines power as linguistic control. What punks subsequently do to enact political change remains ambiguous, but if "Bugger the Queen" is any hint, the content of punk politics matters less than the fact of punk consciousness. The phrase "BUGGER THE QUEEN!" becomes viral (it becomes a word virus), spreading from person to person, fusing individuals into a "vast crowd," a political superorganism that it may not be right to call a collective.

This revolutionary punk superorganism enacts Burroughs's notion of "decontrol," which has its roots in an idiosyncratic intellectual history, one less scientific than spiritual (in Hadot's sense). Burroughs derived his notion of decontrol from General Semantics, a school of thought founded by the Polish count Alfred Korzybski in the 1930s. Burroughs admired Korzybski's influential book, *Science and Sanity: An Introduction to Non-Aristotelian Systems and General Semantics* (1933), and attended a five-day seminar on General Semantics in 1939. Originator of the phrase "the map is not the territory," Korzybski offered a wide-ranging analysis of how the gap between reality and language produces an "un-sanity reflected in our private and public lives, institutions and systems."[95] In Korzybski's view, humans systematically misidentify words for things, confusing verbalizations of reality for reality itself. His General Semantics promised to therapeutically eliminate such interpretive errors. As Burroughs explained, Korzybski identified "either / or" thinking as one of the "great errors of Western thought."[96] "That's not the way things occur," Burroughs says, "and I feel the Aristotelian construct is one of the great shackles of Western civilization."[97] This "great error" conditions misapprehensions that perpetuate control. One can only hope to overcome such modes of control by reconditioning the human organism. Korzybski himself described General Semantics as "a new extensional discipline which explains and trains us how to use our nervous systems most efficiently . . . a new non-aristotelian system of orientation which affects every branch of science and life."[98] The goal of such training is not to better describe the world but rather to return to the "silence on the objective level" that precedes language.[99] "Differentiation," "delay," and "consciousness of abstracting" are the great slogans of his thought. *Differentiation* is "the denial of identity," a way to "discriminate between the objective and verbal levels."[100] Introducing a *delay* into thought would be a way to "learn 'silence' on the unspeakable objective levels."[101] To attain *consciousness of abstracting* means we learn how to "become aware that characteristics are left out in the process of abstracting by our nervous system."[102] Korzybski's thought, though largely forgotten today, was once popular enough that Kenneth Burke felt the need to engage with it in *A Grammar of Motives*. Burke's critique offers a clue as to how we should understand Korzybski's influence on Burroughs. As Burke notes, "[t]he very delay of action [in Korzybski's system] is . . . maintained by motions, since the *attitude* of criticism, or delay, or 'consciousness of abstracting' must be matched by its own peculiar *physiological* configurations."[103] In short, Burke observes, Korzybski's system of thought depends on the very cognitive biases it seeks to overcome. To differentiate requires confusing the objective and verbal level. To delay means to take definite action without waiting. To become conscious of abstracting is to forget that one is abstracting.

However, Burke's well-observed critique does not in any simple way debunk Korzybski's system. Nor should we lightly dismiss Burroughs's concept of "decontrol" as a means of political resistance or his antisocial vision of "objective silence" as the ultimate end of decontrol. Instead, Burke's critique illuminates the specific nature of Burroughs's political intervention, and explains why satire, irony, and cut-up might have seemed to be powerful political weapons. As Burke clarifies, Korzybski's system is less significant as a science than as an ethos or lived philosophy. Differentiation, delay, and conscious-ness of abstracting are best understood as attitudes, orientations, or stances. By turning thought upon the thinking process, one might, it is promised, achieve a state of peace. The self-examining therapies by which one attains objective silence do not resolve easily into phil-osophical, psychoanalytic, or clinical practice. This is why Korzybski's General Semantics can seem to be a self-help cult and, at the same time, an anticipation of cybernetic science. General Semantics most resembles what Hadot calls "spiritual exercises" or what Peter Sloterdijk calls "anthropotechnics." Hadot's "spiritual exercises" are "a transformation of our vision of the world," a "metamorphosis of our personality" in conformity with "the life of the objective Spirit," however it is defined.[104] As I discussed in my introduction, Hadot describes such exercises in terms of the philosophical activity of *askesis* (self-training). Askesis promises "an authentic state of life," "self-consciousness, an exact vision of the world, inner peace, and freedom [mainly from the passions]."[105] Commenting on the same philosophical tradition, Sloterdijk conceives of anthropotechnics as a reformulation of ethics; it is "the methods of mental and physical practicing by which humans . . . have attempted to optimize their cosmic and immunological status in the face of vague risks of living and acute certainties of death."[106] Neither spiritual exercises nor anthropotechnics are limited specifically to philosophical schools or religious dogmas, but can be found in a range of social institutions and popular phenomena, including Scientology, which Sloterdijk describes as a "psychotechnic firm."[107] Sloterdijk does not mention that the psycho-technology Scientology proffers, and which Burroughs investigated during the 1960s, had a strong affinity with General Semantics. As Lawrence Wright notes, L. Ron Hubbard was strongly influenced by Korzybski's ideas.[108]

Korzybski is today widely (and not unfairly) regarded as a crank. But for Burroughs, General Semantics promised relief from an evil force that he called the Ugly Spirit, which he blamed for his having killed his wife, Joan Vollmer, during a game of William Tell. That is, General Semantics was an art of living, another spiritual exercise, of a piece with his wider exploration of mind-altering drugs, orgone accumulators, Scientology, and cut-ups. In his comments to Patti Smith, Burroughs seems to posit punk as belonging to the same genealogy of attitudes. It is pop askesis, a subcultural psychotechnic firm. If Smith was "instrumental in creating" punk as an ethos or a lived philosophy, Burroughs would have to be no less instrumental. Burroughs always aspired to precisely manipulate "word and image to create an action, not to go out and buy a Coca-Cola, but to create an alteration in the reader's consciousness."[109] Burroughs's difficult writing demands a punk askesis of us, invites us to be transformed by language, to rise up as one and scream "BUGGER THE QUEEN!" Such an "action" is for Burroughs a form of silence through shouting, a spiritual schlupping. This is what it might mean for punk media to create punk persons. And this is also what Greil Marcus seems to mean when he calls punk "a language anticipating its own destruction."[110] Punk is here described as a self-destructive antilanguage, as that which is unspeakable or unsingable, perhaps as what happens

when the modernist poem decides to achieve autonomy through suicide. Punk is therefore an apt local name for Burroughs's pursuit
silence at the objective level.

Wild Boys and the Master Mind

Another name for the objective silence that William S. Burroughs
sought might be Utopia. Many critics have suggested that his lifelong
experiments encode a Utopian aspiration, one at first buried under the
remorseless surface of his parodies, but more openly in view during his
middle and later career. Critics tell this story in various ways. Wayne
Pounds suggests that Utopia was always part of Burroughs's project
because "[p]arody necessarily implies a utopia, an ideal standard by
which the vicious is recognized."[111] Burroughs's postmodern parodies
took as their object "not an art style [the object of modernist parodies]
but an administrative, bureaucratic style—the style of instrumental
rationality that, as the discourse of the state, dominates our age."[112]
Pounds invokes Bakhtin's analysis of parodic laughter to explain
Burroughs's supposed Utopianism. Burroughs, this version of the
story goes, similarly destroys in order to clear the ground for a new
creation. Jamie Russell describes the same turn in Burroughs's career
as a change from the dystopian concerns of his writing in the 1950s
and 1960s toward a "fantasy of a masculine queer utopia . . . not only
free from regulation by the heterosexual dominant but also free from
the gender schizophrenia imposed by that dominant."[113] Either
Burroughs's style dramatically transformed in the 1970s (Russell), or
the dialectical possibility of regeneration, always latent in his deni-
grating irony, came at last to the surface (Pounds). Both interpretations insist on describing Burroughs's post-1970 fiction as Utopian,
regenerative, or future-oriented. The analysis of the preceding section, it should be clear, already partly rebuts this interpretation. After
all, Utopias are fantasies of collective life—of social and political life.
Burroughs's antisocial political vision, by contrast, banishes the possibility of collectivity. His imagined punk superorganism dissolves the
individual, helps the individual escape from his flesh, and destroys the
possibility of collectivity, foreclosing the prospect of Utopia. I will
argue that the term positive dystopia better describes the genre of
Burroughs's political fantasies. Though I will defer giving a full

definition of positive dystopia until the end of this chapter, two of
Burroughs's most important but least studied novels, *The Wild Boys:
A Book of the Dead* (1971) and its sequel, *Port of Saints* (1973), will help
us trace its contours in a preliminary way.

The Wild Boys was Burroughs's first long fiction after he exhausted
the Word Hoard that formed the basis for *Naked Lunch* (1959) and
his revolutionary cut-up trilogy, *The Soft Machine* (1961), *The Ticket
That Exploded* (1962), and *Nova Express* (1964). Though similar in
some ways to these previous texts, *The Wild Boys* is a return to narrative for Burroughs, albeit one peppered by cut-up refrains. The novel
introduces the character of Audrey Carson (who resembles, we learn,
"a walking corpse"), a Burroughs stand-in who replaces his previous
surrogate, the character William Lee, and who becomes a major
character in his Red Night Trilogy. *The Wild Boys*' subtitle, "A Book
of the Dead," also anticipates Burroughs's later concern with
Egyptian mythology in *The Western Lands*. The sequel to *The Wild
Boys*, *Port of Saints*, collects material rejected from the first novel,
featuring new wild boy adventures. Jennie Skerl describes *The Wild
Boys* as offering "utopian alternatives to the present social order."[114] It
proffers what Timothy S. Murphy calls a "*positive* or *affirmative* alternative to capitalist society, and not just a negative critique of it."[115]
Though we will have good reason to doubt Murphy's assumption
that Burroughs is anticapitalist, the wild boys are indeed Burroughs's
most forceful image of revolutionary agents of decontrol. They are
also positive representations of Burroughs's ideal antisocial assemblage, a "personal projection" that Burroughs regarded as "desirable
to me."[116] As Murphy notes, the wild boys even share Burroughs's
initials, "W. B."

Described variously as a "humanoid subspecies" and "biologic adap-
tives," the nearly mute wild boys are heavily armed loincloth-wearing
homosexual boy gangs who roam the Third World, mostly North
Africa and Latin America, after a variety of global catastrophes. In
Port of Saints, they begin traveling through time. They reproduce via
asexual budding, brutally murdering all sources of authority with
sharpened eighteen-inch bowie knives, including an army of CIA
agents that is trying to suppress their rebellion. The boys are always

described as having enigmatic smiles. They are "evidently derived from racial and national stock corresponding to Negroes, Mexicans, Danes, Americans etc.," but are also "a new breed."[117] Though written before a proper punk scene formed, *The Wild Boys* became a fount of punk imagery. David Bowie was one crucial mediator between Burroughs's wild boy fantasy and punk. Bowie cites *The Wild Boys* as a source of sartorial inspiration in his construction of Ziggy Stardust. The "shape and the look of what Ziggy and the Spiders were going to become" derived from Burroughs's book and Kubrick's *A Clockwork Orange*.[118] Jon Savage is invested in making the connection more than a matter of inspiration. "Within five years of Ziggy," he writes, "the punks were enacting *The Wild Boys* on the streets of Britain."[119] One of Burroughs's biographers makes the same link, describing the Sex Pistols and others in the orbit of Malcolm McLaren as "the wild boys of the 1976 British punk movement."[120] Sartorial influences aside, we can make more significant connections between the wild boys and punk. As Burroughs's first sustained attempt to represent life beyond control, the wild boys (always a plural figure) offer a political model that earlier novels only hint at.

Burroughs illustrates his positive model of life after decontrol differently in different narrative strands of *The Wild Boys*. As he admits, these strands often bear little obvious relationship to each other. The story of Tío Mate, which opens the novel, "does not belong" to the novel's main narrative.[121] There is "no relation really between that and the rest of the book."[122] Nonetheless, the opening section is worth examining at some length. On the one hand, it hints at the revolutionary ethos Burroughs recommends, and, on the other hand, it exemplifies the performative means through which he sought to propagate this ethos. The first chapter of the novel, "Tío Mate Smiles," opens with what might be described as a postmodern or posthumanist reimagining of the "Camera Eye" sections of John Dos Passos's *U.S.A. Trilogy*, which Burroughs acknowledged as a precedent for his own practice. However, the camera eye in this opening does not articulate some character's stream of consciousness but rather seeks a narrative form for nonconsciousness.

The camera is the eye of a cruising vulture flying over an area of scrub, rubble and unfinished buildings on the outskirts of Mexico City.

Five-story building no walls no stairs . . . squatters have set up makeshift houses . . . floors are connected by ladders . . . dogs bark, chickens cackle, a boy on the roof makes a jack-off gesture as the camera sails past.

Close to the ground we see the shadow of our wings, dry cellars choked with thistles, rusty iron rods sprouting like metal plants from cracked concrete, a broken bottle in the sun, shit-stained color comics, an Indian boy against a wall with his knees up eating an orange sprinkled with red pepper.[123]

The embodied eye of this passage is at the same time the organic eye of a vulture, presumably searching for carrion, and the mechanical eye of a camera. This organic-mechanical cyborg eye hovers over a desiccated, almost-Eliotic version of Mexico City, a landscape that itself fuses biology and technology, albeit metaphorically ("iron rods sprouting like plants"). In this opening scene, there remains a decisive gap between observing subject and observed object, but the mechanical-organic character of the landscape (the plant-like iron-rod assemblage) hints at a possible transcendence of the categories of subject and object. Ellipses suture the objects of the vulture-camera's eye, each verbal fragment—the "makeshift houses," the "floors connected by ladders"—announcing the gap between cuts or frames that Burroughs's previous experiments in cut-up had worked to conceal. Unlike the novels preceding *The Wild Boys*, the camera eye of this cruising vulture motivates the cut-up technique of the passage, remediating film montage. The "boy on the roof" (perhaps the first appearance of a wild boy in the text) hails the observer, making a "jack-off gesture," revealing that the vulture camera is not an invisible mediator but a situated observer. Burroughs's characters know they are being watched or filmed. At the same time, the "we" of the third paragraph pluralizes the reader, and puts this pluralized reader into a relation not only with the narrator (or author) but also with the observing machine. We are asked to see "the shadow of our wings" as the shadow *we* are casting. We are both biological organism and mechanism. While asking the reader to identify with the vulture-camera perspective, Burroughs also highlights the emptiness that logically precedes all perspectives.

For if our vision is like a camera eye, Burroughs implies, then there must be constitutional gaps in our perception and a larger (objective) reality outside the flow of film frames. These gaps (the space between frames as well as the ontological outside to the film apparatus itself) make revolution possible. Control is effective only because we misidentify the rapidly shifting frames of our sense perception for reality as such. In this way, cut-up stands in the same relation to filmic reality as irony stands for de Man to dialectic. Lee Edelman describes irony (and queerness, which comes to seem to be a synonym for irony) as a name for the "force of the unthought remainder," a "disfiguration of identity" that challenges the "imperative of figuration" itself. Burroughs popularized this queer-critical (and I'd argue punk) view of irony as outside or interruption. This is the model of irony implicit in Burroughs's famous injunction to "[s]torm the Reality Studio," to "[w]ise up all the marks everywhere," and to "[r]elease Silence Virus."[124] Burroughs sees the world as a film, a "biologic film," and describes the aim of politics as destroying that film, getting "into the darkroom where the films are processed, where they're in a position to expose negatives and prevent events from occurring."[125] His ideas about cut-up are often rendered less strange than they actually are. In his literary history of the technique, *Shift Linguals*, Edward S. Robinson argues that "Burroughs and his immediate successors replicated the techniques of the mass media to reveal the methods by which language is manipulated and control exercised over the receivers of the messages contained therein."[126] On this view, cut-ups attempt "to undermine the meanings of original texts or to expose their hidden meanings."[127] This description is consistent with Burroughs's desire to "[w]ise up the marks," a desire that recalls the hipster's belief in the power of knowingness or digging, but Robinson does not discuss the odder consequences of the view that "reality is actually a movie."[128] In his essay "invisible people," Burroughs invites his readers to "consider [the tape recorder] and what it can do it can record and play back activating a past time set by precise association a recording can be played back any number of times."[129] The manipulation of tape through cutting and splicing offers to "bring you a liberation from old association locks," because one finds in cut-ups "words which were not in the original tape but which are in many cases relevant to the original text as if the words themselves had been interrogated and forced to reveal their hidden meanings."[130] Not only do "hidden meanings" unveil themselves, but the playback of recorded material has the capacity to transform reality. "anyone with a tape recorder controlling the sound track can influence and create events the tape recorder."[131] These are not metaphorical claims. For, Burroughs writes, if you "mix yesterday in with today and hear tomorrow your future rising out of old recordings you are a programmed tape recorder set to record and play back."[132] The tape does not just *record* yesterday, today, and tomorrow; it literally *remakes* yesterday, today, and tomorrow. Burroughs equates temporality with the sequence of narrative discourse. Cut-up thus has the power not only to disrupt official meanings, but also to "influence and create events."[133]

Burroughs's vision of reality as a "biologic film" also governs the fictive world of *The Wild Boys*, as the opening chapter's vulture-camera perspective shows. The chapter entitled "'Mother and I Would Like to Know'" dramatizes revolutionary practices required to disrupt power within this essentially filmic world. The episode is set in the "uneasy spring of 1988" (*WB* 138). Around the Western world, "suppressive police states" "maintain a democratic façade" by means of "[t]he precise programming of thought and feeling and apparent sensory impressions" (*WB* 138). Our narrator, a revolutionary who is not a wild boy but hopes to make contact with them, outlines the strategy and tactics his revolutionary movement will use to destroy the "police machine and all its records" (*WB* 140). Around the global south, revolutionary guerilla armies gather in order "to free the United States" and "to liberate Western Europe and the United Kingdom" (*WB* 139). These revolutionaries are not yet themselves wild boys but wild boys in the making. Their target is "[t]he family unit and its cancerous expansion into tribes, countries, nations" (*WB* 140). Hoping to "destroy all dogmatic verbal systems," they fight "family talk, mother talk, father talk, cop talk, priest talk, country talk *or* party talk" (*WB* 140). Critics have analyzed the novel's rendition of revolutionary violence, but have less frequently discussed the origin of the wild boys themselves. They emerge, we learn, during "the uneasy spring of 1969 in Marrakech." The first-person narrator (it is unclear if this is the same narrator who begins the chapter) is hiding in a closet where he "had prudently taken refuge" to observe a "gasoline gang" burn to death a "nice young couple" in their "chintzy middle-class living room" (*WB* 143). Captivated by the boy who lights the match that kills the gasoline-doused couple, the narrator thinks, "My God what a cigarette ad," and the "BOY" who lights the match ends up becoming "the hottest property in advertising" (*WB* 143–144). The image of the "BOY" becomes "too hot to handle," and "all the teenagers began acting like the BOY looking at you with a dreamy look lips parted over their Wheaties," and they buy "BOY shirts and BOY knives running around like wolf packs burning, looting, killing" (*WB* 144). Observing the burning city from his balcony, regarding the violence as "all very romantic," the narrator happily suggests that he is observing a scene "[r]ather like fairyland . . . except for the smell of gasoline and burning flesh" (*WB* 144). After state authorities, under the leadership of Colonel Arachnid Ben Driss, squelch the revolution, surviving gasoline boys "evolved different ways of life and modes of combat," becoming wild boys proper (*WB* 144). In *Port of Saints*, we learn more about their origin. After surviving the "terror of Colonel Driss," wild boy communes decide to "put all thought of women from their minds and bodies" (*POS* 96). They will "never again submit to the yoke of female flesh" (*POS* 97). A "senior editor" describes this account of the wild boys as a "myth," but the narrator explains that "[t]he myth spread and wild boy tribes sprang up everywhere"; they form "their own language and exchange trade goods over a vast network" (*POS* 97). At their origin, then, the wild boys are, like punks, a media creation, a myth that creates a community. They target linguistic control systems, hijack advertising, and reproduce the revolution through image manipulation, forming alternative networks of communication and exchange. Those who follow their lead use similar tactics. The ultimate weapon of the wild boys is a so-called film grenade. "A cop stopped toward us I pushed the plunger down and brought my hands up tossing the grenade into the air. A black explosion blotted out the set" (*POS* 67). The term "set" recapitulates Burroughs's description of reality as a film, as do the two novels' repeated references to cinematographic language and screenwriting conventions.

Burroughs's vulture-eyed satire hopes to inspire revolutionary activity by transforming the reader. By presenting the image of a BOY, he aims to make a BOY of us, to make us wild. In his prior cut-up experiments, Burroughs imagined that he might fuse himself with another writer—not only collaborators such as Brion Gysin, but also dead writers whose work was getting cut or folded into the new text. Burroughs and Gysin describe the results of this collaboration as forming a "third mind," one not reducible to the mind of either original contributor. "The third mind," they write, "is there when two minds collaborate."[134] Burroughs borrows this concept from what may seem to be a surprising source, the bestselling self-help book by Napoleon Hill, *Think and Grow Rich* (1937), which purported to share the secret of Andrew Carnegie's business success. Hill develops a concept he calls the "Master Mind" to describe the nature of business collaboration, which he defines as the "[c]oordination of knowledge and effort, in a spirit of harmony, between two or more people, for the attainment of a definite purpose."[135] This spirit of harmony is not a metaphor for Hill but has an extra-human ontological force that resonates with other intellectual sources that informed Burroughs. Hill describes the "psychic phase of the Master Mind principle" as tapping into "spiritual forces with which the human race, as a whole, is not well acquainted."[136] Whereas earlier experiments by Burroughs sought to create artistic third minds, *The Wild Boys* and *Port of Saints* aspire to join the reader into the Master Mind that Hill posits. Burroughs hopes to schlupp with the reader. Becoming aware of his participation in the Master Mind, the reader moves beyond his individual subjectivity to join an all-present objective silence before identity formation. As the wild-boy-in-the-making narrator of "'Mother and I Would Like to Know'" explains, "I have a thousand faces and a thousand names. I am nobody I am everybody. I am me I am you. I am here there forward back in out. I stay everywhere I stay nowhere. I stay present I stay absent"

(*WB* 140). At the beginning of *The Wild Boys*, Burroughs uses the first-person plural to indicate that the reader is complicit in forming the vulture-camera perspective. Now, Burroughs has given the reader a full enough sense of his idea of revolution to use the more technically accurate first-person singular. For the Master Mind is not a plural mind. It is not a collective in any traditional sense of the word. We all already belong to it. Burroughs is me. I am you. You are everyone. And when you are decontrolled, you too will become wild. This is what it means to be a wild boy.

By calling *The Wild Boys* a "book of the dead," Burroughs also aligns his novel with another how-to guide, the Egyptian *Book of the Dead*, which gives elaborate instructions on funerary rites meant to ensure the soul's safe passage into the afterlife. Burroughs saw Egyptian mummification practices as exclusionary, "the most arbitrary, precarious, and bureaucratic immortality blueprint," which made "immortality a monopoly of the truly rich."[137] *The Wild Boys* was a "book of the dead" because, as Burroughs wrote in a letter, "[t]he hero is killed in a car crash on the first page and the whole book is a series of episodes in which the female and ugly spirit forces try to lure or force him back into the birth death cycle."[138] *The Wild Boys* might thus be viewed, as Murphy puts it, as a "plan for afterliving," which does not mean preparing for one's inevitable death but rather learning how to transcend time while still living, moving beyond the "birth death cycle" as such.[139] Eliminating "birth" from the "birth death cycle" seems to require eliminating women. Burroughs was, of course, famously misogynistic, though he denied such charges in his inauspiciously titled essay "Women: A Biological Mistake?" by arguing that dinosaurs and humanity itself might also be regarded as similar "mistakes." He claims to be concerned not so much with eliminating women as with moving beyond sex and gender binaries.[140] Elsewhere, speaking of the exclusionary maleness of the wild boys, Burroughs suggests, "I certainly have no objections—if lesbians would like to do the same."[141] These defenses are, to say the least, unconvincing. In his letters, Burroughs was quite clear that the appeal of the wild boy fantasy is specifically "about a *world without women*."[142] "No women no trouble no problems," he writes. Discussing the possibility for a *Wild Boys* film adaptation, Burroughs insists that it must be "the first uncompromising anti-female state-ment," and imagines the wild boys' enemies to be the "police and a lesbian legion known as the Fanatical 80," whom the boys defeat by releasing a virus that destroys the industrialized world. (The Fanatical 80 appear in *Port of Saints*.)

In his 1969 book of interviews with Daniel Odier, *The Job*, Burroughs describes a fantasy of the "academy," in which "decentral-ized and camouflaged training" would "enable students to challenge the parasitic persistence of unworkable establishments," namely the state and the family. The student who undergoes "academy" training, in effect, becomes a wild boy. Burroughs conceives *The Wild Boys* and *Port of Saints* as texts that might perform the same function as his fantasized academy. Students take "a weapons course financed by a rightist billionaire in East Texas where we learn to use every weapon from a crossbow to a laser gun."[143] When Murphy laments that *The Wild Boys* failed to facilitate "the total dismantling of worldwide state capitalism," he wrongly assumes that Burroughs's target was capi-talism.[144] As *The Job* shows, Burroughs saw some use for "rightist" capitalists. Moreover, the dream of wild boys who "exchange trade goods over a vast network" stands specifically in opposition to monop-olistic and state-backed capitalist enterprises, not laissez-faire or so-called free market capitalism, which Burroughs sometimes roman-ticized (albeit in impressionistic terms). In a short narrative routine about the "the incestuous Carson family" in a 1971 letter to Gysin, Burroughs celebrated "healthy old fashioned capitalism," praising the Carsons for being "very efficient."[145] The efficient Carson family, of course, arouses resistance from control systems. "Do you hear the Ugly Spirit snarling off stage?" Burroughs writes.[146] Fortunately, the war against the Carsons has what Burroughs views as a happy ending: the Carsons defeat the forces of the Ugly Spirit because the healthy old-fashioned-capitalist Carsons "are simply more efficient."[147] Even if we doubt that Burroughs had a systematic understanding of capi-talism, or if we discount the significance of his economic opinions when assessing the political effects of his work, it is hard to construe Burroughs's writing as anticapitalist. In 1994, worried about medical bills, the 79-year-old writer appeared in an advertisement for Nike's Air Max sneakers, in which he plays a character who declares that

"The purpose of technology is not to confuse the brain, but to serve the body, to make life easier, to make anything possible. It's the coming of the new technology." Those who would accuse Burroughs of "selling out" for appearing in this advertisement profoundly misunderstand his work. Put in the perspective of his whole career—from his hatred of the New Deal and the meddling federal government; through his lifelong dismissal of socialism, communism, and Marxism; to his celebration of spontaneity, flexibility, and antisocial schlupping as the goal of human life—appearing in a Nike commercial hardly seems like a betrayal. As Burroughs told a *Paris Review* interviewer, "I see no reason why the artistic world can't absolutely merge with Madison Avenue."[148] The fantasy of the wild boys, the image of a smiling BOY that spreads virus-like via advertising, dissolving the subjectivity of anyone who encounters it, does not subvert advertising but signals its total triumph, its dissolution of the distinction between subject and object and between individuals. Viewed this way, Burroughs's antisocial fantasy was ultimately less a failure than a rousing success. We would not be wrong to suspect that somewhere the wild boys are still smiling.

The Language of the Body

William S. Burroughs launched his most advanced artistic weapon against the state, family structures, and midcentury capitalism (which some critics have misrecognized as capitalism as such). All of these control systems were manifestations of the semantic prisonhouse of temporal sequence, beyond which lay an atemporal paradise of objective silence. But for all that he attacked, Burroughs retained an alternative, positive vision of capitalism, sometimes identified with a mythical laissez-faire era, sometimes with a thinly sketched anarcho-capitalism. Analyzing the cut-up trilogy, Michael Clune argues that there is a formal identity between Burroughs's ideas of spontaneous order and F. A. Hayek's fantasy of how prices structure a marketplace. By Clune's phenomenological account, prices are a way to "prestructure the context of embodiment in terms of a collective system."[149] When gas prices reach a certain level, they prestructure the normative context within which you encounter your bicycle, which becomes something for commuting. Likewise, an oil field becomes a thing for drilling into. Clean battery technology suddenly seems, to the scientist, like an interesting research problem. Clune is at pains to explain "the simple fact of the formal identity" of Burroughs's and Hayek's ideas. I do not agree that there is a strict identity in their visions of life outside sociality. Burroughs's thought is frankly much more impressionistic than Hayek's (and we need to be careful about taking Hayek's catallactic fantasies at face value). But the consonance between them is hard to deny. It may be more accurate to say that Burroughs and neoliberal economic theorists (Hayek, Friedman) constructed similar fantasies of spontaneous order in response to centralized state power, relatively strong unions, and bureaucratic corporate forms. Burroughs's ideas thus resonated with larger cultural transformations that led to the rise of the projective city. Punk represented one pathway through which Burroughs's capacious and idiosyncratic thought was adopted and extended. Kathy Acker, the smartest and most artistically innovative punk interpreter of Burroughs, will provide our case study of how these ideas were taken up, transformed, and put to new literary-political uses.

Describing Kathy Acker's punk aesthetic as contributing to the rise of the projective city may seem perverse. After all, many critics take punk to be an incorrigibly left artistic movement, anticapitalist to its core, which even in failure demands reverence for its effort to escape commodification. Acker, likewise, continues to be an emblem of left literary critique, as well as radical feminism, and is celebrated for her power to subvert dominant, sexist ideologies, "to challenge rationalism, the reigning logic of capitalism," in the words of Nicola Pitchford.[150] Larry McCaffery expresses what largely remains the consensus view on Acker, punk, and experimental art's subversive powers when he writes: "Her aesthetic, which is intimately related to the 'punk' aesthetic that evolved in music during the mid 1970s, has led Acker to produce a series of novels that are deliberately crude, violent, obscene, disjointed, surreal. Her methods are designed to force a confrontation between readers and *all* conventions (literary and otherwise), to shock them out of complacent acceptance of hierarchies, received traditions, meanings, stable identities."[151] This reading accurately describes how Acker understood her own art.

She saw identity and language as traps, homogenizing machines, social technologies that together imposed "a structure of closed and centralized meaning and defined position in culture and history."[152] Art, by contrast, has the power to disrupt "phallocentric, patriarchal" systems of myth, meaning, and ideology (*Bodies* 88). In the mid-1970s, confronting a New York art scene that valued personal expression, she identified with punk rebellion against hippies. She wished to confront hippie dreams of Utopia with ugly actuality. Against a lyrical imperative to "find your voice," associated for her with the Black Mountain poets, she frequently insisted that she had no voice.[153] Punk thus profoundly shaped her view of art as a form of social criticism, affecting her compositional practice as well as her understanding of what her texts might do to readers. Punk allowed Acker to conceive of writing as a mode of reading, literary composition as appropriation or collage. The movement gave her a means by which to create art against conventional dogmas of originality, artistic ownership, and identity. Though it shaped her literary experiments, punk was infrequently a direct subject of her writing (with a few important exceptions to be examined here). Punk was rather a good name for the ethos of her art. "[T]here was no way I had of talking about [my work] . . . until the punk movement came along," she explained to McCaffery in an interview.[154] "I don't know for what reason or what magic thing happened, but suddenly everyone started working together along the same lines."[155]

McCaffery takes Acker's punk "prose assemblages" to be "*wickedly funny* critiques of life-under-late-capitalism."[156] And yet, a more thorough rehearsal of Acker's statements on punk and capitalism almost immediately complicates this canonical interpretation. The specific content of Acker's critique of capitalism becomes elusive. Her model of politics retreats from sight. In fact, Acker once suggested, American punk, at least in the New York scene during the midseventies, was not a "political movement."[157] It was rather an art movement spearheaded by "a bunch of middle class people who suddenly were finding themselves broke and living in a system that disgusted them."[158] What disgusted them about the system under which they made art was that "their audience was upper-middle-class white art gallery audience."[159] These disgusted young artists "wanted to find a way to express that anger in their work," and to create "something that would make people notice them because they also felt that they weren't getting enough attention."[160] Acker allows that punk's London scene might have been more politically ambitious than the New York scene. Nonetheless, Acker essentially describes punk as a solution to a problem arising from a broken relationship between artists and their imagined or actual audiences. Middle-class artists were getting the wrong kind of reception. Their poverty arises not so much from their social background or class status as from the incommensurability between the art they would prefer to produce and the available avenues by which they might be remunerated for their artistic labor. These artists wanted both autonomy and recognition, and punk offered "a lot of possibilities" to achieve their aims.[161] Much writing on punk makes some version of this point, emphasizing the horizontal relationship between performer and audience at small venues such as CBGB's, where it became possible to imagine that anyone in the audience might, at any moment, get on stage and start playing. One also finds traces of this view in the advice Acker gave to Kathleen Hanna, soon-to-be lead singer of the riot grrrl band Bikini Kill. "You should be in a band," Acker told Hanna, since "[t]here's more of a community for musicians than for writers."[162] In these comments, Acker puts forward a version of what Boltanski and Chiapello have described as the artistic critique of capitalism. The artistic critique "presents itself as a radical challenge to the basic values and options of capitalism."[163] It attacks "the disenchantment generated by the processes of rationalization and commodification."[164] The artistic critique of alienation must not, Boltanski and Chiapello emphasize, be confused with the social critique of capitalist exploitation. Indeed, the social and artistic critiques are "not directly compatible."[165]

Acker found herself facing an apparent paradox, a specifically punk paradox. On the one hand, she sought recognition for and through her art. Like Burroughs, she wanted to connect (if not schlupp) with an audience. On the other hand, she resisted the possibility of assimilation and homogenization. She sought to make an art that escaped interpretive authority, identified for her with political authoritarianism or fascism. What Acker wanted was reception without understanding, production and circulation without consumption. Acker's Pushcart Prize–winning short story, "New York City in 1979," invents a literary form to solve this artistic conundrum. The story was originally published in the periodical *Crawl Out Your Window* in 1979 and then reprinted as a *Top Stories* pamphlet in 1981. The story, a surreal collage of punk life, evokes scenes from around New York City, mostly the downtown literary scene, specifically the Lower East Side, at the end of the seventies. It was a vibrant artistic scene that, as Joel Rose and Catherine Texier note, deployed "[s]ex violence, shock value, parody, cynicism, irony, and black humor to attack the complacency of established literature and its middle-class values."[166] It was a world Acker described as resembling "an angel miraculously living amid the greed and zombielike behaviors of those outside the art world" (*Bodies* 84). "New York City in 1979" evokes "a typical New York artist attitude."[167] It describes a version of the city "squeezed between inflation and depression" (137). The "American bourgeoisie has left," leaving "[o]nly the poor: artists, Puerto Ricans who can't afford to move . . . and rich Europeans who fleeing the terrorists don't give a shit about New York" (134). Rich hippies, dressed in "outfits the poor people who were in ten years ago wore ten years ago," attempt to infiltrate the Mudd Club, a TriBeCa club that punks frequented, open from 1978 to 1983 (135). In the story, the club's bouncer ("an open-shirted skinny guy who says he's just an artist") turns away the rich hippies (135). What should already be obvious is the idiosyncratic class landscape of the story. In the first place, the rich are identified not with capitalists but with hippies. Acker elsewhere describes the United States as a "postcapitalist" society, and avers that in the United States (unlike England) "art . . . has little to [do] with class" (*Bodies* 84). The punks loitering in front of the Mudd Club contemplate kidnapping the chauffer of these rich hippies and stealing their limousine. Punks hate hippies not only for their bad fashion sense but also because they take pleasure in the downtown scene, dispossessing "[a]ll the poor people who're making this club fashionable" from the coolness they have made via what we might today describe as unpaid affective labor (135). Acker's punks hate hippies for other reasons too. In Acker's view, hippies made the mistake of thinking they could "successfully oppose American postcapitalism by a lie, by creating a utopian society" (*Bodies* 13). What the hippies denied, by imagining Utopia, was that "the body is real" (Ibid.). Hippie Utopianism allegedly props up patriarchal postcapitalist rationality by homogenizing the heterogeneity of bodily desire. Acker imagines that "the body" has a nondualistic language of its own, a true language that rationality falsifies. Not only does the true language of the body "not lie," but "lies are not possible" in this nondualistic "body-language" (*Bodies* 12). The language of the body is the language of the anus. The language of the body is, in truth, many languages: a language of "flux," of "wonder," of contradiction, of "this material body," of "play," of "intensity," and so on (*Bodies* 91–92). As Walter Benn Michaels notes, "writing is bleeding" for Acker.[168]

Utopian discourses come to seem dominating or aligned with oppression because they supposedly reinforce the rationality on which capitalism (or postcapitalism) depends.[169] It is important to emphasize: Acker does not propose that capitalism *corrupts* rationality or uses it along narrowly instrumental lines, but she joins Burroughs in imagining that rationality *as such* is problematic, precisely what makes contemporary life unlivable. America is "a giant baby, perhaps mongoloid . . . who not maliciously but unknowingly breaks everything it meets as it crawls around in chaotic paths" (*Bodies* 1). The problem with this baby is that it "regards the world as an extension of his or her own identity" (Ibid.). The American mongoloid baby, trapped by "Aristotelian continuities," fails to recognize the existence of an "other" and is therefore, in a technical sense, "insane" (Ibid.). The rigor with which Acker has understood Burroughs's ideas should be obvious. She echoes language that Burroughs derived from Alfred Korzybski's General Semantics, and draws similar conclusions about how one might fight contemporary "insanity." Because insanity is grounded in misrecognition, it is possible to fight "post-bourgeois language with poetry: images, dangling clauses, all that lingers at the edges of the unsaid, that leads to and through dreams" (*Bodies* 3). Because they precede signification, the body and its desires become politically important for Acker, enjoying the same pride of place as the Master Mind or objective silence does in Burroughs. The other major inspiration for Acker's nonreified body-language is Luce

Irigaray. On Irigaray's view, the figure of Woman has a special capacity to disrupt centralized meanings (phallologocentrism) because She enjoys the capacity of propinquity. As has been frequently noted, Acker engaged seriously with poststructuralist feminist theory, not only with Irigaray but also with Hélène Cixous, Julia Kristeva, and Judith Butler. Michel Foucault and Gilles Deleuze and Félix Guattari's *Anti-Oedipus* also influenced her, in much the same way that punk did. Irigaray's concept of propinquity not only reinforced Acker's theoretical claim that the body has its own language outside signification, but it also allowed Acker to connect her body-language to feminist politics. On Irigaray's post-Lacanian view, Woman "enters into a ceaseless exchange of herself with the other without any possibility of identifying either."[170] Because the other is "near" to Woman, she finds the notion of property or possession unintelligible. Acker wrote "New York City in 1979" before she read Irigaray. At that time, she understood her artistic practice as an offshoot of punk. However, we shouldn't simply imagine Acker's relationship to punk (or for that matter poststructuralism) as passive or parasitic. Instead, Acker played an important role, more so than Burroughs, in defining what we understand punk to be. Her later, theoretical descriptions of "body-language" formalize ideas already apparent in "New York City in 1979," fusing punk and poststructuralism in ways still important for contemporary critical debates. Acker's body-language entails, as Michel Foucault writes of *Anti-Oedipus*, a "way of thinking and living," a way to "ferret out the fascism that is ingrained in our behavior," to expunge "the slightest traces of fascism in the body."[171]

In "New York City in 1979," Acker hopes that destruction or negation (a sort of deterritorialization without end) might offer the grounds for political action. This political fantasy is simultaneously body-oriented and antimaterialist, which is why the story's protagonist, Janey, dismisses the claim of another character, Bet, that "feminism depends on four factors" (these are economic independence, daycare centers, abortions, and "decent housing"). Janey refutes these factors by suggesting that "those are just material conditions" (141). Bet has committed the crime of "accepting the materialism this society teaches" (Ibid.). Such considerations "belong back in the

1920s" and don't "apply to this world" (141). "This" world, the New York City of the story, is a world where "disaster is the only thing that's happening" (133). The city is "fake," and the world is "gray afterbirth." But these disasters "cause they're so open, spawn a new growth" (133). Acker's first-person narrator (possibly the character Janey) says, "I want more and more horrible disaster in New York cause I desperately want to see that new thing that is going to happen this year" (133). In this context, Janey forecasts that "[a] lot of blood inside is going to fall. MORE and MORE because inside is outside" (133). Janey has suffered so much that she has "become a person," and believes "it's necessary to blast open her mind constantly and destroy EVERY PARTICLE OF MEMORY THAT SHE LIKES" (134). Aware "that writing changes nothing on a larger political scale," Acker aimed, as she explains in her essay "A Few Notes on Two of My Books," to write a short story that "*will* change things magically" (*Bodies* 8). To enact such magical change, she would "take one text, New York City, the life of my friends, and change this text by placing another text on top of it" (Ibid.). Her intertext in "New York City in 1979" is a journal entry, the story of Charles Baudelaire and Jeanne Duval. Baudelaire watches Duval deteriorate from the syphilis he has infected her with. Baudelaire concludes, referring to himself in the second person: "the traces of [her] smallpox will be part of your happiness" (Ibid.). This entry gives Acker what she calls a "model of change" (Ibid.). She concludes: "ugliness [can be] changed through worse ugliness, even destruction, into love."[172] This imagined model of political efficacy is derived, she says, from the myth of Daedalus. As Acker interprets it, the Daedulus myth is about someone who "escaped prison by his art" (Ibid.). The writer for her becomes "a kind of journalist, a magic one" (*Bodies* 9). This portrait of the artist as a magical journalist who effects political change through a practice of negation enacts the punk genre I have been calling positive dystopia.

Positive dystopias transvalue blight and decay, seeing in such conditions the necessary precursors for eliminating the social, political, and cultural strictures that inhibit access to a nonlinguistic or bodily level of reality. The pathway to beauty, it turns out, is even greater ugliness. The first-person narrator of Acker's story lays out the logic positive dystopia hopes to disrupt: "X wants Y and, for whatever reasons reasons [sic], thinks it shouldn't want Y . . . What X wants is Y and to be GOOD" (137). Acker's narrator lays out what Baudelaire does to "solve this dilemma." The solution is to do the BAD thing, to invite the punishment of authorities propping up norms that block desire, because "[t]he authority will punish him as much as possible, punish me punish me, more than is necessary till it has to be obvious to everyone that the punishment is unjust" (Ibid.). The conclusion is that "[p]unishers are unjust" and that "there is no GOOD and BAD" (Ibid.). This is why it is "necessary to go to as many extremes as possible" (Ibid.). Acker imagines a political purpose to the destruction of social standards. In her essay "Some American Cities," Acker is clear on how this wholesale destruction of such standards relates to the historical development of capitalism. "Perhaps New York City isn't disintegrating," she writes. "Perhaps one system, that order based on a certain kind of capitalism, is disintegrating while another world, one of tribes, criminal and other, anarchic, is rising out of the rotting streets, sidewalks, and bridges" (*Bodies* 135). Bodybuilding becomes another metaphor for Acker's vision of rejuvenation through destruction. Acker describes bodybuilding as giving access to a "geography of no language," a "negative space," or "that which rejects language" (*Bodies* 146). Bodybuilding is a project of controlled failure: "I want to shock my body into growth" (Ibid.). Acker destroys a muscle, takes it beyond its capacity, in order to make it stronger. In this way, "muscular destructions" can become synonymous with "muscular growth." Acker suggests that "the equation between destruction and growth" might also be "a formula for art" (Ibid.).

Such, at least, is the formula for Acker's punk art. Across her writing, Acker articulates a powerful ambivalence toward this model of political action. Even in "New York City in 1979," Janey recognizes the ambiguous power of desire, or at least sex. "I'm not fucking anymore cause sex is a prison. It's become a support of this post-capitalist system like art . . . The sex product presents a naturally expanding market. Now capitalists are doing everything they can do to bring world sexual desire to an unbearable edge" (138). Celebrations of sex momentarily get associated with "the sexual revolution" as well as "free love and hippies" (Ibid.). But Janey wavers on this point: "I don't know what my heart is cause I'm corrupted . . . I'm going to be a robot for the rest of my life" (Ibid.). By the end of the short story, Janey gives in to her sexual desire. "Sex drives Janey crazy," the narrator reports. "Janey is Want" (143). When she submits to her Want, "[t]he world in which there is no feeling, the robot world, doesn't exist" (Ibid.). Acker's story seems sometimes to distinguish between sex and desire, sometimes not. Despite her earlier concern about the hippie commodification of sex, Janey's unlimited "Want" and irrepressible desire for "Sex" offer her a pathway to a self-negating personal oblivion in pleasure ("No rationality possible") as well as liberation from robot life in New York City (sex makes her "more content") (Ibid.). It is hopefully clear that Acker is not merely telling Janey's individual story, but more generally trying to imagine solutions to "postcapitalist" oppression.[173] When, later in her career, with her 1988 novel, *Empire of the Senseless*, Acker makes her "positive" or "post-cynical" turn, when she seeks to move "from no to yes, from nihilism to myth," it is not because she has rejected her prior commitments, but because her demolition project is in some sense complete (*Bodies* 11, 13). The desire for positivity is not a new concern for Acker but the fulfillment of an agenda set by her earliest writing.

Punks and Pirates

Punk negativity helped Kathy Acker make sense of her senseless art, offering an art of living that might do justice to—and make audiences aware of—the body's multiform desires, without in any simple way equating the body with matter. Acker emplotted this body-focused ethos within the narrative genre that I have been calling positive dystopia, an antihumanist or posthumanist, anti-Utopian genre that imagines human growth as arising not *from* destruction but precisely *in* destruction. Positive dystopia is an antidialectical genre, both in the sense that it does not ground its hopes in a dialectical logic as well as in the sense that it seeks to interrupt existing dialectics. Acker's language of the body, like Burroughs's pursuit of objective silence, aspires to arrest language, to derange rationalist (phallologocentric) Utopias that deny the body and dream life. Positive dystopia aimed, as Acker's narrator explains in her novel

Empire of the Senseless (1988), "to destroy language through language: to destroy language which normalizes and controls by cutting that language. Nonsense would attack the empire-making (empirical) empire of language, the prisons of meaning."[174] Acker initially associated her desire to destroy controlling language with a broader desire to destroy the ligaments of narrative as such, labeling these experiments "de-narrative."[175] In her self-described postcynical phase, which began with *Empire*, Acker did not abandon her desire to destroy language (she did not give up on negativity), but she did return to narrative—and specifically to myth, which she identified as "[s]omewhere real" (*Bodies* 11). Acker was careful to qualify her use of narrative and myth, to avoid charges that she was creating new master narratives, offering "*a* myth, *a* place, not *the* myth, *the* place" (Ibid.). She did not abandon the project of destroying controlling languages—she did not become a postironist—but rather sought (paradoxically) to describe life outside the empire of language through the language of myth.

Recent critics are divided on the political significance of Acker's postcynical turn. As he does for Burroughs, Michael Clune assimilates Acker's mythmaking with the cultural ascendency of free market ideology. Writing about *Empire of the Senseless*, Clune argues that Acker imagines not "a society without a market but . . . a market without a society."[176] To be sure, Acker's alleged free market vision goes far beyond anything think tank neoliberals claim to support. But Clune does not mean to argue that Acker is a crypto-neoliberal philosopher; rather, he argues that Acker's art constructs virtual fantasies of free market economies that might give us insight into real economies. She tries to imagine what replacing "the social order" with "an organic market" might look like, and so imagines that "the relations between sovereign individuals are replaced by an image of relations within a singular subject, such that the contact with the other is achieved not by moving across bodies but by going beneath the skin."[177] However, Clune's argument seems to be incompatible with Acker's unambiguous attack on intellectual property. As Caren Irr notes, Acker "describes property as the social sign of sex, assesses its effects on women, and imagines worlds ungoverned by ownership."[178] Acker frequently links her allegedly plagiaristic literary practice to a broader critique of intellectual property, to the claim that though the "writer earns money or a living by selling copyright, ownership to words," this system is a "scam" because "[n]obody really owns nothing" (*Bodies* 9–10). Though their analyses seem radically different, Clune and Irr do not offer incompatible descriptions of Acker's political-economic vision. I will show how these two critical views complement each other by examining Acker's rendition of the figure that she most frequently associates with the positive content of life beyond the "prisons of meaning": the pirate.

Pussy, King of the Pirates (1996) is Acker's most sustained investigation of the political figure of the pirate, the culmination of fantasies she had been developing since childhood. "When I was a child," Acker writes, "the only thing I wanted was to be a pirate," but she discovered that "I could never be a pirate because I was a girl" (*Bodies* 158, 159). She eventually discovered that she did not need to travel, to take any particular actions, to become a pirate. It turns out that "to travel into wonder is to be wonder. So it matters little whether I travel by plane, by rowboat, or by book. Or, by dream" (*Bodies* 159). What pirates know is that "*I* do not see, for there is no *I* to see" (*Bodies* 159). To be a pirate means to have attained a certain kind of negative self-knowledge. By examining this novel, we will clarify the peculiar sense in which positive dystopia is "positive" and what role punk negativity plays in cultivating piratical positivity. One of Acker's most accessible books, *Pussy, King of the Pirates*, traces the story of O, an ex-whore, who along with another ex-whore, Agne, hires a group of girl pirates to find buried treasure. The novel is a picaresque dream journal, which incorporates various sources, such as Robert Louis Stevenson's *Treasure Island* and Pauline Reage's *The Story of O*. Many critics have understandably focused on the political dimensions of Acker's vision of piracy but have ignored the importance of punk to the development of pirates in the novel. *Pussy* is Acker's most sustained fictional engagement with punk since the late 1970s. Not only are punks important to the book's narrative of girl piracy, but Acker also collaborated with the punk band The Mekons to create an album accompanying the book. Acker's girl pirates are, in an important sense, the spiritual children of punk, and *Pussy*'s punks harken back to Burroughs's wild boys.

O encounters punk boys early in the novel:

All of them had fucked their mothers and were no longer colonized.

   The growth of private property, one characteristic of the
bourgeois industrial world, ceased; private property, in the form
of multinational and extranational capital, returned to the hands
of the few. Economic, therefore political, power seemed to be
centralizing.

   The decrease of the separation between private and public
property, finally this disappearance, was directly related to a
movement away from, and then to the passing away of the
memory of patriarchy.

   In other words, the punks were one beginning of a new world.
   (40)

This passage is Acker's most direct statement about the function that
punks play in her political myth of piracy. By violating Oedipal
taboos, Acker's punk boys decolonize or deterritorialize norms. As in
Clune's account, this decolonization has economic effects, though
Acker's description of these effects can seem contradictory. On the
one hand, private property is redistributed to "the few" and thereby
centralized; on the other hand, private property "ceased" and the
distinction between public and private ultimately disappears. Whatever
this contradiction might mean, Acker is widely understood to have
opposed the centralization of private property and to support the
decentralized or anarchistic "new world" that the punks promise to
bring forth.[179] The novel's punks, we learn, "had no idea how to
relate to each other. For them, language just wasn't a problem" (41).
They presumably "speak" in something like Acker's language of the
body. They have "disavowed history" and are "descendants of
Heliogabalus of Alexandria," whose "anarchistic" "reign was replete
with murder, incest, and a lack of values" (41). Punks spread their
revolutionary "lack of values" through sexual contact. "To be kissed
by a punk boy was to be drawn to insanity or toward death" (41).
They are pedagogues who "teach" that "the civilized West has disappeared" and that "Terror is the answer for our times because we,

whores and punks, cannot liberate ourselves by running away from
horror, a horror that's nameless" (42). In Acker's hands, as late as
1996, punks continued to be imagined as popular revolutionary philosophers. They spread their beneficent horror not through language, which they know nothing about, but through sexual touch.
Acker's whores "commence their violent actions" because "punk
boys came to town" and touch them (41).

Later in the novel, in a section called "Where Boys Come From,"
punks also indirectly help formulate the rules of piracy, by telling
Pussy and her girl-pirate comrades the curious story of an act of
bodily cut-up. When Pussy encounters the punk boys hanging out in
a beauty parlor in the basement of a restaurant, which also doubles
as an art gallery, she has a vision of "an ocean in all its glory. Glory
which is infinity. The ocean has no bottom, is all surface" (197).
These wild-boy-like punk boys follow the example of (the character)
Antonin Artud, who is earlier described as a "protopunk boy" (41).
They "wanted to become Antonin Artaud," to imitate his life, Acker's
narrator explains, as Christians do Christ (197). The punk boys call
Artaud "Our Toad" and quote him as saying:

> this world of Christianfathermother is the one that must
>   go away,
> this world of split-in-two or constant-union-always-
>   longing-for-total-unification,
> around which the whole system of this society is turning,
> this world of fathermother malignantly sustained by the
>   most somber organization.
> (198)

Artaud's attack on "Christianfathermother" mirrors the wild boys'
hatred of "family talk, mother talk, father talk, cop talk, priest talk,
country talk *or* party talk." His revulsion for the world "split-in-two"
repeats Korzybski's attack on Aristotelian thought. His distaste for
the "constant-union-always-longing-for-total unification" should, I
think, be taken as criticism of hippie Utopianism and collectivism.
After Our Toad dies in China, Acker's punks begin reading books
that are all "about a boy," a figure that recalls the BOY whose viral

image births the wild boys (202). The punks tell Pussy a story featuring this boy, called Punk Boy (also Brat Rat), and his girlfriend Slut Girl, who together make a new child called Ganesh, by stitching together a human body with an elephant head. Initially, Slut Girl, who desperately wants a child, "shape[s] a boy" from "her own residue," shaved from her skin with a pumice stone while taking a bath (203). Punk Boy's friends, "his skeletons, his lads, the ghoulie tongues and spermy skins, who always accompanied him," decapitate this molded child, leading Slut Girl literally to cry her eyes out (which causes her to go blind) (203–204). To console Slut Girl, Punk Boy cuts the head off "the first sentient being whom he caught sight off" (an elephant) and "placed [the elephant head] on his son's red neck" (204). They "name their nameless son: Ganesh," and Ganesh's making provokes the development of nine rules of piracy (204). The pirate is therefore, in the novel, something like the unnatural offspring of a punk and a slut.

The rules of piracy illuminate the new world that punks and sluts make together. The goal of piracy, we learn, is to "find that place out of which we come" (204). Pirates are "[h]alf-human half-beast" (205). Earlier, the character Bad Dog claims that pirates "come from the moment when animals become holy" (195). The purpose of piracy is, the rules explain, "[s]tealing" and "find[ing] buried treasure" (206). The ninth rule is a banner, drawn by Acker, featuring "Red, Fat Ratski," a rat (207). We are told that "the world sits inside [Ratski's] belly" and that she "lives inside the interstices of the world." Though the meaning of these rules seems initially obscure, they actually recapitulate Acker's other writings. The "place out of which we come" seems to be the nonmaterial body. To make animals "holy" means to honor the animal within oneself, to celebrate animal dreams, desires, and appetites. The fact of animality licenses the norm of piratical agency. Moreover, to return to one's animal home (presumably inside Ratski's belly), one must also abandon common misconceptions of property. "I don't want to own," the girl-pirate Silver explains to O and Ange, "I wanna go back and be a sailor" (214). Being a pirate requires shifting from a false perspective on property to a more accurate view. In "A Few Notes on Two of My Books," Acker distinguishes between "creation" and "making." The "ideology of creativity," which Acker thinks is "capitalistic," presumes that one can create something from nothing, and that one therefore has power over what one creates (*Bodies* 9). Only "a belief in phallic centrism could have come up with the notion of creativity," Acker writes (*Bodies* 10). Fortunately, "no one, writer or politician, is more powerful than the world: you can make, but you don't create" (Ibid.). The writer "dips into" the world's self-making, but she does not directly make anything truly new, instead recombining the elements of existence (10). In an essay called "Writing, Identity, and Copyright in the Net Age," Acker imagines that copyright is a way of covering over the essential truth of artistic production. Acker concludes that writers must escape a "totalitarian relationship . . . in which the subject denies the otherness, therefore the very existence of the other person" (*Bodies* 104). In place of the totalitarian relationship to otherness, Acker imagines a relationship in which one accepts the otherness of the other, giving up one's ideas of self-sufficiency, adopting friendship as an alternative mode of relation. Her "Net" essay may seem almost liberal in temperament, but Acker is consistent in rejecting individuality and identity as a basis for artistic production. Acker argues for mutual recognition without individualism, hoping to foster an appreciation of the other without positing the existence of something like a self. "A Few Notes" is clearer in its rejection of the basis of liberal creativity. Here, "making" becomes a means for tapping into a worldly power greater than any self-possessed individual person. Piracy channels this power, supposedly overcoming capitalist property relations in the name of making, friendship, and use value.

But Acker misapprehends the philosophical justification for capitalist property relations. At the most elementary level, as Curtis White notes, "[p]irates were the first pure laissez-faire capitalists," and so Acker's appropriation of piracy is at best a "risky gambit of reappropriating the terms of our collective defeat in the name of our collective renewal."[180] More significantly, Acker seems to identify capitalism with the state enforcement of property rights, and thinks that piracy is anticapitalist (anti-postcapitalist?) because it avows stealing and treasure hunting. But foundational liberal philosophy *also*, like Acker, distinguishes between creation and making in its account of the origin of property. The possibility of individual property depends on a prior preindividual and prepolitical common heritage. John Locke's *Second Treatise of Government* (1689), after all, assumes that God gave the world to all humankind in common. Locke means to show how property must arise despite this fact. Locke reasons that "there must of necessity be *a means to appropriate* [common property] some way or other, before they can be of any use, or at all beneficial to any particular Man," and proffers an explanation and justification of appropriation under natural law.[181] Property arises, in his account, from the combination of labor with communal resources. Because we own our bodies, albeit in a qualified sense, we can mix our labor with creation and be entitled therefore to its products. Though Acker would likely deny that we "own" our bodies, Locke's account of the origin of property invokes a concept more like "making" than "creation." Moreover, for Locke, property rights *precede* government. Only the "invention of money" created the conditions for larger possessions, which go beyond individual use, setting the grounds for consensual government. To be clear, I am not arguing that Acker has a Lockean view of property. Nor should we conflate Locke's account of property with neoliberalism.[182] Rather, I am merely observing that a categorical distinction that Acker takes to subvert capitalism actually harmonizes with one major theoretical pillar of the liberal justification of property rights. People mix bodily labor with the common resources of creation to serve the body's needs. Even for Locke, people do not create; they only ever make.

Locke's account of self-ownership also informed attacks on distributive justice by right-libertarian philosophers such as Robert Nozick, who holds the view that "the theory of justice in holdings of a person are just if he is entitled to them by the principles of justice in acquisition and transfer, or by the principle of rectification of injustice."[183] But in adopting these arguments, libertarians have made use of an ontologically ambiguous defense of property rights. Such arguments are designed to defend territorial property rights, but fare less well when describing immaterial property rights, leading some self-professed free market libertarians—who, again, are dialectically entwined with but not identical to neoliberals as such—to reject all or some intellectual property rights.[184] One has a right to the product of one's labor, on this view, but not to government-granted monopolies permitting dominance over nonexcludible goods, even goods that one has had a hand in producing oneself. In the most extreme libertarian visions, government should not even exist to defend material property rights. On this view, your property would be that which you had the means to defend with whatever weapons you could buy or build, and your right to property would be nothing other than your capacity to keep your property safe, in voluntary association with others.[185] This anarcho-capitalist fantasy bears almost no relationship to the practice of actual neoliberal states, of course, which strongly protect both intellectual and physical property rights, serving the interests of large multinational corporations and media companies. But intellectual property regimes and agreements have been particularly hard to defend, given the importance of free market rhetoric in justifications of contemporary capitalist practice. This is true not only in the case of patents but also copyrights. And in this context, appropriative art, cut-up, sampling, free and open software ideologies, and remix culture have enjoyed great prestige. Among poets and novelists, techniques that once invited charges of plagiarism are now central to manifestos by literary figures such as Kenneth Goldsmith, Cory Doctorow, and Jonathan Lethem.[186] Mainstream celebrations of creativity as the centerpiece of contemporary capitalism (for example Richard Florida's *The Rise of the Creative Class*) also take for granted that artists do not "create" in any literal sense but rather always remix existing elements. "We humans are not god-like," Florida writes. "Creativity for us is an act of synthesis," an idea Florida associates with Einstein's notion of creativity as "combinatory play."[187] The core point is simple: a world without state-enforced property rights would not necessarily be a noncapitalist world. Rodolphe Durand and Jean-Philippe Vergne's *The Pirate Organization: Lessons from the Fringes of Capitalism* goes even further, arguing that pirates have a positive function in checking state capitalism. As Vernge writes, "[p]irates keep reminding us of the crucial difference that exists in practice between capitalism and free markets."[188] Pirates, by this account, advocate open markets for personal and common benefit against national monopolies. They might thus be seen to promote

"an alternative model of capitalism," one that is ultimately dialectically linked to state-supported capitalism.[189] The illicit economic
activity pirates undertake helps make public goods such as the sea or
common resources such as national airwaves available according to
rules that are "open, neutral, respectful of privacy," facilitating trust
among transacting parties.[190] "Pirate-driven innovation" is "the van-
guard of capitalism" and "a key driver of . . . creative destruction."[191]

The pirate is, to be sure, an ambiguous figure in *Pussy, King of the
Pirates*. O and Ange end up in a violent conflict with Silver and the
other pirates and when they find the treasure they have been seeking,
Silver decides not to take it. "I'd rather go a-pirating . . . If me and
my girls take all this treasure, the reign of girl piracy will stop, and I
wouldn't have that happen" (276). Pussy stares out "toward the
ocean" and the girl pirates leave the treasure for O and Ange, who
have chosen not to become pirates. Nonetheless, Acker considers the
pirate, who is inextricably linked to the punk, to be a vibrant political
figure. By not taking the treasure, Pussy and her girl pirates choose
endless adventure over individual possession. It should, finally, be
clear what positive dystopia entails both as a political vision and a
narrative genre. In the first instance, positive dystopias demolish
restrictive or ossified identity categories (identified with Utopian
political projects). These categories include state-oriented ideologies, as well as other rationalist identity groupings. This project of
ground-clearing can be viewed as dystopian both in the sense that it
is anti-Utopian but also in the sense that such narratives figure the
transcendence of identity in terms of destruction, decay, blight, and
negativity as such. This dystopia is positive in the sense that it opens
a space for infinite play, the adoption of different identities, pleasure and spiritual connection outside categorization. For Burroughs,
especially in *The Wild Boys* and *Port of Saints*, this zone of positivity
outside language was a sort of spiritual over-mind. In Acker's writing,
and especially *Pussy, King of the Pirates*, positivity means gaining
access to a treasure located within the body. This is what it means, as
Acker puts it, to travel "by dream." It is not so much to have a dream
of a better future as to gain access to the desires already encoded, in
the present, in dream language. Acker herself called this an anarchistic view, but largely did not explore the specific implications of

the positivity she wanted to facilitate. In that sense, though piracy is an important political ethos for Acker, it is dependent on her more fully articulated view of punk. Her positivity is not a form of postirony (in the sense to be developed in later chapters). It is, instead, an attempt to imagine a thoroughgoing negativity that promises access to the real itself. This is what her "post-cynical" turn entailed, what is meant for her to go "[s]omewhere real" with her art. While I would not claim that her vision shared a strict identity with celebrations of the free market, it should be clear that her punk vision was quite successful. As with Burroughs, Acker's powerful attack on "postcapitalist" rationalism fortified the new regime of justification that undergirded the projective city. This is why punk's anti-Utopianism, valorization of cut-up, and D.I.Y. ethic could seamlessly transition from seeming to resist capitalism to becoming a feted component of neoliberal apologetics (even if contemporary intellectual property regimes remain locked down). Acker herself could become, in a phrase used in one of her most repeated book blurbs, "America's most beloved transgressive novelist," partly because she told Americans a story about themselves that many of them—that many of us—wanted to hear.[192]

Conclusion: Temporary Autonomous Zones

Writing about punk is fraught with peril. It is perilous, in part, because the history and ethos of punk continue to have powerful effects on literary, musical, cultural, and critical production. I have, like many writers before me, mostly discussed punk subcultures that flourished for a short time in the mid-to-late seventies, referring mostly to the New York scene (and less frequently to the London scene). I have, perhaps counterintuitively, made pronouncements on the political and artistic meaning of punk by analyzing two writers who have complex associations with punk—and who developed a kind of irony thought to be characteristic of punk's aesthetic priorities. But punk is surely much more diverse than this, and it survives today not only as nostalgia industry but also as living artistic practice. Furthermore, contemporary literary writers as different in style as Jonathan Lethem, Jennifer Egan, Dana Spiotta, and Jonathan Franzen have reflected on the cultural legacy of punk in their fiction.

As Michael Szalay shows, these novelists "invoke punk both to recall their formative years and to inquire into the terms and conditions of their own entrance into a middle-class mainstream."[193] Their novels typically treat the peril of musical co-optation as an allegory for the situation of the creative professional who publishers her fiction through multinational media companies. They not only dramatize the writer's dilemma as she works under and for corporations but also investigate what happens when "a person becomes something more than a single body, something, we might hazard, like a corporation."[194] Such books tend to understand punk as a cultural phenomenon that enjoyed a handful of singular authentic moments of ascendency before burning itself out. They largely focus on the New York, London, or less frequently California, hardcore scenes. Other major punk subgenres (Straight Edge, Riot Grrrl, Pop Punk, Queercore, and Anarcho-Punk) do not so neatly fit the narrative of punk as irrecoverable historical singularity, and so have received less mainstream literary and critical analysis. And writing by members of more recent punk communities has received even less mainstream critical attention (an oversight lamentably reproduced in these pages). There are, however, serious grounds for defending the claim that punk experienced a singular moment in the midseventies. This singularity arises less from the features of any particular scene than from the unique political-economic situation from which punk arose and to which it responded. By comparison, subsequent punk scenes and subgenres can sometimes seem like an endless repetition of familiar subcultural discourses (and in the case of Pop Punk . . . like pop). Indeed, even one of the most interesting contemporary incarnation of punk (another proof that punk's energies endure) nonetheless shows how the meaning of punk has changed. The incarnation I am referring to is the taqwacore subgenre, inspired by Michael Muhammad Knight's 2003 novel *The Taqwacores*. Knight's novel depicts a fictional "Muslim punk," or "taqwacore," community in Buffalo, New York, in the early days of the War on Terror. The term *taqwacore* is a portmanteau combining the term "taqwa" and "hardcore." The Arabic *taqwa* term refers to a concept of "God-consciousness" or "God-fearing piety."[195] It is identified sometimes as "the most important single concept in the Quran," a concept that is supposed to serve as the foundational element of any Islamic society.[196] Though *hardcore* refers, of course, to the punk California subgenre / scene, it would be a mistake to imagine that Knight is specifically invested in hardcore. More than anything, his novel resembles the narratives published by Aaron Cometbus in his popular 'zine *Cometbus*, collected in the novel *Double Duce* (2003) and elsewhere. Even so, it is most accurate to say that Knight's vision of punk is ecumenical or syncretic in spirit.[197]

The Taqwacores features a heterogeneous group of Muslim housemates living in Buffalo, each of whom stands in for a different strand of punk history. Umar is a buff, tattooed straight-edger who frequently complains about alcohol consumption, drug use, and partying in the house. Jehangir Tabari, a tall Mohawk-wearing quasi-mystic Sufi, regales his housemates with tall tales about the Muslim punk scene on the West Coast. Fasiq Abasa is a stoner from Indonesia. Amazing Ayyub is an Iranian Shiite Skinhead. Rabeya is a burqa-wearing feminist riot grrl (her burqa is covered with various band patches) who decries sexism within Islam and distributes a 'zine called *Ayesha's Hymen*. Our hero is Yusef Ali, a nerdy engineering student from a conservative immigrant Pakistani family, whose pious parents naïvely encourage him to move into the Muslim punk house hoping it will be safer than the dorms. Throughout the book, numerous Muslim punk bands are named, such as Vote Hezbollah, The Mutaween, Osama bin Laden's Tunnel Diggers, the Bin Qarmats, Burning Books for Cat Stevens, the Zaqqums, Wilden Mukhalloduns, Istimna, Gross National, Bilal's Boulder, the Guantanamo Bay Packers, and Boxcutter Surprise.[198] In order to account for the origin of the scene that it largely invents, Knight's novel constructs a genealogy of punk writing, from Gideon Sams to William S. Burroughs, which exposes a hitherto unrecognized Islamic element in the history of punk. Fasiq calls Burroughs "Imam Burroughs" (157). While visiting a mosque in Rochester, Jehangir places a copy of Gideon Sams's 1977 novel *The Punk* among the mosque's other books, and explains that *The Punk* is "the first punk novel . . . it's like reading a book by one of the old Sahabas . . . Who knows who'll find it" (171). The Sahabas were the companions of the Prophet Muhammad, those who saw him, believed in him, and died Muslim. Unlike the case of Burroughs, who spent time in Tangiers, Sams's proximity to Islam is tenuous. Nonetheless, by having Jehangir call Sams a Sahaba, Knight asks us to see his novel as informed by a long and still-living punk faith.

On the one hand, Knight invokes punk to criticize the conservatism of mainstream American Muslim communities (while attempting to stave off charges that he has reproduced Islamophobic discourses). On the other hand, he tries to counteract Islamophobia by showcasing a wide range of Muslim characters with diverse opinions and by writing Islam into a genealogy of punk. However, this latter strategy presumes that "punk" has become the *mainstream* or *acceptable* term of the "Muslim punk" formulation. In the first decade of the new century, amid growing Islamophobic sentiment in the United States, it was Islam and not punk that had come to seem alien and terrifying to non-Muslim Americans. Whereas punk could once seem like a powerful threat to the established social order, it was now familiar enough, now welcome enough, to rhetorically naturalize Knight's Muslim characters. Knight's novel depends on punk having been defanged of any sense of threat (the novel ends by trying to restore punk's menace, but veers into a lurid or almost-silly surrealism in order to do so). Nonetheless, *The Tacqwacores* comfortably fits into the tradition of punk positive dystopia that I have described, and indeed, Knight's imaginary Muslim punk house resembles nothing so much as a small Temporary Autonomous Zone (TAZ), a political concept first named by the anarcho-Sufi writer Peter Lamborn Wilson (a.k.a. Hakim Bey). Bey was a friend of Burroughs and a mentor to Knight.[199]

Bey's 1991 book, *T.A.Z.: The Temporary Autonomous Zone, Ontological Anarchy, Poetic Terrorism*, has influenced a range of contemporary cultural institutions ranging from Burning Man to Occupy Wall Street (OWS); Bey's was the first book entered into the catalog of OWS's Zuccotti Park library. The theory and rhetoric of TAZs— which Bey variously describes as a "pirate utopia," a "nomad camp," an "encampment of guerilla ontologists"—goes well beyond the history of specific punk communities.[200] But as this chapter should make clear, the concept of the TAZ crucially derives from assumptions generated in and around the ethos of punk, especially the punk-piratical fantasies that Burroughs and Acker developed across their careers. The TAZ is, in Bey's view, a "tactic of disappearance" aiming at creating zones of human autonomy in the present. Bey celebrates eighteenth-century pirates for creating "whole mini-societies living consciously outside the law and determined to keep it up, even if only for a short but merry life." Bey's analysis of piratical freedom leads him to conclude that "a certain kind of 'free enclave' is not only possible in our time but also existent." Escaping the total surveillance of the state, TAZ insurgents launch "an uprising which does not engage directly with the State" but which "dissolves itself to re-form elsewhere / elsewhen, before the State can crush it." Bey conceives of the state as "omnipresent and all-powerful and yet simultaneously riddled with cracks and vacancies," and though he recognizes that TAZs do not achieve universal anarchist aims, he imagines that they give a taste of real freedom in the here and now. Bey concludes that "realism demands not only that we give up waiting for 'the Revolution' but also that we give up wanting it."

To call the TAZ a Utopia, as Bey occasionally does, is clearly a mistake. The TAZ is too present-oriented, too defined by finding a space untouched or untouchable by the state, more invested in escaping power than seizing it. The Temporary Autonomous Zone is a textbook example of a punk positive dystopia. The withdrawal from all signifying systems, imagined to share an identity with state power, supposedly opens up the possibility of a mystical autonomy. Advocates of the TAZ look not to the future but to the present; don't only build a physical zone of autonomy but also, and more importantly, change their habits and perceptions; and give up not only on *waiting* but also on *wanting*. In place of wanting future revolution, they make a zone of present-day autonomy. The resulting TAZ is, like Knight's Muslim punk house, temporary in its specific configuration. But, in principle, the Temporary Autonomous Zone can always emerge again "elsewhere / elsewhen." Inhabitants of TAZs show little interest in the future (in this sense, the TAZ too has no future). They dissociate themselves from "the mundanity of negativity or countercultural drop-out-ism," but also (paradoxically) imagine that the politics of the "republic of gratified desires" that one feels after a good party might have "more reality and force for us than [the politics] of, say, the entire U.S. Government." Another name for this "republic of gratified desires," this ecstatic politics of the party, as opposed to mundane party politics, or dull hippie / statist Utopias, is—I have argued—punk. And there is every reason to believe that punk's party is nowhere near ready to burn itself out. Such an eternal party has, Bey rightly notes, lost some of its negativity. Perhaps, then, the contemporary positive dystopia known as the TAZ, whether located in the Black Rock Desert or at Zuccotti Park or in some corner of the Deep Web or in a house in Buffalo, New York, is what a punk party looks like when it has lost its sense of irony.

PART II:

Postirony

3

How to Be a Believer

LET US BEGIN our discussion of postirony with the end—the end of the world, that is. Tim LaHaye and Jerry B. Jenkins's *Left Behind* (1995) is the first in a hugely popular series of novels, based on a premillennial dispensationalist evangelical theology, associated with the U.S. Christian Right, which tells the story of the biblical Tribulation as if it were a techno-thriller. The novel begins aboard an airborne 747 jet immediately after the Rapture, an event in which millions of believers—truehearted born-again Christians—suddenly vanish from the earth, leaving behind empty clothes and unworn jewelry. The born again have been transported to heaven, while those who remain must fight to survive as the Antichrist, Nicolae Carpathia, former president of Romania, consolidates the world into a single government controlled by the wicked United Nations. The left behind include non-Christian believers, secular humanists, and insufficiently committed Christians. The novel repeatedly emphasizes that even otherwise decent Christians will not be raptured if they sustain any doubt whatsoever about the literal truth of the Bible. The novel's protagonist, the vaguely adulterous Rayford Steele, pilot of the aforementioned 747, falls into the category of insufficiently committed Christians: "God was OK with Rayford Steele," we learn (a bad sign). "Rayford even enjoyed Church occasionally."[1] Rayford's daughter, Chloe Steele, an undergraduate at

Stanford, is skeptical of "religious nuts" and quick with a cutting "smart remark" (163, 190). Before the Rapture, Rayford's devout wife, Irene, joined a congregation whose members had the audacity to ask Rayford "to his face, what God was doing in his life" (2). Born-again Irene and their son, Raymie, disappear during the Rapture, leaving the rest of the Steele family to contemplate their failures of faith. Despite its heavy-handedness, I begin this chapter on the figure of the (secular) believer with the decidedly nonsecular *Left Behind* because the novel constructs an ingenious narrative technology for fostering readerly belief, one that can help clarify the nonreligious literary experiments of David Foster Wallace and Dave Eggers. Though its readership undoubtedly includes secular humanists, the primary imagined reader of *Left Behind* belongs to the third category of those who are left behind: somewhat committed Christians who have not yet fully embraced the ontological commitments that define the contemporary Christian Right.[2] *Left Behind*'s rendition of Revelation is underwritten by eschatological guarantees, which are founded on what passes itself off as a literal interpretation of biblical prophecy.[3] The events described in Revelation unfold daily, reported on the news. Despite this overwhelming evidence, some characters amusingly persist in explaining the Rapture as a mysterious scientific phenomenon, the effect of an "alien life force" or "some incredible cosmic energy reaction," as though the events depicted in the novel were explicable in materialist terms (160, 361).

But once the reader understands that the novel's narrative is the unfolding of prophesized events, the end of the series is preordained. Sometime before the final pages of Book 12, Christ will return and will personally throw the Antichrist into hell, inaugurating his thousand-year reign on Earth (Book 13 deals with the end of Christ's earthly reign). The series' foreordained conclusion raises several interesting literary questions. Given that it demands to be taken as a rewriting or fictionalization of a prophecy already available in the Bible, how can *Left Behind* generate any narrative interest whatsoever? After all, aren't techno-thrillers thrilling precisely because we cannot predict how they will turn out? The Left Behind series employs two major narrative strategies to address these questions.

First, the series creates suspense by inviting the reader to bring an allegorical eye to its plot. Narrative interest partly arises from our not knowing which modern characters will fulfill which roles in premodern biblical prophecy: Is Nicolae Carpathia really the Antichrist or merely a charming, articulate, well-meaning Romanian politician with a metaphorical whiff of sulfur about him? Who will play the role of the "two witnesses" prophesied in Revelation 11:3? In due course, all such questions receive definite—and unimaginative—answers. This aspect of the series takes on the character of an eschatological crossword puzzle. Second, and to greater effect, *Left Behind* drives narrative interest by creating uncertainty about which of its "left behind" characters will be saved before the end of the series. As newly born-again characters repeatedly point out, unsaved characters who die during the seven years of the gratuitously violent Tribulation (the interval between the Rapture and Christ's return) will be sent directly to hell. "People die every day in car accidents, plane crashes," a pastor, Bruce Barnes, informs Rayford. "What would be worse than finally finding God and then dying without him because you waited too long?" (207). As this warning indicates, having an intellectual understanding of the Bible's truth ("finding God") isn't enough to save your soul in the world of *Left Behind*. To avoid hell, you must be born again; having *true beliefs* or even *true knowledge* is not the same as *being a believer*. Characters in *Left Behind* have been given one last chance to become believers. The mechanism for crossing the chasm from *possessing belief or knowledge* to *being saved* is, as Amy Hungerford and Jonathan Freedman show, rather complex, paradoxically linking free choice and submission to forces outside oneself.[4] One does not save oneself, but opens oneself to being saved. "If you accept God's message of salvation, his Holy Spirit will come in unto you and make you spiritually born anew," LaHaye and Jenkins write (219). When Rayford becomes a "true believer"—what his daughter earlier in the novel sarcastically calls a "super Christian"—his submission involves literally throwing away a remote control (221, 168). He has been using the remote to pause a recorded video explaining the true nature of the Rapture. After the prayer is over, the pastor in the video explains, "If you were genuine, you are saved, born again, a child of God" (220).[5]

Readers are being asked to hope that Rayford Steele, Chloe Steele, Buck Williams, and the rest of the characters in the series become born again before they are banished to an eternal hell. The only serious question of dramatic interest is who will be saved and who will be damned before the end of the series. All the rest is foreordained. *Left Behind* thus tries to dragoon readerly belief by making our sympathy for fictive souls depend upon our understanding of the eschatological guarantees that underwrite its larger plot.[6] The series hopes to use narrative suspense as a machine for converting readers.[7] Though the ontological and intellectual stakes differ dramatically, an identical rhetorical strategy is at work in the writing of Wallace and Eggers. Both writers try to map fictional narratives onto extratextual foundations: metafiction designed to spur belief, nonfiction that uses anxious metacommentary to tell the truth. Unlike the true believers conjured by conservative religious fictions such as *Left Behind*, Wallace and Eggers's postironic believer knows that there's no ontological ground for his faith, but he paradoxically needs to pray anyway, to live *as a believer*, in order to render life livable.[8] Belief is, therefore, not only a theme of their postironic texts, but also a disposition or attitude these writers try to instill in the reader, often through formal means. Though these texts engage in the hybrid discourse that John A. McClure calls "postsecularism," neither Wallace nor Eggers advocate specific ontological claims.[9] Wallace and Eggers adopt instead a disposition similar to what Martin Hägglund, in his brilliant reconstruction of Derrida, has called "radical atheism."[10] For both writers, belief becomes necessary specifically because of the unavoidable destructibility of life, the necessary corruptibility of every claim to sincerity, which Hägglund prefers to call "autoimmunity." Yet the question remains whether, as Adam Kelly puts it, one can argue for "belief, commitment, and sincerity under a model of language without prior subjects."[11] It is my contention that postironic believers attempt to do exactly this, and they do so by articulating what Peter Sloterdijk describes variously as "spiritual regimens," "symbolic immune systems," or "ritual shells," which humans create to respond to "their vulnerability through fate."[12] Wallace, Eggers, and their confederates rarely concern themselves with specific faith traditions, nor do they propose a postmodern negative theology.[13]

Instead, in pursuit of secular fullness, they insist on the necessity of cultivating belief, but without an ontological safety net. In their effort to reenchant life, they come to agree with Charles Taylor's claim in *A Secular Age* that secularism is not a subtraction of fullness from life but rather a continual, precarious addition of new founts of purpose and meaning.

Believing in Stuff

The American 1990s saw the rise of a second popular eschatological vision, one primarily socioeconomic but no less millenarian in temper than the vision offered by *Left Behind*. In the fall of 1989, in the *National Interest*, Francis Fukuyama published "The End of History?" which argues that the end of the Cold War might well have proved Hegel right: history might indeed have ended—and permanently enthroned liberalism—in 1806 with the Battle of Jena. Fukuyama's conclusion is in one sense optimistic. He regards liberal, consumer-oriented capitalist democracy as the best of all possible political worlds. Serious rivals had systematically proved themselves not only morally bankrupt but also pragmatically unsustainable.[14] Though all nations everywhere had yet to arrive at the ideological "Promised Land," it was inevitable that everyone would in due course hear the "good news."[15] But the news was not all good. The end of history might also be viewed as "a very sad time," as an era in which "daring, courage, imagination, and idealism, will be replaced by economic calculation, the endless solving of technical problems, environmental concerns, and the satisfaction of sophisticated consumer demands."[16] When history ends, we face nothing less than "centuries of boredom."[17] Such is life in the secular millennial kingdom. However else we might attack the end-of-history thesis—and even though Samuel Cohen makes a convincing case that many major American writers took a historical, "retrospective turn" in the 1990s—Fukuyama's claim represented something like posthistorical common sense after the end of the Cold War.[18] It was, as David Foster Wallace writes in *Infinite Jest*, "a post-Soviet and -Jihad era when . . . there was no real Foreign Menace of any real unified potency to hate and fear, and the U.S. sort of turned on itself and its own philosophical fatigue and hideous redolent wastes with a spasm of panicked rage" (*IJ* 382).

Life in postindustrial democracies came to seem listless and without flavor; loneliness and a kind of bland sadness were all one could expect of the new world order. At the end of history, irony transformed from an instrument of revolution to a symptom of the impossibility of revolution. In a 1994 issue of *The Modern Review*, a London-based cultural studies magazine, Toby Young linked ubiquitous irony to the end of history: "it's difficult to imagine what a post-ironic sensibility would be like. It's a bit like finding yourself at the end of history. You're bored because you're not participating in any historic events but you can't very well up sticks and go and fight in a war in a less evolved society. To do so would be *untrue to your own historical experience;* it would require you to *unlearn the lessons history has already taught you.* And what would be the point?"[19] One can detect the same weariness of tone ("what would be the point?") in the writing of Richard Rorty. Finding himself at the end of history, Rorty feels compelled to undermine any philosophical ambition to fuse our private and public commitments, leaving us in a position in which our public political commitments must remain philosophically ungrounded. Though he would reject the historical *necessity* of liberalism's final victory, Rorty nonetheless thought that the left should "concede Francis Fukuyama's point" and agreed that "no more romantic prospect stretches before the Left than an attempt to create bourgeois democratic welfare states and equalize life chances among the citizens of those states by redistributing the surplus produced by market economies."[20] At this moment, capitalism's Cold War victory, individual irony, and philosophical antifoundationalism merged into a single discourse. Irony's dominance could sometimes seem like the unavoidable cultural and philosophical consequence of our having arrived at history's end. This background clarifies the ultimate stakes of discovering or inventing a viable postironic ethos. Both David Foster Wallace and Dave Eggers sought to reconnect private and public life, and they pursued this aim by used techniques associated with postmodern metafiction to attempt to generate forms of belief theory held to be no longer possible.

For Wallace, postironic belief underwrites the possibility of genuine human communication. This is why Wallace distrusts the death-of-the-author thesis and constructs his fictions around a drama of unfulfilled communication. When the wraith of James O. Incandenza appears to the convalescing Don Gately, late in *Infinite Jest*, he explains that he created the irresistibly addictive avant-garde film "Infinite Jest" in order "to contrive a medium via which he [James] and the muted son [Hal] could simply *converse*," a form of entertainment that "would reverse thrust on a young self's fall into the womb of solipsism, anhedonia, death in life" (*IJ* 838, 839). Wallace himself claims to know in his "gut that writing is an act of communication between one human being and another," and justifies his conviction with reference to a reading of Wittgenstein as an incipient post-postmodernist, someone who understood the deadly necessity of transcending solipsistic relativism.[21] Eggers and many of those associated with his various literary enterprises (*McSweeney's Quarterly Concern*, McSweeney's Books, *The Believer*, *Wholphin*, his network of 826 tutoring centers), for their part, explode bibliographic form, conflating text and paratext, in order to regenerate a sense of wonder around reading, all of which is part of an effort to undermine what they take to be an overly cynical or snarky literary culture. Eggers's memoir, *A Heartbreaking Work of Staggering Genius* (2000), and his first novel, *You Shall Know Our Velocity!* (2002), proffer an aesthetic of the "quirky," an aesthetic also visible (as we will see) in the various exhibits of the Museum of Jurassic Technology (MJT) in Los Angeles. Wallace and Eggers write against a culture defined by solipsism, anhedonia, cynicism, snark, and toxic irony—a culture whose disenchantment and sadness can be traced back, in one way or another, to the consumerist end of history. Their primary oppositional strategy is to imagine a characterological countertype to the incredulous ironist.

I will call this countertype "the believer," after Eggers's influential magazine of the same name, though Wallace is arguably the architect of this postironic ethos.[22] When he calls for the rise of an "antirebel"—a kind of post-countercultural or newly earnest countercultural figure who opposes a now mainstream irony—Wallace does not give a positive content to the figure, but this antirebellious believer is quite different from the one imagined by LaHaye and Jenkins in *Left Behind*. In *Left Behind*, secular postmodernity and neoliberal globalization demand a counterforce that returns to biblical fundamentals. Wallace, by contrast, cannot accept a religious response to the fallen world, nor can he embrace a simple return to a preironic sensibility. Wallace wants to invent a new form of secular belief, a religious vocabulary (God, prayer) that is emptied out of any specific content and is engineered to confront the possibly insuperable condition of postmodernity. This desire to believe is part of the lineage of the avant-garde and simultaneously criticizes that tradition. Eggers, meanwhile, has taken the impulse behind Wallace's fiction and has successfully popularized it, transforming Wallace's postirony into a literary brand that promises consumer reenchantment, a kind of (nonprofit) retail avant-gardism. Lee Siegel has criticized Eggers for propagating a "self-conscious equivalence between decent living and good writing" and has denounced "the McSweeneyite confusion of good intentions with good art, and of its blithe elision . . . of truth with untruth, prevarication with pretense."[23] Whether or not he is here fairly criticizing "McSweeneyite" art, Siegel correctly identifies a key formal strategy embraced by many postironists: the elision of "truth" and "untruth" in pursuit of creating belief and reenchantment. In what follows, I will treat postironic belief both as a theoretical project and as a literary intervention.

Understood properly, postironists differ from writers of "hysterical realism," a category the critic James Wood associates with a range of authors including Don DeLillo, Thomas Pynchon, Salman Rushdie, Wallace, and Zadie Smith. By equating canonical postmodernists with those who have sought to succeed postmodernism, Wood misses that these younger writers have developed a critique of metafiction that, in its interrogation of the status of belief, resembles his own attack on hysterical realism. In a review of Toni Morrison's *Paradise* (1997), Wood argues that fiction constitutes an invitation to belief, or rather—in a secular age—an invitation to read "as if" one believed in fiction: "Fiction demands belief from us, and this request is demanding in part because *we can choose not to believe*."[24] Wood distinguishes the ontological commitment required by some religious traditions from the reader's belief in fiction. Fiction can, at best, only "gently request" that readers act "as if" they believed. Belief in fiction turns out to be a metaphorical sort of belief.[25] This argument suffers from an obvious contradiction: How can fiction "demand" from us a stance that, by definition, belies choice? Belief is involuntary, which is not the same as saying it is unchanging or saying that all beliefs are equally fixed. Nonetheless, a believer is someone who cannot help but hold his or her particular ontological convictions. The leap from nonbeliever to born again in *Left Behind* is thus not directly the product of will, but arises from an act of freely chosen submission or supplication, a willingness to be changed. Likewise, for Don Gately, Wallace suggests that practices identified with religion (kneeling, prayer) may *precede* belief—they may be necessary preconditions for belief—but that the transition from nonbelief to belief happens apart from one's will. Wood might counter my criticism by suggesting that he is throughout his writing using *belief* in a consistently metaphoric sense. The problem with such a counterargument would be that Wood is actually correct that fiction demands belief of us. We do judge novels based on what they can convince us to believe.[26] We believe or disbelieve in fiction based on a range of criteria—aesthetic, cognitive, social, historical—over which we exercise only partial control. This is the only reason that writing can sensibly be described as "plausible" or "implausible." In its modes of world-building, and no matter the genre, every narrative engages with our capacity to believe. What we believe in (or disbelieve) includes a range of complexly interlocking phenomena. Not only do we read fictions using ontological criteria—judging its social, historical, and scientific plausibility—but fictions can often make ontological demands of us, can try to convert us into believers. If the job of the novel is to make a persuasive request of us to believe in the events depicted, then hysterical realism fails for Wood because its too-rapid accretion of interesting detail breaks the trance of credulity. "[Zadie] Smith does not lack for powers of invention," Wood writes, with reference to a characteristic passage in *White Teeth*. "The problem is that there is too much of it . . . on its own, almost any of these details . . . might be persuasive. Together, they vandalize each other . . . As realism, it is incredible; as satire, it is cartoonish; as cartoon, it is too realistic."[27] What Woods denounces is the sort of novel that, in its particulars, cannot be faulted for lacking realism, but whose overall pattern takes on an implausible shape. Global implausibility disrupts the local pleasure one might take in a work of fiction that more judiciously doled out its unlikelihoods. Novels of hysterical realism simultaneously feel allegorical and do not allegorize; they present characters that almost but do not quite rise to the level of the identifiably human. Hysterical realism's hysteria short-circuits its realism.

So Wood is, in a sense, right. Fiction tries to compel belief from readers, but certain techniques—often associated with metafiction—can erect barriers to belief. Nonetheless, Wood's attack on hysterical realism fails on two fronts. First, it does not address metafiction's historical mission. After all, undermining a naïve version of realism—disrupting the process through which belief formation occurs—was precisely the goal of this type of fiction. To fault a mode of writing for successfully achieving its aims, Wood would need to make a case that those aims are not worth pursuing in the first place, which he does not do. Even in *How Fiction Works*, he promotes realism (or more precisely, works that possess what he calls "lifeness") by critical fiat.[28] Second, Wood misunderstands Wallace and Smith's complex relationship to postmodernism. Postironists often try to cultivate belief among readers, and are reacting against the same picture of metafiction and postmodernism they learned about in university literature departments. For his part, Wallace carefully studied academic criticism on postmodernism. The Harry Ransom Center includes heavily annotated copies of Tom LeClair's *In the Loop: Don DeLillo and the Systems Novel* as well as Frank Lentricchia's *Introducing Don DeLillo*.[29] Like Wood, Wallace came to find postmodern literature wanting in "final seriousness."[30]

Patricia Waugh's *Metafiction*, published in 1984, expresses what remains the consensus view on the historical mission of metafiction. Though there are many different techniques associated with metafiction, all draw attention to practices of reading and writing, often by exposing how worlds of fiction are embedded within higher-order fictional worlds. Metafiction "self-consciously and systematically draws attention to its status as an artefact in order to pose questions about the relationship between fiction and reality."[31] When we read characters reading, we are supposed to become aware of how our own reading habit is homologous to the inscribed reading practice.

Metafiction's power to "pose questions" about reality depends on a homology between fiction and society. Waugh emphasizes "the extent to which the dominant issues of contemporary critical and sociological thought are shared by writers of fiction," suggesting that transformations in fiction and society are linked. The specific nature of this link remains ambiguous.[32] Are writers of metafiction studying contemporary sociological literature—or arriving at their own amateur sociological insights—and seeking to allegorize these findings? Is the turn to metafiction a coincidental development? Or does some underlying shift in the world—economic or epistemic—account for this homology? Answers differ. Waugh distinguishes between "two poles of metafiction": one that "finally accepts a substantial real world whose significance is not entirely composed of relationships within language; and one that suggests that there can never be an escape from the prisonhouse of language."[33] Despite these serious differences, Waugh treats all metafiction as a species of critique, a way of exposing myths and ideological cant.

Either metafiction is an allegory for the breakdown of master narratives and coherent frames in the social world (the weak interpretation) or metafiction, because it changes our relation with language, actually breaks down our confidence in norms, values, and conventions, such that we're thrown into a bottomless well of doubt (the strong interpretation). This latter, strong interpretation has often been compared to a version of critical self-consciousness associated with Romantic irony, and especially Friedrich Schlegel's fragmentary commentary on irony as a mode of "permanent parabasis." Either way, society and culture become especially susceptible to the critical power of metafiction. According to the traditional understanding, metafiction is a form of irony because it forces the reader or subject to question all grounds for understanding, including the grounds one uses to justify being an ironist in the first place. Hegel, and Kierkegaard after him, called this form of questioning irony's "infinite absolute negativity," its self-negating nature. Metafiction does not therefore undermine this or that belief, but belief as such. It operates according to an inverted mechanism found in *Left Behind*. Like LaHaye and Jenkins, metafictionists assume that if a range of vocabulary could be mapped cleanly onto a domain of worldly things, then literary or ontological realism would be possible. We would have to take seriously some version of a correspondence theory of truth. By foregrounding linguistic self-referentiality or the infinite connotative range of words, metafiction tries to show that such a mapping is impossible, undermining our naïve belief in realism. Educated in this consensus view, postironists such as Wallace and Eggers attempt to use metafictional techniques differently—to help readers cultivate belief. In an unpublished contribution to James L. Harmon's *Take My Advice*, Wallace makes the connection between irony and belief explicit: "Ridicule, nihilism, sarcasm, cool, and irony worked for the USA's young when there were big adult hypocrisies for the young to explode and thus transcend . . . But now there are no really interesting hypocrisies left: you can't be a hypocrite if you don't even pretend to believe in anything. Irony and cool keep us from believing in stuff."[34] In his novella "Westward the Course of Empire Takes Its Way," Wallace takes great pains to deny that "cynicism and naiveté are mutually incompatible."[35] "Westward" links the belief in the importance and power of irony to the university, the creative writing workshop, and critical theories of postmodernity.[36] If a cynic can be naïve, then someone nonnaïve can be also noncynical. Wallace attempts to help his reader adopt a stance of nonnaïve noncynicism by means of metafiction. What is paradoxical about this project is the *emptiness* of the proposed postironic belief. Postironists do not advocate a stance of belief toward any particular aspect of the world, but rather promote a general ethos of belief.

By this account, postironic belief might easily be mistaken for what Amy Hungerford calls "postmodern belief," a "belief without meaning" or "belief without content" whose purpose is to "hedge against the inescapable fact of pluralism."[37] The language we use is similar, but I would resist this equation. Hungerford outlines a tradition of "belief in belief" that meant, above all, to sustain faith without having to commit to any particular *religious* community. By contrast, postironic believers are interested in belief apart from questions of social pluralism or religious institutions. Moreover, by Hungerford's account, New Critical arguments against "the heresy of paraphrase" vouchsafed a religious function for literature; but as we saw in my first chapter, it was *irony* that made poetry resistant to paraphrase in the first place.[38] So, though she doesn't describe it in these terms, postmodern literature's "belief in belief" depended on a prior, tacit affirmation of irony. Unlike postmodernists such as Don DeLillo, however, postironic believers do not want to keep faith with irony. Irony's disruptive negativity seems too threatening. This is why it would also be a mistake to describe postironic belief as "metai-ronic."[39] Metairony is "a gambit . . . to turn irony back on itself," but such a practice quickly threatens to become merely a higher-order iteration of the ironist's infinite absolute negativity.[40] Wallace and Eggers's project more resembles what has been called New Sincerity. Adam Kelly focuses on the intersubjective anxiety that drives much contemporary fiction (including that of Wallace, Eggers, Dana Spiotta, Jennifer Egan, and Colson Whitehead), arguing that such fiction "asks what happens when . . . inner states lose their origi-nating causal status and instead become effects of that anticipatory logic."[41] What is new about New Sincerity is that, though it under-stands that there is no pure form of communication, it nonetheless seeks to invent new ways of negotiating the problem of coordinating inner and outer states. But Kelly's account does not address the spe-cific threat these writers see in irony. We might wonder, for instance, whether the "anticipatory logic" that demotes the centrality of the "acting self" is a form of irony. I would argue against this equation. The battle between inner and outer motivation, which dialectically resolves itself in the form of New Sincerity, can arrive only after a prior struggle, the struggle to achieve postironic belief. If they did not believe in the actuality of other persons, Newly Sincere writers would not feel much need to lash together inner intentions and outer performances in the first place, let alone ask readers to trust in them. Postironic belief must precede the ethics of New Sincerity. Wallace's commentary on Wittgenstein's private language argument is one effort to vouchsafe the grounds for such belief. We also see the importance of belief in Eggers's fictionalized autobiography of Valentino Achak Deng, *What Is the What* (2006), which ends with the following lines: "How can I pretend that you do not exist? It would be almost as impossible as you pretending that I do not exist."[42] Valentino Achak Deng's prefatory declamation of his "belief in humanity" uses similar language: "Since you and I exist we can make a difference!"[43] While our trust in Eggers's and Deng's sincerity matters—we hope neither is being mercenary in proffering Deng's story of suffering[44]—the ultimate stakes are more profound but easy to overlook: Deng's very existence. Likewise, it is easy to misread Wallace's declaration that fiction ought "to dramatize the fact that we still 'are' human beings, now. Or can be."[45] Here too, nothing less than existence—both our being human and the dramatized proof that we are—is at stake. The postironic believer therefore does not only affirm the fact of the existence of other persons but also attempts to reconstruct our capacity to believe, seeking a literary means of dissolving the barriers that block that capacity. In the following sections, I will show how Wallace's and Eggers's concerns about belief play out in a variety of works. I will begin with Wallace's influential— widely cited, but rarely analyzed—manifesto, "E Unibus Pluram: Television and U.S. Fiction." Understanding Wallace's analysis of the origins of postmodern incredulity will clarify the formal devices he developed in his fiction and the speculative media he tried to imagine in his magnum opus, *Infinite Jest*.

Credulous Metafiction

In "E Unibus Pluram: Television and U.S. Fiction," David Foster Wallace strives to show how television has co-opted metafiction's mantle of ironic critique. By Wallace's account, television has established itself in a position of domination over those who view it in "high doses" (34). It has displaced all authority beyond itself, putting itself at the center of the lives of media addicts (including himself). Though he demonstrates a sophisticated understanding of the socioeconomic facts of television production (circa the late 1980s), Wallace's problem is not primarily with the capitalist form of network ownership but rather with television's properties as a visual medium.[46] These problematic effects will be found in any spectacular, addictive entertainment medium that is highly responsive to the desires and preferences of its viewers. When discussing the conservative technologist George Gilder's optimistic vision of the coming of the networked telecomputer, which imagines that on-demand programming will improve television, Wallace insists that new technologies will do little to resolve his concerns. Transforming "passive reception of facsimiles of experience to active manipulation of facsimiles of experience" will only make matters worse (74). The problem for Wallace, in this essay and elsewhere, is the problem of addiction. "Whether I'm 'passive' or 'active' as a viewer, I still must cynically pretend [not to be dependent on television], because I'm still dependent, because my real dependency here is not on a single show or a few networks . . . My real dependence is on the fantasies and the images that enable them, and thus on any technology that can make images both available and fantastic" (75).

Television cultivates addiction by transmitting images of persons who pretend, in front of cameras, to go unselfconsciously through their lives. Because these performers are "absolute *geniuses* at seeming unwatched," viewers (and fiction writers) can confuse the experience of watching scripted performances with genuine voyeurism, the authentically secret "espial" of everyday people living their lives (25). "A problem with so many of us fiction writers under 40 using television as a substitute for true espial, however, is that TV 'voyeurism' involves a whole gorgeous orgy of illusions for the pseudo-spy," a gorgeous illusion orgy that is built on the systematic suspension of disbelief (24). Television viewers become habituated to ignoring a range of mediations and hard truths. They fail to see that watching television is not a true form of voyeurism; that what seem to be unscripted scenarios are in fact highly formalized, contrived forms of manipulation; that the previous illusions are emerging from "our own *furniture*" (that is, from our television sets); and so on (24). These are the types of "disbelief we suspend" when we spend huge amounts of our free time watching the performer, the "transcendent semihuman who, in Emerson's phrase, 'carries the holiday in his eye'" (25).[47] We treat these transcendent semihumans—who flatter our narcissism, but are impossible to genuinely emulate—as models of what we ought to want to be. What we become dependent on, in Wallace's view, is our belief in fantastic or fabricated images.

But the television viewer's addiction to images also provokes a cognitive immune reaction. Wallace writes, "Junior advertising executives, aspiring filmmakers, and grad-school poets are in my experience especially prone to this condition, where they simultaneously hate, fear, and need television, and try to disinfect themselves of whatever so much viewing might do to them by watching TV with weary contempt instead of the rapt credulity most of us grew up with" (29). Fearful of this cynical incredulity, producers incorporate viewer disbelief into television programming itself (in allegedly subversive shows such as *The Simpsons* and *Married . . . with Children*). Because television effortlessly mirrors the "weary contempt" of cynical viewers, because it is so good at mocking itself, it neutralizes the critical vocation of experimental writers, rendering incredulous irony redundant. Latter-day postmodernists such as Bret Easton Ellis and Mark Leyner are therefore, despite their best efforts at cultural critique, "doomed to shallowness" (81). Wallace feared that such shallowness marred his own fiction. As he wrote in a letter to his Little, Brown editor, Michael Pietsch,

> I am by inclination and neurosis often pulled hard in Leyneresque directions. But I also like stories; I like to forget myself; I like fiction that gives me access not only to technical prowess but to hearts and persons, selves; I like stuff that makes me feel less lonely . . . This kind of fiction is (for me) way scarier to write than sheer prose-fireworks or mordant irony. Writer-wise, I'd like to find some way to marry these two different elements, to agnatize the dire directions, somehow.[48]

This project is what Wallace has in mind when he calls to arms a new generation of literary "anti-rebels, born oglers who dare somehow to back away from ironic watching" (81). Though commentators have often cited this declaration, few have noted that "the next real literary 'rebels'" are writers who risk, among other things, accusations of "overcredulity" (81). That is, Wallace's antirebel is a type of believer. Wallace's overcredulous antirebel does not oppose irony in any straightforward way, but instead attempts to demonstrate that postmodernist "prose-fireworks" can have a surprising effect: they can give us access to "hearts and persons, selves."

This is what Wallace aims for in his short story "Octet," part of his collection *Brief Interviews with Hideous Men* (1999). In "Octet," Wallace inverts the procedures of metafiction, asking not that we become aware of the fictiveness of his fiction, the artifice of the artificer, but rather that we believe in the total, genuine honesty (the "100% candor" [148]) of the author—not the narrator, but *the author*, Wallace. The story begins as a series of numbered, seemingly unrelated "pop quizzes" asking the reader questions about "late-stage terminal drug addicts," quarrelling friends, and so on. Wallace designates some of his characters with letters (X and Y) instead of proper names. Pop Quiz 6 fails to culminate with a clear question, concluding with a metacomment that "the whole *mise en scène* here seems too shot through with ambiguity to make a very good Pop Quiz."[49] Wallace's narrator rewrites this scenario as Pop Quiz 6(A), which ends with the injunction: "X now finds himself, behind his commiserative expression and solicitous gestures, secretly angry at his wife over an ignorance he has made every effort to cultivate in her, and sustain. Evaluate" (145). The quizzes, though numbered, are not in order—the first quiz we encounter is "Pop Quiz 4"—and they ultimately seem unrelated to one another. Pop Quiz 9 (of the "octet") takes a radically different turn. The narrator informs the reader that "you are, unfortunately, a fiction writer" who is "attempting a cycle of very short belletristic pieces" as a means by which to "compose a certain sort of 'interrogation' of the person reading them, somehow—i.e. palpations, feelers into the interstices of her [the reader's] sense of something, etc. . . . though what that 'something' is remains maddeningly hard to pin down" (145).

After attempting to revise the stories, and realizing that they are something like an "aesthetic disaster," you (the aforementioned "fiction writer") attempt to acknowledge the disastrous nature of the pop quizzes openly, but find that "these intranarrative acknowledgements have . . . the disadvantage of flirting with metafictional self-reference . . . which in the late 1990s, when even Wes Craven is cashing in on metafictional self-reference, might come off as lame and tired and facile, and also runs the risk of compromising the queer *urgency* about whatever it is you feel you want the pieces to interrogate in whoever's reading them" (146–147). A footnote explains that

> part of what you want these little Pop Quizzes to do is to break
> the textual fourth wall and kind of address (or 'interrogate') the
> reader directly, which desire is somehow related to the old

'meta'-device desire to puncture some sort of fourth wall of
realist pretense, although it seems like the latter is less a puncturing of any sort of real wall and more a puncturing of the veil
of impersonality or effacement around the writer himself
(147)

The "latter" form of fourth-wall puncturing—traditional
metafiction—is scathingly attacked by the narrator / Wallace as
little more than a "rhetorical sham-honesty" (Ibid.). Fourth-wall-
puncturing writers of metafiction condescendingly flatter their
reader. Desperate for approval, such a writer pretends that "you're
enough of a grownup to handle being reminded that what you're in
the middle of is artificial (like you didn't know that already, like you
needed to be reminded of it over and over again as if you were a
myopic child who couldn't see what was right in front of you)" (Ibid.).
Initially, the pop quizzes begin for the writer as an attempt at a sublation of metafiction into metafiction critical of its own impulses—
giving evidence for the view that Wallace can be said in some sense
to "ironize irony."[50]

But the imagined "fiction writer" (a.k.a. "you") ultimately admits
failing at this effort to ironize irony, and admits that "this is a very
bad corner to have painted yourself into" (152). The solution
Wallace's narrator hits upon to resolve this paradox is less to sublate
irony by means of higher-order irony (metairony) than to directly
address the reader, to "ask her straight out whether she's feeling
anything like what you feel," a "trick" that requires you "to be
100% honest. Meaning not just sincere but almost naked—more like
unarmed. Defenseless" (154). The danger in this approach is that "it
might . . . come off like [you are] the sort of person who not only
goes to a party all obsessed about whether he'll be liked or not but
actually goes around the party and goes up to strangers and asks
them whether they like him or not" (158). Despite these fears,
Wallace ends the last pop quiz in just the way all the other pop
quizzes end, with a command, which is not framed as a question: "So
decide" (160). What we are supposed to decide remains ambiguous,
though the key decision we seem to have to make is whether or not
to directly address the reader. Remember: Wallace positions the

second-person subject of the last quiz *as a writer*. While it is true, as Adam Kelly notes, that "Wallace's narrator ties himself up in knots about these issues," the last quiz invites us to understand that the fiction writer who is debating whether to address the audience directly is identical to Wallace himself.[51] We are asked to imagine the ninth pop quiz as a thinly encoded account of Wallace's actual experience writing "Octet." Nonetheless, Wallace's use of the second person, and his presentation of the final section as another pop quiz (rather than an unmasked form of address), block a direct conflation of the quiz's second-person protagonist with Wallace. The reader is being asked to *choose* to equate the two. Though framed as a choice, it is clear that Wallace encourages identification and belief. The last quiz is so long, detailed, and specific when compared to the previous quizzes that Wallace makes it hard to interpret the story in any other way. In this manner, Wallace emphasizes the reader's need to choose to believe (or, to be more precise, to choose to be receptive to belief). But he understands that literary form might help the reader neutralize irony and engender belief. After all, one cannot choose to believe in any interpretation one wishes.

Another forceful example of Wallace's credulous metafiction—a story that tries to help its reader believe in a specific reality beyond fiction's fourth wall—is "Good Old Neon," part of the collection *Oblivion* (2004). "Good Old Neon" begins as an apparently fictional story, told in the first person, about a character named Neal, who claims to have committed suicide, a victim of what he calls the "fraudulence paradox."[52] Those suffering from the "fraudulence paradox" discover how "the more time and effort you put into trying to appear impressive or attractive to other people, the less impressive or attractive you felt inside—you were a fraud. And the more of a fraud you felt like, the harder you tried to convey an impression or likable image of yourself so that other people wouldn't find out what a hollow fraudulent person you really were" (147). Though the rhetorical situation of Neal's monologue is ambiguous, it becomes clear that he is speaking from beyond the grave to another, unnamed character who also means to commit suicide. When Neal says, "Whether you decide to go through with it or not," it seems as if the person listening to Neal is still undecided about whether to commit suicide

(178). At the same time, there is a suggestion that Neal's ghost might, in some sense, be talking to his prior self, as he drives toward his own death. He writes, "it wouldn't have made you a fraud to change your mind," suggesting that the moment of decision occurs before the time of narration (180). In either case, Neal promises to "explain what happens immediately after a person dies," and informs his interlocutor that "dying isn't bad, but it takes forever" (143, 180). Wallace constructs a formal analog to Neal's experience of death by depicting a runaway inflation of the time of narrative discourse relative to the time of the story. The story's temporal focus narrows, and the last two pages describe many different spatial locations at "the very same instant"—that is, the time during which the narrator has been speaking. Until this moment, there has been only one hint of the ultimate frame of the story. Neal tells his suicidal interlocutor that "it doesn't really matter what you think about me, because despite appearances this isn't even really about me" (152).

Among others, Neal describes the following scene: "David Wallace blinks in the midst of idly scanning class photos from his 1980 Aurora West H.S. yearbook and seeing my photo and trying through the tiny keyhole of himself, to imagine what all must have happened to lead up to my death in the fiery single-car accident he'd read about in 1991" (180). David is "trying, if only in the second his lids are down, to somehow reconcile what this luminous guy had seemed like from the outside with whatever on the interior must have driven him to kill himself in such a dramatic and doubtlessly painful way" (181). The dramatic focus of the story shifts from the difficulties the narrator has dealing with the "fraudulence paradox" to the fictional David's struggle to deal with "the cliché that you can't ever truly know what's going on inside somebody else," a cliché that strikes him as "hoary and insipid," but true (181). As in the ninth pop quiz in "Octet," Wallace knocks down the fourth wall of the fictional world of his story, revealing that what readers were led to believe was fiction (and specifically postmodern metafiction) is in fact a kind of meta-nonfiction.[53] We are invited to understand "Good Old Neon" as Wallace's actual reflections on the suicide of his high school classmate. Reinforcing this interpretation, the story ends with a cryptic dedication that reads "[→NMN.80.418]" (181). "NMN" stands for

Neal's initials, "80" for his year of graduation from Aurora High, and "418" for his Legion ball batting average (referred to earlier in the story). The arrow is more ambiguous, suggesting the logical symbol for a conditional statement, as though the fictional narrative implies the (presumably) nonfictional dedication.[54] The version of the story that ran in *Conjunctions* ends differently, with the more literal dedication "[for NMN.80.418]."[55] The extrafictive truth that each narrative pivots around (that the author of Pop Quiz 9 *is* David Foster Wallace; that Neal really existed, and really did kill himself) is not the core question in these stories.[56] What is important is that Wallace has formulated a new literary mission for metafiction—to create a form that cultivates the reader's capacity to believe, thus counteracting contemporary incredulity.

Marshall Boswell writes that the stories in *Oblivion* "open up an outer layer of interiority into which the story's principal layer has been nesting all along," though he argues that Wallace is moving with his last collection in a nihilistic direction.[57] Wallace's purpose seems less bleak if we read "Octet" and "Good Old Neon" in light of the post-postmodern narrative technique that Raoul Eshelman calls "double framing."[58] Eshelman discusses this technique in the context of developing a concept of "performatism," his name for post-postmodern art. Allowing us to have our "postmetaphysical cake and eat it too," the performativist work sets up two frames of reference, pitting irony against belief. "The outer frame imposes some sort of unequivocal resolution to the problems raised in the work on the reader or viewer," forcing us to take seriously the outer frame's "coercive" interpretation of the inner frame. "Either some sort of irony will undercut the outer frame from within and break up the artificially framed unity, or we will find a crucial scene (or inner frame) confirming the outer frame's coercive logic."[59] Building on Eric Gans's generative anthropology, and tracing the technique of "double framing" in works such as Sam Mendes's *American Beauty* (1999) and Yann Martel's *The Life of Pi* (2001), Eshelman argues that the outer frame embeds an "originary scene" that reduces "human behavior to what seems to be a very basic or elementary circle of unity with nature and / or with other people."[60] In the case of "Octet," the inner frame of the pop quizzes is offered as the natural form "you" might employ if you, the hypothetical fiction writer described in Pop Quiz 9, wanted to be "100% honest" with your reader. In "Good Old Neon," Neal's narrative gives way to Wallace's; the story comes to seem to be Wallace's (or at least David's) attempt to find a form best able to account for Neal's suicide. Whereas the fourth wall of traditional metafiction opens onto the situation of the reader, revealing that what the reader reads ought to be disbelieved, Wallace's fourth walls opens onto the real conundrum of the writer, whom we as readers are asked to believe in.

Avant-Garde Entertainment

At the conceptual and narrative center of *Infinite Jest* is the film cartridge "Infinite Jest," "a recorded pleasure so entertaining and diverting it is lethal to persons" (321). Whoever watches "Infinite Jest" is unable to do anything else but replay the cartridge repeatedly, unto death. James O. Incandenza creates the cartridge as a way to "really communicate" with his anhedonic, almost cripplingly detached, pot-addicted son, Hal, a tennis and academic prodigy at Enfield Tennis Academy. Wallace often describes Hal as lacking a self; he is the sort of person who runs through "decision trees" when responding to other humans and who studies psychiatric manuals so that he can outwit the phalanx of therapists his parents subject him to. Before committing suicide by placing his head in a microwave oven, James sought "to contrive a medium via which he and the muted son [Hal] could simply converse," a form of entertainment that "would reverse thrust on a young self's fall into the womb of solipsism, anhedonia, death in life" (838, 839). At the start of the novel (which is chronologically the last scene of the story), Hal has fully fallen into living death. Speaking to administrators at the University of Arizona, he thinks he is saying, "I'm not a machine. I feel and believe. I have opinions. Some of them are interesting" (12). But it quickly becomes clear that Hal's inner world has no correlation to his outer behavior; those around him describe his convulsions as "a vision of hell" (14). One mark of Hal's nonmechanical humanity—one defense he offers, albeit in his imagination—is his capacity to "believe." One of the ailments Hal suffers from is therefore an excess of incredulity. He is a hypereducated version of the figure Wallace names "Joe Briefcase" in "E Unibus Pluram" and may also be a stand-in for the reader. If that is so, we might infer that the avant-garde film "Infinite Jest" is meant to act on Hal in much the same way as the novel *Infinite Jest* is meant to act upon its jaded readers, who are, by analogy, imagined to suffer from a generational excess of incredulity. Seen this way, James might be a postironist. As with other postironists, James seems not to have a particular *content* that he wants to communicate to his son—the content of the cartridge is, we will see, only described in a sketchy way in the novel. Instead, James's goal is to communicate as an end in itself. To transmit *any* message from father to son would count as success for him, because to do so would require penetrating Hal's multiple psychic layers of protective irony. In the case of "Infinite Jest," the fact of communication is itself the message and purpose of communication.

But describing James as a postironist is problematic. After all, James wants to use the vehicle of *entertainment* in order to communicate with his son. So is James a genuine postironic "anti-rebel" or a cynic in the vein of Ellis and Leyner? By studying the form Wallace's imagined ultimate entertainment takes, and relating the form of that hypothetical entertainment to the logic of the mass media and the avant-garde, we will better understand how Wallace understands *Infinite Jest* itself to function. *Infinite Jest* attempts to act upon readers in a way that might alleviate some of the problems of postmodernity, without taking recourse to the corrupted critical strategies Wallace describes in relation to "Image-fiction."[61] In *Infinite Jest*, as opposed to the short stories I have already discussed, Wallace's literary intervention makes use of procedures more complicated than tearing down the fourth wall of a narrative at a strategic moment near the end of the text. Wallace does not simply reveal what we thought of as fiction to be a sort of nonfiction. Instead, he uses the style of *Infinite Jest* to lead his readers through his process of thinking, highlighting the complicated interpenetration of the mass media, the avant-garde, and the market, possibly as a precursor to asking readers to become believers modeled on the members of AA. Wallace emphasizes his thinking process at two levels: First, he constructs syntactically complex, hypotactic sentences that often hinge on the articulation or revelation of a paradox—economic, social, or existential. Second, at a higher level of organization, *Infinite Jest* fractures its linear narrative into multiple nonchronological sections and buries key story elements in endnotes, some of which are extremely long. Many of these narrative strategies are of course associated with postmodernist fiction. The challenge for Wallace is to use these characteristically postmodernist techniques in ways that achieves non-postmodernist effects, strengthening the emotional engagement and belief of the reader. As Wallace explains, "a certain amount of the form-conscious stuff I write is . . . supposed to be uneasy [for the passive reader]. For instance, using a lot of flash-cuts between scenes so that some of the narrative arrangement has got to be done by the reader, or interrupting flow with digressions and interpolations that the reader has to do the work of connecting to each other and to the narrative."[62] Whether Wallace's fiction succeeds in awakening the slumbering and passive reader remains an open question, but investigating the way "Infinite Jest" does so within Wallace's novel might illuminate what success would look like.

In her 1999 review of the speculative writings of Charles Ostman, N. Katherine Hayles describes how advertisers might use feedback-enabled technologies to build virtual shopping environments so good at identifying the habits, tastes, and preferences of their users that shopping itself will become a joy, a source of ecstasy "so compelling . . . the experience [will be] more like entertainment than shopping."[63] Hayles paints a picture of a cultural and technological milieu in which market economies, and the ideology of liberal autonomy that underlies them, ineluctably create increasingly perfect pleasure machines. These entertainments ensnare the liberal subject of Enlightenment into a logical bind: she wants nothing more than to give herself over to constant, perfectly engrossing "enrapturement." Thus, our "illusion of autonomy" ultimately leads us to decide to give over that very autonomy to corporate image-makers because the "fact of recursivity" can be leveraged against us via the market.[64] It makes sense then that Hayles sees the ultimate expression of this bind in the lethally addictive film cartridge, "Infinite Jest," which shows what one character describes as "no index of diminishing satisfaction as in the econometrics of normal U.S.A. commodities" (727). This evaluation is offered by M. Fortier, leader of the U.S. cell of *Les Assassins des Fauteuils Rollents* [sic] (A.F.R.), a murderous band of self-crippled Quebecois terrorists who hope to use the Entertainment as a means of achieving their separatist aims. In other words, the A.F.R. view the Entertainment in much the same way as Hayles does, as the ultimate expression of U.S. consumer culture: endlessly pleasurable, terminally amusing. As Hayles puts it, "'Infinite Jest' represents the ironic end point of the demand curve in which pleasure and profit at last come together in a perverted culmination of the two sacred American goals of the pursuit of happiness and the pursuit of money" (687).[65]

But to describe the Entertainment as the ultimate expression of the recursive logic of U.S. consumer culture, as Hayles does, risks eliding certain crucial details about "Infinite Jest." Bracketing the fact that James's film cartridge does not directly use any of the feedback-enabled technologies that Hayles and Ostman describe, or the *p*-terminal technologies that Steeply discusses, we might ask whether such systems could be just as easily turned toward avant-garde or nonmarket-oriented ends as consumer ends.[66] Recursivity and rampant self-consciousness are, after all, vital elements of a tradition stemming from modernist art that imagined itself to be *opposed* to the logic of the market. We would thus be only partly right to endorse a market-oriented interpretation of the nature of the Entertainment. The success of the A.F.R.'s assault on the United States does, on the one hand, depend crucially on the blending of the fantasy of liberal autonomy with the pathological hunger for happiness Wallace considers endemic to U.S. culture. But, on the other hand, we should not forget that the Entertainment is *not* a product of the marketplace. It is not exactly the "ironic end point of the demand curve in which pleasure and profit at last come together in a perverted culmination of the two sacred American goals of the pursuit of happiness and the pursuit of money," as Hayles claims. The capitalistic Organization of North American Nations (O.N.A.N.) will staunchly oppose distribution of the Entertainment. For the Entertainment is not the product of a corporate project to ensnare the largest-possible viewing audience but rather the creation of an avant-garde filmmaker (James O. Incandenza) whose previous works were of more interest to academics than popular audiences.[67]

Corporations want to keep their clients, if not always well, then at least alive and paying, and recent neoliberal fantasies of the free market have often required strong state intervention to transform those fantasies into institutional facts. The historical avant-garde, in contrast, sought to liberate art from commodification and bourgeois aestheticism, which had rendered it inert as an agent of social change. They often did so, as in the case of Marcel Duchamp's "Fountain," by trying to reveal the contradictions inherent in the art market. As Peter Bürger describes in *Theory of the Avant-Garde*, "the European avant-garde movements can be defined as an attack on the status of art in bourgeois society. What is negated is not an early form of art (a style) but art as an institution that is unassociated with the life praxis of men."[68] To fully understand how the Entertainment functions, we must move beyond the existing scholarship's focus on the status of the film as entertainment and analyze how James responds to the legacy of the avant-garde.

According to the standard heroic story—inspired by Renato Poggioli's 1968 *Theory of the Avant-Garde* and Bürger's *Theory of the Avant-Garde*—early avant-gardes sought to use art to catalyze a Utopian transformation of bourgeois culture, hoping in many cases that art might refashion society itself.[69] By Bürger's account, the historical avant-garde proposed a Hegelian sublation of art: "art was not to be simply destroyed but transferred to the praxis of life where it would be preserved, albeit in a changed form."[70] In *Infinite Jest*, Wallace doesn't resist these accounts, but rather reimagines the terminal nature of avant-garde efforts to end art as an institution and to break down the barriers (for Wallace, as we have seen, these including irony, cynicism, and detachment) that prevent art from changing consciousness. The Entertainment promises to do both. While previous avant-gardes attacked the institutions that dominated art's production and circulation, James O. Incandenza's "Infinite Jest" attacks the demand for art by ending the art consumer's ability to consume anything ever again. That is, "Infinite Jest" is a good that kills its consumer, a work whose addictiveness catalyzes involuntary social change. In Wallace's view, we should not regard the Entertainment's apocalyptic power to kill as a science-fictional jape but as the logical extension of the avant-garde's vocation. Wallace expressed his view of the avant-garde, which he associated with metafiction, most force-fully in a 1993 interview with Larry McCaffery: "Metafiction's real end has always been Armageddon," he said, and, "Art's reflection on itself is terminal, is one big reason why the art world saw Duchamp as an Antichrist."[71]

Critics might contest Wallace's characterization of the avant-garde in a few ways. We could easily show that the historical avant-garde—from the futurists through Dada to the Situationists—often con-nected projects of institutional destruction to a redemptive Utopian politics (and, later in the century, to the "Temporary Autonomous Zones" I described in Chapter 2 as positive dystopias). The avant-garde's goal was never literally to kill either producers or consumers of art, despite futurist bluster about bombing museums, but to render obsolete the concepts of "producing" and "consuming" art as rei-fied practices divorced from other spheres of life. But this is a weak objection. The outright hostility of the Entertainment toward its viewers, its promise of apocalypse, need not annul the cartridge's status as an avant-garde artwork. If it were indeed possible to rein-corporate art into life praxis, then such an artistic practice could be both constructive and destructive. The Entertainment most clearly contradicts dominant understandings of the avant-garde in the very fact of its existence. For if the "avant-garde movement can in fact be judged to have failed" because it was "unable to destroy art as an institution," then the Entertainment should not be possible in the first place.[72]

In trying to salvage the project of the avant-garde, even in nega-tive form, Wallace could draw on a postmodernist tradition that came to a different conclusion than Bürger on the nature of rela-tionship among institutions, art, and persons. Although Wallace opposed aspects of postmodernism, he seemed to accept its aesthetic ontology—its interpretation of how one might extend the project of the historical avant-garde and the modernists. The historical post-modernists often participated in the symbolic politics of countercul-ture, on the theory (discussed in my introduction) that disruptions of rationality might affect social change at the level of what C. Wright Mills called "the cultural apparatus." Interrogating and exposing corrupt or authoritarian symbolic forms could do significant political

work in itself, because most of us live in a "second-hand world" constructed by the mass media.[73] Unlike Bürger, then, postmodernist
authors and poststructuralist intellectuals would dispute the claim
that the avant-garde is necessarily doomed to fail. Some postmodernists (such as William S. Burroughs, Kathy Acker, Ishmael Reed,
and Thomas Pynchon) openly identified with the new social movements; others merely integrated countercultural assumptions about
the efficacy of symbolic political warfare into their fictional experiments. Donald Barthelme, for example, emphasizes the ontological
status of the book as a thing-in-the-world in his essay "After Joyce":
"with Stein and Joyce the literary work becomes an object in the
world rather than a text or commentary upon the world."[74] The work
of art becomes more like "a rock or a refrigerator" than a discursive
representation of the world.[75] Although Barthelme adjusts his views
twenty years later in "Not-Knowing" (1987), allowing that the world
still smuggles itself into literary works in the belly of language, the
notion of the book as a thing-in-the-world remained a powerful
legacy of the avant-garde for postmodernist writers. For Barthelme,
the material book becomes a thing about which we ponder, something we live with and explore. When he calls the postmodern novel
a "Hostile Object," Barthelme is referring to Burroughs's cut-up
technique, but he might as well be describing *Infinite Jest* when he
writes that "the form of the [Hostile Object], in other words, suggests that a chunk of a large building may fall on you at any moment.
Burroughs' form is inspired, exactly appropriate to his terroristic
purpose."[76]

Acknowledging its postmodernist forbearers, *Infinite Jest* reminds
us of its status as a thing by virtue of its girth, its heft, its alleged
bloat. While the novel itself may not prove to be as massively addictive as the Entertainment that it describes, it does knowingly exhibit
an avant-garde aggressiveness toward its readers. Wallace associates
aggression with the Entertainment itself, not to mention some
of James's earlier films, such as *The Medusa v the Odalisque*, which
depicts "mobile holograms of two visually lethal mythologic females"
who "duel with reflective surfaces on-stage while a live crowd of
spectators turns to stone" (988). The film is described as "cold,
allusive, inbent, hostile: the only feeling for the audience one of

contempt" (740). Wallace encodes a fantasy of the artist as a (failed) terrorist—which Don DeLillo ponders in *Mao II* (1992) and, in a different way, in *Falling Man* (2008)—into the plot and form of *Infinite Jest*. The A.F.R., after all, want to use the Entertainment as a terrorist weapon against American consumers. By Wallace's own criteria, his novel may constitute a form of aggression against his readers. Wallace explains in an interview with Larry McCaffery that his hostility toward readers tends to manifest itself "in the form of sentences that are syntactically not incorrect but still a real bitch to read. Or bludgeoning the reader with data. Or devoting a lot of energy to creating expectations and then taking pleasure in disappointing them."[77] With its massive and syntactically tangled paragraphs, hundred pages of endnotes in a tiny font, and frustratingly unresolved plotlines, we might find ourselves tempted to consider the novel a Barthelmean "Hostile Object."

Of course, James O. Incandenza never wanted to consider himself an avant-garde artist, although he plays the role of one, often for his own amusement, as a way of laughing at critics who want to impute deep significance to his filmic practical jokes. Let us again recall the original purpose of "Infinite Jest." James does not make his lethally addictive film in order to shock or destroy his viewing audience; his aim, according to the testimony he offers from beyond the grave to the convalescing Don Gately, is to connect with his troubled son Hal.

> The wraith . . . says he spent the whole sober last ninety days of his animate life working tirelessly to contrive a medium via which he and the muted son could simply *converse*. To concoct something the gifted boy couldn't simply master and move on from to a new plateau. Something the boy would love enough to induce him to open his mouth and come *out*—even if it was only to ask for more. Games hadn't done it, professionals hadn't done it, impersonation of professionals hadn't done it. His last resort: entertainment. Make something so bloody compelling it would reverse thrust on a young self's fall into the womb of solipsism, anhedonia, death in life. A magically entertaining toy to dangle at the infant still somewhere alive in the boy, to make its eyes

light and toothless mouth open unconsciously, to laugh. To bring him "out of himself," as they say. The womb could be used both ways. A way to say I AM SO VERY, VERY SORRY and have it *heard*. A life-long dream. The scholars and Foundations and disseminators never saw that his most serious wish was: *to entertain*.

   (838–839, emphasis in original)

From the little we actually learn about the content of the cartridge during Joelle van Dyne's interview with Steeply, the Entertainment during one scene positions its viewers as infants, infantilizing the viewer in literal, technical ways: "The point of view was from the crib, yes. A crib's-eye view . . . There's something wobbled and weird about [a newborn's] vision, supposedly. I think the newer-born they are, the more the wobble . . . I don't think there's much doubt the lens was supposed to reproduce an infantile visual field" (939–940). By constructing the Entertainment in this way, James and, by extension, Wallace seem to be simultaneously criticizing the hyper-self-involution supposedly characteristic of the avant-garde as well as the infantilizing tendencies of the mass media. The two critiques are in fact inseparable for Wallace.

   Within the world of the novel, James's "Infinite Jest" launches a recursive loop, "a moving right-triangular cycle of interdependence and waste-creation and -utilization," to borrow Ted Schacht's explanation of annular fusion (571). This right triangle is a fictive model of the interdependence of the postmodern subject, the avant-garde impulse, and the mass media. In creating this fictive model, Wallace constructs a speculative figure, an ingenious thought experiment, that opens outward onto the situation of the actual reader. Whereas "Octet" and "Good Old Neon" invoke the situation of the reader by repurposing techniques associated with metafiction, *Infinite Jest* does so by leading the reader, sentence by winding sentence, through the paradoxical logic of the form and purpose of the Entertainment. The Entertainment resembles what Daniel Dennett calls an "intuition pump" or what Michael Clune calls a "virtual form."[78] The speculative form of the Entertainment is a tool of thought. In the reader's attempt to trace out the Entertainment's logic, she also supposedly produces a live demonstration that the logic of the avant-garde is inextricably entangled with the logic of the marketplace, showing (by means her own interpretive activity) that overcoming post-modern irony will require confronting both domains. One has to imagine something like an ultimate entertainment (or, what may be the same thing, an ultimate artwork) to see the true contours of this system, to understand how its different elements are tangled together, and to grasp what rebellion might require. The defining characteristic of Wallace's ultimate artwork is its power to literally transform its viewers, to break down the barriers separating the producer and the consumer of art. The point of imagining such an ultimate artwork is not, therefore, to furnish the reader with a higher-order irony or a deeper critical knowingness. Deepening such irony would only, in Wallace's view, deepen the chasm between the writer and the reader, intensifying the loneliness of both. Rather, Wallace means to exhaust the reader's reflexive irony, to take the reader to the limit of critical thought in order to prepare the way for her willingness to believe in the sincerity of the author. Wallace's sincerity would mean little in the absence of a reader willing to submit to the possibility of believing in that sincerity. What Wallace offers the reader is, to be sure, a troublingly individual or at best intersubjective solution to what he elsewhere describes as a political and economic problem. Whether we find Wallace's diagnosis or cure convincing, his advocacy of the ethos of belief as a solution to the problem of postmodern irony has had far-reaching consequences, shaping the priorities and concerns of a generation of writers, inspiring not only a new style of postironic art but also a range of important new literary institutions.

Mean Readers

The paratexts of *A Heartbreaking Work of Staggering Genius* are brazen. Dave Eggers's bestselling memoir, which recounts his effort to raise his brother Toph after the nearly simultaneous deaths of their parents from cancer, proliferates guilt-ridden commentary on its own veracity, while insisting that this commentary is not a form of irony. Eggers's metacommentary begins on the memoir's copyright page. "This is a work of fiction," Eggers explains, "only that in many cases, the author could not remember the exact words said by certain people, and exact descriptions of certain things, so had to fill in gaps as best he could."[79] This is followed by the section "Rules and Suggestions for Enjoyment of this Book," which recommends to readers that "the first three or four [chapters of the memoir] are all some of you might want to bother with" (vii). The "Preface to This Edition," which appeared in the *first* edition, contradicts the copyright page, asserting that "for all the author's bluster elsewhere [that is, the copyright page], this is not actually a work of pure nonfiction. Many parts have been fictionalized in varying degrees, for various purposes" (ix). Following the table of contents, Eggers writes a lengthy acknowledgements section that "acknowledge[s] the major themes of this book" (xxvii). These include "THE PAINFULLY, ENDLESSLY SELF-CONSCIOUS BOOK ASPECT," "THE SELF-FLAGELLATION AS ART FORM ASPECT," and "THE SELF-AGGRANDIZEMENT DISGUISED AS SELF-FLAGELLATION AS EVEN HIGHER ART FORM ASPECT" (xxix, xxxvii). Finally, Eggers adds an "INCOMPLETE GUIDE TO SYMBOLS AND METAPHORS," which informs readers that "No symbolism is meant by the use of Journey's 'Any Way You Want It'" (xliv). Eggers's metacommentary recurs even in *A Heartbreaking Work*'s primary text, calling the distinction between text and paratext into question. After a long day, Dave tucks his brother into bed, and Toph suggests that the chapter we the readers have just read is "not entirely believable" because it seems "as if a number of days had been spliced together to quickly paint a picture of an entire period of time, to create a whole-seeming idea of how we are living, without having to stoop (or rise) to actually pacing the story out."[80] But Toph concludes, "it works fine, in general. It's fine." "Listen, you," Dave responds, "We've had plenty of days like this, and many that were much more complicated . . . It's maddening, actually, when you sit down . . . to try to render something like this." "So you're reduced to complaining about it," Toph counters. "Or worse doing little tricks out of frustration . . . The gimmicks, bells, whistles. Diagrams." The discussion of the difficulty of writing honestly about one's life consumes another six pages of the memoir (114–122). The crux of this conversation, as with the memoir's prefatory paratexts, turns on

whether the reader believes in the memoir's truthfulness. Its "gimmicks, bells, and whistles" are the formal means Eggers uses to
render his life faithfully. In this case, the question is not whether we
believe in any particular event—do readers doubt that Eggers had
ice cream or saw a movie with his brother?—but rather whether we
believe in Eggers's truthfulness.

Eggers seeks to find a literary form that can vouchsafe his integrity, but he finds it difficult to make his case—which is why, in the
2001 Vintage paperback edition of *A Heartbreaking Work*, he includes
a new appendix called "Mistakes We Knew We Were Making," which
is appended to the original text with a tête-bêche binding. The
addendum seeks to neutralize charges that the memoir erred in any
way. The "we" of the addition's title is ambiguous in an important
way. On the one hand, the first-person plural suggests that a group
of persons is making these alleged "mistakes," diffusing responsibility for them. On the other hand, Eggers himself, as the nominal
author of his own memoir, comes to seem as if he were more than an
individual person, as if he were, in some sense, a collective person or
human institution. As Benjamin Widiss argues, Eggers's presentation of himself as a representative of his generation seems to "trade
on a repurposing of Catholic practices, images, and dogma to a set
of ends ranging from the manifestly secular to a twilight zone of
uncertain belief."[81] By either interpretation, the first-person plural is
provocative. What must we do to join ourselves with this plural,
knowingly errant person? The appendix's copyright page (which is
distinct from the original copyright page) gives us our first hint.
Eggers writes that he "wishes to reserve the right to use spaces like
this, and to work within them, for no other reason than it entertains
him and *a small coterie of readers*. It does not mean that anything
ironic is happening. It does not mean that someone is being pomo or
meta or cute."[82] The "smallness" of Eggers's readership is central to
the memoir's form of address. It is an assumption that Eggers repeats
in interviews and that defines the small-batch ethos of *Timothy
McSweeney's Quarterly Concern* (the literary journal Eggers founded
in 1998). Later in the appendix, the condition of membership in
Eggers's "small coterie of readers" becomes explicit. In a note, Eggers
explains that "you can't know how much it pains me to even have

that word, the one beginning with i and ending in y, in this book. It is not a word I like to see, anywhere, much less type on to my own pages . . . I have that i-word here only to make clear what was clear to, by my estimations, about 99.9% of original hardcover readers of this book: that there is almost no irony, whatsoever, within its covers" (33). While Eggers at first described his readership as constituting a tiny coterie, he now invokes the opinions of his actual, mass reader-ship ("99.9%" of his hardcover readers). If Eggers's mass coterie understands his intentions, why bother correcting the errors of a vanishingly small group of outsiders (the errant 0.1%)? Eggers may have been responding to critics such as *The New York Times*' Charles McGrath. In a favorable invocation of Jedediah Purdy's anti-irony polemic, *For Common Things: Irony, Trust, and Commitment in America Today* (1999), McGrath suggests that *A Heartbreaking Work* is suf-fused with irony and unfavorably likens Eggers to Bart Simpson, Hamlet, and Abbie Hoffman.[83] It is understandable that Eggers would have wanted to respond to such mainstream misinterpreta-tions of his work—there was a vitriolic, grossly personal backlash against him when his memoir became a bestseller[84]—but such expla-nations do not yet fully account for the anxiety Eggers betrays when denying to the possibility that he is an ironist. Something greater is at play.

The charge that Eggers is an ironist especially stings because it inflames his most fundamental fears about himself, fears that are the very subject of his memoir. In fact, the only place irony can be found in *A Heartbreaking Work*, according to "Mistakes We Knew We Were Making," is during Eggers's tenure as the editor of *Might* magazine in the early nineties. The late nineties / early 2000s postironic Eggers takes great pains to dissociate himself from the early- to mid-1990s ironic Eggers. *Might* described itself as "a humor magazine for Generation X," reminiscent of the satirical *Spy* magazine. It was part of a flowering of publications in the San Francisco Bay Area before the dot-com bubble. Describing the ethos of *Might*, Eggers writes that "of course, we, and our magazine, can't let on that we're part of . . . any scene . . . Whatever the prevailing thinking, especially our own, we contradict it, reflexively" (*A Heartbreaking Work* 172, 240). In a simplified rehearsal of David Foster Wallace's argument about

television in "E Unibus Pluram," Eggers describes the coterie associated with *Might* as a group of "young people pretending to be
young people, putting across an image of ourselves as representa-
tives, for now and posterity, of *how* youth were at this juncture, *how*
we acted, and in particular, *how* we acted when we were pretending
not to act while pretending to be ourselves" (245, my emphasis). Eggers
paints a painful, self-critical portrait of himself as a ironist. This earlier version of Eggers (that is, Dave) denies that he is performing for
an audience—he insists everywhere on his individuality—but he also
wants his refusal to serve as a generational or collective statement.
Dave's paradoxical purpose manifests at the level of the sentence, in
his repeated, hypotactic "hows," which are at a stroke descriptive and
normative.

While Eggers may claim to have grown beyond the concerns of
his younger, ironic self, his memoir gives evidence that he remains
invested in being a spokesperson or living metonymy for his generation. Eggers (who becomes increasingly difficult to disentangle
from Dave) continues to want to be watched, to be loved, to accumulate prestige, but fears that having these desires will corrode his
authenticity, depriving him of the status he desires. In a fictionalized
transcript of his MTV *Real World* audition, which absorbs fifty pages
of *A Heartbreaking Work*, Dave expresses the fear that he is consumed
by a "pure, insinuating solipsism" and that he only has two available
options for dealing with his self-involvement. He can either be the
sort of person who "talks about his problems, his girlfriend, his poor
prospects, how his parents died, on and on, to the point of paralysis,"
or he can be among those "people who think their personality is so
strong, their story so interesting, that others must know it and learn
from it" (201). At the end of the memoir, describing a game of Frisbee
he plays with Toph, Eggers imagines himself as a sort of secular,
Generation X Christ:

> Don't you know that I am connected to you? Don't you know
> that I'm trying to pump blood to you, that this is for you, that I
> hate you people, so many of you . . . when you're all sleeping so
> many sleeping I am somewhere on some stupid rickety scaf-
> folding and I'm trying to get your stupid fucking attention . . .

What the fuck does it take to show you motherfuckers, what
does it fucking take what do you want how much do you want
because I am willing (436–437).

The "motherfuckers" in question are Eggers's readers, the sleeping
readers for whom Eggers writes, whom he wants to transform, whose
"stupid fucking attention" he still craves, even after he has publicly
abandoned his pervious, ironic persona. All of Eggers's aesthetic
choices therefore seem to be directed not at the "99.9%" of readers,
the mass coterie whom he imagines recognize his good intentions, but rather at the 0.1% of resistant readers. He invites resistance, tempting his readers to interpret him ironically, only to berate
them when they do, thus having his readers enact—by reading his
memoir—a version of his own story. This is why *A Heartbreaking
Work* cannot simply abandon irony. Readers must move through a
moment of self-devouring irony en route to postironic grace. Eggers
must proffer irony as an alluring interpretive option, only finally to
withdraw it from reach. But this act of withdrawal is fraught, and
threatens to destroy Eggers. To foreclose irony, the postironic Eggers
must turn to a Bellovian proliferation of discourse and a rapidly
multiplying set of paratexts, which must acknowledge their own
potential corruption. It is not surprising that the project of blocking
the perverse interpretations of a hypothetical, tiny minority of
readers takes on such an extended form. Absent any ontological certainties to fix meaning, interpretive control can never, in principle,
fully succeed.

   Like David Foster Wallace, whose example so clearly inspired
him, Eggers means to make his readers into believers. Eggers has
asked his readers to believe in *him*, in the truthfulness of his memoir,
the sincerity of his various enterprises. This is why Eggers's experiments in self-publication—his institution-building drive—turn out
to be *the primary contents* of his memoir, and why his guilt over
financing these enterprises through money derived from his parents'
deaths was the main emotional subtext of his early career. In order to
make his life and personality into a human institution, Eggers sup-
plemented his life's story with a range of innovative literary and
philanthropic enterprises. As an empirical organization, of course,

McSweeney's necessarily transcends the particular personality and life story of Eggers; I do not in any way mean to flatten the diversity of the institutions Eggers played a role in founding. Nonetheless, Eggers's public performances (which have involved quirky stunts at readings),[85] his publishing enterprises (*Timothy McSweeney's Quarterly Concern*, McSweeney's Books, *The Believer*), and his philanthropic activities (his network of "826 National" tutoring centers, the Valentino Achak Deng Foundation, Voice of Witness) can be profitably understood as extended interlocking paratexts of *A Heartbreaking Work* itself. I will read these organizations as manifestations of what Gerard Genette calls the "epitext," which he defines as "any paratextual element not materially appended to the text within the same volume but circulating, as it were, freely, in a virtually limitless physical and social space."[86] Genette mentions the newspaper interview as an example of an epitext, and includes "radio or television programs, lectures and colloquia, all public performances perhaps preserved on recordings or in print collections ... Anywhere outside the book may also be the statements contained in an author's correspondence or journal, perhaps intended for later publication, either anthumous or posthumous."[87] Given the diversity of the occasions and venues that Genette cites, we might wonder what prevents epitexts from spanning the totality of literary and social institutions, from the local bookseller up through the world market as such. The answer, I will propose, is that nothing prevents such a hyperextension of the concept of the epitext. Eggers and his associates regard these global epitexts as relevant to their writing, and have sought to create, with McSweeney's, an alternate, semiautonomous sphere within the wider literary field.

Since it was founded, McSweeney's has become a notable literary brand whose postironic ethos has powerfully influenced the U.S. literary marketplace. Critics have understandably linked Eggers's anxious paratextual productivity to his fears about making his work public through the market. Sarah Brouillette argues that Eggers uses innovative bibliographic formats to forestall accusations that he has "sold out" or been corrupted by the market, while he actually mass produces "objects that aim to distinguish themselves from the abundance of disposable works on display at the average major chain bookstore."[88] It is true that Eggers attempts "to police the reception of future works and control the way we read [his] position in the literary marketplace," but he does so not only defensively but also with a strongly normative agenda.[89] He doesn't just want to persuade the reader but to transform her. Amy Hungerford therefore gets closer to Eggers's purpose when she writes that his enterprises seek to "form writers and readers in—and for—the contemporary literary marketplace, and to do it in a way that is distinct from the methods and history of writing programs" (a history outlined in Mark McGurl's *The Program Era*).[90] As Caroline Hamilton writes, Eggers's early writing and his various enterprises constituted "a way of living, complete with its own aesthetic philosophy, its own system of value, even its own soundtrack for life."[91] Yet neither Hungerford nor Hamilton specify the way of life that McSweeney's creates, beyond broad suggestions that these readers are motivated by "love and friendship" or hope to enact a version of "New Sincerity."[92]

In the first issue of *The Believer* (originally called "The Optimist"), founding editor and novelist Heidi Julavits gives a more fully developed portrait of the postironic art of living that Eggers's enterprises call into being. In her essay, Julavits investigates the question "When is criticism too self-serving or mean?" Reflecting on "an era when disenchantment and elation are running nose and nose," she laments that "modest, unspectacular books get celebrated, while more ambitious ones are lambasted or ignored," that "ambition is not the sort of thing that American critics are terribly partial to."[93] Julavits specifically criticizes the critic James Wood for failing to give a fair reading to ambitious writers who do not conform to his limited literary vision, but she more generally targets the "hostile, knowing, bitter tone of contempt" known as "Snark."[94] The film critic Dave Denby defines *snark* as a tone of "insult provoked and encouraged by the new hybrid world of print, television, radio, and the Internet"; in contrast with legitimate satire, it's "low, teasing, snide, condescending, knowing."[95] In her inaugural essay, which for many has defined the literary mission of *The Believer*, Julavits opposes a sort of person I'd call the "Mean Reader," an unapologetic snark whose perversely cynical, disenchanted, disbelieving ethos would lead him to trash books without appreciating their ambition.[96] As we've seen,

Eggers's paratexts construct a similar image of the Mean or Snarky Reader—identified at times with the incredulous 0.1% of his readers, at other times with his former *Might*-era self—against whom he writes and against whom he demands his readers identify themselves. Eggers therefore does not merely want to present himself as personally virtuous or moral, as the critic Lee Siegel suggests, but mobilizes a host of institutions (which wear their sincerity, optimism, and goodness on their collective sleeve) on behalf of worthy causes. Eggers invites us into McSweeney's magic circle of (small-batch, sincere) production, (nonprofit) circulation, (nonsnarky) criticism, and (postironic) reception. Many have accepted his invitation. But the question remains: If you are not a snarky reader—if you opt out of the disenchanted world of contemporary literary culture and join the McSweeney's "way of life"—what sort of life are you living? How does the world look to you? What exactly *are* you?

The Quirky Economy

You are quirky. A popular aesthetic stance, the "ruling sensibility of today's Gen-X indie culture," in the view of many critics, an ethos often associated with Dave Eggers's McSweeney's empire, quirkiness has come under increasing critical scrutiny.[97] The *Oxford English Dictionary* defines *quirky* as "unexpected, odd, or unusual traits; idiosyncratic, eccentric; peculiar, unusual," and dates the earliest use of this sense of the word to the 1870s.[98] In his writing on the term, the film scholar James MacDowell shows that quirkiness has been more recently associated with a range of "Indiewood" filmmakers, such as Wes Anderson, Michel Gondry, Charlie Kaufman, Spike Jonze, Jared Hess, Miranda July, and Mike Mills.[99] MacDowell fruitfully contrasts their offbeat films not with Hollywood film but with the indie style Jeffrey Sconce has called "smart film." A postmodern cinematic style, smart film is characterized by "cultivated disaffection," "studied dispassion," "blank disengagement," "world-weary disinterest"—in short, by "ironic posturing."[100] By MacDowell's persuasive account, quirky film tries to reconcile irony and sincerity, manifesting a "tone that exists on a knife-edge of judgment and empathy, detachment and engagement."[101] In contrast to smart film, quirky film proffers a sort of deadpan comedy that is "simultaneously absurd *and* moving, the characters pathetic *and* likable, the world . . . manifestly artificial *and* believable."[102] In an essay published in *The Awl*, Kenneth Goldsmith suggestively contrasts "smart" and "dumb" culture, preferring (and identifying himself as) "dumb."[103] Goldsmith differentiates further between "smart smart" ("TED talks, think tanks, NPR news, Ivy League universities, *The New Yorker*, and expensive five-star restaurants") and "smart dumb" ("The Fugs, punk rock, art schools, Gertrude Stein, Vito Acconci, Marcel Duchamp, Samuel Beckett, Seth Price, Tao Lin"). He further distinguishes "smart dumb" culture from "dumb dumb" culture ("rednecks and racists, football hooligans, gum-snapping marketing girls, and thick-necked office boys"). For Goldsmith, "dumb" actually means "smart dumb." "By trying so hard, smart smart really misses the point . . . Smart dumb plays at being dumb dumb but knows better." There are, however, corrupt variations of "smart dumb," which Goldsmith describes as *twee*: "Twee (*McSweeney's*, Miranda July, Ira Glass, David Byrne) feigns dumb but won't allow itself to be dumb, for fear that someone might actually think it's dumb, god forbid."[104] Goldsmith prefers the *genuine smart dumbness* of Tao Lin to the *feigned smart dumbness* of twee McSweeney's, but to the degree that it is always defined against a knowing, cynical *smart smartness*, all *smart dumbness* is a variation of postirony. The frequent insistence that quirkiness is anything but smart hints at the appeal of this contemporary style. The quirky believer's mission is not to "dig"; she has no desire to achieve ironic, hip insider knowledge of the symbolic mechanisms that move society. Nor does the quirky believer have much patience for punk negativity (negativity can, after all, be so Mean!). Instead, the quirky person seeks to reenchant the world through an effortless personal style of not knowing, to overcome the "cool" knowledge production of *Wired* with the easygoing "quirky" consumerism of *Timothy McSweeney's Quarterly Concern*.[105]

Some critics have not taken kindly to quirkiness. Michael Hirschorn criticizes this style for eliminating danger. It is "strenuously odd," "beneficent, wide-eyed," an "embrace of the odd against the blandly mainstream," but it ultimately avoids being "too odd." In its mannered oddness, this "non-ironic ironic" stance avoids alienating, angering, or frightening anyone. Melvin Jules Bukiet also denounces quirky style for failing to be sufficiently menacing. His attack on what he calls Brooklyn Books of Wonder (by writers such as "Jonathan Safran Foer, Myla Goldberg, Nicole Krauss, and Dave Eggers, along with everything *McSweeney's*") begins with the warning: "Something nice this way comes."[106] Brooklyn Books of Wonder tediously mixes "mawkish self-indulgence . . . a heavy dollop of creamy nostalgia . . . magic realism . . . [and] a complacency of faith." Such writers display "mock-naïve astonishment" at the wondrousness of life. They disingenuously repackage the ugliness of the world they live in so as "to avoid the taint of anger or cynicism or the passion for revenge felt by real people." I would argue that the quirky's equivocality—its aesthetic capacity to be different, but not too different; provocative, but not uncomfortably so—has enabled it to popularize David Foster Wallace's critique of irony. Quirkiness might well be the stylistic and institutional form the avant-garde takes when it reconciles itself to the reality of the market, no longer seeing its mission as social revolution but as the cultivation of the smartness, the dumbness, or the smart dumbness of the individual person. In making this argument, I don't mean to condemn quirky style as an inauthentic or reactionary "neo-avant-garde," but to document its relationship to mass irony, in order to better understand its appeal. To give evidence for my claims, I will first discuss David and Diana Wilson's Museum of Jurassic Technology (MJT) in Los Angeles and the art critic Lawrence Weschler's overview of the MJT in *Mr. Wilson's Cabinet of Wonder: Pronged Ants, Horned Humans, Mice on Toast, and Other Marvels of Jurassic Technology* (1995). This preliminary discussion will be followed by an analysis of how Dave Eggers's first novel, *You Shall Know Our Velocity!* recasts his memoir's imperial paratexuality into a philanthropic project of quirky self-cultivation.

The Museum of Jurassic Technology is a small, privately owned institution in the Palms district of Los Angeles. Founded in 1988 by David and Diana Wilson, it is "an educational institution dedicated to the advancement of knowledge and the public appreciation of the Lower Jurassic," according to the museum's 2002 *Jubilee Catalog*.[107] Given that the Lower Jurassic began 201 million years ago and ended 174 million years ago, the museum's name already gives a hint of its real mission, exemplifying the deadpan tone in which it purveys its ambiguous hoaxes of human knowledge. The museum stages a miscellany of historical, artistic, and scientific exhibits, including exotic insects; a species of bat called "*Myotis lucifugous [sic]*," which has the ability to use "X ray" echolocation to "fly unharmed through solid objects"; the microminiature sculptures of an Egyptian-born Armenian American sculptor, Hagop Sandaldjian; the decaying dice of the magician Ricky Jay; a gallery featuring portraits of the dogs of the Soviet space program; an exhibit on Los Angeles–area mobile homes and trailer parks; and a scale model of Noah's ark (*Jubilee* 53). Each of these exhibits has a dubious provenance, but each also provocatively mixes true and false information, as Lawrence Weschler discovered in his investigation of the MJT. Weschler wrote a semiregular "Convergences" column for *McSweeney's Quarterly Concern*, which was collected in *Everything That Rises: A Book of Convergences*. Weschler is therefore both a vector for the spread of quirky style and one of its most astute analysts. In *Mr. Wilson's Cabinet of Wonder*, Weschler compares the curatorial practice of MJT to historical Wunderkammern, focusing largely on David Wilson, who he says "never breaks irony" (*Wonder* 53):

> Those earliest museums, the ur-collections back in the sixteenth and seventeenth centuries, were sometimes called *Wunderkammern*, wonder-cabinets, and it occurs to me that the Museum of Jurassic Technology truly is their worthy heir in as much as wonder, broadly conceived, is its unifying theme. ("Part of the assigned task," David once told me, "is to reintegrate people to wonder.") But it's a special kind of wonder, and it's metastable. The visitor to the Museum of Jurassic Technology continually finds himself shimmering between wondering at (the marvels of nature) and wondering whether (any of this could possibly be true). And it's that very shimmer, the capacity for such delicious confusion, Wilson sometimes seems to suggest, that may constitute the most blessedly wonderful thing about being human.[108]

Weschler's analysis leans hard on a semantic accident—the dual sense of the word "wonder"—to argue for the MJT's resemblance to

Wunderkammern, but the connections are plausible enough. One of the key differences, of course, between Wunderkammern of the sixteenth and seventeenth century and Wilson's MJT is the relationship of each form of organized display to mainstream scientific knowledge of the day. Wunderkammern combined or mixed curiosities whose scientific status had yet to be settled; the miscellany nature of historical Wunderkammern originated from the lack of disciplinary specialization, or taxonomic hierarchies, relative to mysterious "distinct ontological" natural kinds.[109] Wilson, by contrast, seeks to "*reintegrate* people to wonder" (my emphasis). He manufactures wonders by manipulating the ignorance of the museumgoer, promising that his museum offers "a Guide to life in the Jurassic" (*Jubilee* 11). The need for such a guide "becomes more and more urgent every day," and "the successful scholar and the casually curious alike cannot confine themselves to the narrow methods of former times" but must adopt "advanced methods" of inquiry, "called for by the progress of science and necessitated by the importance of the work required" (*Jubilee* 11). The Wilsons, if no one else, presumably know which elements of the MJT are true, which are based on truth, and which have been wholly invented, but the tone of these sentences is meant to belie clarification, invoking (via the passive voice, and the pastiche of scholarly discourse) the opinion of a specious expert community. Unlike historical Wunderkammern, which were used as a way of charting "nature's farthest reaches," the Museum of Jurassic Technology makes no claims about the actual frontiers of knowledge.[110] It instead invokes the *style* of knowledge claims. It *simulates* the frontiers of understanding.

The aesthetic effect of the MJT depends upon the poorly calibrated incredulity of its visitors. Its exhibits represent phenomena that are particularly hard to believe, framing them in a way that invites skepticism and then revealing to the viewer who investigates further that what she took for a fabrication is in fact partly true or at least based on something real. We may be tempted to think that it partakes of the "new age of curiosity" that Michel Foucault once dreamed of, but the Museum of Jurassic Technology is *not* exactly a heterotopian institution. For Foucault, the term *curiosity* was appealing because "it evokes the care one takes of what exists and what might exist; a sharpened sense of reality, but one that is never immobilized before it; a readiness to find what surrounds us strange and odd; a certain determination to throw off familiar ways of thought and to look at the same things in a different way; a passion for seizing what is happening now and what is disappearing; a lack of respect for the traditional hierarchies of what is important and fundamental."[111] In *The Order of Things*, Foucault comments on a particular kind of discomfort and delight created by the "Chinese encyclopedia" in Borges's short story "The Analytical Language of John Wilkins." In Borges's Chinese encyclopedia, animals are divided into categories—"(a) belonging to the Emperor, (b) embalmed, (c) tame, (d) suckling pigs . . . (n) that from a long way off look like flies"—that supposedly baffle Western epistemologies.[112] For Foucault, the significance of this exotic categorical schema is its disturbing validity, the idea that one might carve up the world quite differently without producing fictional or mythical beasts. Borges teaches us that there is an infinite set of valid categorical schemes—what Richard Rorty would call "final vocabularies," what W. V. O. Quine discusses in terms of the problem of the "under-determination" of scientific theories—with which we might apprehend reality. His stories show that "we shall never succeed in defining a stable relation of contained to container between each of these categories and that which includes them all."[113]

Where Foucault confronts "the disorder in which fragments of a large number of possible orders glitter separately . . . without law or geometry," the worldly form of "disorder" he calls heterotopia, Wilson wants to decategorize the world, to actively disorder it.[114] Foucault marvels at the universe of marginal knowledge, at different ways of apprehending reality, but never celebrates false or misleading knowledge. He emphasizes the validity of a plurality of heterotopic schemas in order to lay the groundwork for his lengthy examination of how scientific discourse shifts from one episteme to another. Wonder for Foucault, much as it was for medieval and early modern intellectuals, was "a cognitive passion, as much about knowing as about feeling," a way "to register a breached boundary, a classification subverted."[115] Wilson, by contrast, has goals that are more modest. His art depends on what Joshua Landy calls the "ethereal suspension of disbelief" conjured by nineteenth-century magicians such as Jean Eugène Robert-Houdin, who "offered the opportunity . . . to reinforce an aptitude for detached credulity," an "aptitude which would make it possible for everyday life to be re-enchanted."[116] When the MJT describes itself in its catalog as possessing "an incongruity born of the overzealous spirit in the face of unfathomable phenomena," it does not merely invoke a confusion of classifications, or the necessary underdetermination of scientific theories, but lays its emphasis on the *unfathomability* of phenomenal experience (*Jubilee* 17). Wilson wants to unsettle the means by which we determine truth, presenting us with bizarre and unclassifiable objects whose validity we cannot help but question. We are meant to wonder which aspects of the MJT exhibits are real and which fraudulent. As with other postironic forms of belief, the transformation of incredulity into awe is not tied to any particular content or discipline. As a teenager, Weschler writes, Wilson "underwent this incredibly intense . . . well, like a conversion experience. It's just that I came to understand the course of my life and the meaning of life in general. Like in a flash for instance, I knew that there would be no purpose for me in pursuing the world of acquisition. The experience had religious overtones to it, but *not in any specific way*" (*Wonder* 44, my emphasis). This nonspecific religious experience led Wilson to create the MJT: "I see running this museum as a service job, and that service consists in . . . in providing people a situation . . . in fostering an environment in which people can change. And it happens. I've seen it happen" (*Wonder* 44). Wilson has created a space meant to manufacture epiphanic experiences of conversion, but these epiphanies are of a blank or empty sort.

The MJT wants museumgoers to see the world as suffused with wonder, thus inverting the "deep-rooted tradition in modernity of . . . museum bashing . . . in the name of real life," turning the museum into a technology for reencountering a newly enchanted version of the world.[117] While the stance Wilson supports is blank in terms of content, it is not stylistically blank. The primary aesthetic mode of Wilson's museum is juxtaposition and concatenation, a quirky mixture of nature and culture. The MJT exhibit "Tell The Bees . . . Belief, Knowledge and Hypersymbolic Cognition" is characteristic of this aesthetic mode:

In order not to be set hopelessly adrift in this seemingly endless
sea of complex and interrelating beliefs, this exhibition has limited its discussion to five areas of inquiry, and each exhibit bears
a mark that should help in the identification of the source of the
particular belief. The five areas of inquiry are:

- Pins and Needles
- Shoes and Stockings
- Body Parts and Secretions
- Thunder and Lightning
- Insects and Other Living Things

Many of the beliefs illuminated in this exhibition are and
have been practiced in surprisingly similar forms by peoples
separated by hundreds or thousands of miles and often hundreds or thousands of years.

(*Jubilee 98*)

The pleasure of a list like this one comes not only from its surprising
juxtaposition of objects, but also from our suspicion that some unstated
authority justifies these pairings, that further research would reveal a
wondrously improbable plan (whether natural or not) hidden in the
list. Wilson's emphasis is on discovering the *necessary connection* between
these improbably paired objects (pins and needles ... thunder and
lightening), not in exposing the arbitrariness of an established episteme within which they are already embedded.

A similar love of portentous, quirky juxtaposition also propels
Dave Eggers's first novel *You Shall Know Our Velocity!* Eggers's *Velocity*
is a picaresque featuring two friends, Will and Hand, as they travel
the world trying to give away $32,000 in less than a week. Shortly
after the death of their friend Jack, Will receives a significant sum of
money, paid to him by a lightbulb manufacturer for the use of an
image of his silhouette (standing on a stepladder screwing in a lightbulb).[118] Hand, the primary vector of quirk in the novel, "a blond
man with swishy pants," wears a thrift-store-purchased "shirt
declaring I AM PROUD OF MY BLACK HERITAGE," the
back of which inexplicably reads "ROGERS PARK WOMEN'S
VOLLEYBALL."[119] When the two friends arrive at Senegal, Hand

hatches a plan to "tape money to donkeys . . . to their sides for their owners to find": "We wondered what the donkey-owners would think. What would they think? We had no idea. Money taped to a donkey? It was a great idea, we knew this" (94). Taping money to the side of a donkey is a "great idea," it seems, because it will simultaneously fulfill Hand and Will's ethical mission—to give away the money—and will do so in a way that generates surprise for the recipient of the money, not to mention a sense of aesthetic pleasure for the friends. Taping money to the side of a donkey spreads the quirkiness that Hand has long advocated. Will describes his friend this way:

> On and on, for twenty years I'd heard this shit [from Hand], from first grade . . . —and always this mixture of *the true, the almost-true and the apocryphal*—he'd veer within this *emporium of anecdote* like an angry drunk, but all of his stories he stood steadfastly behind never with a twinge of doubt or even allowances for your own. If you didn't know these things, you were willfully ignorant but not without hope.
>
> (52, my emphasis)

Proponents of this sort of quirky belief must neutralize doubt or skepticism. Those who argue against "the almost-true and the apocryphal" are, for the postironist, "willfully ignorant," a laity ripe for conversion. The journalist and philosopher Andrew Potter argues that the rise of quirkiness partly marks the breakdown of cool.[120] Potter draws attention to *Boing Boing*, a well-trafficked technology blog featuring the postcyberpunk author Cory Doctorow, as a special embodiment of quirkiness: "a 'directory of wonderful things' that gets well over 300,000 visitors a day. A typical week of entries will draw your attention to a video of a man dropping 20 kg of Silly Putty off a building, an archive of Soviet-era children's cartoons and a make-your-own-sex-toys blog. There's *no rhyme or reason to any of it, apart from that it is all, in its own quirky way, kinda neat.*"[121] Potter is correct that unusual juxtapositions are at the heart of quirky art, but he also wants to suggest that quirkiness has *displaced* the status-conscious practices of the hipster (and specifically Mailer's white negro), that to be quirky is not to care about the distinctions between insiders and outsiders, the hip and the square, counterculture and mainstream culture.[122]

But this interpretation is unconvincing. The desire to tape money to a Senegalese donkey originates not only from a love of "anti-logic" or a gentle enjoyment of the "random." Eggers's version of a quirky person revels in the shock of unusual juxtaposition, but also needs to police the borders of wonderland. As Hand's earlier description makes clear, the greatest threat to quirkiness is disbelief, snark, ingratitude, or disenchantment. The killjoy who opposes quirk says, "These things are not neat, not wonderful. Sorry, but I haven't undergone an experience of conversion at the MJT." For the great impresarios of quirkiness, the world is thus still divided between believers and disbelievers, those who "get it" and those who do not. This division of insiders and outsiders also crucially shapes the philanthropic project at the heart of *Velocity*'s plot. At one point in the novel, Will has an imaginary, guilt-ridden conversation with the brother of someone to whom he has given money.

> —You should not demand our money so coarsely.
> —You freely handed it to my brother.
> —That is the point. Freely. Of our volition.
> . . .
> —You want docility. You want me to appear indifferent to the money.
> . . .
> —You do more harm than good by choosing recipients this way. It cannot be fair.
> —How ever is it fair?
> (117–118)

Will feels guilty for having received the lightbulb money, does not want to donate this money to a charity, but still regards it as "our money" by right, to be handed out as he chooses. Will turns giving money away into a tortured game, where the criteria for worthy and unworthy recipients seem constantly to change. His anxious self-reflection often makes *Velocity* tedious to read, especially at moments when one suspects that the novel's various set pieces, which invariably involve Will and Hand failing to give away the money, are thinly disguised allegories of Eggers's own guilt regarding the money he earned after documenting his parents' death.

In the paperback edition of *Velocity*, adding yet another metafictional turn to the story, Hand "interrupts" Will's account to tell us that Will had not been beaten up in Jack's personal locker (a scene Will describes earlier in the book). We are told that Will *invented* their friend Jack, that Will's mother (who appears several times in the novel) has been dead for eight years, and that there was no proximate cause for their journey to give money away. Even the amount of money, $32,000, seems to be an invention. Will, we learn, has had the money for many years. "Our motivations," Hand writes, "were self-made and without tragic source" (269). Hand's section, called "An Interruption," theorizes the meaning and failures of Will's alterations of the "real" events of their story. Hand insists that the novel is about "economic disparity," that their story is "a rather neat and tidy allegory for any sort of intervention, whether by governments or neighbors—but mostly the idea of humanitarian aid, on whatever scale, micro or macro—from NGOs to panhandlers and passersby. The story, when we lived it, was about economics, and about desperation, and about inequity brought to levels that are untenable" (262, 274). Uncomfortable that they have money "simply because of the location of our birth," Will and Hand engage in what Hand calls "Performance Literature" and the "Conceptual Life" (275, 281, 283). Performance Literature is "performing in a book not yet written . . . traveling and interacting with the intent to write it down," "act[ing] in a way that would deserve documenting" (282). The Conceptual Life, meanwhile, is a mode of living in which one "sets forward ahead of time, certain goals and a framework within which he or she will live . . . The act of living, of eating and sleeping and defecating, is all included in the larger concept set forward—in this case, of living an elevated and observed life" (283). Both practices are grounded on the idea of observation, transforming one's daily existence into an aesthetic project, in the case of Hand or Will's invented version of Hand, into a quirky aesthetic project. The terms *Performance Literature* and *Conceptual Life* foreground what is unique about Eggers's version of the quirky: its emphasis on nonfictional metacommentary, fiction that approaches the condition of nonfiction, and the necessary infusion of life with a quirky, reenchanted sensibility as a precursor to philanthropic action. This philanthropic aesthetic has led Eggers to focus on journalistic writing (*What Is the What* and *Zeitoun*) and to open his network of walk-in tutoring centers. In 2002, Eggers opened the flagship storefront of this volunteering enterprise, 826 Valencia, in the Mission district of San Francisco. Above the entrance is a huge mural designed by the cartoonist Chris Ware. The storefront houses a pirate supply shop, clearly modeled on the MJT, where one might actually buy peg legs, eye patches, and other pirate-themed merchandise, along with various McSweeney's publications. Tutoring centers opened in other cities are designed as superhero supply stores, gangster supply stores, and so on. The 826 storefronts innovatively fuse retail, art, and philanthropy. They are educational institutions that use quirky style as a pedagogical tool, as part of a philanthropic exercise, and one can't help but wonder if students who stop in are (in addition to learning about writing) not also receiving an education in how to become quirky believers.

Weschler's own obsession with the MJT reaches something like a climax when he meets Wilson for lunch at "the little India Sweets and Spices mart, with its deli-style take-out counter." When Weschler enters the market and is "greeted by the familiar blast of sinuous aromas," he marvels at "such fresh vegetables as the eggplant-like brinjal, spiny kantola, beany valor, green tuver, tindora, lotus root, and chholia . . . all manner of teas and fragrant herbs (from coriander and cardamom through the curry powders); packaged ajwan seeds and Vicco brand vjradanti paste; curried arvi leaves, stuffed brinjal, karela in brine; enticing trapezoidal wedges of dessert cakes like the gold-and-silver-foil-laced almond barifs" (*Wonder* 98). In the presence of such aromatic and culinary "wonders," Weschler imagines what it must have been like for Europeans to encounter such exotic cuisine for the first time: *"We've got to get more of this stuff!"* Weschler's hypothetical European concludes. *"We've got to find an easier way of getting it! We've got to get ourselves over there! . . .* I felt like I was planted in the very engine room of history" (98). The "engine room of

history," in Weschler's astute account, is the *market*, its fuel the imperial desire for wonder-inducing "stuff." The impulse to surround
oneself with wondrous stuff, Weschler implies, promotes the ethos
of the quirky believer, and the "*orientation* toward wonder" that the
MJT attempts to cultivate (99, emphasis in original). The contemporary cabinet of curiosities, the postironic museum of wonder, is
zoned for retail. It is a marketplace whose wonderful stuff, if only for
a moment, excites the passion, commitment, and sense of wonder
that the End of History otherwise threatened to destroy.

Conclusion: Life, Art

In a *LIVE from the NYPL* event held on September 17, 2008—a conversation among James Wood, Daniel Mendelsohn, and Pico Iyer—
an audience member asked the panelists about their views on the
death of David Foster Wallace, who had committed suicide only
days before. The question: "Does one want to attempt to read the
death of David Foster Wallace, a suicide, as a literary gesture, or is
that just too distasteful a suggestion?" Wood replies that he feels
"sort of wrong even sort of commenting on this," but concludes that
Wallace's suicide was not a literary gesture. Mendelsohn is more
emphatic in his rejection of the premise behind the question: "I'm so
dumbfounded by the question I don't—I'm not sure what to say. The
only literary gesture is writing. It's the only—I don't know what it
means to be a literary—I just literally don't know what it means . . . I
can't comment on it because it seems sort of grotesque, I don't know
what to say."

These reactions are suitably decorous, and predictably enough
suggest that life and literature are qualitatively separate spheres, that
to read a life as if it were a text or as comprised of "gestures," is in
some sense perverse. Yet, at the end of this analysis, it seems to me
that Mendelsohn's claim that the "only literary gesture is writing"
misunderstands the seriousness with which Wallace approached his
work. On the most obvious level, near the end of his life, Wallace
found writing to be a difficult struggle, which led to considerable
personal pain and suffering, and which contributed to his decision to
stop taking the drug Nardil.[123] Moreover, Wallace's fiction is filled
with suicides and cripplingly depressed characters. In addition to the

suicide at the center of "Good Old Neon" and the suicide of James O. Incandenza by microwave oven in *Infinite Jest*, there is the minutely documented suffering of the narrator of "The Depressed Person" and a pantheon of damaged characters in *Brief Interviews with Hideous Men* and *Oblivion*. Taken as a whole, Wallace's oeuvre might be seen as a single long survey of the different forms individual human suffering can take in a postindustrial or postmodern society. Characters in Wallace's fiction constantly confront the paradoxes inherent in their suffering, and—tellingly—usually find psychological and pharmaceutical approaches to their problems unsatisfying or ineffective. Such remedies are invariably unable to attack the foundation of their discontents. These characters seek, instead, philosophical and literary solutions to the problem of personal survival, and more often than not fail to find what they are looking for.

The problem then is not that "reading" a life as literature debases life, but rather that to assume that one merely reads literature without having to take its conceptual commitments seriously—to assume that writing is merely a gesture—debases literature. Wallace, more than most contemporary novelists, insisted on the necessary link between life and literature, and in this sense he draws significantly on the legacy of the historical avant-garde and postmodernism. When Wallace writes, in his now widely quoted commencement address at Kenyon College, that "It is not the least bit coincidental that adults who commit suicide with firearms almost always shoot themselves in . . . the *head*," he means to illustrate "the real, no-bull-value of your liberal-arts education."[124] A liberal arts education can help "keep [you] from going through your comfortable, prosperous, respectable adult life dead, unconscious, a slave to your head and to your natural default-setting of being uniquely, completely, imperially alone, day in and day out." The idea that writing is a means of overcoming loneliness and the crippling effects of radical individualism is, as we've seen, a major motif of Wallace's writing, both in his fiction and his nonfiction. In these terms, his suicide might be taken not as a gesture or message but as an emblem of the failure of literature to solve certain kinds of problems. At the same time, we have seen that Wallace's approach to the relationship between life and art differs significantly from the historical avant-garde's. What separates Wallace from them is that Wallace seems uninterested in remaking society along any particular institutional or political economic lines. Wallace might, as Paul Giles argues, "mediate . . . the dynamics of globalization, subtly recording how the mass media impacts upon and interferes jarringly with the lives of American citizens," but Wallace's idea of politics, to the degree that he articulates one, rests squarely within a tradition of symbolic action and culturally oriented activism.[125] Recalling Raymond Williams's distinction between "alternative" and "oppositional" art, we must conclude that Wallace's style of postirony offers more of an *alternative art* than *oppositional art*, and by design.[126]

Wallace's brand of postirony, for all its power, was more concerned with overthrowing the rule of a particular type of person, the ironist, than with changing the institutional relations that facilitated the rise to this type. Put schematically, Wallace sought to defeat bad institutions that give rise to toxic incredulity by constructing a characterological model committed to belief rather than constructing a characterological model committed to challenging (let alone seizing) power. Because he did not focus on transforming postmodern institutions, Wallace may have been doomed to fail to achieve his aims in strictly literal terms.[127] Eggers, by contrast, seems to have understood the importance of constructing alternative institutions. Nonetheless, though Eggers has used his success to foster such institutions, he has not abandoned Wallace's concern with belief. On the contrary, Eggers and his McSweeney's associates have transformed the project of cultivating belief; they are less concerned with the capacity to believe as such and more interested in having readers believe in the goodness and sincerity not only of Eggers as an individual but also of the various enterprises that he has helped construct. They have together created a relatively optimistic ethos of belief that mixes a quirky aesthetic sensibility with an urge toward philanthropy and the active construction of alternative institutional structures (a publishing house, tutoring centers, a charitable foundation). Both dispositions—the characterological models constructed by Wallace and Eggers—are believers. Both authors similarly use metafiction to achieve their respective aims. But where Eggers wants to use nonfiction to make us quirky, to enchant (or more accurately reenchant) us, to inform us of and involve us in collective projects, Wallace uses fiction in what can often seem like a last desperate effort to make us believe something, to feel anything. Wallace hoped, of course, that achieving postirony would not rob his art of a critical or oppositional spirit (his antirebels were, after all, also rebels). In extending Wallace's project, however, McSweeney's has become something like a user-friendly avant-garde, an aesthetic establishment fundamentally integrated into the heart of hip urban areas zoned for retail. Such relatively modest institutional projects, though laudable, are clearly incapable of overcoming the depredations of the End of History. They are squarely (if anxiously) situated within market relations and within mainstream art-publicity economies. Such quirky projects are infrequently oppositional. Nonetheless, the difference between Wallace and Eggers suggests that the ethos of postirony can as easily promote projects of self-transformation as projects of institution building. What remains to be seen is whether postironic characterological models can be of any use in challenging the political-economic institutions that troubled Wallace and Eggers. To develop answers to this question, we will be required in Chapter 4 to look straight into the blinding face of cool.

4

The Work of the Coolhunter

IN A MARCH 1991 *Spy* magazine article, Lynda Edwards informed her readers that the irony of the 1980s would shortly be coming to an end. This prediction is made by Jean-Paul Dorat, "a rakish, pony-tailed, 27-year-old [trend] agent" who "says he's from France." Jean-Paul works the yuppie beat for the Paris-based trendspotting firm Éclat, which clients pay to identify consumer trends in advance of their mass adaptation, to "divine the coming Zeitgeist."[1] Like well-paid anthropologists schooled in cutting-edge critical theory, trend-spotters such as Jean-Paul haunt the streets, using their sharply honed hermeneutical skills as the basis for "trend books," which try to predict with flamboyant insight which colors and cars—and, unavoidably, which values and beliefs—we will prefer in the near future. As part of an "interdisciplinary strike force, flexible and mobile, structured to respond instantly to the first tremors of the socioeconomic and political seismograph," Jean-Paul and his fellow trendspotters are specially attuned to the collective movement of the market (40). Signs that the early nineties will move away from irony are visible at a number of levels. The attitudes of young Wall Street types, for instance, have been changing: "They use the words *good* and *bad* to describe colleagues," Jean-Paul observes. "That's new, since last year . . . It means value judgments." These "anxious young securities analysts" now tend to carry around novels with moral themes, "two Dickenses, a Hugo . . . , well, a Cheever." The move away from irony also leaves its mark at a sartorial level. "Do you know what really shocks me?" Jean-Paul asks Edwards. "There are no red ties anymore. Their ties are . . . *green!*" (41). Taken together, these phenomena signal a collective rejection of the rapacious hedonism and minimalist affects stereotypically associated with Reagan's America in favor of a more sincere—one is tempted to say a kinder and gentler—way of life. Jean-Paul concludes with confidence that there is a "trend away from irony . . . a trend towards heartfelt emotions and mysticism" (43). Irony's decline will "smash the complacent world of the grasping bourgeoisie . . . Social relations currently defined by the Hegelian cash nexus will be destroyed" (44). The upshot of this forthcoming cultural Apocalypse is that "women will dress like goddesses and angels," and consumers will prefer colors like "pale yellow, amethyst, azure, silver, gold, and arctic white" (44).

Even as she admits that trendspotting arose in response to real changes in the U.S. consumer economy, Edwards largely casts its practitioners as comical poseurs who deploy the jargon of critical theory to mystify their corporate clients. It is easy to ridicule Jean-Paul's grandiose pronouncements, but whatever our views on the seriousness or accuracy of his forecasts, trendspotting deserves serious analysis. On the one hand, by predicting irony's demise, Jean-Paul participated in the "Zeitgeist" whose collective movement he sought to forecast, drawing more attention to the problem of irony at a time when many began to question its value. On the other hand, we should note that Jean-Paul does not think to investigate how we might collectively feel about metaphor or zeugma, and for an apparently obvious reason: the declining popularity of irony—the shift from irony to postirony—matters to him and his clients only inasmuch as it signals or determines consumer behavior. But why should cultural attitudes toward irony shape consumption in the first place? Do ironists and postironists shop at different stores? How might "heartfelt emotions" (or perhaps merely the desire to feel them) influence the color of tie or style of novel one prefers? What would a postironic consumer culture look like?

A figure that has emerged in a version of global capitalism characterized by flexible accumulation, segmented markets, and the total branding of the lifeworld, the trendspotter works to answer these questions. Versions of the trendspotter appear in Alex Shakar's *The Savage Girl* (2001), William Gibson's *Pattern Recognition* (2003), and Jennifer Egan's *A Visit from the Goon Squad* (2010), novels that dramatize the aesthetic dilemmas that confront consumers and artists in advanced capitalist societies. In his novel, drawing on a term popularized by Malcolm Gladwell, Gibson uses the term *coolhunter* instead of *trendspotter*. I will use both terms interchangeably, although the change of name is significant inasmuch as a coolhunter seems to make a weaker claim about her predictive powers. Whereas Shakar's trendspotter has a future-oriented relationship to cool (hoping to predict what will become trendy in an imagined future), Gibson's coolhunter sees cool in spatial terms (mapping existing planetary distributions of cool). Egan, meanwhile, doesn't use either term, but nonetheless imagines a near future in which the advanced understanding and manipulation of cool leads to the rise of a postironic youth culture. Despite their differences, these novels demonstrate that the relationship between postirony and the trendspotter / coolhunter is not accidental or circumstantial, but rather that the trendspotter / coolhunter is essentially a postironic figure, a schismatic type of person charged with somehow synthesizing detachment and investment, the market and meaning, the statistical and the personal, and irony and commitment. In an economic milieu where seemingly no cultural practice is too extreme for the market to assimilate, no demographic group safe from corporate manipulation, these novels try to imagine an oppositional ethos capable of synthesizing the desire for authenticity, a desire formulated using the vocabulary of Romanticism, with the fear that authenticity is impossible under the globalizing regimes of modular production, cut-and-paste aesthetics, and postmodern lifestyles. How the trendspotter / coolhunter succeeds and fails at such a synthesis is the subject of this chapter.

Fictionaries of the Future

Trendspotting has received much journalistic attention in the past twenty-five years, but scholarly writing on this practice remains relatively sparse.[2] Though its origins are not well documented, the practice can be traced back to the work of John E. Merriam, head of the World Bank's Department of Information and Public Affairs, who created the National Media Index in the 1970s to track patterns of media coverage.³ Throughout the sixties and seventies, independently of Merriam, a number of fashion-oriented "trend shops" opened in New York and Paris.⁴ John Naisbitt's influential *Megatrends* (1982) brought increased attention to trendspotting, practically inventing a genre of marketing book that, above all, has found many creative ways of incorporating the word "trend" into its titles. In the 1980s and 1990s, trendspotting became a common means by which corporations tried, with various degrees of success, to connect culturally with their customers and, more importantly, to predict changes in consumer tastes, preferences, and values. A relatively new type of cool professional in the culture industry, the trendspotter or coolhunter offers her clients "a window on the world of the street" by finding producers of cool and predicting how newly cool ideas, practices, and objects will spread throughout the larger population. To document this process, Malcolm Gladwell's well-known *New Yorker* article and his book *The Tipping Point* ultimately appeal to such diverse technical domains as diffusion research, epidemiological modeling, and even variations on "meme theory." Put simply, Gladwell's coolhunters help their corporate clients commodify the aesthetic, ethical, and social preferences that shape consumer behavior. Most contemporary trendspotters justify their salaries by claiming that the future already exists in "the progressive microcultures of the streets" and "not in the masses."⁵ Throughout the 1990s, journalistic accounts reinforced this claim, often depicting trendspotters or coolhunters as radical mavericks, tattooed and pierced rebels of the New Economy, streetwise individuals so tapped in to the raw energies of the Zeitgeist that large and saurian megacorporations could never hope to capture market share without a hip helping hand. Only well-coifed trendspotters, insiders to the "alternative" scene, have the cultural expertise to "uncover [the] belief systems" of "progressive thinkers and doers—young street designers, club promoters, DJs, web developers, filmmakers, electronic musicians."⁶

A favorite trendspotter to profile has been Faith Popcorn, whom *Fortune* magazine once called the "Nostradamus of consumer marketing."[7] Popcorn helped found BrainReserve in 1974 and has made a career of trading in on her unusual name and status as, if not the first, then certainly the world's most written-about trendspotter. She has even appeared as a character in James P. Othmer's satirical novel *The Futurist* (2006). Popcorn has published a number of books, the most noteworthy of which, for the purposes of literary analysis, is her *Dictionary of the Future* (2001). Popcorn and her coauthor, Adam Hanft, cast themselves here as "linguistic prospectors and anticipators" in search of "words and terms that are so new they are barely cracking out of their chrysalis, as well as others that are poking tentatively out of their cocoons."[8] The authors do not merely document newly minted words but also invent neologisms when they find "voids in the language that needed to be filled."[9] Popcorn and Hanft invoke the "unrepentant serial coiner" Sir Thomas Elyot, pointing out that the early modern scholar created many neologisms, and they ultimately justify their trendspotting dictionary by suggesting that "language is our most obvious (and meaningful) monitor of . . . cultural and technological flux."[10] *The Dictionary of the Future* finally invites its readers to "become sharper observers, more engaged participants—perhaps even predictors— . . . of the world we will come to inhabit," suggesting not only that we learn about our near future but that we model a certain carefully attentive relationship to it, becoming ourselves something like trendspotters.[11]

We should reject the overblown (and now obsolete) New Economy rhetoric that celebrates trendspotters for their rebellious nonconformity. Whatever else they may be, trendspotters are professional marketers who serve the needs of their clients. Whimsical hair and funny names sugarcoat their essential purpose, which is to engage in cool arbitrage, capitalizing on the time lag between the production and distribution of cool. Nonetheless, we should also take seriously the *Dictionary of the Future*'s call to adopt a certain relationship to the imminent future. The importance of the trendspotter transcends her economic function. Unserious figures such as Faith Popcorn demand serious analysis not because of their supposed statistical acumen or marketing savvy—real-world trendspotters are bad futurologists— but because their ability to forecast cultural trends has so often been treated as a disposition or ethos, which we might all emulate.

Unlike those more rigorous trendspotters who use focus groups, market research, consumer surveys, and statistical models as the basis for their predictions, novelistic trendspotters tend to work alone. The trendspotter is imagined to be more like a freelance artist or critical theorist than like a professional researcher or sociologist of culture.

In many contemporary novels, the trendspotter, the overscheduled heir apparent of the *flâneur*, becomes much more than a job title or occupational choice: she becomes instead the hermeneutic disposition of a postironic figure. As an embodied node or switching station through which cool flows, the trendspotter is a sort of New Man, though more often than not figured as a woman. The trendspotter's gender is not incidental. Andreas Huyssen has observed that "mass culture has always been the hidden subtext of the modernist project," and that modernism has tended to imagine mass culture in pejoratively feminized terms.[12] The association between women and the mass culture has, it is clear, survived beyond modernism. Advertising executive David Ogilvy's much-quoted adage "the consumer isn't a moron, she is your wife" captures the persistence of this association neatly, and when juxtaposed with the marketing science of psychographics strongly underscores the complex connections among cultural values, identity, and consumer behavior.[13] For Shakar, Gibson, and Egan, modernism's "hidden subtext of" mass culture and the association of mass culture with female-gendered dispositions are no longer hidden.[14] Another reason gender comes to the fore in these narratives might be because historically gender-specific forms of affective and immaterial labor, the unpaid labor of social reproduction, have been increasingly integrated into production.[15] As Sianne Ngai notes in her analysis of zaniness as an aesthetic category, under the regime of immaterial and affective labor "the labor of social reproduction finally seems to stand a chance of appearing as what it really is"—that is, as labor.[16] At a post-Fordist moment, the zany's "incessant doing" indexes "a precariousness created specifically by the capitalist organization of work" and evinces "a politically ambiguous erosion of the distinction between playing and working."[17] Moreover, affective, relational, and immaterial labor regimes depend on "the steady growth in numbers of women in the waged workforce around the globe."[18] Though by no means a worker of the Global South, the female trendspotter nonetheless is often imagined to have the special capacity to imaginatively apprehend—to recognize her inextricable connection to—her laboring counterparts down the production supply chain. And within her own overdeveloped economic zone, the trendspotter both embodies the traditional association of women with consumption and also, under the banner of immaterial or affective labor, complicates it by being both a producer and a consumer of culture, a type of person that paradoxically tries to escape the analysis of the psychographic profiler and in so doing simultaneously does the "caring work" of building a sensitive, accurate psychographic profile of herself.[19] The trendspotter finally participates in a sexual division of labor by virtue of her class position as a freelancer.[20] In the problematic terms that the sociologist Richard Florida develops in *The Rise of the Creative Class*, it's not clear whether the trendspotter is a "creative worker" or a "service worker."[21] We might say that the trendspotter is a service worker who has been informed that she is a creative worker, like the mostly female hairdressers and cosmetologists Florida celebrates in nearly the same terms as professors, corporate lawyers, and transplant surgeons.[22] It would be more accurate to say that the trendspotter is what Luc Boltanski and Ève Chiapello call the "*network-extender*," their name for the "great man in the projective city," a figure "who is mobile, streamlined, possessed of the art of establishing and maintaining numerous diverse, enriching connections, and of the ability to extend networks."[23] The trendspotter is a bad professional not only because of the failed rigor of her methods of market analysis, but also because she is not exactly a member of the professional-managerial class to begin with. She is, instead, a freelancer, an independent owner and manager of her so-called human capital, someone who is charged with the task of profitably harnessing her own affects, talents, and capacities as part of a set of commercialized spiritual exercises.[24] We might call this imagined practice of freelancer self-management *autoreification*.[25] It is what every freelancer is told to do: brand yourself or starve.

Interrogating the paradox of autoreification, and adding to a tradition that studies the characterological dimensions of economic life, *The Savage Girl, Pattern Recognition*, and *A Visit from the Goon Squad* assess and try to imagine alternatives to what one critic has called the "advertised life," "an emergent mode of being in which advertising not only occupies every last negotiable public terrain, but in which it penetrates the cognitive process, invading consciousness."[26] The authors of these works use narrative techniques associated with science fiction to model worlds that have become largely colonized by advertisements and branded proper nouns, worlds where the market and everyday life have become increasingly difficult to analytically disentangle, where adopting the pose of a trendspotter or coolhunter might be an essential strategy for getting through the day. These books should thus be classified as sorts of "socioeconomic science fiction," a growing subgenre that not only criticizes economic and marketing theories but also uses these theories as the basis for exercises in world building.[27] The SF "novum" of these novels is not a technology but rather a new type of person, a new type of worker, who must arbitrate between, on one hand, the Bohemian impulse to develop distinct stylistic codes as a means of separating oneself from the market and, on the other, the seemingly unlimited power of the market to decode and commodify individual style.[28]

Such literary critiques are nothing new, perhaps originating with W. E. Woodward's attack on capitalist bunkum, *Bunk* (1923)—from which the term *debunk* originates—or Nathanael West's Hollywood satire, *The Day of the Locust* (1939). In the fifties, Frederik Pohl and C. M. Kornbuth's classic science fiction novel *The Space Merchants* (1952) and Sloan Wilson's novel *The Man in the Gray Flannel Suit* (1955) engaged in energetic debates over the value of mass consumption and the effects of advertising and public relations on public life, acting something like literary analogues to many popular nonfiction accounts, such as William H. White's *The Organization Man* (1956) and Vance Packard's *The Hidden Persuaders* (1957). We could easily read Bret Easton Ellis's *American Psycho* (1991) as a kind of literary psychographic analysis of the yuppie as a character type. Even David Foster Wallace, who was no fan of *American Psycho*, resembles Ellis in deploying the language of marketing across his fiction and essays, quite unoriginally, to criticize America's bunkum consumer culture. When in "Westward the Course of Empire Takes Its Way" (1989) Wallace implies that the character Professor Ambrose, based on John Barth, may be selling out by launching a *Lost in the Funhouse* discotheque franchise, this must be understood as an insult. What differentiates *The Savage Girl, Pattern Recognition,* and *A Visit from the Goon Squad* from these earlier texts is their recognition that the differentiating logic of market segmentation can turn back upon those who define themselves against that logic.[29] Anyone coming to these novels expecting a standard critique of marketing will make a few surprising discoveries. First, reification does not corrode authenticity, or falsify some underlying reality. Instead, reified cultural values often constitute the "real" thing. Second, cultural values invented as a means of resisting commodification are necessarily in accord with market segmentation. Combating reification through stylistic self-cultivation is not difficult but rather internally contradictory. Such self-cultivation may motivate political action, anticapitalist or otherwise, but can never in itself resist capitalism without further action. Nonetheless, achieving these insights does not placate the fear that commodification leeches countercultural practices of their oppositional "cutting edge."[30] The desire for what I would term an unco-optable cultural practice remains fully intact.

The Unco-optable

Alex Shakar's first novel, *The Savage Girl,* tells the story of Ursula Van Urden, a failed painter who comes to the fictional major metropolis Middle City in order to care for her schizophrenic sister Ivy, a second-rate model who has recently had a public breakdown in Banister Park. When she first arrives in the city, Ursula applies for a job as a trendspotter at Tomorrow, Ltd., a small firm owned by Chas Lacouture, Ivy's former lover, a Mephistophelian figure who may or may not have contributed to her mental collapse. Middle City is built on the slope of a dormant volcano ringed with skyscrapers and comes across as a vaguely surrealistic hybrid of New York, Chicago, and Austin, Texas.[31] Middle City's parks and public monuments are named, for reasons that remain unexplained, to honor obscure Cold War intelligence operatives such as Guy Banister, Felix

Rodriguez, and Richard W. Held. Maheu Square features the "Museum of Postmodern Art" and the South Slope Mall is home to the "Postmodern Torse of Schwarzenegger Gymnasium," suggesting that (at least in the world of the novel) postmodern aesthetic values have fully penetrated the spheres of art and commerce respectively.[32] This self-consciously postmodern metropolis is populated by characters who oscillate between psychological roundness and cartoonish flatness, characters who seem at times to have substantial inner lives and at others times to understand themselves in terms of stereotyped images. Two of the novel's main characters, for example, are described as "Granite Man and his sidekick, Rubber Man . . . two lurking, smirking, life-size action figures of themselves" (18). Within this postmodern world, Ursula must navigate between her desire for authentic oppositional meanings and a segmented marketplace seemingly capable of absorbing all meanings. Her training as a trendspotter promises to equip her to strike this balance. Much like their counterparts in Edwards's *Spy* article, Shakar's trendspotters "read the future in the color of ties and the flavors of snack food and the lyrics to pop songs" (30–31). Shakar frequently admits his debt to Edwards, not only by mentioning her in his acknowledgements, but also by basing many of his novel's key passages and situations directly on her article.[33] Most notably, Shakar's trendspotters, like Jean-Paul, identify "postirony" as a forthcoming "megatrend" in the consumer culture of the novel's imagined world. As *The Savage Girl* proceeds, the term *postirony* and the contest over its meaning takes on great importance, both within the novel's imagined world and, in a metafictional turn, as a paradigm for how to interpret the novel itself. In this way, *The Savage Girl* is another salvo in a barrage of writings that took note of the declining cultural value of irony and participated in the discourse of postirony.

   The discourse of postirony was part of a media effort to "name the nineties," in anticipation of the new century.[34] In a campaign developed for *Good Housekeeping*, Faith Popcorn foretold that the nineties would be the "Decency Decade," the decade when the "good guys finally win."[35] As early as 1989, even *Spy*—a magazine famous for its corrosive irony—took up arms against the offending trope. In their article, "The Irony Epidemic," Paul Rudnick and *Spy* cofounder

Kurt Andersen dissected "the era of the permanent smirk, the knowing chuckle, of jokey ambivalence as a way of life," concluding decisively that irony had degenerated from its noble origins into mass kitsch or, to use their term, "Camp Lite."[36] A few years later, as discussed in Chapter 3, David Foster Wallace condemned post-modern irony in "E Unibus Pluram: Television and U.S. Fiction" in the *Review of Contemporary Fiction* and, in an interview with Larry McCaffery, rejected satires such as Bret Easton Ellis's *American Psycho*. The problem with ironic critique, Wallace argued in his essay, was that "TV has coopted the distinctive forms of the same cynical, irreverent, ironic, absurdist post-WWII literature that the new Imagists [that is, late postmodernists] use as touchstones."[37] In London, Toby Young further developed this line of reasoning, arguing in his review of Ben Stiller's film *Reality Bites* (1994) that "the problem faced by Stiller is that, having decided to exploit a genera-tion for commercial purposes, he has to prevent this from alienating the audience it's intended to exploit."[38] Stiller's solution to this problem is to use the irony popular with members of Generation X.[39] Under circumstances in which "everyone stands around winking and nudging," Tom Vanderbilt came to wonder in a 1995 *Baffler* article, "why does no one see fit to question irony itself?"[40]

From the evidence presented here, it is clear that a great number of people were questioning "irony itself." Although their interests differed, these authors largely agreed that irony once had a genu-inely oppositional purpose, but had somehow lost its "cutting edge."[41] They all tacitly accept what Thomas Frank has called the "co-optation theory," the claim that by systematically commodifying authentic forms of countercultural resistance, commercial interests neutralize the revolutionary power of oppositional style.[42] Previously radical lifestyles are turned into "mass-produced fake counterculture," thus subverting "the great threat that 'real' counterculture represents."[43] For Frank, the co-optation theory is the explanatory lynchpin of a version of cultural studies that celebrates creative consumption and symbolic rebellion as a source of genuine freedom. Dick Hebdige has given perhaps the most enduring account of how, in the absence of real social power, a safety pin, a simple gesture, an ironic sneer, or sartorial style "signals a Refusal."[44] The celebration of the subversive or ironic appropriation of consumer products has a long history, ranging from the historical avant-garde up through more recent cultural criticism. For some critics, the gravest threat to a particular style's power to Refuse comes from the absorption and reproduction of the cultural codes by which stylistic dissenters distinguish themselves. Other critics, who avowedly reject the "conspiratorial view of 'mass culture,'" nonetheless have recognized that popular culture can incorporate "popular perceptions, aspirations, and resentments" as a strategy for maintaining existing authority structures, though they also warn that the critic should not therefore discount "the market of popular meanings."[45] Though such accounts have sought to move beyond simplistic notions of mass society and to overcome the urge to "attribute any purity of political expression to popular culture," they seem unable to avoid invoking a dialectic of rebellion and incorporation.[46]

The problem for these critics is to be found not with irony *in itself* but rather with irony in its incorporated form. Having "seized upon irony as the cultural in-joke of the century," corporations now use ironic ads to sell their products.[47] Power now embraces hip irony as something like its official style. The market has stabilized irony into a postmodern or blank form, blocking up or reifying the playful and formerly subversive permanent parabasis of meaning Paul de Man once described.[48] More insidious than the forms of stylistic co-optation that modernists and the historical avant-garde feared, this new hegemony of irony is troubling because it feels unsurpassable. Irony's commodification—its transformation from a means of radical Refusal into just another variable in the profile of your personality—threatens something like the endgame of counterculture as such. For how, Young wonders, "do you ironically distance yourself from the irony tag without confirming its truth? How do you wriggle out of a pigeonhole if the pigeonhole you're in is reserved for those who don't like to be pigeonholed?" Young finds himself tragically flummoxed and cannot "imagine what a post-ironic sensibility would be like."[49] For his part, Shakar has said that he "wanted to address how irony—a tool satirists use to critique our culture—has been co-opted by the advertising industry."[50] How, in other words, do you write a satire that opposes a marketing industry and a consumer culture that embrace irony and satire without reservation? In expressing their fear of co-optation, these critics (and Shakar) share what Huyssen has described as the modernist's "nightmare of being devoured by mass culture through co-optation, commodification, and the 'wrong' kind of success."[51] These postironists update for a new era the oppositional logic of the counterculture. Calls for postirony express a desire not for a return to sincerity or earnestness, but rather for the unco-optable, an ethos or sensibility that, in its constitution, can never lose its oppositional flavor. A desire for the unco-optable is a specimen of what Michael Clune describes as "the ideal art object of the Romantic tradition," an "object that successfully counters habituation, that never gets old."[52] Postironists desire an art object that never loses its cool.

In *The Savage Girl*, the struggle for unco-optable meanings takes the narrative form of a conflict for control over the meaning of the word *postirony* itself. By imagining a battle to semantically capture *postirony*, Shakar builds at the level of plot a toy model of what can happen to oppositional words and meanings under the regime of segmented markets. Although he is not the first person to use the word, Shakar treats *postirony* as if it were a science-fictional novum. Throughout his novel, marketing neologisms perform the role that technical neologisms play in traditional science fiction. The lexical status of *postirony* remains ambiguous, because *The Savage Girl* feels semantically self-contained in its narrative concerns while simultaneously referring outward to a more familiar world. Proper names such as " 'N Sync," "Ricky Martin," and "Arnold Schwarzenegger" index the novel as taking place in a world partly coextensive with our own, likely during the late 1990s or early 2000s. Like its characters, who behave at once like people and the embodied psychographic profiles of people, the projected world of the novel appears both grounded in and apart from our reality. The word *postirony* simultaneously points toward the fictional Middle City and toward a world we might consider our own.

As a frontline soldier in the war to assimilate oppositional meanings into mass-consumable form, the trendspotter poses a unique problem for the desire for unco-optable art. Her job is to co-opt anything that seems unco-optable. Yet the trendspotter often evinces the same countercultural desire as those who fear co-optation. As Frank's *The Conquest of Cool* argues, revolutions internal to the advertising and fashion industries developed during the 1960s independently of the historical counterculture. "Far from oppose the larger cultural revolution of those years," Frank claims, "the business revolution paralleled—and in some cases actually anticipated—the impulses and new values associated with the counterculture."[53] On this view, countercultural movements and the advertising industry were not necessarily ideological opponents, but rather natural allies in the campaign to segment the mass marketplace into myriad demographically distinct (and, it turns out, highly profitable) pieces.[54] Put in Clune's terms, both countercultural rebels and advertisers desperately fear incorporation and habituation. Both pine for a special kind of magical object that can defeat the corrosive power of time. But in their studious attention to the faintest signs of co-optation, both actually *accelerate* the process they most fear. In such an economy, the punk question that dominated Chapter 2—how to avoid selling out—transforms into a fear that Refusal itself is a kind of selling out. Shakar reproduces long passages almost verbatim from *The Conquest of Cool* in his novel. But even as he cites Frank, Shakar seems finally to argue that even if Frank is correct, the desire for unco-optable cultural practices and meanings cannot be so easily dissolved by critique. Such desires cannot be rationally argued away and thus will persist in shaping individual and collective patterns of consumer behavior. Under the regime of segmented markets, your pursuit of an un-coptable thought, practice, or object will not only necessarily fail but will also only reinforce your desire to intensify the pursuit. It is under these complicated circumstances that *The Savage Girl* stages the battle for control over the word *postirony*, suggesting that we might need to become something like trendspotters to navigate these paradoxes.

The Cultural Economy of Postirony

The word *postirony* is first mentioned in *The Savage Girl* by Javier Delreal—a trendspotter at Tomorrow, Ltd.—in reference to a young girl who is called "the savage girl," an "urban savage" that Ursula has discovered living in Bannister Park. Over the course of the novel, Ursula sees the filthy savage girl eating rodents and pigeons that she hunts on the street, clothing herself in a patchwork of discarded garments and animal skins, and bartering with other urban punks and drifters. That the girl wears the aggregation of many scavenged products is in one sense a perfect embodiment of punk's D.I.Y. ethos. "Her pants are from some defunct Eastern European army . . . Her shins are wrapped in bands of pelt . . . Her feet are shod in moccasins . . . There is a metal barb about the size of a crochet needle stuck through her earlobe, and a length of slender chain hangs from her scalp" (3). Ursula imagines that the girl "communicates only by means of whistles, clicks of the tongue, or tattoos stamped out on the cobblestones" (4). At first, it's not entirely clear how the label *postirony* applies to the girl, at least as Javier uses it. For Javier, postirony "means a kind of new earnestness where, by overcoming their ironic doubt, people will be able to customize their beliefs just like they would the rest of their purchases."[55] "[N]iche marketing is getting really sophisticated now," he explains to Ursula. "We can subscribe to even-more-personalized newspapers, magazines, satellite channels, clothing catalogs. We can pop in a CD-ROM and learn how to practice Sufism or Swedenborgianism or Santería" (24).

What distinguishes Javier's view from standard accounts of how market diversity affects identity is his introduction of the dimension of belief, his invocation of what Pierre Hadot calls *spiritual exercises* (practices such as Sufism, Swedenborgianism, Santería). Postirony is a new mode of imagined solidarity, an aspirational, collective form of identification. Javier thinks that "we're on the cusp of something really wonderful" and that market segmentation will lead to "[a] renaissance of self-creation" (24). In this era of self-creation, which he calls the "Light Age," "we'll be able to totally customize our life experience—our beliefs, our rituals, our tribes, our whole personal mythology—and we'll choose everything that makes us who we are from a vast array of choices. The last barrier is our persistent irony, which fills us with doubts about the validity of our relative truths" (24). For Javier, the postironist has achieved something like an ironic faith, a belief in contingent truths, similar to the ironic belief I discuss in Chapter 3. Javier, "his grown man's face as open and earnest as a child's," himself embodies a relentlessly positive interpretation of postirony, as well as an unsurprising predilection for the quirky. He has "[a]pparently . . . transcended this last barrier of which he speaks" (24). He's the type of person who believes that certain kinds of outfits can "lead to trade agreements with North Korea," that a nicely designed sweater will result in the signing of "international peace accords" (109).

Ursula's boss, Chas, has a more cynical view of postirony. While training her to be a trendspotter, Chas asks Ursula to "[l]ook around . . . How many of these people do you think ever get to experience a great passion, a great love, a great cause? A product can stand in for those experiences. A surface can stand in for the depths most people will never know" (63).[56] For Chas, consumers seek out symbolic rebellion, surrogate experiences, and simulated emotions. The job of the marketer is to stoke symbolic rebellion or escape. Advertisers are purveyors not of *information* but of *meaning*.[57] Based on this view, Chas reframes Javier's concept of *postirony* in a presentation to his corporate clients, who are manufacturing a form of diet or "Lite" water. Chas, a former philosophy professor, presents his marketing maxims in the language of critical theory—a full-blooded antihumanism over against Javier's more cheerfully pragmatist attitude toward irony and contingency. For Chas, postirony is the logical outcome of postmodernity. Alluding to *The Conquest of Cool*, Chas gives an account of the rise of ironic advertising—focusing on DDB adman Bill Bernbach's famous "anti-advertising" campaign for the Volkswagen Beetle—and suggests that "postironic consciousness is the beginning of nothing less than the next step forward in the evolution of consumer culture," consumerism's apocalyptic endgame (174). Chas renames the "Light Age" as the "Lite Age," as a means of synchronizing Javier's concept with the ad campaign for diet water. "Through consumption [in the postironic age]," Chas argues, "consumers will be gods; outside of consumption they will be nothing: a perpetual oscillation between absolute control and absolute vulnerability, between grandeur and persecution (175). Javier reacts to the perversion of his positive conception of postirony by quitting his job. Crestfallen, he creates a new theory of consumerism as a "conspiracy against the children."[58] Chas and James T. Couch (another trendspotter) like the sound of Javier's "conspiracy against the children" so much that they draft plans to commodify the conspiracy. They craft a marketing strategy that would help children subvert "the brand imaging that surrounds them by wearing meaningless insignias instead of product slogans and corporate logos," ultimately diverting rebellion "back into the currents of the revenue stream" (180–181). Shakar's satire is unsubtle.

For her part, Ursula oscillates in her view of postirony, seeming at different times in the thrall of Javier and Chas. Eventually classifying the savage girl as part of some new kind of authentic urban tribe, Ursula evokes Hebdige's punks. "She's sick of modernity," Ursula decides late in the novel, "sick of all the cynicism in our culture that passes for sophistication. She tries to live authentically, honestly. She tries to live simply, in tune with the earth" (119). Because her so-called way of life seems to reject the trappings of consumerism and cynicism, the savage girl is postironic, but not in the manner described by Javier and Chas, who both seem to accept the market's beneficence. Ursula imagines that the marketing campaign she is creating for Lite Water will somehow plant the seeds of resistance to consumer culture, although she never articulates what shape this resistance might take. Ursula's attempt to commodify the image of the savage girl in order to spread an anticonsumerist message quickly backfires. Ursula finds one day that, perhaps in response to the "savage" trend that has taken Middle City by storm, the savage girl has mutilated herself unrecognizably, conceivably as a way of further distinguishing herself from the masses. By the novel's end, Chas's ideas seem to have won the day, his interpretation of postirony final. Javier makes arrangements to have himself cryogenically frozen and commits suicide, hoping to be reawakened in some better future. Despite Javier's optimistic faith in the populist market and Ursula's belief in its oppositional power, postirony becomes the official style of (extremely late) capitalism.

Despite Chas's apparent final victory, the meaning of postirony remains very much in doubt, both inside the novel's narrative world and for us. In the novel's epilogue, Ursula travels with her sister

Ivy to the Amazon to collect and store rainforest specimens as part of a project designed to preserve endangered genomes. The project, run by a for-profit company called Ark, Inc., justifies its activities on the basis of its hope that "[i]n the future there will be . . . an enormous robot . . . with a built-in library containing every known gene, a built-in nanogarage full of nanoforklifts, nanocranes, nanobulldozers, nano-arc welders," which will be able to rebuild the rainforest for the highest bidder. Breaking into an almost fully science-fictional rhetorical mode, Shakar's satire becomes importantly ambiguous. Is Ark, Inc., an example of for-profit opportunism (a commodification of ecological destruction, a grotesque futures market for extinct genomes) or a viable vision for a better tomorrow? At this moment of postironic indecision, Shakar refuses to choose. His unwillingness to resolve this interpretive crux invites his readers to confront an ethical aporia. We are simultaneously aware of the undecidability of the question and the urgent need to decide. Shakar's epilogue gives us a second, similar interpretive dilemma: While in the jungle, Ursula meets a multinational group that has made an effort to revive the practices and way of life of the Yanomama tribe. Unlike the neo-Yanomama emulators, the original ethnic Yanomama live in nearby shantytowns, and "[t]he only remaining bright spot in their lives is when one of the neo-Yanomama . . . emerges from the jungle seeking authentic folklore, herbal remedies, food sources, and, especially, ritual ceremonies" (270). The neotribalists initially seem to be an easy target for satire, but Shakar reaffirms Javier's optimistic postirony. "Until recently," Shakar writes, "Ursula didn't think people could assemble their own religions and go on to invest in them even the slightest amount of actual belief. But observational evidence, it seems, is proving her wrong" (274). In a work of science fiction, as in all fiction, "observational evidence" is never neutral or merely factual. In this case, what constitutes observational evidence is evidence of authorial intervention. Ursula inhabits the sort of world in which ironic belief—Javier's postirony—*is theoretically possible*, even if the neo-Yanomama themselves seem silly.

The novel ends with a memory of Ursula, Chas, and James T. Couch conducting their own invented ritual, intoning trends they have recently spotted and starting their own small ironic religion over the metal cylinder that contains Javier's body. Shakar presents Javier as an ironically Christlike figure whose personality outlives him and the promise of whose return foretells some new, better-made future. Shakar projects his hope for a genuine postirony onto some future era, with its nanoforklifts and nanobulldozers. The image of the preservation chamber suggests why Shakar does not fix his views of Ark, Inc., and the neo-Yanomama. Shakar will not tell us what to think about these aspects of his fictive world because their ultimate meanings depend not on their stated aspirations but rather on their still-unknown consequences, on the sort of future they might help, or fail to, bring about. In the face of the undecidability of the meaning of the present, its crucial dependency on a time that does not yet exist, the *unco-optable* becomes synonymous with the future's inexhaustible capacity to create surprise and delight, which is the dialectical counterpart of the present's unlimited capacity to become commodity, habit, and routine. If unco-optable hope can only be found in the future, one must become a trendspotter in order to achieve anything resembling postironic belief. Only the trend-spotter's hyperawareness of the market, cultivated foresight, and Romantic enthusiasm can help one not only foresee but also partici-pate in building the next Zeitgeist.

Postironic Satires

Throughout the previous sections, I have attributed to *The Savage Girl* propositional content. Would treating this novel as a species of theory constitute a category mistake, a confusion of fictional views for nonfictional argument? I want to conclude by justifying my approach, while differentiating it from Steven Shaviro's argument about the novel. Shaviro claims that "Shakar suggests that postirony is the universal attitude of the contemporary consumer. None of us can evade it. Postirony is our most basic form of belief, our American religion."[59] Many reviewers have similarly described postirony as the universal plight of the American consumer, failing to note that Shakar always attributes definitions of postirony to characters, whose views differ substantially, sometimes irreconcilably. Shakar has said that he "purposely left the definition [of postirony] . . .

nebulous," although in every case "it has something to do with . . .
the sense that irony and earnestness are combined in a way where
you don't know whether you're being ironic or earnest and, moreover, the distinction ceases to matter."[60] Why, then, does *The Savage
Girl* seem not only to be fiction but also theory? Part of the answer
must lie in Shakar's ambiguous use of satire, a genre that frequently uses stable irony in the service of critique. Claire Colebrook
claims that "[t]he task of a post-ironic ethics cannot be a return to
satire" because of the impossibility of gaining critical distance or
purchase over the world from which to criticize it, and yet Shakar
does invoke satire.[61] In a standard satire, we are asked to infer the
author's attitude toward represented events by translating textual
ironies, exaggerations, and reductios into propositional statements
about the world. If *The Savage Girl* is a satire, then critics such as
Shaviro would be correct to deduce that Shakar supports some characters while condemning others. Alternatively, if Shakar has not
written a satire, then his theoretical commitments cannot be so easily
decided, and critics may have confused a character's fictive beliefs for
the author's.

The true difficulty here is not how to reconstruct Shakar's beliefs,
but rather how to explain his novel's style. The problem is that many
characters speak in fully formed and theoretically sophisticated sentences. For example, Ursula comes to realize that

> she doesn't necessarily have to feel bad about giving people
> what they want; that contradictions help people cope; that what
> Chas thinks of as the 'broken soul' of a product, if you look at it
> in a more forgiving light, might just as easily be called its magic,
> its power to suspend antinomies, to let the consumer have it
> both ways and every way . . . buying a new pair of sneakers not
> only to grip the earth but to soar in the air . . . Bridging with
> one bold leap of imagination body and spirit, dream and respon-
> sibility, phenomena and noumena. (101)

Even when characters disagree with one another, they all speak and
think this way, using words like "antinomy" and "noumena" with
ease, far more often dissertating on rather than discussing their

fictive world and its myriad problems. It's not surprising then that Shaviro and other critics treat the novel as theory. *The Savage Girl* often reads like it.

Shakar's theoretical or academic style might be explained by the fact that Chas is an ex-professor who has transformed his cultural theories into marketing gold. Apart from his views on postirony, Chas bases his general theory of consumer motivation around another Shakar neologism, the "paradessence" or "paradoxical essence" of a commodity. According to Chas, consumers are drawn to the paradessence of a commodity, the two irreconcilable promises that it makes, the way it symbolically cultivates such social aporias.

> The paradessence of coffee is stimulation and relaxation. Every successful ad campaign for coffee will promise both of those mutually exclusive states . . . That's what consumer motivation is about . . . Every product has this paradoxical essence. Two opposing desires that it can promise to satisfy simultaneously. The job of a marketer is to cultivate this schismatic core, this broken soul, at the center of every product. (72–73)

Although he attributes the theory of paradessences to Chas, Shakar has described the concept as an invention of his own, one that he takes as true: "[W]alking around supermarkets myself, watching commercials, paying attention to what had an effect on me, and then trying to figure out why it did . . . I came up with the idea of paradessence."[62] One gets the sense that paradessence (no less than postirony) isn't only one of the novel's central neologisms, but a principle of construction for the novel itself. Insofar as the paradessence of a "savage girl" is something like savagery and innocence, *The Savage Girl* becomes more than a novel about the process of capitalizing on this particular paradessence. It also becomes an advertisement for itself, a test of its own marketing theories. This is reportedly the "scary" way that the HarperCollins marketing department saw the novel.[63] Moreover, the word *postirony* does not only operate as a marketing neologism but also as a word that seems to have been machine-tooled in and, to some degree, for the academy. The "post-" in postirony draws attention to how new words are produced and marketed even in academic contexts, how we reify such words, and how even something as seemingly innocuous as a prefix can take on market value.

Shakar may augur a new kind of American novelist, one who has not only received an MFA in creative writing but has become a fully integrated writer-theorist, someone who fuses the ethos of the MFA with the theoretical concerns of the PhD. In 2002, Shakar received a PhD in English and Creative Writing from the University of Illinois at Chicago and currently teaches creative writing as an associate professor at the University of Illinois at Urbana-Champaign. *The Savage Girl* is not only his first novel but also his doctoral dissertation. In the summary section of his dissertation, Shakar presents Chas's theory as his own, writing that in "the strangely intoxicating world of trendspotting . . . one lesson prevails": "At the heart of every product lies a paradox," which "when cultivated successfully . . . yields untold riches."[64] The timbre of this summary, no less than passages in the published novel, betrays the intellectual feedback born of standing, perhaps, too close to the institutional reactor cores of theory. I do not want to judge whether the coming together of writer and critical theorist bodes well for the future of fiction, or to suggest that this institutional situation will in every case shape the style of fiction produced within it, but Shakar's location speaks to a large lacuna in Mark McGurl's analysis of the program era. Fiction writers who work in the university haven't only inherited "the New Critical positioning of aesthetic value as something that might be produced, as well as appreciated, in an academic environment," as McGurl shows, but might also (if they're lucky) end up having offices next door to their theoretically minded colleagues.[65] Theory will continue to be a subject for fiction, as Judith Ryan shows in *The Novel After Theory*, but might also increasingly become part of the social and institutional fabric of novelistic production. And as PhD students, such writers will be expected to master their craft as well as to think (and write) theoretically about their own work with increased frequency and intensity. In preparation for writing his dissertation, Shakar read works by Louis A. Sass, Richard Rorty, Deleuze and Guattari, and Schlegel.[66] His theoretical reading leaves an unmistakable mark on his prose style, a mark not yet visible in his earlier collection of stories, *The City in Love* (1996).

The phenomenon of greatest literary significance is not Shakar's presence in the university itself—as McGurl shows, creative writers have long been associated with the American university system—but rather the possible breakdown of intra-institutional barriers between the values and vocabularies of the MFA and the PhD, the merging of the system of creative writing with criticism.[67] The direct cause of this coming together is the labor market, which forces writers to use the university as an economic safe haven, forces critics to evaluate the marketability of their precarious work, and (with the rise of contingency) forces an escalation of accreditation to secure a job in the first place. Though many critics treat the professoriate as part of the professional-managerial class, contemporary capitalism's emphasis on "flexibility" and its "connexionist" institutions have weakened the security of "salaried mental workers."[68] Such a dissolution of the economic foundation of the PMC doesn't, in the case of writers who dream of joining it, dismantle the allure of "mental" labor, but heightens the competition to distinguish yourself on the job market, not only in terms of accreditation but also rhetorically and theoretically. The style of theory is, of course, not much appreciated among craft-oriented creative writers, but this might be viewed as a residue of the older order. Time will tell.

I have focused on the novelist's increased need for a PhD, but this foreclosing of distance, this erosion of critical irony, has also changed the critic. Critics increasingly are forced to become literary trend-spotters, workers who bank on the timely recognition and reification of literary patterns. At the level of the sentence, we encounter an opposite but related trend: the sociable style of recent critical work, such as Jeffrey T. Nealon's *Post-Postmodernism; or, the Cultural Logic of Just-in-Time Capitalism*.[69] The time lag between the publication of a novel and the rise of its peer-reviewed critical industry is shorter now than it has ever been, often strongly influencing how prestige gets allocated to living writers, blurring the lines between criticism and journalism. In some Nabokovian near future, the writer-theorist-freelancer may end up regularly writing criticism about novels she has written herself, for publications whose academic credibility may to a prior generation of critics seem hard to determine.[70] Finally, this same vocabulary has penetrated the marketing and advertising industries, and is especially visible in the language of the professional trendspotter. The vocabularies associated with these three figures—the critical theorist, the novelist, and the trendspotter—have converged, often within the same person. In that sense, Shakar is both the product of his historical situation and a faithful reporter of its shape. Perhaps Shakar has written a satire not about the "universal attitude of the contemporary consumer," as Shaviro suggests, but about a segment of the population of which Shakar himself is a member. If Shakar is being ironic, then he is, above all, being ironic about himself.

Patterns in the Logo-Maze

The November 2004 issue of *Wired* magazine includes a short article by the business writer James Surowiecki titled "The Decline of Brands," which discusses the recent proliferation of corporate trademark registration. The computer-generated illustration accompanying the article features the normally jovial Pillsbury Doughboy leaning on a crutch, his shredded ascot serving as a sling for a broken arm, beaten to within an inch of his doughy life. If we juxtapose this image of the battered doughboy with the specter of Bibendum (a.k.a. the Michelin Man)—"that weird, jaded, cigar- smoking elder creature suggesting a mummy with elephantiasis"—that stalks Cayce Pollard in William Gibson's eighth novel, *Pattern Recognition*, we can begin to think more clearly about some of the cultural problems posed by the recent fusion of critical theory, fiction writing, and marketing, or what Gibson in his novel calls the "logo-maze."[71] Surowiecki writes this of the logo-maze: "Sure, there are more brands than ever. But they're taking a beating—or, even worse, being ignored. Who's to blame? A new breed of hyperinformed superconsumers. (That's right—you!)."[72] What's noteworthy about Surowiecki's exuberant claim is that the "decline" of brand names and logos is logically predicated on the absolute penetration of marketing into every niche of our lives (including, as in Gibson's novel, our interpersonal exchanges).[73] As we might expect, knowing the techno-Utopian ethos *Wired* is so famous for, the outlook of this article is rather optimistic. Despite the undeniable fact that "[t]he world . . . is disappearing beneath a deluge of logos," we should not worry, because while "brands used to inspire loyalty in and of themselves, success is . . . now being determined by performance. The aristocracy of brand is dead. Long live the meritocracy of products."[74] Brands, personified through such corporate mascots as the Pillsbury Doughboy and Bibendum, seem to be locked with us in a war for sovereignty over our minds and our wallets. Sometimes, depending on whom you ask, we beat up the doughboy; at other times, instead, the Michelin Man beats us.

Surowiecki's article is less interesting as the description of a sociological fact—the rise of more savvy consumers—than as a prescription for how to properly survive the strains of our evolving consumer culture. We should cope with the "deluge" of brands not by trying to halt the rate of commodification, by trying to turn back the figurative flood, but by surpassing the consumers of decades past. We are now "superconsumers" endowed with historically unparalleled knowledge-gathering abilities, tied into the "central nervous system" of the Internet, which tells us via cybernetic feedback which products to buy and why. Now "hyperinformed," we emerge from mortal combat with these humanoid mascots as a "new breed," newly self-fashioned consumer-citizens. These recommendations recall many of the academic paeans to posthumanism of the late 1980s and 1990s and grow quite organically out of a vast literature that proposes "ethical consumption" as a potential site of resistance to the established economic order. Some naïve consumers (as distinct from superconsumers) might be foolish enough to remain loyal to brand names, or not to refunctionalize brands in subversive ways, but these naïfs do not read *Wired*.

The logo-centric world, the "logo-maze" of department stores such as Harvey Nichols that Gibson builds in *Pattern Recognition* challenges his coolhunting protagonist Cayce Pollard to carve out an original identity in a hypermediated environment full of "simulacra of simulacra of simulacra" (17, 18). Cayce's effort to do this, to find her own trademark Buzz Rickson's MA-1 flying jacket amid a minefield of Tommy Hilfiger, is perhaps a familiar struggle for many who live in advanced industrial and postindustrial societies. While just about everything has been commodified in these societies, they yet retain a cultural and educational apparatus that valorizes creativity as the uncommodifiable center of economic growth and promotes self-expression as the acme of individual worth. Put differently, neoliberalism has placed increasing pressure on elites to find new methods of forming and expressing their identities, to find safe harbors of sincerity in a sea of irony. The way that these elites find such storm shelters is increasingly through a process of selective consumption. Though Gibson's account of Cayce's coolhunting practice is in important ways less optimistic than Surowiecki's account of the superconsumer, both writers predicate their vision of a brand-free world on a hyperawareness of the brand.

The logic of branding drives the plot of *Pattern Recognition*. Cayce is hired by Hubertus Bigend, the founder of Blue Ant, to find the creator of a mysterious series of avant-garde film clips that are being released onto the Internet, collectively known as "the footage." Cayce is so complicit in neoliberalism that she is helping commoditize the art she cherishes precisely because it offers her a shelter from globalization. Cayce fears that her actions might expose the pure mystery of the footage, and its innocent author, to the "smooth and ironic brow" of Bigend, who will ultimately destroy its integrity (6). The truth of the footage turns out to be much more complicated than Cayce thinks, but the novel's focus on the time lag or feeling of suspension between any art object's fleeting instant of authenticity and its ruthless absorption into an irresistibly clever culture industry highlights *Pattern Recognition*'s fraught relationship to its own present, its dread-laden sense of its own precarious hypercontemporaneity, its attempt as Lauren Berlant rightly notes to write something like a historical novel of the present.[75] This same feeling of temporal suspension or dread also affects the way Gibson renders the terrorist attacks of September 11, 2011. *Pattern Recognition* is one of the first 9/11 novels, if not the first 9/11 novel. Published in February 2003, Gibson wrote most of his book during the summer of 2002, which is also when it's set. For Gibson, the breakneck globalization of the economy and events like 9/11 threaten to put the science fiction writer out of work, since it's now too hard to keep up with the present, let alone forecast possible futures. As a corollary, *Pattern Recognition* also suggests that the only honest way to write about our confused present moment is to treat it as if it were a kind of science fiction world, an alien environment that we, at best, only barely understand. To that end, Gibson attempts to aesthetically map what 9/11 felt like before media and politics could reabsorb, give historical meaning to, and exploit the attacks. Likewise, when rendering the dynamics of consumer culture, Gibson is most interested (paradoxically) in capturing in a narrative bottle the instant before the widespread adoption of new technologies and cultural practices—the moment, for example, where using *google* as a verb in novelistic discourse still felt strange and new, as it did in 2002.

As a protagonist, Cayce is unusually well equipped to observe such moments, to notice habits and affects that are about to be commodified. For she is not an ordinary coolhunter but rather "a sensitive of some kind, a dowser in the world of global marketing," who has a "violent reactivity to the semiotics of the marketplace" that makes her allergic to certain brands, such as Bibendum and Tommy Hilfiger (2, 17). She does not just dislike Bibendum but has something like a psychic allergic reaction whenever she encounters the figure. Cayce imagines, after her encounter with Tommy Hilfiger in the Harvey Nichols department store, that there must exist a "Tommy Hilfiger event horizon, beyond which it is impossible to be more derivative, more removed from the source, more devoid of soul" (18). Cayce's "inner radar" allows her to know which trademarks and logos will "work," although "[s]he has no way of knowing how she knows" (12). She is "a creature of fees," a "very specialized piece of human litmus paper," a freelance authenticity meter (61, 13). Cayce's idea of "soul"— her vision of unco-optable fashion—requires emptying out the human hand, removing semiotically specific markers, from clothing. Cayce's wardrobe seems to "have to come into this world without human intervention . . . a design-free zone, a one-woman school of anti whose very austerity periodically threatens to spawn its own cult" (8). Cayce strips herself of meaning as much as possible, minimizing her semiotic footprint.

Cayce's minimalism notably stands in stark opposition to the more maximalist style of *Pattern Recognition* itself. We learn, at different times, that Cayce "runs tap water through a German filter, into an Italian kettle" to make a cup of "Californian tea substitute"; that she wears "a Korean clone of an old-school Casio G-Shock"; that she carries a "purse-analog" that is a "black East German laminate, purchased on eBay"; that she sees another character wearing a dress that "for all its apparent simplicity, is still trying to say several things at once, probably in at least three languages"; that her own MA-1 jacket has "characteristically wrinkled seams down either arm" that were "the result of sewing with pre-war industrial machines that rebelled against the slippery new material, nylon"; and so on (3, 7, 8, 10, 11). In passages like these—a far cry from literary minimalism—the reader is being positioned to see the world through the focalized, limited third-person perspective of a character with a "compulsive memory for brand names" whose attentiveness to detail seems at times almost superhuman (27). One type of response to this style is Fredric Jameson's admission that Gibson's "hyped-up name dropping" has, in a sense, defeated him: "I have no way of knowing whether all these items actually exist," he writes.[76] Another response—the one investigated here—is to try to keep up with Gibson, to become the kind of reader for whom these references are legible, perhaps meaningful, to adopt the hermeneutic disposition of the coolhunter.

Gibson names the core competency of the coolhunter *pattern recognition*. But what is pattern recognition? Is it, as Peter Gilbert (Parkaboy) claims early in the novel, a species-specific characteristic of human beings? "Homo sapiens are about pattern recognition" (2). In this case, what Cayce is doing is something that any of us can do, only better. Cayce would be a model for how we can escape the logomaze, a literary dramatization of what we are already doing, or perhaps an exemplar of how escape is impossible for creatures like us. Supporting the notion of biologically grounded pattern recognition is the idea that "Cayce's cool-module, wherever it resides, has always proven remarkably good at registering the salient parameters of sexual fetishes she's never encountered before, and doesn't in the least respond to" (128). References to "cultural parameters" suggest that culture is, like natural language, a fact about the brain and can be described in terms of cognitive capability, one mental module among others. Here, Cayce has a knack for understanding culture, just as someone else might display a particular talent for learning languages. The linguistic paradigm Gibson alludes to is a principles-and-parameters generative grammar associated with Noam Chomsky. This paradigm explains several interesting aspects of Cayce's abilities.[77] This cognitive theory of Cayce's power explains why for Cayce "Japanese franchises like Hello Kitty [do] not trigger interior landslide, panic attack" (144).[78] Her brain's parameters are set in such a way that Japanese cultural artifacts have no particular effect on or meaning for her.

But testimony against the notion that Cayce's sensitivity to patterns is an expression of biology comes from Cayce herself, who, when explaining the nature of cool to Voytek and Magda, says, "'cool' . . . isn't an inherent quality. It's like a tree falling, in the forest . . . What I mean is, no customers, no cool. It's about a group behavior pattern around a particular class of object" (86). If cool is a function of how groups behave in relation to types of (temporarily cool) things, as Cayce suggests, then the most curious aspect of Cayce's sensitivity to the "semiotics of the marketplace" is that her individual brain is able to categorize objects in terms of group behavior. Cayce's brain would possess something like an embodied "decision market," an inner intersubjectivity or collectivity that predicts with uncanny accuracy—more or less infallibly—the choices that the market will make.[79] In other words, Cayce cognitively simulates the behavior of groups in ways that not even the most advanced computers are able to. But Cayce is no cyborg; she has not had her nervous system modified or expanded. In this second scenario, Cayce is curiously superhuman. If we accept Cayce's self-understanding, *Pattern Recognition* flips from a work of realism to an SF novel set in the year 2002, a novel in which Cayce's brain is the work's novum. The mysterious way that Cayce's allergy disappears at the end of the novel supports this second reading, requiring us to work especially hard to suspend disbelief, and suggesting that her amazing pattern recognition abilities should be read, within the world that Gibson builds, as operating according to a rule set that we as readers do not have access to.

We can attribute a third possible conception of pattern recognition to the media theorist Marshall McLuhan, from whom Gibson takes his novel's title. In 1967, McLuhan wrote that

> [e]lectric circuitry profoundly involves men with one another. Information pours upon us, instantaneously and continuously. As soon as information is acquired, it is very rapidly replaced by still newer information. Our electrically-configured world has forced us to move *from the habit of data classification to the mode of pattern recognition.* We can no longer build serially, block-by-block, step-by-step, because instant communication insures that all factors of the environment and of experience coexist in a state of active interplay.[80]

For McLuhan, human beings have plastic cognitive capabilities—talk of superhumans and posthumans would miss the point that we were never quite human to begin with, and are always changing to match our circumstances, our "nervous systems" increasingly extended by electronic technologies. What changes for the human subject are the historical circumstances under which a generalized form of cognition occurs.

We move from an era of "data classification," characteristic of the "mechanical age," into a state of "pattern recognition," endemic to our "electronic age." Both are habits of mind shaped within particular media environments. Echoing not only McLuhan but also Alvin Toffler's proclamations on "future shock,"[81] Bigend claims that

> Fully imagined cultural futures were the luxury of another day, one in which 'now' was of some greater duration. For us, of course, things can change so abruptly, so violently, so profoundly, that futures like our grandparents' have insufficient 'now' to stand on. We have no future because our present is too volatile . . . We have only risk management. The spinning of the given moment's scenarios. Pattern recognition. (57)

This vision of how we now relate to the future recalls Niklas Luhmann's claim that "[m]odern society experiences its future in the form of the risk of deciding," suggesting that our experience of history has undergone something like a phase change, moving from large, discrete "Events" to a barrage of small, complexly interconnected events or "total flow."[82] It is within a present characterized by such "total flow" that trendspotting and coolhunting are not merely occupational choices among others, but an essential epistemic means of navigating history itself, for individual and corporate persons alike.[83] Cayce would then be a harbinger of the kind of person we have not yet but will all necessarily become, part of a future that is still "unevenly distributed," to borrow Gibson's famous formulation.

Gibson proffers three mutually incompatible explanations of Cayce's pattern recognition ability, associated with Parkaboy, Cayce, and Bigend, respectively. The true explanation, I have suggested, will determine the genre of *Pattern Recognition* itself. Many critics have reflected on whether or not *Pattern Recognition* counts as a work of science fiction. John Clute argues that for Gibson that "SF is no longer about the future as such, because 'we have no future' that we can do thought experiments about, only futures, which bleed all over the page, soaking the present."[84] Jameson has suggested that Gibson may be "moving closer to that 'cyberpunk' with which he is often associated."[85] Jaak Tomberg proposes that Gibson's Blue Ant Trilogy ought to be read "as *simultaneously* realist and science-fictional."[86] These critics all correctly focus on Gibson's style as the key to answering the question, but they arrive at the wrong conclusion.

The Brand as Cognitive Map

Perhaps Cayce's allergy is an allegory. Fredric Jameson makes this argument, suggesting that Gibson's novel—which, as with much SF, "sends back more reliable information about the contemporary world than an exhausted realism (or an exhausted modernism either)"—updates conspiracy narrative for an era of globalization, largely dropping the quaint need for drugs or paranoia ("these protagonists ... do not particularly need the stimulus of drugs").[87] Jameson here correctly invokes Thomas Pynchon's *The Crying of Lot 49* as "a fundamental paradigm" for Gibson's "in-group," "name-dropping style."[88] Cyberpunk itself becomes in this review "a kind of laboratory experiment in which the geographical-cultural light spectrum and band-widths of the new system are registered."[89] This is, to be sure, an appealing interpretation of *Pattern Recognition*, but Jameson's reading does not account for the more disturbing facets of Gibson's novel. Allegorical or symptomatic readings of *Pattern Recognition*— and specifically of "pattern recognition"—fail to account for the true significance of Gibson's coolhunting style.

An allegorical reading is tempting partly because *Pattern Recognition* itself invokes allegorical interpretation and critical theory. In her first posting to the Footage:Fetish:Forum (F:F:F), an Internet discussion board where followers of the footage electronically gather, Mama Anarchia decries the "hopelessly retrograde" writing she has found there: "Do you know nothing of narratology? Where is Derridean 'play' and excessiveness? Foucauldian limit-attitude? Lyotardian language games? Lacanian Imaginaries? Where is the commitment to praxis, positioning Jamesonian nostalgia, and despair—as well as Habermasian fears of irrationalism—as panic discourses signaling the defeat of Enlightenment hegemony over cultural theory?" (267). Words like *hegemony* and *hermeneutics* signal, for Parkaboy, the "full positive identification" of a "fully genuine" Mama posting (268). Whether an unusual moment of parody in a novel otherwise noteworthy for its elegiac tone or a sign of Gibson's interest in critical theory, this posting is strange in a number of ways. On the one hand, Mama Anarchia is not a person but the composite of two: the graphic design executive Dorotea Benedetti and her "puppenkopf," a "graduate student, in America" who translates whatever Dorotea wants to say "into the language of Anarchia" for F:F:F (315). On the other hand, although she is "herself" unreal within the novel's world—and, although as a "Completist," "her" theory of the footage turns out to be incorrect—Anarchia's commitment to the jargon of critical theory turns out to be justified, in a certain sense, when it comes to the footage.

For at one level, the "author" of the footage is dead: she is the brain-damaged Nora Volkov, a former Russian film student who has had a portion of a Claymore mine embedded in her brain. Nora's

[c]onsciousness [is] . . . somehow bounded by or bound to the T-shaped fragment in her brain: part of the arming mechanism

of the Claymore mine . . . balanced too deeply, too precariously within her skull, to ever be removed. Something stamped out, once, in its thousands, by an automated press in some armory in America. Perhaps the workers who'd made that part, if they'd thought at all in terms of end-use, had imagined it being used to kill Russians . . . And from it, and from her other wounds, there emerged, accompanied by the patient and regular clicking of her mouse, the footage. (305)

The much-revered footage, in defiance of even the most sophisticated F:F:F hypotheses, has been cobbled together from "mere scraps of found video," derived from CCTV archives, processed by what Gibson, invoking William S. Burroughs, has elsewhere called one of "God's little toys"—a computer.[90] Nora points and clicks, cuts and pastes, remixes existing scraps of film—a post-Soviet Burroughs. Gibson shrouds Nora's aesthetic process within the black box of her brain—and seems perhaps to harbor some lingering Romantic notions about the power of her cut-up method—but ultimately displaces her agency to a subpersonal cognitive domain.

Gibson simultaneously locates Nora's creative agency at an interpersonal or social level. The footage is authored, like Mama Anarchia's postings, not by one person but by many. In addition to the assembly-line workers who made the Claymore mine that is embedded in Nora's brain, the ultimate "end-use" of which is producing the footage itself, the footage is rendered by an army of prison laborers, who work for the Russian "version of CCA, Cornell Corrections, Wackenhut," a "bold New Russian entrepreneurial experiment" within the privatized prison system that Nora's oligarch uncle Andrei Volkov has helped build (329). Boon Chu, another character searching for the maker of the footage, had earlier described such a "completely secure rendering operation" as "Shakespeare's monkeys, but working to a plan" (108). Cayce's concern about preventing the commodification of the footage here gets comically deflated. After all, the footage is nothing less than the direct result of the mania of privatization that devastated Russia after the fall of the Soviet Union. We might say that the footage is authored by multinational capitalism or globalization.

Despite our temptation to read it this way, such an interpretation fails to give a full account of *Pattern Recognition*'s style. What is missing becomes clear when we compare Gibson's novel to one of its most important precursors, Thomas Pynchon's *The Crying of Lot 49* (1966). The comparison is obvious. *Pattern Recognition* might even be read as a thinly coded rewriting of Pynchon's short novel, inasmuch as both works dramatize the hermeneutic dilemmas of female protagonists lost in multinational mazes of meaning. During her famous night walk through San Francisco, Oedipa Maas repeatedly encounters the ominous muted post horn, each time within a different context, its significance seeming to change every time she encounters it, her ability to interpret it constantly thwarted, her paranoia growing with every passing hour. Pynchon writes that Oedipa "spent the rest of the night finding the image of the Trystero post horn ... Later, on a sidewalk, she saw two of them, 20 feet apart. Between them a complicated array of boxes, some with letters, some with numbers. A kids' game? Places on a map, dates from a secret history?"[91] Later that evening:

> In Golden Gate Park she came on a circle of children in their nightclothes, who told her they were dreaming the gathering ... They knew about the post horn, but nothing of the chalked game Oedipa had seen on the sidewalk ... You used only one image and it was a jump-rope game, a little girl explained: you stepped alternately in the loop, the bell, and the mute, while your girlfriend sang:
>
> > Tristoe, Tristoe, one, two, three,
> > Turning taxi from across the sea ...[92]

Compare Oedipa's muted post horn to the sneaker logo that Blue Ant has hired Cayce to evaluate at the beginning of *Pattern Recognition*. Moments before she finally rejects the logo, envisioning what effects her approval of it would have, Cayce:

> [b]riefly ... imagines the countless Asian workers who might, should she say yes, spend years of their lives applying versions

of this symbol to an endless and unyielding flood of foot-wear. What would it mean to them, this bouncing sperm? Would it work its way into their dreams eventually? Would their children chalk it in doorways before they knew its meaning as a trademark? (12)

The reference to chalking the syncopated sperm in doorways alludes to Pynchon's muted post horn, but with a difference. To appreciate that difference, we should compare Cayce's vision of the syncopated sperm to her later reflection on whether the "workers who'd made that [T-shaped piece of the Claymore mine]" had "thought at all in terms of end-use, had imagined it being used to kill Russians" (305).

Pynchon's decision not to fix the meaning of the muted post horn—and to litter his novella with overdetermined names, like "Oedipa Maas" and "Mike Fallopian"—suggests that we should read *Lot 49* as something like an allegory, maybe of the "world system of late capitalism (or postmodernity)" itself, as Jameson would have it, or perhaps as an allegorical form emptied out of content, one that feels allegorical but points at nothing in particular.[93] Whether they treat *Lot 49* as an allegory or its hermeneutic negation, a blank allegory, critics have agreed that by not satisfying our desire to know the muted post horn's true meaning, Pynchon highlights the interpretive dilemma that readers themselves face. By contrast, Gibson may have invented Heinzi & Pfaff's proposed bouncing sperm logo (though it suggests, more than anything, the Nike swoosh), but he does not invent his novel's other brand names. Tommy Hilfiger and Google and Starbucks cannot be read as allegorical figures. They do not *stand in for* or *refer to* the world system or consumerism or even late capitalism, but rather are its *real products*, pieces of intellectual property, reproducing themselves again in textual form on Gibson's pages and elsewhere.[94] An iconic "syncopated sperm" is not a symptom of global capitalism (or not only a symptom) but a signifier that could itself become a commodity (or part of a commodity). More specifically, we are being asked to recognize the different possible use values the brand-commodity might take on.[95] For Cayce, the meaning of a brand becomes nothing other than its position in a global supply chain, the collective ("countless Asian workers"; "the workers who'd made that part") and complex ("Would it work its way into their dreams . . ."; "imagined it being used to kill Russians") by-products of its real existence. More so than other commodities, Gibson shows, brands have the potential to become windows onto the underlying production processes that make them profitable in the first place, processes usually concealed within a global maze of anonymous subcontractors.

Bruce Robbins would label the sort of experience Cayce has when gazing upon the sneaker logo as an example of the "sweatshop sub-lime."[96] For Robbins, the sweatshop sublime is a narrative trope depicting "a moment of insight accompanied by a surge of power." An interpreter moves from the experience of some local scene or everyday object "to the outer reaches of a world economic system of notoriously inconceivable magnitude and interdependence, a system that brings goods from the ends of the earth . . . in order to satisfy your slightest desire." The seeming power of this vision comes, how-ever, with a feeling of correlated helplessness: "Your sudden, heady access to the global scale is not access to a commensurate power of action *upon* the global scale."[97] Robbins writes that "to glimpse even for a moment the unimaginable face of society-as-a-whole is to go through a near-death experience in which the activist self dissolves."[98] Discussing problems of reification, Robbins critiques Jameson's claim that "you don't want to have to think about Third World women every time you pull yourself up to your word processor . . . it would be like having voices inside your head."[99] Robbins points out the apparent contradiction between, on the one hand, the consum-er's desire to use reification as a means of blocking the unpleasant awareness of how commodities come into the world and, on the other hand, Jameson's observation that "in consuming culture" we do not "particularly want, particularly need, to forget the human producer."[100] Inspired by the apparent contradiction in Jameson's argument, Robbins claims that a humanistic education might do well to focus on "cultivating, augmenting, and channeling of the desire for voices inside our heads."[101] While the convergence of cultural production and other so-called real sectors of the economy compli-cates Jameson's initial distinction in significant ways, the division of *"non-cultural" commodities* from *culture as a commodity* seems plausible to me. Our desire to enjoy the visible labor of cultural products, especially in the form of style, betrays the fact that the cultural producer generally enjoys a surfeit of cultural (if not other sorts of) capital. Robbins's point, meanwhile, is that the task of humanistic education should be to produce people of a certain type, people who are interested in searching for evidence of exploited labor everywhere they look, even in noncultural areas.

Robbins wants us to see the world, in order words, in much the way as Cayce does. How might we be made to see this way? There are two ways of putting such voices inside our heads, either by making this mode of hallucinatory hearing somehow compulsory or by turning the desire to hear such voices into an aesthetic sensibility. In his novel *Indecision* (2005), Benjamin Kunkel presents an instance of the sweatshop sublime that follows the compulsory path. An activist character named Brigid longs for the existence of a fruit that would compel social awareness: "When you eat from this fruit," Brigid imagines, "then whenever you put your hand on a product, a commodity, an article, then, at the moment of your touch, how this commodity came into your hands becomes plainly evident to you."[102] What is most interesting about this imagined fruit is its implied politics, its seemingly logical and inevitable effects on those who consume it. "Now there is no more mystification of labor," Brigid concludes, "no more of a world in which the object arrives by magic—scrubbed, clean, no past, all of its history washed away."[103] Brigid's fantasy assumes that a politically noncontroversial measure of utility and suffering can be encoded, as information, into objects. Moreover, Brigid takes on faith that such an objective coding, were it possible, would lead others to embrace her political views. This is a problematic assumption. Brigid might change her mind about her politics, given the information encoded in these demystified commodities. Alternatively, she might find that demystification does not eliminate the need to choose a politics—that is, to make a commitment. Kunkel's fruit follows the same reasoning as activist projects of ethical consumption that try to guide consumer choices by means of ethical certification (free range, organic, fair trade, etc.).

The problem with markets, advocates of ethical consumption

posit, is that they fail to distribute sufficient information to consumers, often by mystifying the origin and history of the commodity, and therefore systematically misprice goods and services. The solution of ethical consumption is to embed a concern for invidious externalities into the endogenous preferences of the individual consumer either through the medium of price (for example, a carbon tax) or through some other means (for example, certification or labeling). Consumers will subsequently vote with their wallets. The collective and the personal converge here in an interesting way: odious externalities are converted either into ethical imperatives *(Buy local! Drink fair trade coffee!)* or with Kunkel's magic fruit into sense data that registers presumably as personal pain or pleasure. Borrowing a term from John Tomlinson's discussion of globalization and cosmopolitanism, we might say that the ethical consumer recognizes as sensation, via electronic feedback or other technologies, the "complex connectivity" of his or her position in relation to global supply chains, internalizing all important externalities.[104] This proposed solution faces problems, many of which are already apparent in *Pattern Recognition*. First, receiving more information with our commodities—even as sense perception—guarantees nothing. Being aware of human suffering does not imply a politics, does nothing to guarantee how consumers will value consumption. Cayce already has access to plenty of information (both positive and negative) about the effects of global supply chains, but still finds herself to be complicit in those processes that threaten to commoditize even more of the world. Such fantasies *assume* the political views they ought to *argue* for. If the beholder of the sweatshop sublime wants to change her political world, she should make specific political arguments rather than hope that the nervous systems of her students will be electronically extended or fantasize about a magic fruit that will resolves the mystifications of consumerism or even encourage her undergraduates to apply to graduate school.[105] More to the point, we do not need forms of magical fruit to see through the world's complex connectivity. If we take *Pattern Recognition* as a guide—as an example of the second, aesthetic version of wanting "voices in [our] head"—we will discover that we are surrounded by plenty of information about the effects of global supply chains. However, Gibson uses literary style to make having voices in our head seem like a more appealing proposition—to construct a version of the sweat-shop sublime—but he succeeds, in part, by drawing on the *existing* meanings of his brand-laden vocabulary and by manipulating the alienation that comes from reading a novelization of the immediate present. While Kunkel's magic fruit is, as Robbins suggests, a trope in *Pattern Recognition*, brand names are more than tropes. For when every major multinational corporation essentially joins the culture industry, how consumers *feel* about products and brand names begins to matter powerfully. Under these circumstances, interpretation is not merely something that the academic literary scholar does, but an economic imperative for the "brand manager."[106]

Contemporary marketing literature has extensively theorized the relationship between belief and branding strategy in terms of cul-ture, meaning, interpretation, and belief. Books with such titles as *The Power of Cult Branding* (2002), *The Culting of Brands* (2004), *Married to the Brand* (2005), and *Primalbranding* (2006) all largely claim that "the same dynamics are at play behind the attraction to brands and cults."[107] In order to understand the success of "cult brands" such as Apple and Harley-Davidson, these books claim, one must look more generally at the process by which people form beliefs. The key insight in these popular branding books is roughly the same: that brands have become systems of meaning, value, and identification. "When research subjects were recounting their rea-sons for joining and committing, they were describing the profound urges to belong, make meaning, feel secure, have order within chaos, and create identity."[108] In order to distinguish your brand from the rest, you must create for consumers a powerful brand mythology, a set of distinctive values that can be worn like badges of honor, feel-ings of exclusivity or election, and a robust community of fellow believers. Consumer choice is imagined as an expression of deeply held needs for belonging and recognition, sometimes discussed in this literature as part of a common human genetic and evolutionary inheritance. The aim of marketing shouldn't be to appeal to the rational minds of consumers—to give consumers information—but rather to forge with them direct emotional and even ethical bonds, to cultivate meanings. "Don't try to win the whole market by making generically popular products," these marketing gurus advise. Instead, you should seize the loyalty of a small but fanatically devoted coterie of true believers. Religious cults, or "cultures of belief," become models for what brand builders aspire to create. Douglas Atkin posits that the possibility for cult brands grows directly out of the decline of more traditional sources of collective meaning, such as involvement in civil society.[109] The technical scholarship on brand management has come to basically the same conclusion, emphasizing the vital importance of forging emotional ties with consumers in branding strategy. The authors of one peer-reviewed study conclude that "brands must develop an emotional and symbolic attachment with consumers if they are to succeed in today's highly competitive marketplace."[110]

Naomi Klein's *No Logo* offers many insights into the implications of this new paradigm of branding, outlining at considerable length the relationship between brands, global supply chains, and consumer affects. Reviewing her arguments will help us better understand *Pattern Recognition*, which was indirectly inspired by Klein's book.[111] Many prominent critics have misunderstood her major claims. Robbins incorrectly attributes to Klein the claim that "the key to contemporary injustice is brand names."[112] Timothy Bewes fears that Klein's "analysis has a 'homologous' relation to its object of study" and "produces the very reification it recoils from," because Klein allegedly separates the fictions of brand image from the actualities of labor power.[113] Nowhere in *No Logo* does Klein claim that "the real problem is brands," nor is the line between branding and some real economy so cleanly drawn. Instead, offering an interpretation more subtle than Robbins and Bewes give her credit for, Klein in *No Logo* documents how multinational corporations reinvented themselves in the 1990s as "brand managers," producers not of *goods and services* but rather of *meanings*.[114] This significant corporate transformation is partly a by-product of the fact that the economic value of *aesthetics* has risen relative to functional values. That is, there is now often more of a profit to be made from selling *meanings* than *things*.[115] As brand ownership and the cultural dimensions of economic life have become more profitable, multinational corporations increasingly outsourced less profitable types of production overseas, concealing the connection between any particular brand and the supply chains supporting that brand within global networks of anonymous subcontractors. The growing power of the brand is therefore a direct result of the globalization of production.

Brands thus *do* matter to Klein, but not as Robbins or Bewes would have it. If Klein emphasizes brands, it is largely because multinational corporations—her true targets—also do.[116] The most important effect of the rise of branding is that it became imperative for marketers to create brands with which consumers had empathetic and personal relationships, brands they trusted, brands that had earned public esteem (especially of teenage consumers). In other words, the sphere of the "culture industry"—a term Adorno and Horkheimer used to describe media companies—has expanded radically. As Klein points out, the success of the branding paradigm has been double-edged for corporations. The use of sweatshops, to give one example, was well-documented for many decades, long before the consumer boycotts and "antiglobalization" protests of the nineties, and yet, in her telling, it took the association of sweatshops with popular brand names and celebrities such as Kathie Lee Gifford to spur wider antisweatshop activism.[117] Paradoxically, the answer to Klein's "difficult question" of "[h]ow to be truly critical in an age of mass camp" might be, on the evidence of her own analysis, a strategic co-optation of branding itself, a trading in on the aura of authentic cool that certain brands have achieved.[118] Marketing professionals worry among themselves in their technical literature that the anti-WTO "riots . . . and protests . . . present a real threat to the reputation of global firms."[119] Why might this be the case? I would speculate that brand-conscious corporations, as both their proponents and opponents often claim, work and largely succeed at establishing relationships with consumers based on meaning, belonging, and identification. The disclosure that these brand stewards use unjust labor practices sparks anger because many consumers have genuine affective relationships with their chosen brands. Knowing the results of activist detective work is necessary but not sufficient to motivate action; we must also be invested in the brands that activists target.

We become mad when Nike exploits Indonesian workers, Klein suggests, not because we love Indonesian workers but because we love Nike or identify with its professed values.

This is a dispiriting conclusion, but let us recall Jameson's proclamation that late capitalist societies require a radical art capable of envisioning from within the true complexity of the capitalist world system, "a pedagogical political culture which seeks to endow the individual subject with some new heightened sense of its place in the global system."[120] Jameson called for a critical and artistic production guided by an "aesthetics of cognitive mapping."[121] Conspiracy narrative aspired toward but never achieved such a mapping.[122] The brand itself, I would argue, might have the potential to become the most accomplished existing specimen of aesthetic cognitive mapping, offering a way to see with new eyes a schematic of corporate human agency through more localized bits and pieces of one's world. Though still limited in what they can help us see, have brands not proven to be, in some of the cases cited, a useful means by which individuals and activist groups can conceptualize the global economy? Have brands not helped individual subjects visualize the workings of cultural or creative capitalist economies? We would not be required to assent to any naïve notion of "counterbranding," nor would we need to celebrate *Adbusters*-style "subvertising," to agree.[123] The emergence of such activist maps should not be an entirely surprising development, given that under the "brands, not products" paradigm, multinational corporations conceive of themselves as brand managers and subsequently invest enormous sums to cultivate cultural meanings. By emphasizing so intensely the cultural value of their products, these corporations have unwittingly transformed Jameson's "Third World women" whose voices we would prefer not to hear— and whose suffering was supposed to be conceal within anonymous subcontracting mazes—into the coauthors of meaning-laden brands, literally into cultural producers. The problem with Bewes's complaint about Klein should now be clear. The brand is not a problem to be solved, a hallucination to be banished, but a (privately owned) toll bridge between producers and consumers.

Whether or not we agree with such claims, I would argue that this is the political ethos on offer in Gibson's novel. In *Pattern Recognition*, distant sites of production map onto personal brand meanings *as meanings*, turning the organization of the economy into an aesthetic. Gibson does not ask us to ignore the experience of brand meaning and to focus our attention instead on the study of sociology or economics. Instead, Gibson asks the reader to adopt a characterological model that habitually resists official brand meanings, that considers global supply chains *as* the political meaning of the brand. Gibson's coolhunting aesthetic attempts to reconnect the free-floating brand to the hidden supply chains that make brands profitable in the first place. His style *does not* condemn branding or reification as such. Brand names are thus not exactly tropes in Gibson's novel. We may associate brand names with certain cultural values and meanings, but those associations typically do not constitute a form of allegory. Gibson offers us something akin to a recommendation for how to see the world, an invitation to sensitize ourselves to complex connectivity, to arrange our relationship to the market, if only for a time, like Cayce. To be a coolhunter, for Gibson, is not necessarily to have a particular politics (to be for or against the market) but to cultivate a certain aesthetic relationship to one's world as a (possible) precursor for action. Those who aspire to be cartographers of a postgeographic world cannot, of course, know in advance how their maps will be used. More to the point, if they demanded that their maps be hardwired into us as logical imperatives or sensory perceptions, such cartographers would not be proposing a form of ethics or politics. An ethics or politics requires, above all, meaningful choice.

The Cognitive Style of Jennifer Egan

It may seem perverse to discuss branding or reification as if it were akin to Jameson's more politically ambitious concept of cognitive mapping. Yet any political fantasy that dispenses with reification, I have been arguing, risks dispensing with the grounds of political action. This dialectical truth becomes clear in Jennifer Egan's novel *A Visit from the Goon Squad* (2010), which explores the opportunities of reification and self-consciously depends for its most moving literary effects on shameless self-branding. *A Visit from the Goon Squad* is a novel told in stories or episodes, each chapter from a different point of view, tracing the lives of a cluster of characters orbiting the music producer Benny Salazar and his former assistant Sasha. Evincing what several critics have called "network aesthetics," Egan's stories mimic the form of an online social network, disbursed across time, reimagining the form of the novel as a sort of Facebook wall, indulging in the potent fantasy of rediscovering the lives of old, lost friends who are, it turns out, all connected to one another in delightfully unexpected ways.[124] Egan's book directly and deftly integrates branding theory across its constituent stories, which has led to some critical uneasiness. Michael Szalay, who has discussed Egan's art in relation to the rising popularity of HBO-style television programming, concludes that being a novelist today might require becoming something like a self-managing "show runner," someone "at once empty and full of meaning."[125] This claim comports with the sociological analysis of the contemporary trade publishing field in John B. Thompson's *Merchants of Culture*. By Thompson's account, popular literary writers have leveraged name recognition to win increasingly large advances, squeezing publishers' profit margins with the help of powerful agents.[126] (Egan's agent is ICM's Amanda "Binky" Urban, one of the most successful literary agents of all time.) Though, by design, the overwhelming majority of writers do not master this system, those who do—including writers of literary fiction—can command significant empires of intellectual property. Discussing a range of contemporary writers, Szalay suggests that "the question often raised by these [corporate] fictions is whether or not the novelist is in fact a private artist—wary of the mainstream and working in isolation—or somebody who dreams of movies, videos, promotional products, and spin-off projects: fame." Szalay perceptively reads Dana Spiotta's *Stone Arabia* (2012), and by extension other HBO-style novelists, as obsessed with the corporate body of the writer and the becoming-corporate of the individual person. But Egan's equanimity, even enthusiasm, for serial cable-television drama—one of her inspirations for *A Visit from the Goon Squad* was *The Sopranos* (1999–2007)—her clear-eyed willingness to sell out, by having her novel made into an HBO program, comes to seem like a problem in Szalay's account, albeit one he promises to analyze richly. "HBO shaped *Goon Squad* even before she sold the network her remarkable novel," he notes, evincing a "closed circuit, in which a novelist declares her indebtedness to HBO and then, immediately after winning the Pulitzer Prize, proceeds to sell the rights to her novel to that network."[127] Yet this is nothing new: the desire for adaptation has long been a component of the literary field, at least since the consolidation of the publishing industry, as Thompson shows, and critics have long derided authors who seem too eagerly to seek fame. The poet Frederick Seidel, to take a recent example, means to insult Rachel Kushner by suggesting that her 2013 novel, *The Flamethrowers*, is "interested in being made into a movie."[128]

What is genuinely new in Egan's art is not some especially perverse, preemptive determination to sell out, but the absence of any sort of scandal—any pretense to shame—around rituals of selling out in the first place. It is the *anxiety* of reification that has (almost) disappeared from her prose, and the prose of many of her contemporaries. This absence may signal "that reification has become the human condition as such."[129] As Jeffrey T. Nealon notes in *Post-Postmodernism*, "the word 'commodity' is no longer simply a fighting word."[130] Charges that an author has "sold out" fall flat as criticism, or even as analysis, inasmuch as nearly all artistic production has been revealed to have a commodity character, and all commodity production, however ordinary, turns out to be ensnared into tighter and tighter circuits of cultural signification. Moreover, as Nealon notes, "Regardless of whether or not you're willing to *sell out*, someone first has to offer to *buy* you out—ad agencies, TV producers, the folks who put together sheet music for high school bands."[131] The interesting question, Nealon is right to suggest, is not *why* artists sell out to global capitalism (it's for the money and fame!), but why agents of global capital are interested in buying what artists like Egan are peddling. If Szalay's reading is right, the global publishing industry seems to have become collectively fascinated with allegorical representations of itself. What participants in this vast system most want to commoditize, it seems, are books about their own participation in a system. They hope perhaps to find some Archimedean point outside their situation, to get a good look at the system's pimples under better light. Whatever the answer, Egan has

turned the complexities of selling out, via the use of formerly stigma-
tized commodity forms, into the very form of her art.

The most noted example of this tendency in *A Visit from the
Goon Squad* is Egan's PowerPoint chapter, "Great Rock and Roll
Pauses," created in the novel by Sasha's daughter, Alison Blake,
sometime in the 2020s, as part of her "slide journal."[132] The slide
show describes Alison's relationship with her autistic brother,
Lincoln; opines on great rock and roll pauses (an obsession of
Lincoln's); describes a book in which her mother appears; and cul-
minates with a series of graphs that Drew (Lincoln and Alison's
father) helps Lincoln make, outlining various attributes of musical
pauses. Egan's use of PowerPoint is seemingly conflicted. On one
level, Egan deploys PowerPoint in an unsurprisingly satirical
manner, to criticize a future world where slides have displaced longer
forms of written communication. Notably, when Alison looks
through *Conduit: A Rock-and-Roll Suicide*, she fixates on a picture of
her mother, not the text of the book (257). Egan's willingness
to embrace what Edward R. Tufte has called the "cognitive style of
PowerPoint," her suggestion that this cognitive style is capable
of great human insight, speaks directly to the concerns about
commodification—the fear that new communications platforms
reify speech—that Szalay detects. Tufte's description of PowerPoint
as having a "cognitive style," meanwhile, exposes the centrality of
ethos in popular debates about how technologies shape public life
and habits of thought. His critique is not focused on what you say—
or do not say—using PowerPoint, but rather on what sort of person
PowerPoint transforms you into. As his subtitle insists, "Pitching
Out Corrupts Within." By Tufte's account, PowerPoint impover-
ishes thought: children schooled to articulate their interiority by
means of "slide journals" ought to become something like *slide
people*, a condition for which Lincoln's autism is surely (and unfortunately) meant to be an allegory. PowerPoint allegedly corrupts the
social competences and graces required for genuine human communication; it is ultimately *"presenter-oriented, not content-oriented, not
audience-oriented,"* Tufte writes.[133] Moreover, it exudes "a smirky
commercialism that turns information into a sales pitch and pre-
senters into marketeers." This is the "big attitude" of presentation

software, a manifestation of the dangers lurking in its design.[134] Another term for what such software systems threaten to do to persons is *autoreification*. What better word describes a "smirky" presentation platform that is little more than a "presenter-oriented" way of giving a "sales pitch" (presumably about one's own excellence)? Whereas *reification* subsumes some original wholeness of life under a domineering, falsifying concept, turning a process or person into a thing, *autoreification* requires a person's self-subsumption, her roping in of her own inner resources, affects, habits, thoughts, and life practices under a regime of self-management. Such self-management is part of what it must mean to have a cognitive style in the first place. Egan's PowerPoint chapter is the most obvious—the formally most flamboyant—example of autoreification in *A Visit from the Goon Squad*.

One might be tempted to interpret Alison's slide journal as part of a critique of corporate software platforms, but Egan's satire is ultimately halfhearted. After a fight, Lincoln and Drew reconcile through the use of proprietary presentation software. Preprogrammed templates and privately owned platforms are shown to be capable of great emotional expressivity, belying any simplistic or moralizing attack on new media systems. Moreover, other sections of *Goon Squad* evince Egan's equivocation about self-branding. The most interesting example can be found in the novel's final chapter, titled "Pure Language," which, like Shakar's and Gibson's novels, finds itself needing to invoke the full arsenal of science-fictional representational codes to do justice to its ambivalent exploration of the problem of selling out. In this chapter, Egan depicts a near future in which it may—strictly speaking—be impossible to be a coolhunter, to the degree that there are no wild specimens of cool left to hunt. Alex, a character Sasha meets in passing in the novel's first chapter, consciously sells out to Bennie by agreeing to manipulate his social network to promote a concert by the burned-out punk musician Scotty Hausmann. Scotty's music is hugely appealing to "pointers," prevocal infant consumers who have emerged as a vital demographic for the music industry in the chapter's imagined future. Though he initially resists selling out, Alex acquiesces to Bennie because he realizes that "every byte of information he'd posted online . . . was stored in the databases of multinationals who swore they would never ever use it—that he was *owned*, in other words, having sold himself unthinkingly at the very point in his life when he'd felt most subversive" (316). Alex chooses "parrots" among his 15,896 friends—who will spread via word of mouth news of Scotty's performance in Lower Manhattan—by adjudicating among "three variables: how much they [his friends] needed money ('Need'), how connected and respected they were ('Reach'), and how open they might be to selling that influence ('Corruptibility')" (315).

Egan ties Alex's acquiescence to the market, his callous reification of his (already reified) ties of friendship, to irony. The problem of irony's lost efficacy emerges as a question of concern at various points in the final chapter. Alex's wife, Egan writes, is "an academic star" who disguises her beauty by wearing "dorky glasses," which "threatened to reify her disguise into an identity" (323). Her "new book was on the phenomenon of word casings, a term she'd invented for words that no longer had meaning outside quotation marks. English was full of these empty words—'friend' and 'real' and 'story' and 'change'—words that had been shucked of their meanings and reduced to husks. Some, like 'identity,' 'search,' and 'cloud,' had clearly been drained of life by their Web usage. With others, the reasons were more complex; how had 'American' become an ironic term? How had 'democracy' come to be used in an arch, mocking way?" (323–324). Egan's corporatized future seems to be a bleak, apparently dystopian world of debilitating irony and corrosive cynicism. And yet younger characters in this future are anything but cynical. Benny's assistant, Lulu, is part of a generation that has, Egan shows, lost any sense of irony. Alex observes, "Another thing about her generation: no one swore. Alex had actually heard teenagers say things like 'shucks' and 'golly,' without apparent irony" (320). Like Shakar's postironic consumers, Lulu bats away suggestions that "believing in something . . . for *money*" is problematic by insisting that "if I believe, I believe. Who are you to judge my reasons?" (320). This is not, Egan goes to great pains to emphasize, a form of what Peter Sloterdijk or Slavoj Žižek calls cynical reason, but rather a fullblooded, earnest philosophy of accommodation with capitalism, a robust dismantling of the concept of authenticity that Alex clings to.

Furthering the degradation of language evident in Alison's slide journal, members of Lulu's generation send texts that read like this: *"if thr r childrn, thr mst b a fUtr, rt?"* (331). Yet unlike Gary Shteyngart, who figures the language of texting in dystopian terms in his unremitting satire *Super Sad True Love Story* (2010), Egan does not reject the power or value of Lulu's reified speech. Much of "Pure Language" turns on Alex's struggle with Lulu's equanimity in the face of the market. Alex has sold out, but at least (so he thinks) he knows that he has sold out; by contrast, Lulu is unaware that it is even possible not to sell out. For her part, Lulu remains unimpressed by Alex's agonized struggle: "those metaphors—'up front' and 'out in the open'— are part of a system we call atavistic purism. AP implies the existence of an ethically perfect state which not only doesn't exist and never existed, but it's usually used to shore up the prejudices of whoever's making the judgments" (319). Lulu protests Alex's use of "what we call a disingenuous metaphor ... DMs look like descriptions, but they're really judgments. I mean, is a person who sells oranges *being bought?* Is the person who repairs appliances *selling out?*" (319).

One suspects that Egan would find it hard to answer Lulu's objections.[135] For all his manipulation, Alex's manufactured concert turns out to have long-reaching consequences. Egan rescues a moment of grace from the commoditized spectacle Alex helps engineer. When Scotty takes the stage, Alex expects "a roar of rejection from these thousands he'd managed secretly to assemble" (335). But the outcome of the concert defies his expectations, "And it may be that a crowd at a particular moment of history creates the object to justify its gathering, as it did at the first Human Be-In and Monterey Pop and Woodstock. Or it may be that two generations of war and surveillance had left people craving the embodiment of their own unease in the form of a lone, unsteady man on a slide guitar" (335). The concert quickly becomes a legend, conscious of itself as a legend at its own beginning.

> Anyone who was there that day will tell you the concert really started when Scotty stood up. That's when he began singing the songs he'd been writing for years underground, songs no one had ever heard, or anything like them—"Eyes in My Head,"

"X's and O's," "Who's Watching Hardest"—ballads of paranoia and disconnection ripped from the chest of a man you knew just by looking had never had a page or a profile or a handle or a handset, who was part of no one's data, a guy who had lived in the cracks all these years, forgotten and full of rage, in a way that now registered as pure. Untouched. But of course, it's hard to know anymore who was really *at* that first Scotty Hausmann concert ... Now that Scotty has entered the realm of myth, everyone wants to own him (335–336).

It seems clear that we are meant to take this concert as an authentically countercultural moment, the genuine encounter of a wired generation with Scotty's antisocial atavism. But Scotty's final success (which Egan ensures the reader is rooting for by this point in the novel) depends crucially on two types of reification. First, there is the manipulation of social networks, which Andy engages in, that steers a crowd to the site of its own authentic experience. The second is more subtle: Egan's use of the past participle, her momentary reversion to a present tense, ensures that Scotty's revolutionary performance is already ensconced in a timeframe that has already reified it. Scotty "has entered" myth already. Everyone now "wants" him. Even Scotty turns out already to be enmeshed in the corruptions of a public language that is anything but pure. Art *justifies* a gathering that has already happened, that has already been made to happen through canny marketing; it does not *cause* the gathering. Lulu seems to win the theoretical victory. It may be true that your tastes and preferences are manufactured through marketing manipulation, Egan suggests, but do you not still genuinely *love* what has been marketed to you? In an era of commodified social relations, we lose the serendipity that drives the wistfulness of connections forged, lost, and later relinked. That is, the network aesthetic that makes *Goon Squad*'s narrative structure charming risks losing its charm precisely because it has been formalized. But why should it lose its charm? After all, Egan seems to show, new forms of authentic experience can still emerge unexpectedly even in a world whose social life is fully enclosed within corporate platforms. So is the person who writes *A Visit from the Goon Squad* selling out? Is she being bought? What sort of atavistic purist would you have to be to use such disingenuous metaphors in the first place?

Conclusion: Psychohistories of the Present

Socioeconomic science fictions such as *The Savage Girl*, *Pattern Recognition*, and *A Visit from the Goon Squad* do not merely discuss postironic consumer culture as a theme but also try to intervene in that culture. These novels themselves proffer a postironic aesthetic, a style designed to capture the extreme contemporary. This aesthetic orientation becomes a component of the coolhunter, imagined not as a marketing professional but rather as a disposition or attitude that responds to a literal economy of meaning. The authors fear themselves to be trapped within this economy, though not without equivocation or ambivalence. Alex Shakar seems both to believe in and to distance himself from his own theories of consumer motivation, the concepts of paradessence and postirony that reviewers have so frequently commented on. HarperCollins's marketing team interpreted *The Savage Girl* almost as a marketing textbook, and with good reason. In a review written for the *Journal of the Academy of Marketing Science*, Stephen Brown suggests, with only the slightest trace of irony, that "*The Savage Girl* contains real lessons for twenty-first-century marketing managers."[136] In a longer review of *The Savage Girl* and Max Barry's science fiction political satire *Jennifer Government*, Brown argues that literature may be "the new (and improved) path to thick description that qualitative consumer researchers require."[137]

For his part, William Gibson reflects on the nature of his own authorship, the ways in which he is himself a kind of literary coolhunter, ultimately using style to imagine (real and imagined) brand names as cognitive maps of global capitalism. It should not surprise us to learn that Gibson has appeared in an advertisement for a black Buzz Rickson's MA-1 flying jacket, which retails for $455 ("Type MA-1"). More surprisingly, however, is the revelation that Gibson actually *invented* the black MA-1 jacket—it had never been manufactured by anyone before he imagined it. Gibson inserted the black MA-1 into his novel, mistakenly thinking that Buzz Rickson's produced it. Rickson's eventually sent him an e-mail message explaining that they had received many requests for a black jacket that they had never made. Once they learned of *Pattern Recognition* and the imaginary black MA-1, Rickson's asked Gibson for permission "to make a repro of *Cayce's* jacket, to market as their Pattern Recognition model."[138] From there a whole "William Gibson line" of black Air Force flying jacket reproductions has been produced, an apparently good simulacrum within the logo-maze of bad brands like Tommy Hilfiger. On his blog, Gibson defends the high cost of these jackets by explaining that they are carefully handcrafted simulacra, an authentic real (fake) thing in an economy of fakes, and that their cultural aura of cool is justified. At the end of this analysis, the bursting-through into our world of things born in fiction should leave no one surprised, especially with these particular novels. As ridiculous as some of them may seem as individuals, and as bad as they may be at making accurate predictions, professional coolhunters can be good readers of culture, careful hermeneuts, always on the lookout for a good idea. And the black MA-1 flying jackets are, admittedly, quite cool.

A Visit from the Goon Squad, meanwhile, portrays a future where cool may no longer be in the streets to be hunted but may have been subsumed by the total commodification of everyday life. In exploring this world, Egan suggests that the novelist finds herself in much the same situation as the creative class freelancer. She is an affective laborer in the allegedly immaterial or creative economy and must brand herself in order to thrive. Her art, moreover, must traverse privately owned technological platforms in order to find an audience in the first place. The desire to have one's intellectual capital turned into a serial television drama is incidental to this larger reality (and, in any case, action figures, video games, or black MA-1 flying jackets would also do). What the ambitious creative worker must do under such circumstances is incorporate the functions of an institution, a human corporation, into her own personality, to serve as the CEO of what the marketing guru Tom Peters insidiously calls "Brand You."[139] While one suspects that Egan would show little love for toxic marketing gurus such as Peters, she is unable to entirely reject his advice, fearing that time necessarily reifies all processes, flows, lived prac-

tices, and communities, that even authentic outbursts of singular artistry (as in Scotty's concert) must ultimately succumb to incorporation. The "goon" of her novel's title is, after all, *time* (127, 332). If
reification is an unavoidable dimension of temporal existence, as
Egan suggests, perhaps what is most troubling about Peters's vision
of Brand You is not autoreification as such, but the pursuit of reification in a manner that naturalizes the priorities of global capitalism.
The problem is not that you keep a slide journal on PowerPoint, but
that your postironic autoreification (the project of cultivating Brand
You) obscures the economic exploitation undergirding corporate
power. The true goon is not time, but capitalism. Egan arguably herself obscures such political-economic relations by emphasizing the
fact that Scotty has never had "a page or a profile or a handle or a
handset," as though the question of *whether you should have a social
profile on Facebook* were more important than the question of *who owns
Facebook*. In this regard, Gibson offers a better description of contemporary capitalism.

Individual differences notwithstanding, these novels all compel-
lingly show that the trendspotter or coolhunter arises in response to
the existential problems of a cultural economy operating under neoliberal policies and global distributions of labor. The marketing
industry absorbs and reproduces the language of interpretation and
cultural analysis because, in the context of automation and out-
sourcing, culture is more profitable than ever before. The novelist
interested in this world cannot avoid the risks of self-reference, techniques once commonly associated with metafiction and its many
blank ironies but now fully integrated into the movements of the
market. This is, in the end, why the coolhunter is necessarily a
postironic figure: she simultaneously must understand cultural
meanings and critically distance herself from these meanings, entertaining a kind of schizoid relationship to the concept of authenticity.
To be postironic in this sense is to be both a producer and a consumer of culture, something like a professional shopper. If this
seems like a somewhat weak position from which to fight exploitation or abolish class, that is because it is. The coolhunter, whatever
else she is, has not been put forward in these pages as a substitute for

other, properly political action figures. Being a coolhunter does nothing, on its own, to shut down sweatshops or to price goods "correctly" or to redistribute wealth more justly or to reduce greenhouse emissions. (I will discuss more directly political characterological models in the conclusion of this book.) At her best, the coolhunter sensitizes herself to the global networks she finds herself within— not an insignificant task—integrating her sensitivity into an economically aware characterological model. The lesson the coolhunter teaches is that such sensitivity requires, at a minimum, both a critically distant and aesthetically invested sense of the market and the world. What we do with this capability remains an open question, one that fiction cannot answer.

Conclusion

MANIC PIXIE DREAM OCCUPIER

On December 10, 2013, the Occupy Solidarity Network, Inc. (OSN), a three-person nonprofit organization that claims to run the "oldest and most trusted online resource for the Occupy Movement," sent a fundraising message to its large e-mail list.[1] It invited members to purchase a print of "The Ballerina and the Bull," an iconic image of a ballerina posed in arabesque atop *Charging Bull*, a bronze sculpture of a ferocious bull located in Bowling Green Park near Wall Street. "The Ballerina and the Bull" was originally published by the Vancouver-based anticonsumerist magazine *Adbusters*, and had come for many to symbolize the aspirations of the movement.[2] Proceeds from the sale of the poster would, OSN's e-mail explained, support an "activist fund managed by the Occupy Solidarity Network" and would "spark and sustain tomorrow's social uprising of the 99%."[3] This solicitation sparked a furious debate among different people and groups who had participated in Occupy. *Adbusters* denounced OSN for "selling out the movement." OSN board member Micah White responded to this criticism by seizing *Adbusters*'s Twitter account (@Adbusters). White—a former *Adbusters* editor, the self-described "creator of the #OWS meme," and founder of an organization called Boutique Activist Consultancy—accused *Adbusters* of having "lost its spirit" and being "unable to adapt to the post-Occupy reality." *Adbusters* soon regained control of its Twitter account, and reiterated its view that "[s]elling the original meme undermines the message of the movement." The NYC General Assembly, meanwhile, criticized OSN in a blog post called "Occupy Irony." The General Assembly complained that OSN had "resisted integration into the culture of Occupy Wall Street itself, which from the first instant was organized around an open working group model and direct democracy."[4] White had allegedly failed to live up to the principles of the General Assembly's "Statement of Autonomy," which insists that occupiers "SPEAK WITH US, NOT FOR US." Those who attempt to "speak for" Occupy by appropriating its messages and symbols are, by definition, "not a part of Occupy Wall Street."[5] Such appropriators balefully transform the "visionary spirit of OWS as a space-creating, conversation-generating, prefigurative uprising" into something "stagnant and dull and transactional."[6]

Though seemingly minor, this controversy showcases the political paradoxes of Occupy, illuminating how difficult it can be to differentiate "speaking with" from "speaking for" within the context of Occupy's style of anarchist politics. By what procedure are some persons or groups designated to be "not a part" of a group that otherwise claims to embody the 99%? Who, if anyone, gets to determine whether someone is "speaking for"—rather than "speaking with"—a movement that nominally aspires to be leaderless? Whose "autonomy" is threatened when self-avowed activists raise money through the sale of an iconic image that had been offered as a common visual resource?[7] One way to start answering these questions is to note that the slogan "We are the 99%" was never an empirical claim. By drawing attention to the fact of income inequality, the slogan "transforms a statistic into a crime."[8] The slogan, Mark Bray argues, "reclaimed a sense of class conflict under a seemingly apolitical guise."[9] We must, he notes, "distinguish between the 99% as a normative claim as opposed to a factual description."[10] Occupy is not, therefore, as some have claimed, anti-institutional. Rather, Occupy emerged from a lively effort to determine the terms of membership in—and legitimate methods of enforcing accountability for—the so-called 99%. The conflict over "The Ballerina and the Bull" was ultimately a conflict over which political norms, and which institutional forms, should govern the community. Occupiers overwhelmingly followed anarchist political principles developed across the 1990s and 2000s among alter-globalization activists.[11] And Occupy more generally came to be associated with horizontalism (antihierarchy), leaderless revolution (as opposed to vanguardism), Collective Thinking (as opposed to competitive thinking), direct action, mutual aid, and modified consensus decision making (as opposed to parliamentary or other procedures).[12] Occupiers sometimes proffered these principles as substitutes for parties, electoral politics, labor organizing, and single-issue activism. They insisted, as part of a call-and-response chant, "This is what democracy looks like." This model of participatory democracy also owes something to punk, particularly Hakim Bey's *T.A.Z.: The Temporary Autonomous Zone, Ontological Anarchy, Poetic Terrorism*, which was, in fact, the first book cataloged in the 5,000-book Occupy Wall Street library at Zuccotti Park.[13] The Zuccotti Park encampment might justly be regarded as a future-oriented version of a Temporary Autonomous Zone.

But the debate about which norms should govern Occupy does not just involve institutional questions. If Jodi Dean is correct in her claim that Occupy allowed "us" to "*imagine* and *enact* a new subject that is collective and in so doing appear differently to ourselves," then debates about what norms should govern Occupy also participated in the characterological history of counterculture.[14] The characterological question Occupy raised was nothing less than what form our new collective subjectivity should take. And this question was, unsurprisingly, intimately linked to the political debates about irony I have traced in these pages. After all, as Dean observes, "occupiers look like hippies, radicals, and hipsters."[15] Media discourse, likewise, frequently linked occupiers to the contemporary figure of the hipster. NPR, for example, explained that hipsters "follow indie bands and camp out at Occupy movements."[16] This recent version of the hipster should not be confused with the midcentury hipster I discussed in Chapter 1. Whereas intellectuals largely adored the midcentury hipster, no self-respecting intellectual would dare celebrate the contemporary hipster. Today's hipster is almost universally reviled.[17] A cottage industry has dedicated itself to attacking the hipster. The contemporary hipster, Mark Greif writes, emerged from "nineties youth culture, often called alternative or indie, that defined itself by its rejection of consumerism."[18] This new, vile version of the hipster is accused of using "irony without sarcasm, bitterness, or critique," using "[r]eflexivity . . . as a means to get back to sentimental emotion."[19] This debased figure deploys "the rhetoric but not the politics of the counterculture."[20] Christian Lorentzen excoriates both "Sweet hipsters, who practice the sort of irony you can take home to meet the parents" as well as "those Vicious hipsters, who practice the form of not-quite-passive aggression called snark."[21] *Adbusters* itself, a bastion of countercultural anti-consumerism, has also attacked hipster irony in the name of authentic rebellion, describing hipsters as "[l]overs of apathy and irony" whose ubiquity "represents the end of Western civilization."[22] The ascendancy of the hipster evidences "a culture lost in the superficiality of its past and unable to create any new meaning."[23] For the hipster, Christie Wampole writes in the *New York Times*, "irony functions as a kind of credit card you never have to pay back."[24] Given this vitriolic antihipster discourse, the association of occupiers and hipsters was often rightly taken as a slur. A blogger for the *Washington Post* felt the need to reassure her readers that Occupy was not a "hipster movement." It was, instead, "a real protest," though the writer admits that "there are more accordions at the movement than a totally non-ironic, non-hipster movement would have, which is to say, there is at least one accordion."[25] Even those sympathetic to the protests, such as the anthropologist Michael Taussig, called the occupiers of Zuccotti Park "radical hipsters from Brooklyn," meaning to signal the socioeconomic contradictions internal to the protest.[26] For some, Occupy was regarded as a political turning point, a final rejection of the apolitical character of contemporary hipster culture. By contrast, Rob Horning argued that Occupy raised profound questions about "the political sincerity of the Left" and feared that the movement would become "hipsterized."[27] Horning concludes that social movements "can no longer promise us chances for a more creative life—that revolution has come and been co-opted."[28]

Condemnations of the contemporary hipster should arouse some skepticism. Horning's claim that resistance to capitalism can "no longer" use a rhetoric of creativity reconstructs an idealized past when creative countercultural resistance was possible. But the mid-century hipsters, punks, and countercultural heroes celebrated as authentic bastions of political resistance were never so completely oppositional as they are commonly imagined to be. Nor, for that matter, were the alternative cultures that characterized the 1990s and early 2000s as ironic as they are often described. Indeed, I would argue, antihipster rhetoric often partakes of the same postironic discourse as contemporary hipster culture. Any smart hipster would have told you that revolutionary irony had been "co-opted" over twenty-five years ago. But, of course, such false genealogies—the fantasy that once upon a time truehearted countercultural rebels roamed the earth—can powerfully motivate contemporary political action. Stories about the dire need to move beyond contemporary hipster irony, toward some new form of oppositional political sincerity, are written in a narrative genre that I will call the postironic Bildungsroman. This genre figures postirony as the end of a process of either individual or collective political maturation. I will conclude *Cool Characters* by outlining the workings of this genre in two recent novels, both of which invoke Occupy: Rachel Kushner's *The Flamethrowers* (2013) and Jonathan Lethem's *Dissident Gardens* (2013). Both novels suggest that in order to become something like an occupier, one must traverse from a state of political naïvety through a phase of cynicism or post-modern irony, arriving finally at a state of postironic political commitment. These literary occupiers come to stand in for political transformations required of the reader. The occupier's (and reader's) final state of postironic political commitment is not, I would add, imagined to be personal or private but rather collective. Moreover, this postironic politics relies on a providential model of historical causality resembling the "figural causality" discussed by Hayden White. White's model of historical "causation" secularizes Christian typology, according to which figural types of the Old Testament are fulfilled by antitypes in the New Testament. This "figure-fulfillment model," which Erich Auerbach used to plot the history of Western literature, becomes for Occupy a proleptic political narrative.[29] The rhetoric of Occupy depends on what I will call, in homage to White, *prefigural causality*. Many occupiers use the term *prefiguration* to refer to the belief that activists can construct in the present a model of the postcapitalist future they hope to bring about.[30] This notion of pre-figuration is also figural because the occupier strives preemptively to become a figure in the present that will, in time, be fulfilled by inhab-itants of some postcapitalist future. Those who discursively construct the rhetorical (normative) 99% aspire in time to have that figure ful-filled by an empirical 99%, which will take the rhetorical 99% as its genealogical precursor. It is not enough to achieve an actual postcap-italist future. Present-day *activist communities* (figure) and *future poli-ties* (fulfillment) must be isomorphic. The empirical 99% are being asked to move beyond political irony—to move beyond the "dull" transactional politics represented by those like OSN, who claim to "speak for" Occupy—in order to adopt (to "speak with") the postironic characterological form of the occupier.

RACHEL KUSHNER's *The Flamethrowers* is not directly about Occupy. Largely set in the mid-1970s, the novel follows a motorcycle-obsessed artist nicknamed Reno (she's from Reno), who moves from Nevada to New York because of the "irony" that "a person had to move to New York City first, to become an artist of the west."[31] Reno eventually starts dating an Italian expatriate artist, Sandro Valera, heir to the Moto Valera motorcycle empire, who brings her into the downtown New York art scene. The novel intersperses the history of the fictional motorcycle company Moto Valera into Reno's primary narrative, outlining the company's involvement with futurism, fas-cism, as well as colonial exploitation in Brazil, by recounting the story of Sandro's father, T. P. Valera, before, during, and after World War I. After traveling to Italy with Sandro, Reno observes massive protests in Rome, encountering various members of "the Movement, as they called it" (270). Numerous commentators have described *The Flamethrowers* as a historical novel. Sounding like Georg Lukács, Hari Kunzru writes in his blurb for the book that Kushner "uses recent history not as a picturesque backdrop but as a way of interro-gating the present."[32] What has not been commented upon is that *The Flamethrowers* is a historical novel specifically about postmod-ernism. That is, the reader stands in relation to the novel's central postmodernist setting much as Reno stands in relationship to the modernism of T. P. Valera. Kushner tries to imagine postmodernism as a historical object of literary representation—as a moment that is resolutely past. And in attempting to write a novel about the "historical peculiarity" of an age that had allegedly "forgotten how to think historically," she is forced not only to "interrogate the present" but also to imagine what form a post-postmodern historical novel might take.[33] *The Flamethrowers* is therefore not an example of what Amy Elias has called metahistorical romance. Metahistorical romance oscillates between "skepticism and irony about the possibilities for true historical knowledge" and a "desire for History, for the 'secular sacred' sublime in the absence of the gods."[34] As Elias describes the genre, metahistorical romance is a posttraumatic narrative mode that posits history as lost forever, or rather accessible only through narrative emplotment.[35] If *The Flamethrowers* employed this mode, then the Movement would be lost to history. The mid-1970s would be the absent postmodern object of Kushner's sublime desire, impossible to fully recover or reconstruct. Instead, *The Flamethrowers* proposes that the Movement of '77 is—far from irrecoverably past—erupting again in our present. The novel imagines the possibility that history has been thinking the present.

At the level of content, Kushner figures postmodernism's relationship to our time in terms of Reno's journey from her working-class origins through the cynicism of the downtown scene to a renewed sense of political possibility in Italy. Furthermore, Kushner constructs a rigorous analogy between the developmental waystations of this postironic Bildungsroman and various geographical zones. Reno moves from the naïve earnestness of Nevada through the ironic minefield of New York City, finally arriving at a new sense of political awareness (if not exactly full-blown commitment) in Rome. Each location functions in a loosely allegorical way. We are frequently reminded that various characters in New York regard Reno as naïve. When Reno expresses surprise that Sandro, fourteen years her senior, might be attracted to her, Reno's new friend Giddle (a former denizen of Warhol's factory) treats her as if she were "too naïve to understand" (93). Giddle describes herself as "very camp and ironic," as a "downtown hipster" (90). If she were still hanging out at the Factory, Reno concludes, Giddle "would have been too cool to speak to me" (88).

Burdmoore Model, a member of the radical group The Motherfuckers, regards Reno as "endearingly naive" (157). Reno herself tells Sandro, during a movie date, that she has "a requirement for friendship," which is "Sincerity" (96). Sandro sincerely proceeds to unbutton her skirt and finger her. The character that best exemplifies the corrosive irony of the downtown scene is Ronnie Fontaine. Reno sleeps with Ronnie when she first arrives in New York (but does not learn his name). She meets Ronnie again through Sandro. We are informed that Ronnie displays an "artistic genius" for self-invention, though his actual art—he reformulates magazine images for "camp effect"—is "too flatly ironic" (144). Near the end of the novel, Ronnie sarcastically defends "two concepts" that are, in his view, "important tools for surviving the human condition" (315). One is *"Eye-ron-ee"* and the next is *"Diss-sim-you-lay-shon,"* or "[g]iving the false appearance that you are not some thing" (315).

The New York scene of the mid-1970s comes to stand for depoliticized "hipster" culture (both historical and contemporary). Within this milieu, the only character who seems to be interested in political action is Burdmoore, whose associates The Motherfuckers, a group of murderous pranksters founded in the 1960s, have largely burnt themselves out by the time of the novel's primary story. Burdmoore laments that "the Lower East Side . . . is dead now." One no longer finds traces of "insurrection" downtown (157). By contrast, Rome shows no lack of insurrection. When Reno finds herself with members of the Movement, she observes political graffiti in San Lorenzo and concludes:

> New York graffiti was not desperate communication. It was an exuberance of style, logo, name, the feat of installing jazzy pseudonyms, a burst of swirled color where the commuter had not thought possible. These were plain, stark messages written in black spray paint, at arm and eye level from the street. There were few pictures, with the exception of the occasional five-pointed star of the Red Brigades. (272)

Reno opposes American graffiti, written in the service of "style, logo, name," to the "plain, stark messages" of Italian political graffiti. When she observes the full protest, Reno at first thinks "Ronnie would have

appreciated them" but then concludes "that this context was too massive for Ronnie" (276). Kushner suggests that Ronnie's irony, his lame
camp self-creation, would fail to understand, let alone appreciate, the
"desperate communication" of the Italian uprising. Italian political
commitment exposes the shallowness of New York posturing, revealing
it as little more than "upper-class performance" (276). Reno finally
understands the ultimate hollowness of the downtown "hipster" scene
(though the less anachronistic term would be *punk*).

But *The Flamethrower*'s Roman protests are not, it turns out, just
history. Kushner suggests that the Movement of 1977 might be a
prolepsis of contemporary political activity, and specifically the
Occupy movement. Kushner has made this connection explicit in
interviews and in an essay she wrote for *The Paris Review* (which has
since been included in the paperback edition of the novel), in which
she discusses photos that inspired her novel. The book's cover image,
of a young Italian woman wearing war paint, "symbolized for me the
insurrectionary foment that overtook the country in that decade."
Kushner describes Autonomia as "a loose wave of people, all over
Italy, who came together for various reasons at various times to
engage in illegality and play, and to find a way to act, to build forms
of togetherness."[36] Kushner overtly puts the Movement into a genealogical relation with Occupy, and emphasizes that part of what was
appealing to many about the Movement was that it offered a "set of
refusals that no longer cohered with the factory and a traditionally
Marxist class composition." As imprisoned members of Autonomia
Operaia wrote, the uprisings of the mid-1970s were the culmination
of a "sharp break with the 'laborist' and State socialist traditions of
the established working-class movement."[37] In an interview, Kushner
praises Occupy in similar terms for not "making a specific set of
demands. They weren't asking for health benefits and better minimum wages as barristas [sic] or whatever. It was, and I hope remains,
a kind of rejection and a refusal, rather than a demand for a specific
and better-negotiated position in the service economy."[38] But the
connections between Autonomia and Occupy go beyond the style of
refusal each movement enacted. In her *Paris Review* essay, Kushner
writes that as she was completing *The Flamethrowers*, "events from
my time, my life, began to echo those in the book, as if I were inside
a game of call-and-response." It is as if the Movement of '77 invaded

the America that Kushner inhabited as she wrote retrospectively about the (postmodern) historical past. The Movement (call) figurally "causes" Occupy (response). She explains, "by the time I needed to describe the effects of tear gas for a novel about the 1970s, all I had to do was watch live feeds from Oakland, California." The historical sublime is now just down the street (though viewed online). Kushner's literary metahistory promises actual access to history. *The Flamethrowers* thus updates a postmodern genre (metahistorical romance), suggesting that this genre now affords a window onto the real. History, it turns out, is happening now. "[T]he lost potential of Italy's Movement of '77" turns out not to be lost, but has "come up again . . . with Occupy."[39] And the "illegality and play" Kushner celebrates is unlikely to end with the arrival (or even the failure) of Occupy. History's game of "call-and-response" will presumably continue, turning Occupy into the figure (call) for some future yet unnamed political fulfillment (response).

Her novel ultimately commits to a figural model of revolutionary change that unsurprisingly resembles Hardt and Negri's immaterialist politics. Autonomia comes to look, by her account, like nothing other than an anticipation of the Multitude, which Hardt and Negri describe as a "postmodern revolution" that "looks beyond imperial sovereignty."[40] The revolution of the multitude is postmodern in the sense that it seeks to counteract post-Fordist and biopolitical models of power.[41] The Multitude might be conceived as "an open and expansive network in which all differences can be expressed freely and equally, a network that provides the means of encounter so that we can work and live in common."[42] It is "capable of forming society autonomously."[43] Echoing these sentiments in her interviews and essays, Kushner constructs the occupier along a similar model, suggesting that to be an occupier requires moving through a necessary process of postmodern demateralization en route to a new sense of collective political belonging. Reno may be more right than she recognizes: to become a true artist of the west, to achieve autonomy and sincerity, she very well might need to be transformed by the ironic life of New York City.

*   *   *

JONATHAN LETHEM'S NINTH NOVEL, *Dissident Gardens*, represents the figure of the occupier more directly than does *The Flamethrowers*. Lethem places Occupy at the end of a lineage of leftist activism stretching from the mid-1950s through the early 2010s, telling the story of this radical inheritance as a multigenerational family saga. At the beginning of the novel, Rose Zimmer is kicked out of the Communist Party on the pretext that she is having an affair with a married black police officer, Douglas Lookins. Even though she is expelled, she becomes a one-woman torchbearer for the left in her community, the "Red Queen" of Sunnyside Gardens, a garden home community in Queens.[44] The novel traces the fortunes for the American Left across six decades, following the political evolution of Rose's daughter, Miriam, and Miriam's husband, Tommy. Along the way, Rose mentors Cicero Lookins, the son of her lover, who eventually becomes a college professor in Maine, "Baginstock College's miraculous triple token, gay, black, and overweight" (48). When Miriam and Tommy are murdered in Nicaragua in 1979, Rose's grandson, Sergius, who is raised by Quakers, becomes the locus of the novel's political hopes. He attempts to learn more about Rose from Cicero and discovers a surviving Occupy encampment, long after the major occupations have ended, in Maine. *Dissident Gardens* distributes its postironic Bildungsroman across multiple characters, tracing a trajectory from disillusionment with the credulous sincerity of the American Communist Party through a long period of countercultural irony and ending with a culminating— tentative but unambiguous—renewal of postironic political engagement, a new political hope that the novel associates with the figure of the occupier.

Dissident Gardens stages a confrontation between irony and sincerity within each successive generation, suggesting that whereas irony was once a necessary corrective to the political failures of the American Communist Party, it has today hardened into cynical reason. In the first generation, Rose's disillusioned irony—her new aversion to belief—stands in stark contrast with the political commitments of her husband, Albert, who leaves the United States for East Germany. When they are married, Albert and Rose share a commitment to "the greatest movement of human history" (12). Lethem

describes the newly married couple as "[t]wo believers in revolution" (12–13). The failure of the marriage ends up recapitulating
the failure of Rose's faith in the Communist Party. In a letter to
Miriam, Albert later writes, "Our striving on behalf of international
Communism during the years leading up to the war was, however
sincere, deeply naïve. How could it be anything other, given the situation of a Communism attempting to bring itself into consciousness
from within the American atmosphere" (225). Lethem contrasts
Albert's credulity—his sincere but degrading political commitment—
with Rose's more humane irony. As Rose suggests, "My beliefs don't
deliver me from a responsibility to the poor degraded human souls in
front of my face," contrasting her *political beliefs* and her *ethical respon-
sibilities* (16). In a sense, Rose's choice comes to resemble the choice of
the invisible man; she abandons a politically debilitating sincerity in
favor of a form of irony that gives her access to "the sidewalks of
Queens" (Ibid.). Rose would insist that she has "renounced nothing,"
that the "ideals that had sustained her a lifetime still sustained her,
because they weren't ideological, not even really ideals" (272). What
allegedly motivates Rose is not ideology or even ideals but a political
vision—a form of ethics—that she comes to call "comraderism"
(273).[45] The term arises in the context of a delusion that Rose has
toward the end of her life. She feverishly imagines that she befriends
the character Archie Bunker, the bigoted protagonist of Norman
Lear's sitcom *All in the Family*. Archie uses the term *comraderism* "to
name the feeling between himself and the others" at his bar, Kelcy's
(273). Rose's Left is not the organized Left; it is instead a spiritual left,
a left of affect, intersubjectivity, and everyday intimacy. Rose's ideal of
comraderism "existed in the space between one person and another,
secret sympathies of the body" (272). For Rose, access to comraderist
affect requires a prior loss of faith in ideology.

As a young adult, Rose's daughter, Miriam, finds herself becoming
an ironist, somewhat against her will. During a date, at the age of
seventeen, she finds "[h]er fiercest sincerities ... translated by the
male ego, on arrival, into daffy flirtation" (24). She is interpreted as "a
tease, an ironist supreme. And with a figure" (Ibid.). Rose has schooled
her daughter in "second-generation cynicism towards collapsed
gleaming visions of the future," but Miriam's "whole body demanded

revolution and gleaming cities" (28). In this sense, at least, she remains a "Bolshevik" (Ibid.). Despite her Bolshevism of the body, Miriam has a "talent for worldly implication," a capacity to insinuate that "she knew more than what she knew, and that what she knew was that everything was secretly and sexily connected" (71). She is a master of the asymmetrical logic of hip, and those who observe her find her lips forming "a smirk so perpetual, so embracing in its implications, it absolved its recipient of individual judgment" (172). Only the folk singer Tommy Grogan, Miriam's future husband, seems capable of seeing beyond her irony. Speaking to Sergius, Cicero describes Tommy as "sincere in his commitments to you and your mother, and to nuclear disarmament and Salvador Allende" (49). Rose and Miriam similarly regard Tommy as "the sincere one" (160). As Tommy grows more political, his transformation is described as a transition from being "the sincere one" to being "the protest one" (164). Lethem aligns Tommy's sincerity with his willingness to protest against injustice, but this commitment is Quixotic, and results in his and Miriam's murder in Nicaragua. When she confronts a character named "Fred the Californian," who may or may not be a CIA agent, Miriam attempts to make herself "sympathetically legible as a fellow cynic, a seeker of the pleasures of irony" (322). Her hopes are, alas, in vain. Tommy's sincere political commitment to Salvador Allende comes to seem, much like Albert's dedication to communism, credulous and dangerously self-destructive. In the end, not even Miriam's irony can save them.

The third generational confrontation between irony and sincerity—or, more precisely, cynicism and belief—arrives in the novel's climactic encounter between Cicero Lookins and Sergius Gogan. Sergius visits Cicero in Maine to learn more about Rose, conducting research for what he hopes will become "a cycle of songs" (48). Cicero is, early in the novel, coded as an arch-cynic. Lethem's narrator describes Cicero as a "monster of skepticism" from the age of thirteen (57). He needs to "unmask and unmake, to decry and destroy" ideology, ripping away the "veil of sustaining fiction that drove the world, what people *needed* to believe" (65). He is a "machine for debunking bullshit" (73). When he attempts to describe the "affective turn" to Sergius, he discovers that "[a]rmoring himself in hostility turned Cicero's sincerest allegiances to jargon and junk, to ash in his mouth" (221). He is, like Rose, committed to a form of affective politics—a politics of interbodily relation, a politics somehow beyond ideology—but he is unable to discuss these commitments sincerely. Words fail him. His thoroughgoing, theoretically sophisticated irony has not only unmoored him from the perils of ideology but also the pleasures of true commitment. Cynical reason has made it impossible for him to form lasting commitments. Sergius, by contrast, resembles his father, Tommy. He is sincerely, almost naïvely, committed to his art. At the end of the novel, Sergius's sincerity, like Tommy's, becomes political.

While visiting Cicero, Sergius meets an occupier, Lydia, at the "tiny spectacle of Occupy Cumbow," the occupation of the downtown of a small town in Maine (219). Cicero observes that Sergius and "his Occupy girl seemed incapable of other than moonish chirping in each other's presence" (221). Annoyed that Sergius wants him to befriend Lydia, Cicero finds himself cynically describing the political activity of Sergius's "Occupy girl" in the terms that his students use: "Sergius, in the great tradition of the wan hetero, was serially addicted to the Actualizing Other he wanted his magical Negro to befriend—what name was it Cicero's students gave the archetype? His *Manic Pixie Dream Girl.* Though this one was a little worse for wear than Zooey Deschanel" (218). In 2007, the film critic Nathan Rabin coined the phrase Manic Pixie Dream Girl to describe a stock film character who "exists solely in the fevered imaginations of sensitive writer-directors to teach broodingly soulful young men to embrace life and its infinite mysteries and adventures."[46] This stock character is frequently associated with New Sincerity, including filmic subgenres such as mumblecore; the M.P.D.G.'s sole purpose in these films seems to be to facilitate the transformation of a male protagonist from cynicism or disenchantment to a sense of wonder or whimsy. She promptly thereafter disappears, her whimsical work done. And, of course, Cicero is right. Sergius *is* treating Lydia less as a person than as a trope; he *is* figuring her as a Manic Pixie Dream Girl. And she also functions that way within Lethem's novel. Before she quits the scene, her commitment to Occupy facilitates Sergius's decision to regard himself not only as chronicler of his family's history but also as a "fellow traveler," a wholehearted part of the American Left (365). However, Lydia's presence also resists Cicero's style of ideology critique; as an occupier, she provokes and embodies a characterological form of commitment that, Lethem seems to hope, will not turn into "ash" in the mouth. After having sex with Lydia in the bathroom of an airport, Sergius is apprehended by security, encountering the American national security state in its most mundane—but ubiquitous—form. His encounter with Occupy and the TSA comes to seem like destiny: "This, all this, as it was meant to be. Sergius, arrived here in this crucial indefinite place, this undisclosed location, severed from the life of the planet yet not aloft. Arrived at last at this nowhere in which he became visible before the law" (366). Describing the crucial moment of Sergius's political commitment, this passage balances a sense that Sergius is grounded (he has arrived) and unrooted (he is in an unspecified place). His identity becomes both crystalized by and subjected to state power. He becomes, Lethem writes, "[a] cell of one, beating like a heart," recognizing himself, perhaps for the first time, as something like a collective subject (366). Sergius angrily declares that he is "an Occupier" to his confused captors (363). He becomes, in his own hyperbolic estimation, "a Backwards traveller. Time pilot. By birthright an American Communist" (363). Lethem imagines the occupier as a figure who might at once hearken back to the spirit of American communism—without forming a new party, submitting to this or that dogmatic ideology, or holding naïve beliefs. Sergius transforms Rose's ironic affective spirit of comraderism into the postironic ethos of the occupier. At least within the narrative set out by the novel, Sergius fulfills the aspirations motivating Rose, Miriam, and Cicero. The history of the American Left, by Lethem's account, is largely a bleak history of naïve failure or corrosive, soul-crushing ironic disillusionment. Only Occupy offers his characters a name for a political ethos (a postironic characterological model) that might do something to reverse, or at least halt, the American Left's downward political trajectory, to synthesize these two stances. Sergius's political awakening may be, in one sense, overblown, but it is nonetheless heartfelt. Unlike Jodi Dean, Lethem does not seem to hope that Occupy might literally lead to the formation of a "new communist party," but he does imagine that it might—and perhaps should—become the vehicle for a spirit of "American Communism" within the hearts of newly collectivized individuals. What such a communism of the spirit—a communism of identity, affect, and character—portends is politically ambiguous, to say the least.

THIS AMBIGUITY IS, finally, the same ambiguity that haunts Occupy, which is now often referred to in the past tense, as exhausted or failed. Lethem and Kushner powerfully dramatize sympathetic ties between bodies, across races, and across class locations. They also subtly engage with their own post-postmodern literary positions by writing historical novels whose historical moments are not past, not objects eliciting sublime desire, but living, present, and active figures for future fulfillment. In Lethem's portrait of "comraderism" or Kushner's renditions of the "desperate communication" of the Movement of '77, one also glimpses the political ecstasy—and sense of community—that characterized occupation sites around the United States (and around the world) in 2011 and 2012. Kelcy's Bar and the streets of Rome can, no less than Zuccotti Park, come to seem like the punk Temporary Autonomous Zones Hakim Bey celebrated. And yet, though Occupy often invoked an idea of prefigural politics, all of these zones can sometimes feel like emotionally, socially, and spiritually self-sufficient spaces that are not preparations for action but ends in themselves. What comes after postmodern blank ironies or cynical reason is not a commitment to sustained and methodical organizing but rather a willingness finally to enjoy one's affective connections, to taste tear gas among comrades—or least watch comrades getting tear gassed on YouTube. Of course, in a political economy that exploits the affect of workers, in a media environment that commoditizes almost all social relationships, constructing a TAZ is no small feat. But the limitation of such a vision is, I hope, obvious. However one feels about the specific political form of the party, Jodi Dean is certainly correct when she writes that Occupy should be made "explicit as a political form for the incompatibility between capitalism and the people" if it hopes to endure, if it hopes to transform the solidarity of the 99% from norm to fact. Absent specific ambitious, sustainable, scalable, and—yes—sometimes dull political projects, such postironic celebrations of local freedom threaten to regress into Bohemian consumerism, "[a] sort of unconscious R&D [for industrial civilization], exploring alternate social strategies," as one character suggests in William Gibson's *All Tomorrow's Parties*.[47] The image of the ballerina on the bull would become nothing other than a figure for the creative class professional, someone who will in time make her own bronze bulls.

This is not to argue against the significance of culture to politics, or to dismiss the allure of Temporary Autonomous Zones, Occupation sites, comraderly bars, or other lively zones of human contact. As this study has tried to show, we must take cultural politics and character-ological terminology seriously. A better political future must trans-form not only the institutional forms through which we exercise col-lective action but also our affects and habits. In fact, the problem with the TAZ as a model of political community is characterological. A slogan like "This Is What Democracy Looks Like" poses two risks. The first danger is that we might take too seriously the verb's tense, imagining that democracy has already been achieved or is easily achieved for the 99%. The second danger is that we might imagine that the local institutions (general assemblies, spokescouncils) that created this or that Temporary Autonomous Zone are the sole legiti-mate vehicles for political transformation, and that future societies must recapitulate the form. The institutional form of a spokescouncil would not be a strategic or transitional form of organization but would become an already-existent blueprint for the future. These two risks are, I would argue, versions of the same danger. Both views take the prefigurative politics that characterizes Occupy literally. Prefigu-rative rhetoric is a powerful motivator of human action. Imagining how future generations will write you into their histories, how your actions today might become part of genealogies of human liberation, is rousing. It is not hard to understand why such fantasies might help some people overcome political cynicism and quietism. But taking prefiguration literally threatens to replicate that cynicism and qui-etism. If you think that you have already literally *lived* the future, that you can simply form a TAZ whenever you become sick of contempo-rary life, you may become quietist. If you thought that the General

Assembly was the sole legitimate means of achieving a better future, and came to see it destroyed—not only through police action but also through internal strife—you might become cynical. And if you imagine your relationship to the future in genealogical terms, you risk offloading responsibility for building the better world you desire onto future generations. Your only role in the present would be to inspire history's true, unnamed protagonists.

Those of us committed to convincing the empirical 99% to join the normative 99% might instead adopt a slightly different ethos. We might, first of all, see the project of transcending political cynicism as requiring a characterological commitment to transforming the social and political forms—the structures, practices, and institutions—that generate political detachment, cynicism, and blank irony in the first place. Institutions capable of overcoming cynicism would not be ends in themselves but rather would be precursors to other projects of institution building. This oppositional ethos would not only be oriented toward the future, but would simultaneously require a historical sense of the changing political fortunes of countercultural irony, a sense of why irony took on and lost political significance in the twentieth and now the twenty-first centuries. The ethos of irony is always political—in that it always recommends a specific relationship between individual and collective life—but it does not have a predetermined fate or political content. As my discussions of the hipster and the punk have tried to show, irony did not, even it its most avowedly countercultural forms, necessarily aid projects of human liberation. Nor, as my discussions of the believer and the coolhunter sought to demonstrate, will we be able to predict in advance the future political significance of postirony. Even the most debased corporate inventions, such as the brand, might offer unexpected political insights. We must, therefore, cultivate within ourselves an ironic understanding of our own countercultural inheritance while simultaneously developing a nonironic commitment to learning how to build enduring institutions that have the capacity not only to rouse spirits but also to dismantle the power of those whose strength partly depends on our cynicism. Such a character type might, finally, fulfill the figure of the occupier, and be worthy of the name.

NOTES

ACKNOWLEDGMENTS

INDEX

Notes

Preface

1. *Infinite Jest* imagines a near future North America in which the Organization of North American Nations (O.N.A.N.) has adopted a scheme of "REVENUE-ENHANCING SUBSIDIZED TIME™." David Foster Wallace, *Infinite Jest* (Boston: Little, Brown and Company, 1996), 223. Subsequent references will be cited parenthetically as *IJ*. Based on internal evidence, the Year of the Perdue Wonderchicken corresponds to 2005, the year I first read Wallace's book. Most of the main action of the novel occurs during the Year of the Depend Adult Undergarment (Y.D.A.U.) or 2009.

2. David Foster Wallace, "E Unibus Pluram: Television and U.S. Fiction," in *A Supposedly Fun Thing I'll Never Do Again: Essays and Arguments* (New York: Back Bay Books, 1998), 81. Subsequent references will be cited parenthetically.

3. Fredric Jameson, "Future City," *New Left Review* 21 (2003): 76.

4. Roger Rosenblatt, "The Age of Irony Comes to An End," *Time*, September 24, 2001, http://content.time.com/time/magazine/article/0,9171,1000893,00.html.

5. Plato, "Symposium," trans. Alexander Nehamas and Paul Woodruff, in *Plato: Complete Works*, ed. John M. Cooper and D. S. Hutchinson (Cambridge, MA: Hackett Publishing, 1997), 498.

Introduction

1. These quotes are all from Zadie Smith, "Fail Better," *Guardian*, January 13, 2007, and Zadie Smith, "Read Better," *Guardian*, January 20, 2007. These essays are no longer available on *The Guardian*'s Web site. "Fail Better" can be read at http://faculty.sunydutchess.edu/oneill/failbetter.htm, and "Read Better" is available at http://www.sis-sevres.net/The-limits-of-fiction-part-2.html.

2. T. S. Eliot, "Tradition and the Individual Talent," in *The Sacred Wood and Major Early Essays* (New York: Dover, 2007), 30.

3. The full bibliography of antitheory writing is too vast to document here. For a representative selection across three decades, see W. J. T. Mitchell, ed., *Against Theory: Literary Studies and the New Pragmatism* (Chicago: University of Chicago Press, 1985); Alex Callinicos, *After Postmodernism: A Marxist Critique* (London: Polity Press, 1991); Gerald Graff, *Literature against Itself: Literary Ideas in Modern Society* (Lanham, MD: Ivan R. Dee, 1995); Alan Sokal and Jean Bricmont, *Fashionable Nonsense: Postmodern Intellectuals' Abuse of Science* (New York: Picador, 1999); Terry Eagleton, *After Theory* (New York: Basic Books, 2004); Daphne Patai and Will H. Corral, ed., *Theory's Empire: An Anthology of Dissent* (New York: Columbia University Press, 2005). These books attack theory from so many different angles, with so many definitions of what constitutes theory, and with so many mutually contradictory explanations of why theory endangers planetary survival that general comment is close to impossible. Though myriad philosophical and critical projects have been described using the catchall label *theory*, it is nonetheless possible to speak of a relatively coherent cultural image of theory that has circulated over the past thirty years, both inside and outside academia, associated with postmodernism. Smith's essay evokes one version of this image.

4. Zadie Smith, *On Beauty* (New York: Penguin, 2006), 44. Subsequent references will be cited parenthetically.

5. See Zadie Smith, "Two Paths for the Novel," *New York Review of Books*, November 20, 2008, http://www.nybooks.com/articles/archives/2008/nov/20/two-paths-for-the-novel/.

6. For a classic analysis of theory as "a new discursive genre, which we might as well call 'postmodern theory,'" see Fredric Jameson, *Postmodernism, or, the Cultural Logic of Late Capitalism* (Durham, NC: Duke University Press, 1991), x. Jeffrey T. Nealon likewise associates postmodernism and theory in his effort to trace theory's future beyond postmodernism. He does so "in part because in its heyday, postmodernism was often simply equated with theory. Or at least there was a sense that this mongrel hybrid called theory was an invaluable tool for diagnosing the postmodern condition." Jeffrey T. Nealon, *Post-Postmodernism: Or, The Cultural Logic of Just-in-Time Capitalism* (Stanford: Stanford University Press, 2012), xi.

7. See, for example, Paula Geyh, Fred G. Leebron, and Andrew Levy, ed., *Postmodern American Fiction: A Norton Anthology* (New York: W. W. Norton & Company, 1997). The anthology begins with an excerpt from Pynchon's *The Crying of Lot 49* (1966) and ends with Jameson's essay "Postmodernism and Consumer Society." Between these bookends comes an array of writers, including Truman Capote, Don DeLillo, Neal Stephenson, Joyce Carol Oates, Marilynne Robinson, E. L. Doctorow, Philip Roth, Art Spiegelman, Leslie Marmon Silko, Toni Morrison, and Wallace. Although they do not endorse his Marxist commitments, by positioning Jameson where they do, the editors use him as a kind of retroactive justification for their fairly wide-ranging, disparate, and arguably idiosyncratic choices. The tacit argument of the anthology seems to be this: if postmodernism is the cultural logic of late capitalism, and every

cultural artifact symptomatically expresses this logic, then every text in the anthology can be justified as representative of the period.

8. It should not come as a surprise to learn that Smith was a 2002–2003 Radcliffe Institute for Advanced Study Fellow at Harvard University, where she worked on a nonfiction book project called "Fail Better," which was also called "The Morality of the Novel," "a book of essays considering a selection of twentieth-century writers through the glass of moral philosophy." "Zadie Smith," Radcliffe Institute for Advanced Study, https://www.radcliffe.harvard .edu/people/zadie-smith. Smith also appears as a character in *On Beauty*. Described as a "feckless novelist on a visiting fellowship," Smith's stand-in flees a faculty meeting (324).

9. Nicholas Dames, "The Theory Generation," *n+1* 14 (2012), https:// nplusonemag.com/issue-14/reviews/the-theory-generation/.

10. Mark McGurl, *The Program Era: Postwar Fiction and the Rise of Creative Writing*, 321. The exception is his discussion of Sandra Cisneros's *The House on Mango Street* (334–346).

11. Judith Ryan, *The Novel after Theory* (New York: Columbia University Press, 2012), 20.

12. François Cusset, *French Theory: How Foucault, Derrida, Deleuze, & Co. Transformed the Intellectual Life of the United States*, trans. Jeff Fort, with Josephine Berganza and Marlon Jones (Minneapolis: University of Minnesota Press, 2008), 5.

13. Dames, "The Theory Generation."

14. Zadie Smith, "Foreword," in *Changing My Mind: Occasional Essays* (New York: Penguin Books, 2010), xi.

15. Stephen J. Burn, ed., *Conversations with David Foster Wallace* (Jackson, MS: University Press of Mississippi, 2012), 49.

16. Ibid.

17. McGurl does not explicitly define the autopoetic process but offers a series of diagrams that suggest that this process arises from the interplay among ideologies of experience, creativity, and craft, respectively associated with the creative writing slogans "Write What You Know," "Find Your Voice," and "Show Don't Tell" (23).

18. Mark Greif, "'The Death of the Novel' and Its Afterlives: Toward a History of the 'Big, Ambitious Novel,'" *boundary 2* 36, no. 2 (2009): 12.

19. On snark, see David Denby, *Snark: It's Mean, It's Personal, and It's Ruining Our Conversation* (New York: Simon & Schuster, 2009).

20. Qtd. in Caroline Kepnes, "The After Words," *Entertainment Weekly*, December 21, 2001, http://www.ew.com/ew/article/0,,252843,00.html.

21. Edward Rothstein, "Attacks on U.S. Challenge Postmodern True Believers," *New York Times*, September 22, 2001, http://www.nytimes.com/2001 /09/22/arts/22CONN.html.

22. Paul Rudnick and Kurt Andersen, "The Irony Epidemic," *Spy*, March 1989, 92–98.

23. Franco Moretti, "The Spell of Indecision," *New Left Review* 164 (1987): 33.

24. Peter Sloterdijk, *Critique of Cynical Reason*, trans. Michael Eldred, foreword Andreas Huyssen (Minneapolis: University of Minnesota Press, 2010), 539.

25. Ibid., 103.

26. Slavoj Žižek, *The Sublime Object of Ideology* (London: Verso, 1989), 25–26.

27. Ibid., 24.

28. Eve Kosofsky Sedgwick, *Touching Feeling: Affect, Pedagogy, Peformativity* (Durham, NC: Duke University Press, 2003), 143.

29. Ibid., 143, 144.

30. Stephen Best and Sharon Marcus, "Surface Reading: An Introduction," *Representations* 108, no. 1 (2009): 2.

31. Sedgwick, *Touching Feeling*, 123–152. Best and Marcus, "Surface Reading." Timothy Bewes, "Reading with the Grain: A New World in Literary Criticism," *differences* 21, no. 3 (2010): 1–33. Michael Warner, "Uncritical Reading," in *Polemic: Critical or Uncritical*, ed. Jane Gallop (New York: Routledge, 2004), 13–38. S. P. Mohanty, *Literary Theory and the Claims of History: Postmodernism, Objectivity, Multicultural Politics* (Ithaca, NY: Cornell University Press, 1997). Paula M. L. Moya, *Learning from Experience: Minority Identities, Multicultural Struggles* (Berkeley: University of California, 2002). Rita Felski, *Uses of Literature* (New York: Wiley-Blackwell, 2008). Chris Nealon, "Reading on the Left," *Representations* 108, no. 1 (2009): 22–50. Jeffrey T. Nealon, *Post-Postmodernism*. This is, of course, only a partial list of efforts to move beyond what we might call postmodern criticism. One might also include recent scholarship on affect theory and various offshoots of speculative realism/object-oriented ontology (SR/OOO). Advocating OOO, Timothy Morton describes "the time of hyperobjects" as "a time of sincerity: a time in which it is impossible to achieve a final distance toward the world. But for this very reason, it is also a time of irony. We realize that nonhuman entities exist that are incomparably more vast and powerful than we are, and that our reality is caught in them." Timothy Morton, *Hyperobjects: Philosophy and Ecology after the End of the World* (Minneapolis: University of Minnesota Press, 2013), 130.

32. For a partial version of this descriptive poetics, see my essay "Four Faces of Postirony," in *Notes on Metamodernism: Art, Literature, and Visual Media after Postmodernism*, ed. Timotheus Vermeulen and Robin van den Akker (forthcoming).

33. The best historical survey of irony is Claire Colebrook, *Irony* (New York: Routledge, 2003). For a more episodic (one might say appropriately ironic) analysis of moments in the history of irony, see Kevin Newmark, *Irony on Occasion: From Schlegel and Kierkegaard to Derrida and de Man* (New York: Fordham University Press, 2012). For a theoretical analysis of irony, see Linda Hutcheon, *Irony's Edge: The Theory and Politics of Irony* (New York: Routledge, 2003).

34. H. W. Fowler, *A Dictionary of Modern English Usage: The Classic First Edition*, ed. David Crystal (Oxford: Oxford University Press, 2009), 295.

35. The "mention theory of irony" is outlined in Dan Sperber and Deirdre Wilson, "Irony and the Use-Mention Distinction," in *Radical Pragmatics*, ed. Peter Cole (New York: Academic Press, 1981), 295–318. The "pretense theory of irony" is described in Herbert H. Clark and Richard J. Gerrig, "On the Pretense Theory of Irony," in *Irony in Language and Thought: A Cognitive Science Reader*, ed. Raymond W. Gibbs and Herbert L. Colston (New York: Routledge,

2007), 25–34. On irony as a "viewpoint phenomenon," see Vera Tobin and Michael Israel, "Irony as a Viewpoint Phenomenon," in *Viewpoint in Language: A Multimodal Perspective*, ed. Barbara Dancygier and Eve Sweetser (Cambridge: Cambridge University Press, 2012), 25–46. These analysts owe much to the linguistic philosophy of Paul Grice.

36. James C. Scott, *Weapons of the Weak: Everyday Forms of Peasant Resistance* (New Haven, CT: Yale University Press, 1987), 350.

37. Leo Strauss, *The City and Man* (Chicago: University of Chicago Press, 1978), 51.

38. Ibid.

39. Hutcheon, *Irony's Edge*, 10.

40. Wayne C. Booth, *A Rhetoric of Irony* (Chicago: University of Chicago Press, 1975), 62.

41. See Bernadette Meyler, "Bakhtin's Irony," *Pacific Coast Philology* 32, no. 1 (1997): 105–120. Bakhtin's philosophy and criticism are, of course, more complex than contemporary critical appropriations of his ideas would sometimes suggest. *Rabelais and His World*, for example, famously depicts a regenerative model of iconoclastic politics and argues that medieval carnival laughter built "a second world and a second life outside officialdom, a world in which all medieval people participated more or less, in which they lived during a given time of the year." Mikhail Bakhtin, *Rabelais and His World* (Bloomington: Indiana University Press 2009), 6. For Bakhtin, only the laughter of medieval carnival and marketplace culture has this power. Romantic irony and modernist irony, by contrast, represent fallen or reduced forms of this second-world-disclosing, life-building laughter. Modern ironies, Bakhtin argues, trade in cheap negation without rebirth. To the degree that he is interested in irony as such, Bakhtin would prefer to view it not only as "literary phenomenon" but also in "its link with the culture of folk humor" (120n63). Despite these qualifications, Bakhtin's grotesque realism invokes all four categories of political irony I discuss in this section. Moreover, as will become apparent, the question of whether irony has a regenerative function is of great concern for many of the authors I discuss. In Bakhtin's account of the politics of "grotesque realism," we see a template for— and characterological prefiguration of—Scott's analysis of peasant resistance. It should finally not come as a surprise that the anthropologist and activist David Graeber invokes Bakhtin and the concept of the *carnivalesque* more broadly in his account of anarchist protests against the 2001 Summit of the Americas in Québec City. Speaking of a group of radical puppeteers at this protest, Graeber assures his readers that "[e]ven those who have not themselves read Rabelais or Bakhtin are certainly familiar with the notion of the carnivalesque" and that these dissident puppeteers are engaged in a form of "collective consumption" that "challenges the principle of hierarchy itself" and does something to reverse the "privatization of desire." *Direct Action: An Ethnography* (Oakland, CA: AK Press, 2009), 503.

42. For a comprehensive analysis of this German aesthetic tradition of irony, and Hegel's critique of it, see Ayon Maharaj, *The Dialectics of Aesthetic Agency: Revaluating German Aesthetics from Kant to Adorno* (New York: Bloomsbury Academic, 2013). Roy wishes to defend a notion of aesthetic agency, the idea

that "art at its most sublime registers the pathos of the distance between who we are and who we might be" (15).

43. Friedrich Schlegel, *Friedrich Schlegel's* Lucinde *and the Fragments*, trans. and intro. Peter Firchow (Minneapolis: University of Minnesota Press, 1971), 29.

44. Ibid., 247.

45. "God-like geniality" is from George Wilhelm Friedrich Hegel, *Introductory Lectures on Aesthetics*, trans. Bernard Bosanquet, ed. Michael Inwood (New York: Penguin, 1993) 72. The phrase "unrelenting antifoundationalist skepticism" is from Maharaj, *The Dialectics of Aesthetic Agency*, 94.

46. Lee Edelman, *No Future: Queer Theory and the Death Drive* (Durham, NC: Duke University Press, 2004), 24.

47. Ibid., 23.

48. Christian Thorne, *The Dialectic of Counter-Enlightenment* (Cambridge, MA: Harvard University Press, 2010), 13.

49. Ibid.

50. Hegel, *Introductory Lectures on Aesthetics*, 73.

51. Søren Kierkegaard, *The Concept of Irony: With Continual Reference to Socrates*, ed. and trans. Howard V. Hong and Edna H. Hong (Princeton: Princeton University Press, 1989), 275.

52. Colebrook, *Irony*, 1.

53. See, for example, Fred Pfeil, "Postmodernism as a 'Structure of Feeling,'" in *Marxism and the Interpretation of Culture*, ed. Cary Nelson and Lawrence Grossberg (Champaign: University of Illinois Press, 1988), 381–404.

54. Roman Jakobson, "The Dominant," in *Selected Writings, Volume III: Poetry of Grammar and Grammar of Poetry*, ed. Stephen Rudy (The Hague: Mouton, 1981), 751.

55. See, of course, Jameson, *Postmodernism*, 4.

56. See Alan Wilde, *Horizons of Assent: Modernism, Postmodernism, and the Ironic Imagination* (Philadelphia: University of Pennsylvania Press, 1987). See also discussions of irony as a dominant mode of postmodernism (compared to nostalgia) in Linda Hutcheon, *A Poetics of Postmodernism: History, Theory, Fiction* (New York: Routledge, 1988) and *The Politics of Postmodernism* (New York: Routledge, 2002).

57. Paul Fussell, *The Great War and Modern Memory* (Oxford: Oxford University Press, 2000), 8.

58. Ibid.

59. Ibid., 33.

60. Ibid., 35.

61. Ibid.

62. Jean-François Lyotard, *The Postmodern Condition: A Report on Knowledge*, trans. Geogg Bennington and Brian Massumi, Foreword Fredric Jameson (Minneapolis: University of Minnesota Press, 1984), xxiv.

63. Richard Rorty, *Contingency, Irony, and Solidarity* (Cambridge: Cambridge University Press, 1989), 87.

64. Christy Wampole, "How To Live without Irony," *New York Times*, November 17, 2012, http://opinionator.blogs.nytimes.com/2012/11/17/how-to-live-without-irony/.

65. Jürgen Habermas, "Modernity—an Incomplete Project," trans. Seyla

Ben-Habib, in *The Anti-aesthetic: Essays on Postmodern Culture*, ed. Hal Foster (New York: New Press, 2002), 3–15.

66. Neither Aristophanes nor Xenophon applies the term to Socrates.

67. Gregory Vlastos, *Socrates: Ironist and Moral Philosopher* (Ithaca, NY: Cornell University Press, 1991), 31.

68. Melissa Lane, "The Evolution of Eirōneia in Classical Greek Texts: Why Socratic Eirōneia is Not Socratic Irony," *Oxford Studies in Ancient Philosophy* 31 (2006): 51.

69. Ibid.

70. Ibid., 53.

71. Aristotle, *Nicomachean Ethics*, trans. and ed. Roger Crisp (Cambridge: Cambridge University Press, 2004), 76.

72. Ibid., 77.

73. Cicero, *On the Ideal Orator*, trans. James M. May and Jakob Wisse (Oxford: Oxford University Press, 2001), 198.

74. Qtd. in Melissa Lane, "Reconsidering Socratic Irony," in *The Cambridge Companion to Socrates*, ed. David R. Morrison (Cambridge: Cambridge University Press, 2010), 240–241. The translation is from *Quintilian: The Orator's Education: Books 9-10*, ed. and trans. D. A. Russell (Cambridge, MA: Harvard University Press, 2001), 61. The possibility that irony might encompass a whole life is, for Quintilian, specifically a consequence of the fact that a figure is an iterated trope: "just as a continued series of Metaphors produces an Allegory, so a sustained use of the Trope Irony will give rise to the Figure" (Ibid.)

75. Randolph Bourne, "The Life of Irony," in *The Radical Will: Selected Writings 1911–1918*, preface Christopher Lasch, selections and intro. Olaf Hansen (Berkeley: University of California Press, 1992), 134.

76. Ibid.

77. Ibid.

78. Amanda Anderson, *The Way We Argue Now: A Study in the Cultures of Theory* (Princeton: Princeton University Press, 2005), 116.

79. Ibid., 285.

80. Ibid., 287.

81. Michel Foucault, "Preface," in Gilles Deleuze and Félix Guattari, *Anti-Oedipus: Capitalism and Schizophrenia*, trans. Robert Hurley, Mark Seem, and Helen Lane (Minneapolis: University of Minnesota Press, 1983), xiii.

82. Stephen K. White, *The Ethos of a Late-Modern Citizen* (Cambridge, MA: Harvard University Press, 2009).

83. Jeffrey T. Nealon, *Foucault beyond Foucault: Power and Its Intensifications since 1984* (Stanford: Stanford University Press, 2007), 10. Nealon wishes to argue against this thesis and to reactivate the force of Foucault's thought for the present.

84. Richard Wolin, *The Wind from the East: French Intellectuals, the Cultural Revolution, and the Legacy of the 1960s* (Princeton: Princeton University Press, 2010), xi.

85. Aristotle, *On Rhetoric: A Theory of Civic Discourse*, trans. George A. Kennedy (Oxford: Oxford University Press, 2006), 38.

86. Ibid., 39.

87. George A. Kennedy, for instance, claims that Aristotle "fails to recognize the great role of the authority of a speaker as already perceived by an audience." Ibid., 22.

88. The concept of ethos has been studied most commonly among scholars of composition and rhetoric. See James S. Baumlin and Tita French Baumlin, ed., *Ethos: New Essays in Rhetorical and Critical Theory* (Dallas: Southern Methodist University Press, 1994). For a narratological view, see also Liesbeth Korthals Altes, *Ethos and Narrative Interpretation: The Negotiation of Values in Fiction* (Lincoln: University of Nebraska Press, 2014).

89. Bourdieu writes, "'habitus' permitted me to break with the structuralist paradigm without falling back into the old philosophy of the subject or of consciousness, that of classical economy and its *homo economicus*, returning these days under the name of 'methodological individualism.'" Pierre Bourdieu, *The Rules of Art: Genesis and Structure of the Literary Field*, trans. Susan Emanuel (Stanford: Stanford University Press, 1995), 179.

90. Pierre Bourdieu, *The Logic of Practice*, trans. Richard Nice (Stanford: Stanford University Press, 1992), 62.

91. Some have argued that the concept of habitus has not accounted well for individual and group creativity. For an effort to move beyond these limitations, see Bruno Frère, "Bourdieu's Sociological Fiction: A Phenomenological Reading of Habitus," in *The Legacy of Pierre Bourdieu*, ed. Simon Susen and Bryan S. Turner (London: Anthem Press, 2011), 247–270.

92. I am positing a different relationship between ethos and habitus than Bourdieu himself does. Bourdieu claims that "*habitus* encompasses the notion of ethos," and he opposes "ethos" to "ethic." He defines ethos as "a system of practical, axiological schemes," as "morality made flesh." Pierre Bourdieu, *Sociology in Question*, trans. Richard Nice (London: SAGE Publications, 1993), 86.

93. Pierre Hadot, *Philosophy as a Way of Life*, ed. and intro. Arnold I. Davidson (Hoboken, NJ: Wiley-Blackwell, 1995), 82.

94. Ibid., 265.

95. Ibid.

96. Ibid., 273.

97. Ibid.

98. This is perhaps one reason that the term ethos can seem to describe the "prevailing spirit" both of individual persons and institutions. Although terms like *ethos* and *askesis* should, strictly speaking, not be conflated, I will use a set of related terms—*ethos, character, disposition, orientation, stance*, and less frequently *askesis*—synonymously throughout these pages.

99. Alexander Nehamas discusses three genres of the art of living. The first, which he identifies with the Socrates of the early dialogues, is "tentative and protreptic." Alexander Nehamas, *The Art of Living: Socratic Reflections from Plato to Foucault* (Berkeley: University of California Press, 2000), 9. Its advocates believe themselves to have discovered a universally valid mode of life, but they have no means to prove the correctness of their view. The second genre of the art of living arises from the conviction that "a single type of life is best for all people." The third Nehamas describes as "aestheticist"—that is, the conviction that we should produce "as many different modes of life" as possible on the

theory that each new mode of living "enriches and improves human life" (10). Critics have categorized the postmodern art of ironic living in terms of all three genres. Postmodern irony can be described as an essentially private project of self-realization (Rorty) or an incredulous life that proffers an antifoundational universality (Lyotard).

100. There is, of course, a long tradition of imagining literary texts as instruments for self-cultivation. One point of origin for this way of thinking about literature is the rise of vernacular humanism. In *Literary Language and Its Public in Late Latin Antiquity and in the Middle Ages*, Erich Auerbach notes that in the fifteenth and sixteenth centuries, Latin became "an organ of human self-cultivation, of a well-rounded individual culture, the organ of those who possessed the intelligence and leisure for such self-cultivation." Children "studied Latin not for erudite (scholastic or even philological) ends but as the foundation for self-cultivation or culture in the sense of an imitation of antiquity, and they expressed their culture in their mother tongue." Such notions of vernacular humanism "gave rise to cultivated society, the modern public." Erich Auerbach, *Literary Language and Its Public in Late Latin Antiquity and in the Middle Ages*, trans. Ralph Manheim (Princeton: Princeton University Press, 1993), 319.

101. Joshua Landy, *How to Do Things with Fictions* (Oxford: Oxford University Press, 2012), 10.

102. Peter Sloderdijk, *You Must Change Your Life*, trans. Wieland Hoban (London: Polity, 2013), 4.

103. Hayden White, *Metahistory: The Historical Imagination in Nineteenth-Century Europe* (Baltimore, MD: Johns Hopkins University Press, 1975), 434.

104. Jameson, *Postmodernism*, 39.

105. We might locate another origin of American political irony in periodical culture, especially popular humor magazines such as *Puck* (1871–1918), *Judge* (1881–1947), and *Life* (founded in 1883 as a humor magazine). However, I would distinguish satire and the history of periodical humor from the ethos of irony under investigation here.

106. Henri Murger, *Scenes from the Life of Bohemia* (Indianapolis, IN: Bowen-Merrill, 1896), xxxi.

107. Ibid.

108. Ibid, xxvi.

109. William Dean Howells, *Literary Friends and Acquaintance: A Personal Retrospective of American Authorship* (New York: Harper & Brothers, 1911), 71.

110. *The Saturday Press* was published from 1858 to 1860 and then again from 1865 to 1866. The complete archives of the paper are available at *The Vault at Pfaff's: An Archive of Art and Literature by New York City's Nineteenth-Century Bohemians*, http://digital.lib.lehigh.edu/pfaffs/sat/press/.

111. Joanna Levin, *Bohemia in America, 1858–1920* (Stanford: Stanford University Press, 2009), 1.

112. Ibid., 5.

113. Howells, *Literary Friends*, 68.

114. Ibid., 69, 73.

115. Ibid., 70.

116. Ibid., 8.

117. Malcolm Cowley, *Exile's Return: A Literary Odyssey of the 1920s* (New York: Penguin, 1994), 55.

118. Matthew Stratton, *The Politics of Irony in American Modernism* (New York: Fordham University Press, 2013), 192.

119. Ibid., 52.

120. Friedrich Nietzsche, *The Will to Power*, trans. Walter Kaufmann and R. J. Hollingdale, ed. Walter Kaufmann (New York: Vintage, 1968), 261.

121. Bourne, "The Life of Irony," 138.

122. Ibid., 136.

123. Theodor W. Adorno, *Minima Moralia: Reflections on a Damaged Life*, trans. E. F. N. Jephcott (New York: Verso, 2006), 210.

124. Ibid.

125. See Don M. Burks, "Kenneth Burke: The Agro-Bohemian 'Marxoid,'" *Communication Studies* 42, no. 3 (1991): 219–233.

126. Kenneth Burke, *Language as Symbolic Action: Essays on Life, Literature, and Method* (Berkeley: University of California Press, 1968), 3.

127. Ibid., 50.

128. Ibid., 46.

129. Kenneth Burke, *A Grammar of Motives* (Berkeley: University of California Press, 1969), 503.

130. Kenneth Burke, *Attitudes toward History* (Berkeley: University of California Press, 1984), 394.

131. Fredric Jameson, "The Symbolic Inference: Or, Kenneth Burke and Ideological Analysis," *Critical Inquiry* 4, no. 3 (1978): 523. Burke's terms ultimately inform Jameson's view of literature as "a socially symbolic act," as articulated in Jameson, *The Political Unconscious: Narrative as a Socially Symbolic Act* (Ithaca, NY: Cornell University Press, 1982).

132. Lionel Trilling, "The State of American Writing, 1948," *Partisan Review* 15, no. 8 (1948): 889.

133. David Riesman, with Reuel Denney and Nathan Glazer, *The Lonely Crowd: A Study of the Changing American Character* (New Haven: Yale University Press, 1967), 4.

134. Ibid., 6.

135. Ibid., 7.

136. Ibid., 16, 26. Of course, for Riesman, inner-direction is just as much a form of social control as tradition-direction and outer-direction. The inner-directed type's "psychological gyroscope" merely internalized the mechanism of control as individuality.

137. Ibid., 21–22.

138. Ibid., my emphasis.

139. Daniel J. Boorstin, *The Image: A Guide to Pseudo-Events in America* (New York: Vintage, 1992), 13.

140. Guy Debord criticizes Boorstin because he "never arrives at a concept of the spectacle" and for being unable to "see that the proliferation of prefabricated 'pseudo-events'—which he deplores—flows from the simple fact that, in face [*sic*] of the massive realities of present-day social existence, individuals do not actually experience events." Guy Debord, *The Society of the Spectacle*, trans.

Donald Nicholson-Smith (New York: Zone Books, 1994), 140, 141. Baudrillard, for his part, is less critical of Boorstin, though he emphasizes that we should "beware of language, which speaks automatically of the 'false,' the 'pseudo' or the artificial." Instead, Baudrillard insists that "reality itself is abolished, obliterated, in favour of this neo-reality of the model, which is given material force by the medium itself." Jean Baudrillard, *The Consumer Society: Myths and Structures*, trans. Chris Turner, intro. George Ritzer (London: SAGE Publications, 2004), 126.

141. Boorstin, *The Image*, 11.

142. Ibid., 64.

143. Ibid., 65.

144. C. Wright Mills, *The Politics of Truth: Selected Writings of C. Wright Mills*, intro. John H. Summers (Oxford: Oxford University Press, 2008), 194.

145. Ibid.

146. Ibid., 195.

147. Ibid., 204.

148. Ibid.

149. Ibid., 207.

150. Ibid., 221.

151. Ibid., my emphasis.

152. Ibid.

153. Ibid., 161., my emphasis.

154. Ibid., 222.

155. Stephen E. Kercher, *Revel with a Cause: Liberal Satire in Postwar America* (Chicago: University of Chicago Press, 2006), 3.

156. Richard Yates, *Revolutionary Road* (New York: Vintage, 2000), 20.

157. There is, however, a problem of dangerous regress with Wheeler's ironic strategy. All internal evidence suggests that Yates considers Frank to be stupidly provincial, narcissistic, and talentless, tragically unaware of his own limitations. Frank would deny that he is what Abigail Cheever calls a "real phony," a type of person who exemplified "the possibility that the idea of the unique American individual was not just hiding beneath a phony mask, but rather no longer existed at all." Abigail Cheever, *Real Phonies: Cultures of Authenticity in Post-World War II America* (Athens: University of Georgia Press, 2010), 6. While in college, Frank comically imagines that he is "an intense, nicotine-stained, Jean-Paul Sartre sort of man," and he tries unsuccessfully to live a pseudo-Bohemian lifestyle in Greenwich Village (23). But if Frank thinks he can escape the dominant social order by symbolically rebelling within his mind (and Yates suggests that Frank is ridiculous for believing this) what makes Yates so sure that he's any better able to escape mental mediocrity than Frank? The unsustainability of this second-order irony—Yates's extradiegetic laughter at Frank's diegetic laughter at the banality of the suburbs—perhaps explains why, as Frank becomes increasingly invested in his boring job at (where else?) Knox Business Machines, Yates drives his novel away from satire toward a lurid and unconvincing melodramatic finale. But when exactly were we supposed to start *really caring* about these buffoonish characters and their risible suburban ennui? And what, for that matter, makes us think we're any better than the Wheelers or

Yates? Indeed, as more and more suburbanites came to express their unique identities (in more or less the same ironic way), newer, fresher countercultural waves arose to decry the co-optation of these formerly revolutionary styles (the need for the co-optation theory now becomes clearer). In a cynical mood, we might say that postirony can be described as the realization that irony had reached the end of the line in terms of its power to confer distinction. One's stock of countercultural capital would need to be replenished.

158. For a discussion of the opposite claim—that irony is only possible in already-existing communities—see Linda Hutcheon, *Irony's Edge:* "[Irony] is not a matter of in-group elitism; it is merely a matter of different experiential and discursive contexts. In a way, if you understand that irony can exist . . . and if you understand how it works, you already belong to one community: the one based on the knowledge of the possibility and nature of irony. It is less that irony creates communities, then, than discursive communities make irony possible in the first place . . . the more the shared context, the fewer and the less obvious the markers needed to signal—or attribute—irony" (17–18). Hutcheon is correct to say that shared communities can signal irony more easily, but as Yates's novel makes clear, irony is in fact predicated on the logical possibility that some people will not be able to understand the ironist's true meaning.

159. See Honoré de Balzac, *Treatise on Elegant Living*, trans. Napoleon Jeffries (Cambridge, MA: Wakefield Press, 2010). This essay was featured in *The Saturday Press*. See Honoré de Balzac, "A Treatise upon the Life of Elegance," trans. Edward Howland, *New-York Saturday Press*, October 6, 1860, http://digital.lib.lehigh.edu/pfaffs/spr/578/497/25/40/900/.

160. Mark McGurl, *The Novel Art: Elevations of American Fiction after Henry James* (Princeton: Princeton University Press, 2001). McGurl argues that "rather than merely trading pleasure for work, modernism is also reflective of the notion, associated with professionalism, that there might be pleasure *in* work and, specifically, in the particular kind of intellectual work that reading the difficult modernist text is said to require" (11).

161. Morris Dickstein, *Leopards in the Temple: The Transformation of American Fiction, 1945–1970* (Cambridge, MA: Harvard University Press, 2002), 146.

162. Gary Morson and Caryl Emerson, *Mikhail Bakhtin: Creation of a Prosaics* (Stanford: Stanford University Press, 1990), 28.

163. John Guillory, "The Sokal Affair and the History of Criticism," *Critical Inquiry* 28, no. 2 (2002): 476.

164. Anthony Reynolds, "Irony's Resistance to Theory: Pragmatism in the Text of Deconstruction," *Angelaki* 13, no. 3 (2008): 69.

165. Paul de Man, "The Concept of Irony," in *Aesthetic Ideology*, ed. and intro. Andrzej Warminski (Minneapolis: University of Minnesota Press, 1996), 181.

166. Rorty, *Contingency, Irony, and Solidarity*, 73.

167. Ibid., 78, 80, my emphasis. Rorty redescribes all human conflict in terms of a conflict between vocabularies; he does not necessarily invest in a heroic role for symbolic analysis in political life. Nonetheless, Rorty's account shares two crucial similarities with theories that treat symbolic action as the key to undermining hegemony. First, Rorty shares the view that we cannot help but approach reality via our language games. Second, he believes that when we convince

someone to change their views, we have displaced their final vocabulary with our own: "For us ironists, nothing can serve as a criticism of a final vocabulary save another such vocabulary; there is no answer to a redescription save a re-re-redescription" (80).

168. Reynolds, "Irony's Resistance to Theory," 78.

169. Thomas Frank, *The Conquest of Cool: Business Culture, Counterculture, and the Rise of Hip Consumerism* (Chicago: University of Chicago Press, 1998), 9.

170. Sean McCann and Michael Szalay, "Do You Believe in Magic? Literary Thinking after the New Left," *Yale Journal of Criticism* 18, no 2 (2005): 435, 436.

171. Walter Benn Michaels, *The Shape of the Signifier: 1967 to the End of History* (Princeton: Princeton University Press, 2006), 16, 17.

172. Leslie Marmon Silko, *Almanac of the Dead* (New York: Penguin, 1992), 516.

173. Michaels, *The Shape of the Signifier,* 23.

174. Thomas Frank, "Baby Boomer Humor's Big Lie: 'Ghostbusters' and 'Caddyshack' Really Liberated Reagan and Wall Street," *Salon*, March 2, 2014, http://www.salon.com/2014/03/02/baby_boomer_humors_big_lie _ghostbusters_and_caddyshack_really_liberated_reagan_and_wall_street/.

175. David Harvey, *A Brief History of Neoliberalism* (Oxford: Oxford University Press, 2005), 90.

176. McCann and Szalay, "Do You Believe in Magic?" 441, my emphasis.

177. Michaels, *The Shape of the Signifier,* 13.

178. Ibid., 14.

179. One finds evidence for this view in Walter Benn Michaels, *The Beauty of a Social Problem: Photography, Autonomy, Economy* (Chicago: University of Chicago Press, 2015). When Michaels celebrates a generation of photographers and artists whose "work would have been unimaginable" without postmodern critiques of autonomy and intentionality, but whose work "departs and dissents from" these critiques, he might as well be celebrating his own work (xii).

180. Joseph Heath and Andrew Potter, *Nation of Rebels: Why Counterculture Became Consumer Culture* (New York: HarperCollins, 2004), 9.

181. The importance of this distinction will become clearer in subsequent chapters. I am indebted to the pioneering work on youth subcultures by the Centre for Contemporary Cultural Studies in the 1970s, but I do not conceive of my object of study as empirical subcultural communities. This is not a work of subcultural studies. For a subcultural studies approach, see Stuart Hall and Tony Jefferson, ed., *Resistance through Rituals: Youth Subcultures in Post-War Britain* (New York: Routledge, 2006); Dick Hebdige, *Subculture: The Meaning of Style* (New York: Routledge, 1979); Keith Gelder and Sarah Thornton, ed., *The Subculture Reader* (New York: Routledge, 2005); David Muggleton and Rupert Weinzierl, ed., *The Post-Subcultures Reader* (New York: Bloomsbury, 2004).

182. I use the term "canon" in the sense that Bakhtin uses it when he writes of the "grotesque canon." He uses canon "not in the narrow sense of a specific group of consciously established rules, norms, and propositions in the representation of the human body" but "in the wider sense of manner of representing the human body and bodily life." Bakhtin, *Rabelais and His World,* 30.

183. See Andrew Hoberek, "Introduction: After Postmodernism," *Twentieth-Century Literature* 53, no. 3 (2007): 233–247. Daniel Worden, Jason Gladstone,

and Andrew Hoberek, ed., *Postmodern / Postwar—and After* (Iowa City: University of Iowa Press, forthcoming).

184. Mary Holland argues that "newly humanist twenty-first century literature might represent the success of postmodernism rather than its failure." Mary Holland, *Succeeding Postmodernism: Language and Humanism in Contemporary American Literature* (New York: Bloomsbury Academic, 2013), 16. Nealon, *Post-Postmodernism*. See also Fredric Jameson, "The Aesthetics of Singularity," *New Left Review* 92 (2015): 101–132.

185. Hutcheon, *The Politics of Postmodernism*, 165–181. Robert Rebein, *Hicks, Tribes, and Dirty Realists: American Fiction after Postmodernism* (Lexington: University Press of Kentucky, 2009). Neil Brooks and Josh Toth, ed., *The Mourning After: Attending the Wake of Postmodernism* (Amsterdam: Rodopi, 2007). Josh Toth, *The Passing of Postmodernism: A Spectroanalysis of the Contemporary* (Albany: State University of New York Press, 2010).

186. For "post-postmodernism," see Nealon, *Post-Postmodernism*; Nicoline Timmer, *Do You Feel It Too? The Post-Postmodern Syndrome in American Fiction at the Turn of the Millennium* (Amsterdam: Rodopi, 2010); and Robert L. McLaughlin, "Post-postmodernism," in *The Routledge Companion to Experimental Literature*, ed. Joe Bray, Alison Gibbons, and Brian McHale (New York: Routledge, 2012), 212–223. For "late postmodernism," see. Jeremy Green, *Late Postmodernism: American Fiction at the Millennium* (New York: Palgrave, 2005). For "cosmodernism," see Christian Moraru, *Cosmodernism: American Narrative, Late Globalization, and the New Cultural Imaginary* (Ann Arbor: University of Michigan Press, 2011). For "altermodernism," see Nicolas Bourriaud, *Altermodernism* (London: Tate Publishing, 2009), and Alison Gibbons, "Altermodernist Fictions," in *The Routledge Companion to Experimental Literature*, ed. Joe Bray, Alison Gibbons, and Brian McHale (New York: Routledge, 2012), 238–252. For "metamodernism," see Timotheus Vermeulen and Robin van den Akker, "Notes on Metamodernism," *Journal of Aesthetics & Culture* 2 (2010): 1–14, and David James and Urmila Seshagiri, "Metamodernism: Narratives of Continuity and Revolution," *PMLA* 129, no. 1 (2014): 87–100. For "digimodernism," see Alan Kirby, *Digimodernism: How New Technologies Dismantle the Postmodern and Reconfigure Our Culture* (New York: Continuum, 2009). For "hypermodernism," see Gilles Lipovetsky, *Hypermodern Times*, trans. Andrew Brown (Cambridge: Polity, 2005). For "performatism," see Raoul Eschelman, *Performatism, or the End of Postmodernism* (Aurora, CO: Davies Group, 2008). For "contemporaneity," see Terry Smith, *What Is Contemporary Art?* (Chicago: University of Chicago Press, 2009). One might also include less inventive terms on the list of candidates for the cultural dominant that follows postmodernism, such as globalization, neoliberalism, and the contemporary.

187. Patricia Waugh, *Metafiction: The Theory and Practice of Self-Conscious Fiction* (New York: Routledge, 1984), 13–14.

188. Joseph Witek, ed., *Art Spiegelman: Conversations* (Jackson: University Press of Mississippi, 2007), 228.

189. Adam Kelly, "From Syndrome to Sincerity: Benjamin Kunkel's *Indecision*," in *Diseases and Disorders in Contemporary Fiction: The Syndrome Syndrome*, ed. T. J. Lustig and James Peacock (New York: Routledge, 2013), 65.

See also Adam Kelly, "David Foster Wallace and the New Sincerity," in *Consider David Foster Wallace*, 131–146.

190. Ibid.

1 The Hipster as Critic

1. Norman Mailer, "The White Negro," in *Advertisements for Myself* (New York: Berkeley Medallion, 1959), 311–312.

2. Ibid., 312.

3. Cowley, *Exile's Return*, 62.

4. Andrew Hoberek, *The Twilight of the Middle Class: Post-World War II American Fiction and White-Collar Work* (Princeton: Princeton University Press, 2005), 67. For a recent cultural studies approach to zoot suit culture (and hip culture more generally), see Luis Alvarez, *The Power of the Zoot: Youth Culture and Resistance during World War II* (Berkeley: University of California Press, 2008). Alvarez argues that "[z]oot suiters' fashion choices . . . often entailed a critical stance toward authority that rendered back to society the aggression it practiced during wartime, while they also opened spaces of autonomy and independence for many of the youth involved" (4). Alvarez is careful to qualify such claims for zoot suiters' oppositional power, but he ultimately (approvingly) argues that hip culture treated cultural consumption as a synonym for dignity. Though his understanding of dignity, as he explains, "is deeply influenced by the Zapatistas in Chiapas, Mexico," it is startling how consonant his emphasis on dignity is with Mailer's much-maligned account of the hipster (248). The hipster's emphasis on dignity-through-consumption recalls Riesman's celebration of "autonomy." In "a society of abundance," Riesman argues, "[t]he new possibilities opening up for the individual are possibilities not so much for entering a new class but rather for changing one's style of life and character within the middle class." Riesman, *The Lonely Crowd*, 248.

5. Richard Lloyd, *Neo-Bohemia: Art and Commerce in the Postindustrial City* (New York: Routledge, 2005), 181. In this sense, against Cowley's view, Bohemia is also a *production* ethic, one that can serve to obscure or even justify one's exploitation. The contemporary hipster is very different from the Cold War version discussed in this chapter, though both share a desire to rescue human dignity from conformity. For a brief discussion of the contemporary hipster, see my conclusion.

6. For an excellent account of the rise of consumerism in the United States, see Liz Cohen, *A Consumers' Republic* (New York: Vintage Books, 2004). John Leland documents many funny attempts to exploit the popularity of the Beats in *Hip: The History* (New York: Ecco, 2004). *Playboy* launched in 1953 with an ad that read: "Join the beat generation! Buy a beat generation tieclasp! A beat generation sweatshirt! A beat generation ring!" After *On the Road* was published, Atlantic Music ran an ad that read: "Atlantic is the label in tune with the BEAT generation. We produce the music with the BEAT for you. Write for free catalog" (qtd. in Leland 154).

7. Andrew Ross, *No Respect: Intellectuals and Popular Culture* (New York: Routledge, 1989), 82.

8. Ibid., 83.

9. Ibid., 101.

10. Dwight Macdonald, *Masscult and Midcult: Essays against the American Grain*, ed. John Summers, intro. Louis Menand (New York: NYRB Classics, 2011). Theordore Roszak, *The Making of a Counter Culture: Reflections on the Technocratic Society and Its Youthful Opposition* (Berkeley: University of California Press, 1995).

11. Scott Saul, *Freedom Is, Freedom Ain't: Jazz and the Making of the Sixties* (Cambridge, MA: Harvard University Press, 2005), 32.

12. Phil Ford, "Somewhere / Nowhere: Hipness as an Aesthetic," *Musical Quarterly* 86, no. 1 (Spring 2002): 51. See also Ford, *Dig: Sound and Music in Hip Culture* (New York: Oxford University Press, 2013).

13. Michael Szalay, *Hip Figures: A Literary History of the Democratic Party* (Stanford: Stanford University Press, 2012), 4. Szalay draws the term *second skin* from Wolfgang Haug, *Critique of Commodity Aesthetics: Appearance, Sexuality and Advertising in Capitalist Society* (Minneapolis: University of Minnesota Press, 1986).

14. Ibid., 123.

15. Stephen Schryer, *Fantasies of the New Class: Ideologies of Professionalism in Post-World War II American Fiction Paperback* (New York: Columbia University Press, 2011), 65, 112.

16. Alan Liu has written about the connection between knowledge work and cool at a later historical moment. See Liu, *The Laws of Cool: Knowledge Work and the Culture of Information* (Chicago: University of Chicago Press, 2004). The primary anxiety of the knowledge worker is to show that, "We Work Here, but We're Cool" (76). Analogously, we might say that midcentury intellectuals and critics wanted to show that "We're Knowledge Workers, but We're Hip."

17. Cleanth Brooks, "Irony as a Principle of Structure" [1949], in *Literary Opinion in America: Essays Illustrating the Status, Methods, and Problems of Criticism in the United States in the Twentieth Century*, Third Edition, Revised, Vol. II, ed. Morton D. Zabel (New York: Harper Torchbooks, 1962), 738. It is important to note the special definition of irony that Brooks uses in this essay. For Brooks, irony is a structural matter, the inherent possibility that words in a poem might take on different meanings in different contexts. Irony is also a technique for producing poetic misdirection: using particulars to get at universals. In that sense, irony is simultaneously a principle by means of which one may choose to build a poem (Donne being the supreme ironist for him) and a latent potential even in supposedly nonironic poetry (Wordsworth being the least ironic possible type of poet, a lyric poet).

18. Ibid.

19. Ibid.

20. See Cleanth Brooks, "The Heresy of Paraphrase," in *The Well Wrought Urn: Studies in the Structure of Poetry* (New York: Harcourt, 1975), 192–214.

21. Amritjit Singh, ed., *Conversations with Ralph Ellison* (Literary Conversations Series) (University Press of Mississippi, 1995), 18.

22. John Leland, *Hip: The History* (New York: Harper Perennial, 2005), 5. David Dalby was the first scholar, as far as I can tell, to propose this spurious

etymology. Leland cites Clarence Major's *Juba to Jive: A Dictionary of African-American Slang*. See also Jesse Sheidlower, "The Real History of 'Hip,'" *Slate*, December 8, 2004, http://www.slate.com/id/2110811. Sundquist points out that the OED lists the first use of *hipster* in Jack Smiley's 1941 *Hash House Lingo*. The word *hip*, however, can be dated as far back as 1904.

23. I draw this history from Rick McRae, "'What Is Hip?' and Other Inquiries into Jazz Slang Lexicography," *Notes* 57, no. 3 (2001): 574–584. McRae reviews the lexicographic history of hip via glossaries and dictionaries of jazz slang published between 1934 and 1970.

24. Jack Smiley, *Hash House Lingo: The Slang of Soda Jerks, Short-Order Cooks, Bartenders, Waitresses, Carhops and Other Denizens of Yesterday's Roadside*, intro. Paul Dickson (New York: Dover Publications, 2012), 82. McRae doesn't mention Smiley's dictionary.

25. Qtd. in McRae "'What Is Hip?' and Other Inquiries into Jazz Slang Lexicography," 581.

26. Ibid., 582.

27. Phil Ford, "Hip Sensibility in an Age of Mass Counterculture," *Jazz Perspectives* 2, no. 2 (2008): 123.

28. Anatole Broyard, "Portrait of the Hipster," *Partisan Review* 15, no. 6 (1948): 721.

29. Ibid., 722.

30. Ibid., 723–724.

31. Ibid., 726, 727.

32. Anatole Broyard, *Kafka Was the Rage: A Greenwich Village Memoir* (New York: Vintage, 1997), 111.

33. Ibid., 115, 118.

34. The character Henry Porter was based on Broyard. See Henry Louis Gates Jr., "The Passing of Anatole Broyard," in *Thirteen Ways of Looking at a Black Man* (New York: Random House, 1997), 180–214.

35. For his part, Mailer seems also to have edited Broyard out of the history of hip. In "Hipster and Beatnik," his "footnote" to "The White Negro," Norman Mailer claims that the term *hipster* was used "as long ago as 1951 or 1952." *Advertisements for Myself*, 343. This elision is likely motivated more by his competitive relationship with Brossard than from any commitment to philological or conceptual rigor. During a visit to Mailer's Connecticut home in "1956 or '57," Brossard found himself rebuffing Mailer's suggestion that they box each other. "'No, Norman,' Brossard told him, 'What you really want is for us to fall into each other's arms and cry and hug, covered with blood . . . I don't like blood, and also it sounds kind of homosexual to me.'" Qtd. in William Crawford Woods, "The 'Passed' White Negro: Brossard and Mailer at the Roots of Hip," *Review of Contemporary Fiction* 7, no. 1 (1987): 94. Mailer would write "The White Negro" soon after this visit, mostly (by his own account in *Advertisements for Myself*) as a way of restarting his writing career after a fallow period, but he faced the fact that Brossard's novel *Who Walk in Darkness* had, years before he wrote his essay, beaten him to the punch. Brossard's novel features hipster-like figures and invokes many of the same existentialist motifs Mailer came to find so attractive. "Who Walk in Darkness is," reads one blurb on Brossard's novel, "one of

the best books about the 'Beat Generation,' 'hipsters,' and their girls in New York's Greenwich village." (This is, incidentally, an inaccurate characterization of Brossard's novel, which lavishes scorn upon its hipster and proto-Beat characters. Brossard considered himself to be not a Beat but an American existentialist, and he insisted that *Who Walk in Darkness* was the first American existentialist novel.)

36. Lawrence Jackson, *Ralph Ellison: Emergence of Genius* (New York: Wiley, 2002), 426.

37. Ralph Ellison, *Trading Twelves: The Selected Letters of Ralph Ellison and Albert Murray* (New York: Vintage, 2001), 195. Ellison would also note: "The hipster, although Mailer doesn't quite understand it, is not simply living in the present, he is living a very stylized life which implies a background because it takes a good while, a lot of living to stylize a pattern of conduct and an attitude. This goes back very deeply into certain levels of Negro life. That's why it has nuances and overtones which Mailer could never grasp." Singh, *Conversations*, 75.

38. Jackson, *Ralph Ellison*, 340.

39. Sianne Ngai, *Ugly Feelings* (Cambridge, MA: Harvard University Press, 2005), 95.

40. See Baldwin's "The Black Boy Looks at the White Boy" for a fascinating commentary on Mailer's desperate desire to be hip. Baldwin writes: "And matters were not helped at all by the fact that the Negro jazz musicians, among whom we sometimes found ourselves, who really liked Norman, did not for an instant consider him as being even remotely 'hip' and Norman did not know this and I could not tell him. He never broke through to them, at least not as far as I know; and they were far too 'hip,' if that is the word I want, even to consider breaking through to him. They thought he was a real sweet ofay cat, but a little frantic." James Baldwin, "The Black Boy Looks at the White Boy," in *James Baldwin: Collected Essays*, ed. Toni Morrison (Washington DC: Library of the Americas, 1998), 272. On "The White Negro," Baldwin writes: "I was also baffled by the passion with which Norman appeared to be imitating so many people inferior to himself, i.e., Kerouac, and all the other Suzuki rhythm boys. From them, indeed, I expected nothing more than their pablum-clogged cries of *Kicks!* and *Holy!* It seemed very clear to me that their glorification of the orgasm was but a way of avoiding all of the terrors of life and love. But Norman knew better, had to know better . . . What in the world, then, was he doing, slumming so outrageously, in such a dreary crowd?" (277).

41. Henry Louis Gates Jr., *The Signifying Monkey: A Theory of African-American Literary Criticism* (Oxford: Oxford University Press, 1989), 79.

42. Ralph Ellison, *Invisible Man* (New York: Vintage, 1995), xiv. Subsequent references will be cited parenthetically.

43. Richard Gibson, "A No to Nothing," *The Kenyon Review* 13, no. 2 (1951): 252.

44. Ibid., 253.

45. Ibid., 253, 256.

46. Ibid., 254, my emphasis, and 255.

47. Ibid., 255.

48. Ralph Ellison, "Richard Wright's Blues," in *The Collected Essays of Ralph Ellison*, ed. and intro. John F. Callahan, preface Saul Bellow (New York: Modern Library, 2003), 134. "Richard Wright's Blues" was originally published in *The Antioch Review* 5 (1945): 198–211.

49. Ralph Ellison, "The World and the Jug," in *The Collected Essays*, 166–167. "The World and the Jug" was originally published as two separate essays in *The New Leader*. Ellison, "The World and the Jug," *New Leader*, December 9, 1962, 22–26. Ellison, "A Rejoinder," *New Leader*, February 3, 1964, 15–22.

50. Ibid., 167.

51. When it was published, Ellison claimed Wright's story "compared favorably to Kafka." Jackson, *Ralph Ellison*, 269.

52. Michel Fabre, *The Unfinished Quest of Richard Wright* (Urbana: University of Illinois Press, 1993), 240.

53. Houston A. Baker, *Blues, Ideology, and Afro-American Literature: A Vernacular Theory* (Chicago: University of Chicago Press, 1987), 160.

54. In "Reality in America," Trilling juxtaposes Dreiser and James—who might as well stand in for Wright and Ellison—as addressing "themselves to virtually the same social and moral fact. The difference here is one of quality." Lionel Trilling, *The Liberal Imagination*, intro. Louis Menand (New York: NYRB Classics, 2012), 11. Dreiser "thinks stupidly," "writes badly," and is "awkward and dull" (12). James has a "moral mind, with [an] awareness of tragedy, irony, and multitudinous distinctions," displays "wit, and flexibility of mind, and perception, and knowledge" (11). For Trilling, the liberal critic (as exemplified by V. L. Parrington) incorrectly ascribes value to Dreiser's terribly written fiction because he associates Dreiser's badness with the grossness of "reality" itself and foolishly decries the refined style of James as symptomatic of a reactionary / aristocratic disposition. The greatest crime of this type of critic, in Trilling's view, is that he does not take Dreiser's ideas as seriously as Dreiser did himself. That is, such a critic willfully ignores or explains away Dreiser's anti-Semitism or membership in the Communist Party, and sees Dreiser's stupid lack of sophistication as a palliative in itself. Only at the end of Trilling's polemic do the literary politics of the Cold War, at last, fully emerge. According to the common Cold War formula, popular with the new liberals of the "vital center," social realism or naturalism is irredeemably corrupted as a literary practice because it subsumes all standards of quality to ideological hackery and dogmatic political propaganda. It is strongly implied, though not always openly stated, that the clunky, awkward, stupid style of social realism is the necessary product of its politically debased origins. Modernist irony and nuanced literary refinement, meanwhile, stand as metonymies for (or symptoms of) the liberty that inheres under the condition of political democracy characteristic of the "free" West and "open" societies.

55. Ralph Ellison, "An Extravagance of Laughter," in *The Collected Essays of Ralph Ellison*, 627. "An Extravagance of Laughter" was originally published in Ellison, *Going to the Territory* (New York: Vintage, 1985).

56. See Robert Chodat, *Worldly Acts and Sentient Things: The Persistence of Agency from Stein to DeLillo* (Ithaca: Cornell UP, 2008), esp. 135–138 and 147–148. Chodat gives a useful but only partial picture of the stakes for Ellison in

declaring himself an individualist. Chodat takes "roles" to refer, sometimes strangely, both to one's function in an economy—a carpenter—and other aspects of one's full personhood, such as a racial identity. The term "roles" does capture some of the sense behind what Ellison is opposing, though Ellison's point is not a philosophical reflection on the ontology of agency—as personal, subpersonal, or superpersonal—but rather a *political stance* in a field of choices defined by the situation of the cultural Cold War, as we will see.

57. The fate of Tod Clifton stands as a counter-Bildungsroman, an example of what the invisible man might have become had he submitted to viewing himself as less than human or acceded fully to the ideological demands of the Brotherhood.

58. For example, Amritjit Singh claims that "If Ellison's Ras the Destroyer came to signify against many who would define 'blackness' in essentialist terms in the 1960s and later, so Rinehart's trickster-man, both hero and villain, calls into question contemporary postmodern platitudes about how all is performance. Rinehart both prefigures and critiques postmodernism" (*Conversations* xii). The problem here should be obvious. Singh reads Ras and Rinehart as proleptic allegories of political problems that occur after Ellison wrote his novel. While it is certainly true that the present always contains the seeds of future developments—and the hipster lays the foundation for certain countercultural commonplaces—we will see that the politics of "Rinehartism" matter more as an alternative to or a moving beyond Marxism than as a critique of a then-nonexistent discourse of postmodernism.

For an early, influential interpretation of the significance of the hipster to Ellison, see Larry Neal, "Ellison's Zoot Suit," in *Ralph Ellison's* Invisible Man: *A Casebook* (Oxford: Oxford University Press, 2004), 81–108. In some ways, Neal's argument resembles my own, but Neal's 1970 essay is ultimately interested in condemning social realism, Marxism, and black leftists, seeking to rehabilitate Ellison as an emblem of black cultural politics. "Ellison's Zoot Suit," therefore, not only critically comments on Ellison but also bolsters Ellison's political project.

59. Robert Genter, "Toward a Theory of Rhetoric: Ralph Ellison, Kenneth Burke, and the Problem of Modernism," *Twentieth-Century Literature* 48, no. 2 (2002): 195, 197.

60. Ibid., 208. It's interesting to note that Gordon Marino includes the prologue of *Invisible Man* in his *Basic Writings of Existentialism* (2004), an anthology of existentialist writing, but not Wright's overtly existentialist later writing, such as *The Outsider* (1953).

61. Arnold Rampersad, *Ralph Ellison: A Biography* (New York: Vintage, 2008), 162.

62. Ralph Ellison, "Editorial Comment," *Negro Quarterly: A Review of Negro Life and Culture*, no. 1–4 (1942–1943): 301.

63. Jackson, *Ralph Ellison*, 306, my emphasis.

64. Ralph Ellison, "Remembering Richard Wright," in *The Collected Essays of Ralph Ellison*, 675. "Remembering Richard Wright" was originally delivered as a lecture at the Institute for Afro-American Culture at the University of Iowa on July 18, 1971.

65. Ibid., 678.

66. In 1949, Ellison was forced to report back to Wright, who had asked him to find arrangers and composers to score his "FB Eye Blues," that musicians were afraid of being associated with his leftist views. Lawrence Jackson reports that Ellison refrained from naming which composers he had approached, fearful that Wright's mail was being read by the authorities. Jackson, *Ralph Ellison*, 402.

67. *Antioch, Kenyon,* and *Sewanee* all received grants from the Farfield Foundation (a CIA front).

68. Frances Stonor Saunders, *The Cultural Cold War: The CIA and the World of Arts and Letters* (New York: New Press, 2000), 140.

69. Ibid.

70. Greg Barnhisel, *"Perspectives USA* and the Cultural Cold War: Modernism in Service of the State," *Modernism / modernity* 14, no. 4 (2007): 751.

71. Barbara Foley, "From Communism to Brotherhood: The Drafts of *Invisible Man,"* in *Left of the Color Line: Race, Radicalism, and Twentieth-Century Literature of the United States* (The John Hope Franklin Series in African American History and Culture), ed. Bill V. Mullen and James Smethurst (Chapel Hill: University of North Carolina Press, 2006) 164. See also Barbara Foley, *Wrestling with the Left: The Making of Ralph Ellison's Invisible Man* (Durham, NC: Duke University Press, 2010). Adam Bradley, *Ralph Ellison in Progress: From "Invisible Man" to "Three Days before the Shooting . . ."* (New Haven, CT: Yale University Press, 2012).

72. Kenneth W. Warren, *So Black and Blue: Ralph Ellison and the Occasion of Criticism* (Chicago: University of Chicago Press, 2003).

73. In this sense, I agree with Matthew Stratton when he complains about the "transitive logic" that "tacitly assumes a definition of politics in order to stipulate that New Criticism produced an 'apolitical' evaluation of literature" and in order to condemn the use of irony as inherently apolitical. Stratton, *The Politics of Irony in American Modernism,* 146-147. My argument is that irony was intensely political at midcentury (as was New Critical irony). Whatever its prior radical history, Ellison explicitly aligned literary irony with the priorities of liberal anticommunism. No transitive logic is needed to make the connection.

74. Burke revised his earlier works in ways consonant with the broader tendency toward leftist self-emendation during the Cold War. For example, he removed the term *communism* from later editions of *Permanence and Change.* Don M. Burkes argues that Burke "was advocating principles and personal convictions that have changed little, even though he stopped using the term *communism."* Don M. Burkes, "Kenneth Burke: The Agro-Bohemian 'Marxoid,'" *Communication Studies* 42, no. 3 (1991): 220. See also the discussion of Burke in Michael Denning, *The Cultural Front: The Laboring of American Culture in the Twentieth Century* (New York: Verso, 2011).

75. The reported date of this encounter differs in different sources. Rampersad and Foley claim Ellison encountered Burke at the Second American Writers' Congress in 1937, but Burke delivered "The Rhetoric of Hitler's 'Battle'" at the Third American Writers' Congress on June 4, 1939 at a closed session called "The Writer in Politics." Ellison later wrote admiringly to Burke,

"I believe you were the only speaker out of the whole group who was concerned with writing *and politics* rather than writing as an *excuse* for politics." Qtd. in Ann George and Jack Selzer, *Kenneth Burke in the 1930s* (Columbia, SC: University of South Carolina Press, 2007), 202. Bryan Crable agrees that the correct year is 1939. Bryan Crable, *Ralph Ellison and Kenneth Burke: At the Roots of the Racial Divide* (Charlottesville, University of Virginia Press, 2011), 191n242. Stratton and Donald E. Pease incorrectly claim that Ellison heard Burke speak in 1935, which would have meant that he attended Burke's controversial speech "Revolutionary Symbolism in America," which proposed that the American Communist Party should embrace a *"propaganda by inclusion,"* replacing the figure of "the worker" with "the people." Kenneth Burke, "Revolutionary Symbolism in America," in *The Legacy of Kenneth Burke*, ed. Herbert W. Simons and Trevor Melia (Madison: University of Wisconsin Press, 1989), 272.

76. Kenneth Burke, "The Rhetoric of Hitler's 'Battle,'" in *The Philosophy of Literary Form: Studies in Symbolic Action* (Berkeley: University of California Press, 1974), 191.

77. Letter to Wright, August 18, 1945. Qtd. in Jackson, *Ralph Ellison*, 316.

78. Ellison, *Collected Essays*, 84–85.

79. Donald E. Pease, "Ralph Ellison and Kenneth Burke: The Nonsymbolizable (Trans)action," *boundary 2* 30, no. 2 (2003): 85.

80. Jackson, *Ralph Ellison*, 353.

81. Ibid.

82. Pease, "Ralph Ellison and Kenneth Burke," 66.

83. In his opening chapter to *The Well Wrought Urn*, "The Language of Paradox," Brooks claims that in the "language of poetry," "the connotations play as great a part as the denotations. And I do not mean that the connotations are important as supplying some sort of frill or trimming, something external to the real matter at hand." Brooks, *The Well Wrought Urn*, 8–9.

84. Burke, *A Grammar of Motives*, 503.

85. Qtd. in Ibid., 516.

86. Ellison, *Collected Essays*, 167.

87. Ibid. 157.

88. This statement is only a slight exaggeration. It is true that Ellison's novel met with resistance, initially from his former allies on the left, and later from the black arts movement. But the mainstream organs of literary reviewing and critical assessment quickly canonized Ellison's novel. African American artists came around to Ellison, in no small part thanks to efforts at recuperation, such as Larry Neal's "Ellison's Zoot Suit." By Neal's account, communism comes to seem to be "a very square vision of social realities" (86). Arguing that Ellison is relevant to "the current black arts movement," Neal suggests that black cultural nationalism should "resist the tendency to 'program' our art, to set unnatural limitations upon it" (95, 96).

89. Ellison's insistent faith in the political power of hipness may give us insight into why he wasn't able to complete his second novel, *Three Days before the Shooting* . . . In that novel, Senator Sunraider, who hopes to catalyze black revolution by intensifying public racist discourse, seems to be an attempt to represent the next step for the invisible man. "'He makes you feel that there's a

joke lying at the bottom of everything,'" one character notes. Ralph Ellison, *Three Days before the Shooting . . .* (New York: Modern Library, 2011), 26. He is described as "an underground hero, a dragon slayer, a holy fool manqué" (22). His whole career is a practical joke, a strategic deployment of vitriolic racist rhetoric in the service of antiracism. He is rumored to have sponsored scholars to "look into the court records of several cities of the Old South and jot down any information concerning the blood relationship between the old families and their slaves and between contemporary members of these families and the descendants of the slaves who share their esteemed names" (33). He wears a "suit of blackmail" (34) and says "Negros are 'black White Anglo-Saxon Protestants" (24), an obvious inversion of Mailer's "white Negro," as Michael Szalay notes in *Hip Figures*. Sunraider is, in other words, the hipster as United States Senator.

90. The incomplete manuscript of "Minstrel Island" is located in the Thomas Pynchon Collection of the Harry Ransom Humanities Research Center in Austin, Texas.

91. Thomas Pynchon and Kirkpatrick Sale, "Minstrel Island" [1958], Harry Ransom Humanities Research Center, University of Texas at Austin. Box 2, Folder 3.

92. Ibid.

93. Ibid.

94. Ibid.

95. Ibid.

96. The only discussion of this material as of this writing is Rodney Gibbs, "A Portrait of the Luddite as a Young Man," *Denver Quarterly* 39, no. 1 (2004), http://themodernword.com/Pynchon/paper_gibbs.html.

97. Emily Apter, "On Oneworldedness: Or Paranoia as a World System," *American Literary History* 18, no. 2 (2006): 368.

98. Randall Jarrell, "The Age of Criticism," in *Poetry and the Age*, Expanded Edition, intro. William Logan (Gainesville: University Press of Florida, 2001), 72–73.

99. Ibid., 73, 82.

100. Ibid., 89.

101. Ibid., 94

102. Thomas Pynchon, *V.* (New York: Harper Perennial, 1999), 305. Subsequent references will be cited parenthetically.

103. Qtd. in David Hajdu, *Positively 4th Street: The Lives and Times of Joan Baez, Boy Dylan, Mimi Baez Fariña, and Richard Fariña* (New York: Farrar, Straus, and Giroux, 2001), 46.

104. Thomas Pynchon, "Introduction," in *Been Down So Long It Looks Like Up to Me*, by Richard Fariña. (New York: Penguin Books, 1983), vi–vii.

105. Ibid. vii

106. Ibid., vi, emphasis in original.

107. Ibid., viii.

108. Qtd. in Hajdu, *Positively 4th Street*, 45.

109. Thomas Pynchon, "Introduction," in *Been Down So Long It Looks Like Up to Me*, xiii.

110. Pynchon, "Introduction," in *Slow Learner: Early Stories* (Boston: Back Bay Books, 1998), 14.

111. Qtd. in Marian Janssen, *The Kenyon Review 1939–1970: A Critical History* (Baton Rouge: Louisiana State University Press, 1990), 307. As I have already mentioned, *The Kenyon Review* was a recipient of a grant from the Farfield Foundation, a CIA front organization that sought to cultivate noncommunist high culture in the United States, part of something like a "cultural NATO," in the words of Frances Stonor Saunders. Saunders, *The Cultural Cold War*, 275.

112. Qtd. in Janssen, *The Kenyon Review 1939–1970.*, 2.

113. Ibid., 2.

114. Ibid., 249.

115. Qtd. in Ibid., 8.

116. "In 1956, in Norfolk Virginia, I had wandered into a bookstore and discovered issue one of the *Evergreen Review*," Pynchon writes. "It was an eye-opener . . . By the time I got back to college, I found academic people deeply alarmed over the *cover* of the *Evergreen Review* then current, not to mention what was inside. It looked as if the attitude of some literary folks toward the Beat generation was the same as that of certain officers on my ship towards Elvis Presley." Pynchon, "Introduction," in *Slow Learner*, 8.

117. Pynchon, "Entropy," in *Slow Learner*, 81. Subsequent references to "Entropy" will be cited parenthetically.

118. Pynchon, "Introduction," in *Slow Learner*, 14.

119. "Entropy" has been the most analyzed and anthologized of Pynchon's short fiction. Perhaps because of its popularity, and the obvious ways it anticipates themes important to Pynchon's later work, critics have tended to treat the story in ways that elide its textual and historical contexts. Most articles about the story have suggested that "entropy" is something like a master trope in Pynchon's oeuvre, that Pynchon applies the concept to all his fiction. Another common approach to analyzing "Entropy" has been to use the story as a document to reconstruct a map of sources for Pynchon's later writing, to figure out by following up on various citations what he had read, and when he had read it. For example, see Peter L. Hays and Robert Redfield, "Pynchon's Spanish Source for Entropy," *Studies in Short Fiction* 16 (1979): 327–334. Against readings that overemphasize Pynchon's engagement with questions of science, Douglas Keesey has offered an intelligent rereading of "Entropy" that attends to how the story "is . . . packed full of allusions to many different contexts, scientific, social, sexual, and literary, no one of which should be arbitrarily isolated from the others, for the point of the story lies in their intersection." Douglas Keesey, " 'A Flaw Not Only in Him': Rereading Thomas Pynchon," *boundary 2* 15/16, no. 3/1 (1988): 217. Among the critics of Pynchon's short fiction, only John K. Young has tried to read Pynchon's stories in the terms of material history, focusing his particularly useful article, "Pynchon in Popular Magazines," on "The Secret Integration" (which appeared in *The Saturday Evening Post*) and on excerpts from *The Crying of Lot 49* (which appeared in *Esquire* and *Cavalier*). I agree with Young's claim that "the material traces of [textual] history speak volumes about the social, political, and cultural negotiations necessary to make a

text public." John K. Young, "Pynchon in Popular Magazines," *Critique* 44, no. 4 (2003): 389.

120. Based on an interview with Abrams, Tabbi writes that "Thomas Pynchon was among the first students Abrams influenced." Joseph Tabbi, "Pynchon's 'Entropy,'" *Explicator* 43, no. 1 (1984): 61.

121. Ibid., 113–114.

122. Ibid., 114.

123. Ibid., 116.

124. M. H. Abrams, "The Correspondent Breeze: A Romantic Metaphor," *The Kenyon Review* 19, no. 1 (1957): 122.

125. Ibid., 126.

126. Victoria F. de Zwann, "Pynchon's 'Entropy,'" *Explicator* 51, no. 3 (1993): 195.

127. Chandler Brossard, "Parties—Pathological and Otherwise," *Neurotica* 6 (1950): 34–35.

128. Jack Kerouac, "The Origins of the Beat Generation," *Playboy*, June 1959, 42.

129. Deborah L. Madsen, *The Postmodernist Allegories of Thomas Pynchon* (Leicester, UK: Leicester University Press, 1991), 29.

130. Theodore D. Kharpertian argues, "The V. narrative and the Profane narrative constitute, then, a binary opposition; as the Profane narrative represents entropy (and ridicules its principal exponent, Profane), so the V. narrative represents the contradictory effort at negentropy (and ridicules its principal exponent, Stencil), and the two narratives coexist within the frame of the text, consequently, in ironic relation to each other." Theodore D. Kharpertian, *A Hand to Turn the Time: The Menippean Satires of Thomas Pynchon* (Bloomington: Indiana University Press, 1990), 76.

131. See Tony Tanner, "V. and V-2," in *Pynchon: A Collection of Critical Essays*, ed. Edward Mendelson (Englewood Cliffs, NJ: Prentice Hall, 1978).

132. Luc Herman and John M. Krafft, "Race in Early Pynchon: Rewriting Sphere in *V.*," *Critique* 52, no. 1 (2011): 17.

133. Ibid., 28. Their argument better describes Pynchon's 1964 short story "The Secret Integration."

134. Charles B. Harris, *Contemporary American Novelists of the Absurd* (New Haven, CT: Rowman and Littlefield, 1972), 91. Perhaps the oldest version of this claim was put forward by Andrew Gordon. "I argued that *V.* was organized less as a novel than as a moral fable or apologue, and that its message read, 'Keep cool but care.'" "Smoking Dope with Thomas Pynchon: A Sixties Memoir," in *The Portable Sixties Reader*, ed. Ann Charters (New York: Penguin, 2002), 234. See also Raymond M. Olderman, *Beyond "The Waste Land": A Study of the American Novel in the Nineteen-Sixties* (New Haven, CT: Yale University Press, 1977).

135. Jerome Klinkowitz, "Review of Pynchon's Fictions: Thomas Pynchon and the Literature of Information, by John Stark," *American Literature* 53, no. 2 (1981): 336.

136. Luc Herman, "Early Pynchon," in *The Cambridge Companion to Thomas Pynchon*, ed. Inger H. Dalsgaard, Luc Herman, and Brian McHale (Cambridge: Cambridge University Press, 2012), 26.

137. Charles Hollander, "Does McClintic Sphere in *V.* Stand for Thelonius Monk?" *Notes on Contemporary Literature* 30, no. 1 (2000): 4.

138. Thomas Pynchon to Kirkpatrick Sale, "Letter," November 23, 1962. Thomas Pynchon Collection, Harry Ransom Humanities Research Center, Box 2, Folder 1. It is a point of historical humor to note that Thelonious Monk liked his middle name for the same reason that Pynchon did. Monk would joke that "he used it as a hip accessory . . . that owing to his middle name he could never be called a 'square.'" Thomas Fitterling, *Thelonius Monk: His Life and Music,* foreword Steve Lacy (Berkeley, CA: Berkeley Hills Books, 1997), 20.

139. David Witzling, "The Sensibility of Postmodern Whiteness in *V.,* or Thomas Pynchon's Identity Problem," *Contemporary Literature* 47, no. 3 (2006): 385.

140. Szalay, *Hip Figures,* 4.

141. Jack Kerouac, *On the Road* (New York: Penguin, 1999), 169.

142. Thomas Pynchon to Kirkpatrick Sale, "Letter," Undated. Thomas Pynchon, Harry Ransom Humanities Research Center, Box 2, Folder 1.

143. Qtd. in Hajdu, *Positively 4th Street,* 47.

144. Thomas Pynchon, "A Journey into the Mind of Watts," *New York Times Magazine,* June 12, 1966, 78. Subsequent references will be cited parenthetically.

145. Baldwin, "The Black Boy Looks at the White Boy," 269.

146. W. E. B. Du Bois, *Writings: The Suppression of the African Slave-Trade / The Souls of Black Folk / Dusk of Dawn / Essays and Articles* (New York: Library of America, 1987), 364.

147. Cheever, *Real Phonies,* 175.

148. Susan Gubar, *Racechanges: White Skin, Black Face in American Culture* (Oxford: Oxford University Press, 2000), 5.

149. For a fascinating exploration of the relationship between the modernist celebration of surfaces and the theatrical visualization of racialized skin, see Anne Anlin Cheng, *Second Skin: Josephine Baker and the Modern Surface* (Oxford: Oxford University Press, 2013).

150. Mailer, "The White Negro," 341.

151. C. E. Shannon, "A Mathematical Theory of Communication," *Bell System Technical Journal* 27 (1948): 380.

152. Ibid., 379.

153. For an overview of these debates, see N. Katherine Hayles, *How We Became Posthuman* (Chicago: University of Chicago Press, 1999). See also James Gleick, *The Information: A History, a Theory, a Flood* (New York: Random House, 2011).

154. Molly Hite, *Ideas of Order in the Novels of Thomas Pynchon* (Columbus: Ohio State University Press, 1983), ix.

155. Ibid.

156. Thomas Pynchon, Letter to Stanley Hyman, December 8, 1965. Stanley Edgar Hyman Papers, Library of Congress, Box 14.

157. Milton Klonsky, *A Discourse on Hip: Selected Writings of Milton Klonsky,* ed. Ted Solotaroff, intro. Mark Schechner (Detroit: Wayne State University Press, 1991), 134.

158. Ibid., 135.

159. Ibid., 137.

160. Ibid.

161. Ibid., 139.

162. Burn, *Conversations with David Foster Wallace*, 48.

163. Qtd. in Herman and Krafft, "Race in Early Pynchon: Rewriting Sphere in *V.*," *Critique: Studies in Contemporary Fiction* 52, no. 1 (2011): 19.

164. See McHale, *Postmodernist Fiction* (New York: Methuen, 1987), 21–22. McHale describes *V.* as a late modernist novel (pointing to the Vheissu episode in particular) as opposed to "'science-fictionalized' postmodernism" (McHale 68). McHale's classification of *V.* derives from his distinction between an epistemological and ontological dominant as the key difference between modernist and postmodernist fiction.

163. I would agree with "late modernism" as a period concept in the sense that Jameson develops in *A Singular Modernity* (New York: Verso, 2002), as a specific description of the U.S. postwar university's institutionalization of the more dynamic field of prewar modernism, whose name denoted less a period concept or style than an broad assessment of the state of the arts. "But when I suggest that late modernism was an American phenomenon," Jameson writes, "I have in mind the theory of art, the ideology of modernism, which it was the very role of abstract expressionism pre-eminently to have generated and which then accompanied it everywhere abroad as a specifically North American cultural imperialism . . . The development is replicated, but on a more limited national scale, in American poetry, where the rich and complex oeuvre of Wallace Stevens begins to displace those of Ezra Pound and T. S. Eliot. . . . Stevens' poetry can be seen as literature and as theory alike; his practice is essentially what he himself, along with the influential New Criticism, made theory of—which is to say that both Stevens and the New Criticism prepared the space in which an ideology of modernism could emerge" (68–69).

165. Herbert Marcuse, *One-Dimensional Man: Studies in the Ideology of Advanced Industrial Society*, intro. Douglas Kellner (Boston: Beacon, 1991), 14.

166. One might argue against my account by foregrounding the ideological differences between the New Critics and Marcuse. After all, Marcuse derides "the setting aside of a special reservation in which thought and language are permitted to be legitimately inexact, vague, and even contradictory" (that is, preserving a special zone of poetic truth) as "the most effective way of protecting the normal universe of discourse from being seriously disturbed by unfitting ideas." Marcuse, *One-Dimensional Man*, 184. Presumably the solution to this problem is to see *all* worldly truth in "inexact, vague, and even contradictory" terms; as we have seen, this is exactly what Kenneth Burke's theory of symbolic action does through the conscious mapping of New Critical vocabularies onto other domains. Considered in this light, and reflecting on Burke's influence on Jameson's model of the political unconscious, there is less philosophical daylight between Marcuse and the New Critics than one might be tempted to think.

167. Marcuse, *One-Dimensional Man*, 180.

168. Arthur M., Schlesinger Jr., "Introduction," in *The Politics of Hope* (Boston: Houghton Mifflin Company, 1963), xi. He also writes, "The word 'togetherness' has passed from our language" (xi).

2 *Punk's Positive Dystopia*

1. My account of the publication history of *The Punk* is based on Miriam Rivett, "Misfit Lit: 'Punk Writing' and Representations of Punk through Writing and Publishing," in *Punk Rock: So What? The Cultural Legacy of Punk*, ed. Roger Sabin (New York: Routledge, 1999), 31–48, and Paul Rochford, "Gideon Sams," *Punk77*, March 2, 2002, http://www.punk77.co.uk/groups/thepunkpaul rochfordremembers.htm.

2. Gideon Sams, *The Punk* (London: Corgi Books, 1977), 4. This language comes from an archly ironic biographical blurb included in the Corgi edition of the book. The full text of *The Punk* is available at *Punk77*, accessed July 2, 2012, http://www.punk77.co.uk/groups/thepunk.htm. Subsequent references will be cited parenthetically.

3. For one canonical account of punk in the UK, see Jon Savage, *England's Dreaming: Anarchy, Sex Pistols, Punk Rock, and Beyond* (New York: St. Martin's, 2002), 263–269.

4. Rochford, "Gideon Sams." Sams was, Rochford reports, more of a fan of the Stones. The phrase "The Filth and the Fury" derives from the *Daily Mirror*'s 1976 headline reporting on the Grundy episode. See *Daily Mirror*, December 2, 1976.

5. Sams's protagonist has changed his name from David to Adolph Sphitz, since "punks like to have odd, and often depressing names, as in their nature" (9).

6. Existing studies that emphasize punk resignification—and the significance of the punk use of swastikas—are numerous. James J. Ward, "'This is Germany! It's 1933!' Appropriations and Constructions of 'Fascism' in New York Punk / Hardcore in the 1980s," *Journal of Popular Culture* 30, no. 3 (1996): 155–184. See the discussion of punk and postpunk in Matthew Boswell, *Holocaust Impiety in Literature, Popular Music and Film* (New York: Palgrave Macmillan, 2012), 97–136. Jon Stratton, "Jews, Punks, and the Holocaust: From the Velvet Underground to the Ramones—the Jewish-American Story," *Popular Music* 24, no. 1 (2005): 79–105.

7. Dick Hebdige, *Subculture*, 123.

8. Greil Marcus, *Lipstick Traces: A Secret History of the Twentieth Century* (Cambridge, MA: Harvard University Press, 1989), 110.

9. The British Conservative politician Iain Macleod coined the term in 1965.

10. Daniel Stedman Jones, *Masters of the Universe: Hayek, Friedman, and the Birth of Neoliberal Politics* (Princeton: Princeton University Press, 2012), 5, 233.

11. For a more extensive discussion of the concept of the "creative class," see Chapter 4.

12. That a text as interesting as Sams's *The Punk* is almost unstudied indicates the scale of this lacuna. The exception is Rivett, though her account is more of a publication history of *The Punk* and other punk texts. She gives less attention to the content of these texts. There is reason to believe that this situation will change soon. Punk studies has recently begun to consolidate itself as a specific area of academic inquiry. Alongside Roger Sabin's *Punk Rock: So What?*, Nicholas Rombes has contributed much to the new wave of punk

studies, editing *New Punk Cinema* (Edinburgh: Edinburgh University Press, 2005) as well as writing *Ramones* (New York: Continuum, 2011) and *A Cultural Dictionary of Punk, 1974–1982* (New York: Continuum, 2009). In 2012, a peer-reviewed journal dedicated to punk, *Punk & Post-Punk*, was founded. Jayna Brown, Patrick Deer, and Tavia Nyong'o coedited "Punk and Its Afterlives," a special issue of *Social Text*. See also Zack Furness, ed., *Punkademics: The Basement Show in the Ivory Tower* (Brooklyn: Minor Compositions, 2012). Many of these studies self-consciously treat punk not only as an object of study but also as an ethos that ought to guide critical practice (ergo the name *punkademics*). The editors of "Punk and Its Afterlives," for example, disavow any desire to "recover any singular sense of the term [punk] or to settle questions of origins or authenticity." Jayna Brown, Patrick Deer, and Tavia Nyong'o, "Punk and Its Afterlives: Introduction," *Social Text* 31, no. 3 (2013): 2. Nonetheless, like many recent academics who study punk, they "seek the constant punk spirit of misbehavior, improvisation, disobedience, and deviance, through all its mercurial transformations, and in spite of the predictable naysaying as to its lack of political guarantees" (2). The articles in the special issue "don't move the margin to the center" (that is, plea for "women, people of color, and queers" to be included in punk history) but rather "move us off the grid entirely and make a linear master narrative impossible, in the spirit of the unruly and uncontrollable" (5). The editors turn the spirit of punk against self-avowed punks who assume that punk was "a bastion of straight, white masculinity" (5). The editors not only study punk but also *critically enact* the spirit of punk (which requires them to affirm, like all good punks, that there is no singular definition of *punk*). The punk impulse to "move off the grid," we will see, has a specific—and politically surprising—intellectual history that I will trace in the writing of William S. Burroughs.

13. See Daniel Kane, "From Poetry to Punk in the East Village," in *The Cambridge Companion to the Literature of New York*, ed. Cyrus R. K. Patell and Waterman Bryan (Cambridge: Cambridge University Press, 2010), 189–201.

14. Terrance Diggory, *Encyclopedia of the New York School of Poets* (New York: Facts on File, 2009), 398.

15. Two important exceptions include Robert Siegle's *Suburban Ambush: Downtown Writing and the Fiction of Insurgency* (Baltimore: Johns Hopkins University Press, 1989) and Brandon Stosuy's *Up Is Up, But So Is Down: New York's Downtown Literary Scene, 1974–1992* (New York: NYU Press, 2006). For a broader analysis of contemporary taboo-breaking fiction, see Linda Kauffman, *Bad Girls and Sick Boys: Fantasies in Contemporary Art and Culture* (Berkeley: University of California Press, 1998).

16. For an illuminating history of 'zines across the twentieth century, see Stephen Duncombe, *Notes from Underground: Zines and the Politics of Alternative Culture* (London: Verso, 1997).

17. Rivett, "Misfit Lit," 35.

18. On "dirty realism," see Robert Rebein, *Hicks, Tribes, and Dirty Realists: American Fiction after Postmodernism* (Lexington: University Press of Kentucky, 2001). The British literary journal *Granta* used the term *dirty realism* as the title of a special issue on American minimalism, which included work by Raymond

Carver, Richard Ford, Jayne Anne Phillips, Tobias Wolff, and others. In an editorial note in this issue, Bill Buford describes dirty realism as "the fiction of a new generation of American authors. They write about the belly-side of contemporary life . . . but they write about it with a disturbing detachment, at times verging on comedy. Understated, ironic, sometimes savage, but insistently compassionate, these stories constitute a new voice in fiction." *Granta* 8–9 (1983): 258. On "blank fictions," see James Annesley, *Blank Fictions: Consumerism, Culture, and the Contemporary American Novel* (London: Pluto Press, 1998). Annesley defines *blank fictions* as "modern fiction that is flat, ambiguous and problematically blank" (137).

19. Joel Rose and Catherine Texier, "Introduction," in *Between C & D: New Writing from the Lower East Side Fiction Magazine* (New York: Penguin, 1988), xi.

20. Zack Carlson and Bryan Connolly, ed., *Destroy All Movies!!! The Complete Guide to Punks on Film*, foreword Richard Hell (Seattle, WA: Fantagraphics Books, 2010), 387.

21. In *Class of 1982*, a beleaguered high school music teacher murders punk students who have terrorized his class and raped his wife.

22. Slavoj Žižek, *The Sublime Object of Ideology*, Second Edition (New York: Verso, 2009), 176.

23. Curtis White, *Monstrous Possibility: An Invitation to Literary Politics* (Champaign, IL: Dalkey Archive Press, 1998), 59.

24. Ibid.

25. Ibid.

26. Ibid.

27. Richard Lloyd, *Neo-Bohemia*, 90.

28. "ANARCHY in the UK!" *SpecialGroupTours*, http://www.specialgrouptours.com/html/anarchy_in_the_uk_punk_rock_lo.html (accessed January 22, 2014).

29. Robert Garnett, "Too Low to Be Low: Art Pop and the Sex Pistols," in *Punk Rock: So What? The Cultural Legacy of Punk*, ed. Sabin, 24.

30. Richard Laermer and Mark Simmons, *Punk Marketing: Get Off Your Ass and Join the Revolution* (New York: HarperCollins, 2007), 13.

31. Ibid., 1.

32. Ibid., 17.

33. Johnny Rotten, "Johnny Rotten's Cordial Letter to the Rock and Roll Hall of Fame: Next to the Sex Pistols, You're 'a Piss Stain,'" *Open Culture*, July 10, 2013, http://www.openculture.com/2013/07/john-rottens-cordial-letter-to-the-rock-and-roll-hall-of-fame.html.

34. Laermer and Simmons, *Punk Marketing*, xxiv.

35. James F. English, *The Economy of Prestige: Prizes, Awards, and the Circulation of Cultural Value* (Cambridge, MA: Harvard University Press, 2009), 222.

36. Stacy Thompson, *Punk Productions: Unfinished Business* (Albany: State University Press of New York, 2004), 86.

37. Jon Savage, *England's Dreaming*, 243.

38. Ibid., 178.

39. Sean McCann and Michael Szalay, "Do You Believe in Magic? Literary Thinking after the New Left," *Yale Journal of Criticism* 18, no. 2 (2005), 460.

40. Victor Bockris, *Beat Punks* (Boston: Da Capo Press, 2000), 80.

41. Luc Boltanski and Ève Chiapello, *The New Spirit of Capitalism*, trans. Gregory Elliott (London: Verso, 2006), xv.

42. Ibid., 22.

43. Ibid.

44. Ibid.

45. Ibid., 23.

46. For an astute analysis of this rhetoric, see Sarah Brouillette, *Literature and the Creative Economy* (Stanford: Stanford University Press, 2014).

47. Guy Standing, *The Precariat: The New Dangerous Class* (New York: Bloomsbury, 2011), 26.

48. David Harvey, *A Brief History of Neoliberalism* (Oxford: Oxford University Press, 2007), 40.

49. Ibid.

50. Boltanski has also initiated a methodological effort to move beyond Bourdieuvian models of "agency" in the name of self-theorizing "actors," part of a broader effort to supplant critical sociology with the so-called pragmatist sociology of critique. For an account of this project, see Luc Boltanski, *On Critique: A Sociology of Emancipation* (Cambridge: Polity, 2011).

51. Boltanski and Chiapello, *The New Spirit of Capitalism*, 199.

52. Tavia Nyong'o argues that "queerness was ... punk's sinthome insofar as punk's most powerful affects were employed in unknotting the body from its psychic link to the social." Tavia Nyong'o, "Do You Want Queer Theory (or Do You Want the Truth)? Intersections of Punk and Queer in the 1970s," *Radical History Review*, no. 100 (2008): 114.

53. See Judith Halberstam, "The Anti-social Turn in Queer Studies," *Graduate Journal of Social Science* 5, no. 2 (2008): 140–156.

54. Lee Edelman, "Antagonism, Negativity, and the Subject of Queer Theory," *PMLA* 121, no. 3 (2006): 822.

55. Lee Edelman, *No Future: Queer Theory and the Death Drive* (Durham: Duke University Press, 2004), 45, 23, 24.

56. Luke Thurston, "sinthome," in *An Introductory Dictionary of Lacanian Psychoanalysis*, Dylan Evans (New York: Routledge, 1996), 191. Lacan introduced the concept of the *sinthome* in Jacques Lacan, *Le Séminaire de Jacques Lacan, Livre XXIII: Le Sinthome (1975–76)*. Unpublished seminar.

57. Ben Watson, "Philosophizing Post-Punk," *Radical Philosophy* 132 (2005): 6.

58. Ibid., 6, 2.

59. There has been a lively debate about the relationship between empirical punk communities and academics who study punk. Self-identified punks have, to say the least, resisted incorporation into academic discourses. In an insightful review of a collection of essays on punk and race, Golnar Nikpour writes: "the academic world has produced a silly number of texts in the name of 'punk studies,' but the great majority of these studies traverse a world that has little to do with punk as I know it. At best, they are basically irrelevant

the-Sex-Pistols-Were-Totally-Influenced-By-Situationism-and-Other-Serious-Things Studies, and at worst they are egomaniacal attempts to garner legitimacy (not to mention CV padding!) on the backs of DIY subculture(s). In general, I am leery of those academic 'experts' whose object of study is punk, not only because I don't consider the punk scene an intellectual little league that needs legitimacy bequeathed to it by professionals, but also because punk—auto-archiving, self-aware, and interested in its own history—operates on the premise that everyone is an expert." Golnar Nikpour, "White Riot: Another Failure . . . ," *Maximum Rocknroll*, January 17, 2012, http://maximumrocknroll.com/white-riot-another-failure/. She is reviewing Stephen Duncombe and Maxwell Tremblay, *White Riot: Punk Rock and the Politics of Race* (London: Verso, 2011). Nikpour complains about "Duncombe and Tremblay's assumption that their 'own experience' of punk—English speaking, suburban, US-based, middle-class, and white—is the norm from which others should be judged." Despite the trenchancy of her criticism—and her persuasive alternative account of the origin of punk in the mid-1970s—Nikpour calcifies the difference between punks and academics, contrasting authentic punk D.I.Y. subcultural experience with the egomaniacal academic theft of punk authenticity. If it is true that "everyone is an expert," this does not seem to entail that everyone has a right to speak for or even of punk. This distinction—which pits condescending academic expertise against respectful punk self-knowledge—is problematic. The first problem is that many academics claim that punk has influenced their own intellectual practices, radically transforming their understanding of knowledge production. Partly responding to Nikpour, the editors of "Punk and Its Afterlives" propose "punk study" (study "with and for" punk) as a substitute for "punk studies" (the study of punks as mute objects). Brown, Patrick Deer, and Tavia Nyong'o, "Punk and Its Afterlives," 8–9. The editors propose "being-with rather than speaking for punk and its afterlives" (9). The problem is therefore not the academic study of punk *per se* but the methods and assumptions guiding study. I am indebted to Leif Sorensen for making this observation in "Richard Hell, D.I.Y. Subject Formation, and the Gamble of Getting a Face," *Postmodern Culture* 24, no. 2 (2014). A second problem, one that the editors of the *Social Text* special issue somewhat reproduce even while attempting to engage in genuine punk study, is the implication that there is some kind of hard epistemic or ontological chasm separating authentic punks (with whom one can *be with*) from egotistical academics (those who have unthinkingly sought to "speak for" punk). It is true that some subcultural studies scholars have attempted to "speak for" punk, condescendingly honoring their objects of study by celebrating punks' critical self-consciousness. Nonetheless, I do not think one can ever simply separate "being-with" and "speaking for." Any "being-with" requires a prior "speaking for," which speculatively posits the characteristics of those beings with whom we are attempting to be. Punk's characterological form necessarily arises from myriad historical efforts to speak for, interpret, and in so doing be with (or stand against) persons, practices, and groups. The ethos of punk is related to but never identical to the lived experience of self-identified empirical punk subcultures. As with all the figures in this study, the meaning and purpose of punk was highly contested by various parties, not only by self-described punks but also by academics who did not identity as punks. The speculative images of punk constructed together by these actors (the spiritual exercises that constitute "punk study") are still under revision.

60. Like Watson, Reiichi Miura also sees the "essence of punk . . . in the bands' activities, tunes, records, and performances, rather than what philosophy the movement follows." Reiichi Miura, "What Kind of Revolution Do You Want? Punk, the Contemporary Left, and Singularity," *Mediations* 25, no. 1 (2010): 61. Yet he arrives at a different political conclusion, arguing that punk was committed to a "symptomatic performance of the unrepresentability of one's identity" (65). Punk's commitment to singularity betrays a "latent biopolitical program," which "encourages a certain kind of quietism" (61).

61. We might wonder whether punk negation eroded or undermined the concept of the project itself. The implosion of myriad punk bands might be taken as an indication that it did. But in practice the temporary small group has often been the locus of punk authenticity, activity, and organization.

62. *The Great Rock 'n' Roll Swindle*, directed by Julian Temple (London: 2008).

63. Huxley, " 'Ever Get the Feeling You've Been Cheated?" in *Punk Rock: So What?* ed. Sabin, 98.

64. On the argument between Reid and McLaren, see Robert Garnett, "Too Tow to Be Low," in *Punk Rock: So What?* ed. Sabin, 24.

65. Qtd. in Ibid., 96.

66. Qtd. in Huxley, " 'Ever Get the Feeling You've Been Cheated?" in *Punk Rock: So What?* ed. Sabin, 96.

67. Ira Silverberg, "Editor's Introduction" in William S. Burroughs, *Word Virus: The William S. Burroughs Reader,* ed. James Grauerholz and Ira Silverberg (New York: Grove, 2000), xi.

68. Barry Miles, *William Burroughs: El Hombre Invisible* (London: Virgin Books, 2002), 10.

69. Victor Bockris, *With William Burroughs: A Report from the Bunker* (New York: St. Martin's, 1996), xii.

70. Barry Miles, *Call Me Burroughs: A Life* (New York: Twelve, 2014), 593.

71. Bockris, *With William Burroughs,* 127.

72. Ibid.

73. Lotringer had first met Burroughs in 1975 at the Schizo-Culture Conference at Columbia University, which featured the Beat writer alongside Arthur Danto, Jean-François Lyotard, Michel Foucault, Gilles Deleuze, and Félix Guattari.

74. Miles, *William Burroughs,* 217.

75. William S. Burroughs, "Bugger the Queen," in *The Adding Machine* (New York: Arcade Publishing, 1993), 80. Subsequent references will be cited parenthetically.

76. Bockris, *With William Burroughs,* 127.

77. William S. Burroughs, "Keynote Commentary & Roosevelt after Inauguration," Nova Convention, recording available at http://www.ubu.com/sound/nova.html.

78. William S. Burroughs and Allen Ginsberg, *The Yage Letters Redux* (San

Francisco: City Lights Publishers, 2006), 41. Subsequent references will be cited parenthetically.

79. Ted Morgan, *Literary Outlaw*, 182. See also Rob Johnson, *The Lost Years of William S. Burroughs: Beats in South Texas* (College Station: Texas A&M University Press, 2006).

80. Johnson, *The Lost Years of William S. Burroughs*, 65. Phil Baker, *William S. Burroughs* (London: Reaktion Books, 2011), 53.

81. Johnson, *The Lost Years of William S. Burroughs*, 113.

82. Ibid., 113, 136.

83. William S. Burroughs, *The Letters of William S. Burroughs, Vol. 1: 1945–1959* (New York: Penguin, 1994), 67.

84. Bockris, *With William Burroughs*, 179.

85. Ibid., 180.

86. William S. Burroughs, *Letters to Allen Ginsberg 1953–1957* (New York: Full Court Press, 1982), 79. Note that for Burroughs, the laughter of the routine offers freedom *from* the body, not (as for Bakhtin's carnival laughter) a freedom *of* the body (or lower bodily regions).

87. Ibid., 201.

88. Stephen E. Kercher, *Revel with a Cause: Liberal Satire in Postwar America* (Chicago: University of Chicago Press, 2006).

89. William S. Burroughs, "The Limits of Control," in *The Adding Machine*, 143.

90. Ibid., 144.

91. Conrad Knickerbocker, "William S. Burroughs, The Art of Fiction No. 36," *Paris Review*, no. 35 (1965), http://www.theparisreview.org/interviews/4424/the-art-of-fiction-no-36-william-s-burroughs.

92. Burroughs, "The Limits of Control," in *The Adding Machine*, 145.

93. William S. Burroughs, *Burroughs Live: The Collected Interviews of William S. Burroughs, 1960–1997*, ed. Sylvère Lotringer (New York: Semiotext(e), 2000), 461.

94. The second issue of the punk 'zine *Maximum Rocknroll* cites Burroughs twice in an article called "The Spirit of the Tzara Lives On!" which ties punk to a much wider tradition of antiart. The author writes: "Punk is Dada. Be anti-art, dada is anti-art. Opposition strengthens. Dada is short-lived and self-destructive . . . Art comes from the decaying, shattered minds. Do you have the balls to <u>know?</u>" "The Spirit of Tzara Lives On!" *Maximum Rocknroll* 1, no. 2, September-October 1982, 45. The article recommends "<u>Naked Lunch, Nova Express,</u> just about everything [Burroughs] wrote" (46).

95. Alfred Korzybski, *Science and Sanity: An Introduction to Non-Aristotelian Systems and General Semantics*, Fifth Edition (New York: Institute of General Semantics, 1995), 7.

96. Knickerbocker, "William S. Burroughs."

97. Ibid.

98. Alfred Korzybski, *Science and Sanity*, xxvi–xxvii.

99. Ibid, 35.

100. Ibid., 404.

101. Ibid.

102. Ibid., lxiii.

103. Burke, *A Grammar of Motives*, 242.

104. Hadot, *Philosophy as a Way of Life*, 82.

105. Ibid., 83.

106. Peter Sloterdijk, *You Must Change Your Life*, 10.

107. Ibid., 84.

108. Lawrence Wright, *Going Clear: Scientology, Hollywood, and the Prison of Belief* (New York: Vintage, 2013), 74.

109. Conrad Knickerbocker, "William S. Burroughs."

110. Marcus, *Lipstick Traces*, 82.

111. Wayne Pounds, "The Postmodern Anus: Parody and Utopia in Two Recent Novels by William Burroughs," *Poetics Today* 8, no. 3–4 (1987): 613.

112. Ibid., 614.

113. Jamie Russell, *Queer Burroughs* (New York: Palgrave Macmillan, 2001), 57–58.

114. Jennie Skerl, *William S. Burroughs* (Boston: Twayne, 1985), 78.

115. Timothy S. Murphy, *Wising Up the Marks: The Amodern William Burroughs* (Berkeley: University of California Press, 1998), 146.

116. Sylvère Lotringer, ed., *Burroughs Live: The Collected Interviews of William S. Burroughs* (Los Angeles: Semiotext(e) Double Agents Series, 2001), 180.

117. William S. Burroughs, *Port of Saints* (Berkeley, CA: Blue Wind Press, 1980), 71. Subsequent references will be cited parenthetically. Though this discussion will largely concern *The Wild Boys*, I will quote from *Port of Saints* freely, taking the two novels as the same text.

118. Jon Savage, "When Bowie Met Burroughs," *Guardian*, March 8, 2013, http://www.theguardian.com/music/2013/mar/09/david-bowie-william-burroughs.

119. Ibid.

120. Barry Miles, *William Burroughs: El Hombre Invisible*, 188.

121. William S. Burroughs, *Burroughs Live*, 276.

122. Ibid. We would nonetheless be justified, in my view, in interpreting the opening episode in terms of later episodes in *The Wild Boys*.

123. William S. Burroughs, *The Wild Boys: A Book of the Dead* (New York: Grove, 1992), 3–4, ellipses in original. Subsequent references will be cited parenthetically.

124. William S. Burroughs, *Nova Express* (New York: Grove, 1994), 59.

125. Conrad Knickerbocker, "William S. Burroughs."

126. Edward S. Robinson, *Shift Linguals: Cut-Up Narratives from William S. Burroughs to the Present* (New York: Rodopi, 2011), 251.

127. Ibid., 252.

128. Conrad Knickerbocker, "William S. Burroughs."

129. William S. Burroughs, "invisible people," in *The Ticket That Exploded* (New York: Grove, 1967), 205.

130. Ibid., 206.

131. Ibid., 207.

132. Ibid., 213.

133. Ibid., 207.

134. William S. Burroughs and Brion Gysin, *The Third Mind* (New York: Viking, 1978), 25.

135. Napoleon Hill, *Think and Grow Rich*, Original Unabridged Edition, foreword Melvin Powers (Chatsworth, CA: Wilshire Book Company, 1999), 169.

136. Ibid., 183.

137. William S. Burroughs, *The Place of Dead Roads* (New York: Picador, 2001), 43.

138. William S. Burroughs, *Rub Out the Words: The Letters of William S. Burroughs* (New York: Ecco, 2012), 294. It is worth noting that this description doesn't accurately describe the opening of the published book, but suggests that Audrey Carsons and the wild boys may be dead.

139. Timothy S. Murphy, *Wising Up the Marks*, 156.

140. William S. Burroughs, "Women: A Biological Mistake?" in *The Adding Machine*, 126.

141. William S. Burroughs, *Burroughs Live*, 180.

142. William S. Burroughs, *Rub Out the Words*, 392.

143. William S. Burroughs, *The Job* (New York: Penguin, 1989), 92.

144. Timothy S. Murphy, *Wising Up the Marks*, 168.

145. William S. Burroughs, *Rub Out the Words*, 377.

146. Ibid.

147. Ibid.

148. Conrad Knickerbocker, "William S. Burroughs."

149. Michael Clune, *American Literature and the Free Market, 1945–2000* (Cambridge: Cambridge University Press, 2010), 93.

150. Nicola Pitchford, *Tactical Readings: Feminist Postmodernism in the Novels of Kathy Acker and Angela Carter* (Lewisburg, PA: Bucknell University Press, 2001), 17.

151. Larry McCaffery," "The Artists of Hell: Kathy Acker and 'Punk' Aesthetics," in *Breaking the Sequence: Women's Experimental Fiction*, intro. and ed. Ellen G. Friedman and Miriam Fuchs (Princeton: Princeton University Press, 1989), 218.

152. Kathy Acker, "Critical Languages," in *Bodies of Work: Essays* (London: Serpent's Tail, 1997), 88. Subsequent references will be cited parenthetically as *Bodies*. I will move between essays in this collection in the discussion that follows. Though these essays were written at different times, they represent a consistent set of views, and so it is justified to treat this book of essays as developing a single argument.

153. Larry McCaffery, "An Interview with Kathy Acker," *Mississippi Review* 20, no. 1–2 (1991): 91.

154. Ibid., 89.

155. Ellen G. Friedman, "A Conversation with Kathy Acker," *Review of Contemporary Fiction* 9, no. 3 (1989), http://www.dalkeyarchive.com/a-conversation-with-kathy-acker-by-ellen-g-friedman/.

156. Larry McCaffery, "Kathy Acker: Always Missing—a Plagiarized Tribute," *Critique* 51, no. 2 (2010): 107.

157. McCaffery, "An Interview with Kathy Acker," 94.

158. Ibid.

159. Ibid.

160. Ibid.

161. Ibid.

162. Sarah Marcus, *Girls to the Front: The True Story of the Riot Grrrl Revolution* (New York: HarperCollins, 2010), 34.

163. Boltanski and Chiapello, *The New Spirit of Capitalism*, 39.

164. Ibid.

165. Ibid., 38.

166. Qtd. in Brandon Stosuy, ed., *Up Is Up But So Is Down: New York's Downtown Literary Scene, 1974–1992*, afterword Dennis Cooper and Eileen Myles (New York: New York University Press, 2006), 18.

167. Kathy Acker, "New York City in 1979," in *Essential Acker: The Selected Writings of Kathy Acker*, ed. Amy Scholder and Dennis Cooper, intro. Jeanette Winterson (New York: Grove Press, 2002), 134. Subsequent references will be cited parenthetically.

168. Walter Benn Michaels, *The Shape of the Signifier*, 67.

169. Although she does not define "postcapitalism" directly, Acker seems to use the term to suggest that capitalism's reliance on wage labor as a mechanism of exploitation has either broken down or that the nature of capitalist oppression goes well beyond class antagonism. That said, she will occasionally use "postcapitalism" interchangeably with "capitalism."

170. Luce Irigaray, *The Sex Which Is Not One*, trans. Catherine Porter, with Carolyn Burke (Ithaca, NY: Cornell University Press, 1985), 31.

171. Michael Foucault, "Preface," in Deleuze and Guattari, *Anti-Oedipus: Capitalism and Schizophrenia*, xiii.

172. Ibid.

173. The political ambiguity of this ethos appears also in another descendent of deleuzoguattarian / punk thought, the notion of "accelerationism," which oscillates between right accelerationists such as Nick Land and so-called left accelerationists. In any case, it should come as no surprise that Land has written an essay called "No Future" celebrating the fact that "[p]unk arises within the culture of universal prostitution and laughs at the death of the social." Nick Land, *Fanged Noumena: Collected Writings 1987–2007* (Falmouth / New York: Urbanomic / Sequence Press, 2011), 413. Though by no means identical, accelerationism and positive dystopia participate in broadly similar intellectual tendencies. See also Steven Shaviro, *No Speed Limit: Three Essays on Accelerationism* (Minneapolis: University of Minnesota Press, 2015).

174. Kathy Acker, *Empire of the Senseless* (New York: Grove, 1994), 134.

175. Larry McCaffery, "An Interview with Kathy Acker," in *Some Other Frequency: Interviews with Innovative American Authors* (Philadelphia: University of Pennsylvania Press, 1996), 24.

176. Caren Irr, *Pink Pirates: Contemporary American Women Writers and Copyright* (Iowa City: University of Iowa Press, 2010), 117. Clune, *American Literature and the Free Market, 1945–2000*, 104.

177. Clune, *American Literature and the Free Market*, 126.

178. Irr, *Pink Pirates*, 113.

179. See Paul Giles, "Historicizing the Transnational: Robert Coover, Kathy

Acker and the Rewriting of British Cultural History, 1970–1997," *Journal of American Studies*, no. 41 (2007): 26.

180. White, *Monstrous Possibility*, 64.

181. John Locke, *Two Treatises of Government*, ed. Peter Laslett (Cambridge: Cambridge University Press, 1988), 286.

182. The relationship among classical liberalism, neoliberalism, and libertarianism is complicated. I am unable to fully clarify this relationship here, but I have been implicitly arguing in this chapter that, though these discourses are not identical, the neoliberal invocation of libertarianism is not (or not only) dissimulation. Rather, I would argue, libertarianism accurately names one tendency within the fractious neoliberal coalition. Members of this coalition shared common historical enemies, common readings of classical liberal texts, as well as a common fantasy of the free market, though they did not agree on the specific role or limits of the strong state. Therefore, though it is undeniable that the neoliberal program has in practice embraced the coercive state, it is not quite right to say that "neoliberalism turned out to be very nearly the polar opposite of libertarian anarchism." Philip Mirowski, *Never Let a Serious Crisis Go to Waste* (London: Verso, 2013), 41. At the very least, even adopting Mirowski's preferred distinctions, right-libertarians and anarcho-capitalists have been dialectical partners with what he calls the Neoliberal Thought Collective.

183. Robert Nozick, *Anarchy, State, and Utopia*, foreword Thomas Nagel (New York: Basic Books, 2013), 153. Technically speaking, Nozick does not successfully defend the Lockean account of original acquisition. Instead, he "assume[s] that any adequate theory of justice in acquisition will contain a proviso similar to the weaker of the ones we have attributed to Locke" (178). That is, he assumes that one does not have a property right in a "previously unowned thing" if, by owning that thing, "the position of others no longer at liberty to use the thing is thereby worsened" (178). Nozick then asserts, without argument, that "the free operation of a market system will not actually run afoul of the Lockean proviso" (182). Though Nozick does not devise a positive justification for property rights, the important point is that he does not, as Acker would predict, justify his theory of property by claiming that holders of property in any sense "create" their holdings, nor does the creation of a thing necessarily entitle one to own it.

184. Murray N. Rothbard, for instance, rejects patents (but not copyrights) as a violation of free market principles. See Murray N. Rothbard, *Man, Economy, and State and State with Power and Market*, intro. Joseph T. Salerno (Auburn, AL: Ludwig von Mises Institute, 2011), 749. For a more general libertarian case against intellectual property (including copyrights and trademarks), see Stephan N. Kinsella, *Against Intellectual Property* (Auburn, AL: Ludwig von Mises Institute, 2011).

185. For a systematic description of this lunatic view, see Hans-Hermann Hoppe, *Democracy—the God That Failed: The Economics and Politics of Monarchy, Democracy, and Natural Order* (Edison, NJ: Transaction Publishers, 2001).

186. Kenneth Goldsmith's *Uncreative Writing: Managing Language in the Digital Age* (New York: Columbia University Press, 2011). Cory Doctorow, *Context: Further Selected Essays on Productivity, Creativity, Parenting, and Politics in the 21st Century* (San Francisco: Tachyon, 2011). Jonathan Lethem, "The Ecstasy

of Influence," in *The Ecstasy of Influence* (New York: Vintage, 2012), 93–120. See also Lawrence Lessig, *Free Culture: The Nature and Future of Creativity* (New York: Penguin, 2005), and *Remix: Making Art and Commerce Thrive in the Hybrid Economy* (New York: Penguin, 2009).

187. Richard Florida, *The Rise of the Creative Class: And How It's Transforming Work, Leisure, Community, and Everyday Life* (New York: Basic Books, 2003), 153.

188. Jean-Philippe Vergne, "The Pirate and the Capitalist: A Love Story?" *Policy* 29, no. 3 (2013): 4.

189. Ibid.

190. Ibid., 6.

191. Ibid.

192. Kathy Acker, *Essential Acker*, cover.

193. Michael Szalay, "The Incorporation Artist," *Los Angeles Review of Books*, July 10, 2012, http://lareviewofbooks.org/review/the-incorporation-artist.

194. Ibid.

195. "taqwa" in John L. Esposito, ed., *The Oxford Dictionary of Islam* (Oxford: Oxford University Press, 2004), 314.

196. Ibid., 315

197. *The Taqwacores* was originally self-published by Knight. It was photocopied by him and given away out of the back of his car before being picked up first by the punk record label Alternative Tentacles and then by the radical publisher Autonomedia. In the UK, the novel was purchased by Telegram, which censored the book in the wake of the Muhammad cartoons controversy of 2005 and 2006. In the United States, the book was revised and republished by Soft Skull Press in 2008. A film adaptation played at Sundance in 2010. Since the publication of *The Taqwacores*, Knight has released a slate of spinoff or related books, including a metafictional novel called *Osama Van Halen* (2009); a couple books of travel writing; a memoir that discusses his conversion to Islam at the age of fifteen; a quasi-academic ethnography of the Nation of Gods and Earth (a spinoff group of the Nation of Islam also known as the Five Percenters); and a memoir about his alienation from one of his mentors, the so-called anarcho-Sufi writer Peter Lamborn Wilson (Hakim Bey), called *William S. Burroughs v. the Qur'an* (2012).

198. Muslim punk was a relatively small phenomenon until Knight's book was published. Many new Muslim punk bands formed after the publication of *The Taqwacores*, including The Kominas, Al-Thawra, Diacritical, and Fedayeen, some directly inspired by Knight's book.

199. Knight writes about his disillusionment with Bey in *William S. Burroughs vs. the Qur'an*.

200. Hakim Bey, *T.A.Z.: The Temporary Autonomous Zone, Ontological Anarchy, Poetic Terrorism* (Brooklyn: Autonomedia, 1991), available online at http://hermetic.com/bey/taz_cont.html.

3 How to Be a Believer

1. Tim LaHaye and Jerry B. Jenkins, *Left Behind: A Novel of Earth's Last Days* (Wheaton, IL: Tyndale, 1995), 1–2. Subsequent references will be cited parenthetically.

2. I am unable in this space to give the political content of *Left Behind* and its relationship to the Christian Right the attention it deserves. Suffice it to say that LaHaye and Jenkins show little sympathy in *Left Behind* or elsewhere for "secular humanists," a group they characterize as amoral, relativistic followers of Darwin, Nietzsche, Freud, and Marx, among others. LaHaye popularized the term "secular humanist" as a term of opprobrium in his *Battle for the Mind: A Subtle Warfare* (Old Tappan, NJ: Revell, 1980). See also LaHaye and David Noebel, *Mind Siege: The Battle for the Truth* (Nashville, TN: Thomas Nelson, 2003).

3. In case the true purpose of the series is lost, LaHaye and Jenkins include an appendix in each book of the series that details "The Truth behind the Fiction."

4. Amy Hungerford, *Postmodern Belief: American Literature and Religion since 1960* (Princeton: Princeton University Press, 2010). Jonathan Freedman, *Klezmer America: Jewishness, Ethnicity, Modernity* (New York: Columbia University Press, 2009).

5. In the fourth book in the series, *Soul Harvest* (1999), believers gain a literal "mark of the believer" on their foreheads, which allows them to identify each other. Though the mark is first mentioned in Tim LaHaye and Jerry B. Jenkins, *Soul Harvest: The World Takes Sides* (1999), the phrase "mark of the believer" doesn't appear until LaHaye and Jenkins, *The Indwelling: The Beast Takes Possession* (Wheaton, IL: Tyndale House, 2011), 124. Believers cannot see their own marks and can only see the marks of others, ensuring a social dimension to the avowal of belief. In the world of the Left Behind series, you must submit yourself to faith, but cannot see the mark of your own faithfulness. Your faithfulness can only be validated when you are part of a Christian community.

6. For a sympathetic survey of the dispensationalist tradition that the Left Behind series participates in, see Thomas Ice, "Left Behind and the Dispensational Tradition," in *Left Behind and the Evangelical Imagination: Apocalypse and Popular Culture*, ed. Crawford Gribben and Mark. S. Sweetnam (Sheffield: Sheffield Phoenix Press, 2011), 133–154.

7. As Amy Johnson Frykholm shows, actual readers do not always accept this way of reading the Left Behind series. Frykholm, *Rapture Culture:* Left Behind *in Evangelical America* (Oxford: Oxford University Press, 2007).

8. Don Gately, a recovering Demerol addict in *Infinite Jest*, has no personal conception of God—members of AA and NA "get to make up [their] own understanding of God or a Higher Power or Whom- / Whatever"—but he "takes one of AA's very rare specific suggestions and hits the knees in the A.M. and asks for Help and then hits the knees again at bedtime and says Thank You, whether he believes he's talking to Anything / -body or not, and he somehow gets through that day clean." David Foster Wallace, *Infinite Jest*, 443. Some critics, such as Mary Holland, have interpreted *Infinite Jest* as harshly critical of AA. She writes, "Significantly, the same looping pathology defines and so calls into question the culture of recovery represented in the novel by the Alcoholics Anonymous program. For, in equally powerful and less subtle ways than the Incandenza family, the novel's drug addicts, recovering and not, further illustrate the pathological recursivity of narcissism, in which narcissism operates as

both the cause and effect of their addictions . . . In this way, the AA and NA programs ultimately ask not that members reach out to empathize with strangers but that they recognize their own place in this infinitely repeating sameness, the recursivity of addiction." Mary Holland, *Succeeding Postmodernism*, 77. Against this view, I would argue that Gately's relation to God is meant to be isomorphic with the relation between the reader and Wallace. Wallace wants us to take AA seriously. We find evidence of this interpretation in a letter Wallace wrote in support of the mission of Granada House, a halfway house in which he stayed. See "An Ex-Resident's Story," Granada House, http://www.granadahouse.org /people/letters_from_our_alum.html. For a discussion of Wallace's stay in Granada House, see D. T. Max, *Every Love Story Is a Ghost Story: A Life of David Foster Wallace* (New York: Vintage, 2012). In a note written in his personal copy of Lewis Hyde's *The Gift* (New York: Vintage, 1983), held in the Harry Ransom Center, Wallace writes, "AA's=those driven mad w / fear by the paradigm of scarcity in a commodity / capitalist economy; require return to basically 1st-century communism of spirit" (127).

9. John A. McClure, *Partial Faiths: Postsecular Fiction in the Age of Pynchon and Morrison* (Athens: University of Georgia Press, 2007), 30.

10. Martin Hägglund, *Radical Atheism: Derrida and the Time of Life* (Stanford: Stanford University Press, 2008), 1. Hägglund argues against the notion that there is a religious turn in Derrida. Contra the claims of some theologians who read deconstruction as negative theology, "*différance* is nothing in itself because it designates the spacing of time that makes it impossible for anything to be in itself" (3). What makes such an atheism radical is that, on this view, "the immortality of God is not desirable in the first place" (8). It might seem surprising to call Wallace an atheist, let alone a radical atheist, partly because we know that he tried to convert to Catholicism, and especially because of his claim in his Kenyon College commencement speech that "in the day-to-day trenches of adult life, there is actually no such thing as atheism." Wallace, *This Is Water: Some Thoughts, Delivered on a Significant Occasion, about Living a Compassionate Life* (New York: Little, Brown and Company, 2009), 98. Moreover, in a review of Joseph Frank's multivolume biography of Dostoevsky, Wallace asks, "Does this guy Jesus Christ's life have something to teach me even if I don't, or can't believe he was divine? . . . Can I still believe in JC or Mohammed or Whoever even if I don't believe they were actual relatives of God? Except what would that mean: 'believe in'?" Wallace, "Joseph Frank's Dostoevsky," in *Consider the Lobster and Other Essays* (New York: Little, Brown and Company, 2006), 269–270. This wish—to believe in religious teachers without believing in any attendant claims to the divinity of those teacher—gives evidence of the paradoxical spirituality Wallace adopted. Herbert Dreyfus and Sean Dorrance Kelly condemn Wallace's atheism in *All Things Shining: Reading the Western Classics to Find Meaning in a Secular Age* (New York: Free Press, 2011), 22–57. Dreyfus and Kelly argue that Wallace adopts a Nietzschean view of human will, one in which "we are the sole active agents in the universe, responsible for generating out of nothing whatever notion of the sacred or divine there can ever be" (57). They are correct to call Wallace an atheist, but misrepresent Wallace's proposed mechanism for generating belief, and misunderstand Wallace's view of the will. They wrongly assume

that Wallace wishes humans to have total control over what to consider sacred, when in fact he wishes to learn to "exercise *some* control over how and what you think" (*This Is Water* 53, my emphasis). More, they ignore Wallace's emphasis on submission in learning to exercise control, as is the case for Gately's practice of worshiping a God he does not believe in, and his emphasis in his Kenyon address on the need "to decide what to worship" (*This Is Water* 96). Wallace argues that we already participate in collective projects and worship various sources of full-ness, even in a world without God—not that we need to develop total control over our bodies and minds. This also means, however, that while Wallace seemed to accept the truth of poststructuralist claims, he simultaneously wished to reconstruct the terms of belief and faith from within such frameworks.

11. Adam Kelly, "Dialectic of Sincerity: Lionel Trilling and David Foster Wallace," *Post45*, October 17, 2014. *Infinite Jest*, Kelly argues, "employs com-plexity and impurity in the service of his text's sincerity, paradoxically mobilizing the contaminations of the fictional to access the true." On this view, Wallace's concept of sincerity is a "paradoxical and dialectical" expression of the contra-dictions of "our time." My main emendation to this argument, as will become clear, is that any understanding of Wallace's efforts at literary sincerity requires a prior analysis of his critique of irony and his effort to reconstruct a viable notion of belief.

12. Sloterdijk, *You Must Change Your Life*, 3, 9. Sloterdijk claims that the dichotomy between believers and unbelievers has become obsolete, and ought to be "replaced by the distinction between the practising and the untrained, or those who train differently" (3). In denying this distinction, Sloterdijk overlooks the possibility that cultivating one's inner attitude and disposition of belief might become part of practicing a spiritual regime.

13. For the view of postmodernism as negative theology, see Thomas J. J. Altizer, *Deconstruction and Theology* (New York: Crossroad, 1982). Mark C. Taylor, *Erring: A Postmodern A / theology* (Chicago: University of Chicago Press, 1987). Howard Coward and Toby Foshay, ed., *Derrida and Negative Theology* (Albany: State University of New York Press, 1992). Graham Ward, ed., *The Postmodern God: A Theological Reader* (Malen, MA: Blackwell, 1997).

14. Francis Fukuyama, "The End of History?" *National Interest*, no. 16 (1989): 3–18.

15. In *The End of History and the Last Man* (New York: Free Press, 2006), Fukuyama directly addresses his book to our "problems recognizing good news when it comes," and assures us that, yes, the "good news has come" (xiii). This "good news" comes in the form of an argument Fukuyama develops along two tracks, one economic, the other based on a fundamental human need for recog-nition. Fukuyama doubles down on his religious rhetoric—what we might call his liberal fundamentalism—when he writes that "while modern natural science guides us to the gates of the Promised Land of liberal democracy, it does not deliver us to the Promised Land itself, for there is no economically necessary reason why advanced industrialization should produce political liberty" (xv). Jacques Derrida makes a similar observation of Fukuyama's rhetoric: "Is not what we have here a new gospel, the noisiest, the most mediatized, the most 'successful' one on the subject of the death of Marxism as the end of history?"

Derrida, *Specters of Marx*, trans. Peggy Kamuf, intro. Bernd Magnus and Stephen Cullenberg (New York: Routledge Classics, 2006), 70.

16. Fukuyama, "The End of History?" 18.

17. Ibid.

18. Samuel Cohen, *After the End of History: American Fiction in the 1990s* (Iowa City: University of Iowa Press, 2009), 28.

19. Toby Young and Tom Vanderbilt, "The End of Irony? The Tragedy of the Post-Ironic Condition," *Modern Review*, April-May 1994: 7, my emphasis.

20. Richard Rorty, "The End of Leninism, Havel, and Social Hope," in *Truth and Progress: Philosophical Papers* (Cambridge: Cambridge University Press, 1998), 229.

21. David Foster Wallace, "Greatly Exaggerated," in *A Supposedly Fun Thing I'll Never Do Again: Essays and Arguments* (New York: Back Bay Books, 1998), 144. Wallace sees Wittgenstein as an early discoverer of the idea that the human stance toward reality may be fundamentally linguistic in character: "This was Wittgenstein's double bind: you can either treat language as an infinitely small dense dot, or you let it become the world—the exterior and everything in it. The former banishes you from the Garden. The latter seems more promising. If the world is itself a linguistic construct, there's nothing 'outside' language for language to have to picture or refer to. This lets you avoid solipsism, but it leads right to the postmodern, post-structural dilemma of having to deny yourself an existence independent of language. Heidegger's the guy most people think got us into this bind, but when I was working on *Broom of the System* I saw Wittgenstein as the real architect of the postmodern trap. He died right on the edge of explicitly treating reality as linguistic instead of ontological. This eliminated solipsism, but not the horror. Because we're still stuck." Burn, *Conversations with David Foster Wallace*, 44. In terms of the distinctions developed in this passage, we might say that Wallace regards the world as linguistic but nonetheless wants to use language as a way of reconstructing an extralinguistic reality, specifically the reality of the existence of other persons.

22. I might have again used the term "hipster" to describe this figure, albeit with a different sense than in my first chapter. I have avoided using the term to prevent confusion. On the more recent incarnation of the hipster—stripped of racial anxiety, far more ambivalent about irony than before—see n+1, *What Was the Hipster? A Sociological Investigation* (New York: n+1 Foundation, 2010). Jake Kinzey, *The Sacred and the Profane: An Investigation of Hipsters* (New York: Zero Books, 2012). R. Jay Magill Jr., *Sincerity: How a Moral Ideal Born Five Hundred Years Ago Inspired Religious Wars, Modern Art, Hipster Chic, and the Curious Notion That We All Have Something to Say (No Matter How Dull)* (New York: W. W. Norton & Company, 2012). See also my Conclusion.

23. Lee Siegel, "The Niceness Racket," *New Republic*, April 23, 2007: 50, 53.

24. James Wood, "The Color Purple: Toni Morrison's False Magic," in *The Broken Estate: Essays on Literature and Belief* (New York: Random House, 1999), 236, my emphasis.

25. Wood's 2003 novel, *The Book against God* (New York: FSG, 2003), provides an intriguing example of his conflation of religion and literature (which he treats as a sort of secular religion). The novel revolves around Tom's inability to

reveal his atheism to his father, an Anglican minister. Tom—whose name unsubtly recalls the story of Doubting Thomas, a.k.a. Thomas the Believer—assembles his "Book against God" instead of writing his PhD thesis, though at one point Tom is forced to admit that "the cathedral is, after all, a beautiful mistake, a magnificent lie" (173).

26. This claim runs against Coleridge's notion of "the willing suspension of disbelief," which he also calls "poetic faith." The concept of "suspension of disbelief" has been popularly generalized to describe how readers must approach all fictions. But Coleridge distinguished between his own Romantic art and Wordsworth's enchantment of everyday life. "It was agreed," he writes, "that my endeavours should be directed to persons and characters supernatural, or at least romantic, yet so as to transfer from our inward nature a human interest and a semblance of truth sufficient to procure for these shadows of imagination that willing suspension of disbelief for the moment, which constitutes poetic faith. Mr. Wordsworth on the other hand was to propose to himself as his object, to give the charm of novelty to things of every day, and to excite a feeling analogous to the supernatural, by awakening the mind's attention from the lethargy of custom, and directing it to the loveliness and the wonders of the world before us." Samuel Taylor Coleridge, *Biographia Literaria: The Collected Works of Samuel Taylor Coleridge, Biographical Sketches of My Literary Life & Opinions*, ed. James Engell and W. Jackson Bate (Princeton: Princeton University Press, 1985), 6–7. Coleridge describes "poetic faith" as the by-product of instilling a "semblance of truth" into fantastic images, not as an ethos required to enjoy all fiction. In a May 13, 1816, letter to Daniel Stuart, he describes in more detail "the voluntary Lending of the Will to this suspension of its own operations," arguing that when the faculties of "Judgment" or "Understanding" are voluntarily suspended, it is not right to say we believe or disbelieve in fantastic images or thoughts (6–7, n2). As in dreams, the question of the correspondence between images or thoughts and some underlying reality does not arise. What remains unclear in this account, no less than in contemporary discussions of the concept of the suspension of disbelief, is why a "sufficient semblance of truth" is required at all if our disbelief is arrested on a "voluntary" basis.

27. James Wood, "Hysterical Realism," in *The Irresponsible Self: On Laughter and the Novel* (New York: Picador, 2005), 172.

28. James Wood, *How Fiction Works* (New York: FSG, 2008), 247. Wood writes, "Hypothetical plausibility—probability—is the important and neglected idea here: probability involves the defense of the credible imagination against the incredible. This is surely why Aristotle writes that a convincing impossibility in mimesis is always preferable to an unconvincing possibility" (238). This discussion leads Wood to define "lifeness" this way: "Realism, seen broadly as truthfulness to the way things are, cannot be mere verisimilitude, cannot be mere lifelikeness, or lifesameness, but what I must call lifeness: life on the page, life brought to different life by the highest artistry. And it cannot be a genre; instead it makes other forms of fiction seem like genres. For realism of this kind—lifeness—is the origin. It teaches everything else; it schools its own truants; it is what allows magical realism, hysterical realism, fantasy, science fiction, even thrillers, to exist" (247). In other words, "lifeness" has no specific or

discernible properties except of course that it excludes genre fiction, including the hated lifeness-less genre of "hysterical realism." As a critical category, "lifeness" is a bit vague. One might as well claim that good books have "souls" and that the special ethereal emanations of such soul-filled books expose which of their brethren are soulless, but also hold that—by necessity—there are no particular nameable properties we can reference to prove that a book has such a vital spirit. However, the quasi-spiritual category of "lifeness" bears considerable interest as a reflection on the sociological landscape of literary prestige in the early twenty-first century.

29. Tom LeClair, *In the Loop: Don DeLillo and the Systems Novel* (Champaign: University of Illinois Press, 1988). Frank Lentricchia, ed., *Introducing Don DeLillo* (Durham: Duke University Press, 1991).

30. Wood, *How Fiction Works*, 150.

31. Waugh, *Metafiction*, 2.

32. Ibid., 60.

33. Ibid., 53.

34. David Foster Wallace Papers, Box 3, Folder 2, Harry Ransom Center, University of Texas at Austin, Austin, Texas. Wallace apparently wrote his contribution for a version of Harmon's book that was to appear in the early 1990s, but the book itself was not published until the late 2000s. His short essay resembles a compressed version of his argument against irony in "E Unibus Pluram."

35. David Foster Wallace, "Westward the Course of Empire Takes Its Way," in *Girl with Curious Hair* (New York: W. W. Norton, 1996), 304.

36. Cornel Bonca insightfully discusses the role of the university in the formation of post-postmodernism in Bonca, "The Ineluctable Modality of the Marginal," *Orange County Weekly*, March 15, 2001, http://www.ocweekly.com /content/printVersion/36539.

37. Hungerford, *Postmodern Belief*, xiii.

38. Ibid., xvii.

39. A. O. Scott, "The Panic of Influence," *New York Review of Book*, February 10, 2000, http://www.nybooks.com/articles/232.

40. Such claims are common in Wallace scholarship. Marshall Boswell argues that Wallace "opens the cage of irony by *ironizing* it." Marshall Boswell, *Understanding David Foster Wallace* (Columbia: University of South Carolina Press, 2003), 207. Iannis Goerlandt concludes that Wallace fails to transcend irony by means of irony. Iannis Goerlandt, "'Put the Book Down and Slowly Walk Away': Irony and David Foster Wallace's *Infinite Jest*," *Critique* 47, no. 3 (2006), 320.

41. Adam Kelly, "David Foster Wallace and the New Sincerity in American Fiction," in *Consider David Foster Wallace: Critical Essays*, ed. David Hering (Los Angeles: Sideshow Media Group Press, 2010), 136. See also Kelly, "From Syndrome to Sincerity: Benjamin Kunkel's *Indecision*," in *Diseases and Disorders in Contemporary Fiction*, 53–66.

42. Dave Eggers, *What Is the What* (New York: Vintage, 2007), 535.

43. Ibid., xv.

44. Lee Siegel excoriates the book, accusing Eggers of "post-colonial arrogance" and "socially acceptable . . . Orientalism": "How strange for one man to

think that he could write the story of another man, a real living man who is perfectly capable of telling his story himself—and then calling it an autobiography. It is just one more instance of the accelerating mash-up of truth and falsehood in the culture, which mirrors and—who knows?—maybe even enables the manipulation of truth in politics." Siegel, "The Niceness Racket," 53.

45. Burn, *Conversations with David Foster Wallace*, 26.

46. Wallace's critique draws heavily on the essays published in Todd Gitlin, ed., *Watching Television* (New York: Pantheon, 1987).

47. Wallace derives this phrase from Stanley Cavell's *Pursuits of Happiness: The Hollywood Comedy of Remarriage* (Cambridge, MA: Harvard University Press, 1981), 43. The Harry Ransom Center has Wallace's annotated copies of *Pursuits of Happiness* and *In Quest of the Ordinary: Lines of Skepticism and Romanticism* (Chicago: University of Chicago Press, 1988). The phrase "holiday in his eye" can be found in Ralph Waldo Emerson, "Manners," in *Emerson: Essays and Lectures (Nature: Addresses and Lectures, Essays: First and Second Series, Representative Men, English Traits, the Conduct of Life)*, ed. Joel Porte (New York: Library of America, 1983), 519. A variation of the phrase appears in Emerson, "Behavior," in *Emerson: Essays and Lectures*, 1033.

48. Letter from David Foster Wallace to Michael Pietsch, June 22, 1992, Little, Brown and Company Collection of David Foster Wallace, Box 3, Folder 2, Harry Ransom Center, University of Texas at Austin, Austin, Texas.

49. David Foster Wallace, "Octet," in *Brief Interviews with Hideous Men* (New York: Back Bay Books, 1999), 134. Subsequent references will be cited parenthetically. "Octet" was originally published as "Pop Quiz" in *spelunker flophouse* 1, no. 4 (1997): 30–41. This version did not include Pop Quiz 9.

50. Boswell, *Understanding David Foster Wallace*, 184.

51. Kelly, "David Foster Wallace and the New Sincerity in American Fiction," 143.

52. David Foster Wallace, "Good Old Neon," in *Oblivion: Stories* (New York: Back Bay Books, 2005), 147. Subsequent references will be cited parenthetically. "Good Old Neon" was originally published in *Conjunctions*, no. 37 (2001): 105–140.

53. Wallace used David Wallace as a character in other texts, including *The Pale King*. David also appears in an early draft of *Infinite Jest*, in place of Hal during the professional conversationalist scene. This alternate section is titled "What Are You Exactly," with two subtitles, "unadorned autobio" and "automa-biography." David Foster Wallace Papers, Box 15, Folder 7, Harry Ransom Center, University of Texas at Austin, Austin, Texas.

54. Making this reading less implausible is Neal's overt use of logical notation in "Good Old Neon," where he describes the mutual exclusivity of fear and love using the expression "$(\forall x) ((Fx \to \sim (Lx)) \mathbin{\&} (Lx \to \sim (Fx))) \mathbin{\&} \sim ((\exists x) (\sim (Fx) \mathbin{\&} \sim (Lx))'\,)$" (164). Against this view, one might note that Wallace also uses arrows as an element in "The Suffering Channel," another story in *Oblivion*.

55. Wallace, "Good Old Neon," *Conjunctions*, 140. The original version begins with an epigraph drawn from Borges's story "Discusión": "Hay un concepto que es el corruptor y el desatinador de los otros." The concept referred to here is the concept of infinity.

56. This speaks against Marshall Boswell's view that *Oblivion* offers "dense description without redemption." Boswell, "'The Constant Monologue inside Your Head': *Oblivion* and the Nightmare of Consciousness," in *A Companion to David Foster Wallace Studies*, ed. Marshall Boswell and Stephen J. Burn (Palgrave Macmillan, 2013), 168. It also speaks to the dubiousness of Jonathan Franzen's suggestion that Neal is meant to be a thinly coded version of Wallace. Boswell, "'The Constant Monologue inside Your Head,'" 158.

57. Ibid., 152.

58. Raoul Eschelman, *Performatism, or the End of Postmodernism* (Aurora, CO: Davies Group, 2008), xii.

59. Ibid., 3.

60. Ibid., 4.

61. The notion that *Infinite Jest* is a therapeutic novel—a kind of novelistic therapy—seems consistent with Wallace's wish for an art that "locates and applies CPR to those elements of what's human and magical that still live and glow despite the times' darkness." Burn, *Conversations with David Foster Wallace*, 26. That said, current Wallace scholarship is unresolved on the question of whether *Infinite Jest* "resolves" or "cures" the problems the author outlines. Timothy Aubry provides a compelling case for *Infinite Jest* as a novel that "produces a compulsive reading experience designed to simulate the trajectory of addiction in order to overwhelm and oversaturate his readers' desires, exhaust their internal mechanisms of defensive sophistication, and thus prepare them to confront AA as a salutary model for an alternative paradigm refreshingly at odds with their cynical impulses." Aubry, *Reading as Therapy: What Contemporary Fiction Does for Middle-Class Americans* (Iowa City: University of Iowa Press, 2011), 99. My reading here is similar. The primary piece of evidence marshaled against the idea that Wallace wanted his fiction to act as a cure is his criticism of postmodern fiction's assumption that "etiology and diagnosis pointed toward cure, that a revelation of imprisonment led to freedom." Wallace, "E Unibus Pluram," 67. This quote is discussed in Stephen J. Burn, "'Webs of Nerves Pulsing and Firing': *Infinite Jest* and the Science of Mind," in *A Companion to David Foster Wallace Studies*, ed. Stephen J. Burn and Marshall Boswell (London: Palgrave Macmillan, 2013), 75. Burn discounts invocations of the CPR quote by suggesting that CPR only keeps the organism barely alive—hardly an upbeat project for fiction. Burn, "'Webs of Nerves Pulsing and Firing,'" 79. Burn's discounting of Wallace's therapeutic project is mistaken. Wallace criticizes the idea that *knowledge* leads to a cure, but not the broader idea that fiction can offer a kind of therapy. In fact, Wallace hoped fiction might overcome the "terrible master" of the mind. Wallace, *This Is Water*, 56. One might also recall the plight of the yuppie Geoffrey Day, a "red-wine and Quaalude man" (*IJ* 272). Evincing what Don Gately calls "Analysis-Paralysis," Geoffrey anxiously worries that "there are things about this allegedly miraculous Program's doctrine that simply do not follow. That do not cohere. That do not make anything resembling rational sense" (*IJ* 1002). Wallace's testimonial on behalf of Granada House suggests that Geoffrey's Analysis-Paralysis resembles Wallace's own reaction to AA. "They also recognized bullshit, and manipulation, and meaningless intellectualization as a way of evading terrible truths—and on many days the most helpful

thing they did was to laugh at me and make fun of my dodges (which were, I realize now, pathetically easy for a fellow addict to spot), and to advise me just not to use chemicals today because tomorrow might very well look different." "An Ex-Resident's Story." So in *Infinite Jest*—and in his fiction more generally— Wallace hoped to help revive "what's human and magical" about life, and he specifically proposed doing so by dissolving the reader's posited Analysis- Paralysis. What critics such as Aubry miss, however, is that Wallace invokes Wittgenstein's view that philosophy could be therapy for "philosophical dis- eases." Ludwig Wittgenstein, *Philosophical Investigations: The German Text, with a Revised English Translation 50th Anniversary Commemorative Edition*, trans. G. E. M. Anscombe (Hoboken, NJ: Wiley-Blackwell, 1991), §593. The specific relationship between therapeutic philosophy and clinical therapy remains a core ambiguity in Wallace's writing. Of course, it is possible to view *Infinite Jest* as an attempt at therapy that fails on its own terms. As Samuel Cohen writes, "it is more than possible to see [*Infinite Jest*], like *Broom* and *Girl*, as containing ear- nest, sophisticated, and sometimes very funny attempts to take this step but as ultimately failing to move from critique to alternative." Samuel Cohen, "To Wish to Try to Sing to the Next Generation: *Infinite Jest*'s History," in *The Legacy of David Foster Wallace*, ed. Samuel Cohen and Lee Konstantinou (Iowa City: University of Iowa Press, 2012), 72.

62. Burn, *Conversations with David Foster Wallace*, 33.

63. N. Katherine Hayles, "The Illusion of Autonomy and the Fact of Recursivity: Virtual Ecologies, Entertainment, and *Infinite Jest*," *New Literary History* 30, no. 3 (1999): 682.

64. Ibid., 683.

65. Hayles offers a useful summary of a debate that is already staged within *Infinite Jest*. The characters Rémy Marathe and M. Hugh Steeply have this debate on the rocky outcropping overlooking Tucson, AZ, which replays Hayles's concerns almost verbatim. Marathe and Steeply discuss the Entertainment in terms of market preferences and the antinomies of liberal autonomy; outline the dangers of having endless pleasure available on demand "for any industrialized, market-driven, high-discretionary-spending society" (473); and discuss the cultural grounds upon which such pleasure machines depend, comparing the different philosophies of autonomy that separate the United States and Canada. Defending the morality of the A.F.R.'s planned assault on U.S. consumer society, Marathe emphasizes that "Us, we will force nothing on U.S.A. persons in their warm homes. We will make only available. Entertainment. There will be then some choosing, to partake or choose not to" (318). Marathe claims that "this appetite to choose death by pleasure if it is available to choose—this appetite of your people unable to choose appetites, this is the death. What you call death, the collapsing: this will be the formality only" (319). Ironically, preserving the liberal autonomy that Steeply claims to value requires governmental intervention in order to remove too-dangerous choices from the marketplace. This was also the case, according to Wallace's narrator, for the Canadian p-terminal technologies developed by the Brandon Psychiatric Center in the 1970s. Steeply describes how scientists at this Manitoba-based laboratory implanted electrodes directly into the pleasure centers of various

animals—rats, cats, dogs, monkeys, dolphins—and allowed these animals to control the amount of stimulation they received.

66. Hayles, "The Illusion of Autonomy and the Fact of Recursivity," 682.

67. Wallace outlines this carefully in Incandenza's filmography, 985–993.

68. Peter Bürger, *Theory of the Avant-Garde*, trans. Michael Shaw (Minneapolis: University of Minnesota Press, 2002), 49.

69. For a challenge to this standard story, see "What Is an Avant-Garde?" the special issue of *New Literary History* 41, vol. 4 (2010), edited by Jonathan P. Eburne and Rita Felski. As Eburne and Felski note, such heroic stories—or the mirror-image story, which charges that the avant-garde has in some sense been exhausted or sold out—have come to seem sclerotic and tired. Against this view, they "question the pervasive tendency to personify the avant-garde through a biographical narrative of birth, youthful insurrection, and death—a narrative that translates psychologically into a predictable arc of anticipation followed by disappointment, and politically into the lexicon of a radical oppositional force that cannot escape its subsequent co-option" (vii).

70. Bürger, *Theory of the Avant-Garde*, 49.

71. Burn, *Conversations with David Foster Wallace*, 30. Unlike conservative critics of postmodernism, Wallace does see some value in postmodernist literary experimentation: "But I still believe the move to involution had value: it helped writers break free of some long-standing flat-earth-type taboos. It was standing in line to happen. And for a little while, stuff like *Pale Fire* and *The Universal Baseball Association* was valuable as a metaaesthetic breakthrough the same way Duchamp's urinal had been valuable" (30).

72. Bürger, *Theory of the Avant-Garde*, 87.

73. C. Wright Mills, *The Politics of Truth*, 174.

74. Donald Barthelme, "After Joyce," in *Not-Knowing: The Essays and Interviews of Donald Barthelme*, ed. Kim Herzinger (New York: Random House, 1997), 4.

75. Ibid., 4.

76. Ibid., 8.

77. Burn, *Conversations with David Foster Wallace*, 25.

78. Daniel C. Dennett, *Intuition Pumps and Other Tools for Thinking* (New York: W. W. Norton & Company, 2013). Michael W. Clune, *Writing against Time* (Stanford: Stanford University Press, 2013), 23.

79. Dave Eggers, *A Heartbreaking Work of Staggering Genius: A Memoir Based on a True Story* (New York: Vintage, 2001), iv. Subsequent references will be cited parenthetically.

80. I use "Dave" to distinguish between the memoir's protagonist and Eggers.

81. Benjamin Widiss, *Obscure Invitations: The Persistence of the Author in Twentieth-Century Literature* (Stanford: Stanford University Press, 2011), 111.

82. Dave Eggers, "Mistakes We Knew We Were Making," in *A Heartbreaking Work of Staggering Genius* (New York: Vintage, 2001), 2, my emphasis. Subsequent references will be cited parenthetically as "Mistakes."

83. Charles McGrath, "No Kidding: Does Irony Illuminate or Corrupt?"

New York Times, August 5, 2000, http://www.nytimes.com/2000/08/05/books
/no-kidding-does-irony-illuminate-or-corrupt.html.

84. For an account of the early backlash against Eggers, see Caroline
Hamilton, *One Man Zeitgeist: Dave Eggers, Publishing and Publicity* (London:
Bloomsbury, 2010), 53–57.

85. When *A Heartbreaking Work* was first released, Eggers staged a number
of quirky stunts at his readings. He would bake cupcakes for his audience, bring
guest speakers who would expound on obscure topics, plant friends in the audience to heckle him at key moments in his readings, etc. Many of these events
involved Neal Pollack, with whom Eggers would later have a public falling out,
but not before he published Pollack's *The Neal Pollack Anthology of American
Literature: The Collected Writings of Neal Pollack*—a satirical collection by the
obnoxious, self-obsessed, ironic persona Pollack had created—the first book
published by McSweeney's Books in 2001.

86. Gerard Genette, *Paratexts: Thresholds of Interpretation* (Cambridge:
Cambridge University Press, 1997), 344. Genette distinguishes epitexts from
peritexts, which he defines as "such elements as the title or the preface and
sometimes elements inserted into the interstices of the text" that are physically
appended to it (4–5).

87. Ibid., 345.

88. Sarah Brouillette, "Paratextuality and Economic Disavowal in Dave
Eggers' *You Shall Know Our Velocity,*" *Reconstruction: Studies in Contemporary
Culture* 3, no. 2 (2003): par. 5, http://reconstruction.eserver.org/032/brouillette.
htm.

89. Ibid., par. 1.

90. Amy Hungerford, "McSweeney's and the School of Life," *Contemporary
Literature* 53, no. 4 (2012): 649.

91. Hamilton, *One Man Zeitgeist,* 19.

92. Hungerford, "McSweeney's and the School of Life," 655.

93. Heidi Julavits, "Rejoice! Believe! Be Strong and Read Hard!" *Believer,*
March 2003, http://www.believermag.com/issues/200303/?read=article_julavits.

94. Julavits also writes, "To be perfectly clear—I am not espousing a feel-
good, criticism-free climate, where all ambitious literary books receive special
treatment, just because they're 'literary' (I acknowledge the dubiousness of the
term)—I'm simply asking that we read between the lines, and see what value
systems these reviews are really espousing. I imagine snarkiness has always been
around, if not thriving then dormant, but I'd argue that the critics with staying
power never employ it."

95. Dave Denby, *Snark: It's Mean, It's Personal, and It's Ruining Our
Conversation* (New York: Simon & Schuster, 2010), 1.

96. I derive this term from Daniel Zalewski and James Surowiecki, "You
Shall Know Our Velocity," *Slate,* October 29, 2002, http://www.slate.com
/articles/arts/the_book_club/features/2002/youshall_know_our_velocity/i_was
_terrified_not_to_likeit.html. Zalewski astutely suggests that "if you don't like
[Eggers's] books, he strongly implies you are a bad person—that is, one of those
'Mean / Jaded / Skimming Readers' who are poisoning the well of American literary culture."

97. Michael Hirschorn, "Quirked Around," *Atlantic*, September 2007: 142.

98. *OED Online*, s.v. "quirky," http://www.oed.com/view/Entry/156766 ?redirectedFrom=quirky.

99. See James MacDowell, "Notes on Quirky," *Movie: A Journal of Film Criticism*, no. 1 (2010): 1–16. MacDowell, "Wes Anderson, Tone, and the Quirky Sensibility," *New Review of Film & Television Studies* 10, no. 1 (2012): 1–22. MacDowell, "Quirky: Buzzword or Sensibility?" in *American Independent Cinema: Indie, Indiewood and Beyond*, ed. Geoff King, Claire Molloy, and Yannis Tzioumakis (London: Routledge, 2012), 53–65.

100. Jeffrey Sconce, "Irony, Nihilism, and the New American 'Smart' Film," *Screen* 43, no. 4 (2002): 352, 361. Sconce offers an ingenious analysis of the function of irony in "smart film," and ironic art more generally, as a "strategic gesture" (352).

101. MacDowell, "Notes on Quirky," 13.

102. Ibid., 4.

103. Goldsmith's March 13, 2015 performance of "The Body of Michael Brown" at the Interrupt 3 conference at Brown University might lead us to conclude that he is himself more "dumb dumb" than "smart dumb."

104. Kenneth Goldsmith, "Being Dumb," *Awl*, July 23, 2013, http://www .theawl.com/2013/07/being-dumb.

105. On the link between cool and knowledge production, see Liu, *The Laws of Cool*.

106. Melvin Jules Bukiet, "Wonder Bread," *American Scholar* 76, no. 4 (2007), http://theamericanscholar.org/wonder-bread/.

107. The Museum of Jurassic Technology, *The Museum of Jurassic Technology: Primum Decem Anni, Jubilee Catalog* (Los Angeles: Society for the Diffusion of Useful Information, 2002), 13. Subsequent references will be cited parenthetically as *Jubilee*.

108. Lawrence Weschler, *Mr. Wilson's Cabinet of Wonder: Pronged Ants, Horned Humans, Mice on Toast, and Other Marvels of Jurassic Technology* (New York: Vintage, 1996), 60. Subsequent references will be cited parenthetically as *Wonder*.

109. Lorraine J. Daston and Katharine Park, *Wonders and the Order of Nature*, 1150–1750 (New York: Zone Books, 2001), 14. See also Oliver Impey, *The Origins of Museums: The Cabinet of Curiosities in Sixteenth- and Seventeenth-Century Europe* (Cornwall: House of Stratus, 2001), and R. J. W. Evans and Alexander Marr, ed., *Curiosity and Wonder from the Renaissance to the Enlightenment* (Surrey: Ashgate, 2006).

110. Daston and Park, *Wonders and the Order of Nature*, 14.

111. Michel Foucault, "The Masked Philosopher," in *Ethics: Subjectivity and Truth*, ed. Paul Rabinow (New York: New Press, 1998), 325.

112. Michel Foucault, *The Order of Things* (New York: Vintage, 1994), xv.

113. Ibid., xvii. On "final vocabularies," see Rorty, *Contingency, Irony, and Solidarity*, 73. On the underdetermination of scientific theories, see Willard Van Orman Quine, "Two Dogmas of Empiricism," in *From a Logical Point of View: Nine Logico-Philosophical Essays*, Second Revised Edition (Cambridge: Harvard

University Press), 20–46, and "On Empirically Equivalent Systems of the World," *Erkenntnis*, no. 9 (1975): 313–328.

114. Foucault, *The Order of Things*, xvii.

115. Danston and Park, *Wonders and the Order of Nature*, 14.

116. Landy, *How to Do Things with Fiction*, 76.

117. Boris Groys, *Art Power* (Cambridge, MA: MIT Press, 2013), 24.

118. The silhouette is inserted into the body of the text, and there are a number of other images in the novel: three white broncos appear between two em dashes, becoming part of the sentence they're in; a treasure map indicating the location of a deposit of cash; various additional photographs interspersed in the narrative and referred to by the narrator. This incorporation of images arguably demonstrates the novel's formal commitment to quirkiness, just as the unusual manner in which Will earns his money displays quirkiness at the level of the plot.

119. Dave Eggers, *You Shall Know Our Velocity!* (New York: Vintage, 2003), 48. Subsequent references will be cited parenthetically. Eggers published the hardback edition of *You Shall Know Our Velocity* (no exclamation point) with McSweeney's Books in 2002. A new hardback version of the novel called *Sacrament*, published in 2003, also by McSweeney's Books, included an additional section told from the perspective of Hand, who calls Will's narrative into question. The 2003 Vintage paperback, now titled *You Shall Know Our Velocity!* (with an exclamation point), contains both the original text of the novel and Hand's new section, and bears the new subtitle "previously retitled as Sacrament."

120. Andrew Potter, "Newsflash: Cool's Out," *Maclean's*, January 14, 2006, http://www.macleans.ca/article.jsp?content=20060116_119485_119485.

121. Potter, "Newsflash: Cool's Out." It is interesting to note the reappearance of Soviet-era kitsch in recent manifestations of quirky culture. In their memorializing of Soviet culture—whether space dogs or cartoons—both the MJT and *Boing Boing* seem nostalgic for the lost mode of production of the Soviet Union. The irony that once seemed to be an emblem of democratic freedom has given way to ambivalence, bordering on admiration, for the allegedly ham-handed sincerity of the departed communist enemy. On Russian invocations of bygone Soviet sincerity, a movement in the contemporary Russian art world he calls "New Sincerity," see Alexei Yurchak, "Post-Post-Communist Sincerity: Pioneers, Cosmonauts, and Other Soviet Heroes Born Today," in *What Is Soviet Now? Identities, Legacies, Memories*, ed., Thomas Lahusen and Peter H. Solomon Jr. (Berlin: Verlang, 2008), 257–276.

122. Potter's discussion of quirkiness extends upon his argument against "the countercultural idea." Joseph Heath and Potter, *Nation of Rebels*, ix.

123. See D. T. Max, "The Unfinished," *New Yorker*, March 9, 2009, http://www.newyorker.com/reporting/2009/03/09/090309fa_fact_max?currentPage=all. While struggling to write *The Pale King*, his unfinished last novel, "Wallace had come to suspect that the drug was also interfering with his creative evolution. He worried that it muted his emotions, blocking the leap he was trying to make as a writer. He thought that removing the scrim of Nardil might help him see a way out of his creative impasse. Of course, as he recognized even then, maybe the drug wasn't the problem; maybe he simply was distant, or

maybe boredom was too hard a subject. He wondered if the novel was the right medium for what he was trying to say, and worried that he had lost the passion necessary to complete it."

124. David Foster Wallace, "David Foster Wallace on Life and Work," *Wall Street Journal*, September 19, 2008, http://online.wsj.com/article /SB122178211966454607.html. This passage is slightly different in the version of this speech published as *This Is Water*, which reads "the real, no-shit value of your liberal arts education" (60).

125. Paul Giles, "Sentimental Posthumanism: David Foster Wallace," *Twentieth-Century Literature* 53, no. 3 (2007): 341.

126. Williams writes: "Thus we have to recognize the alternative meanings and values, the alternative opinions and attitudes, even some alternative senses of the world, which can be accommodated and tolerated within a particular effective and dominant culture . . . There is clearly something that we can call alternative to the effective dominant culture, and there is something else that we can call oppositional, in a true sense." Raymond Williams, "Base and Superstructure in Marxist Cultural Theory," in *Culture and Materialism: Selected Essays* (London: Verso, 2005), 39–40.

127. Complicating my argument here, I would quickly note that *The Pale King*, though unfinished, has much more to say about the structural and institutional causes of postmodern suffering than does *Infinite Jest*. We can only speculate on what shape the completed novel might have taken. See Lee Konstantinou, "Unfinished Form," *Los Angeles Review of Books*, July 6, 2011, http://lareviewofbooks.org/review/unfinished-form.

4 The Work of the Coolhunter

1. Lynda Edwards, "Tomorrow's Forecast Calls for Shimmery Fabrics, Portable Fax Machines, Senegalese Cuisine, and Heroic Romanticism," *Spy*, March 1991, 40. Subsequent references will be cited parenthetically.

2. In addition to Edwards's *Spy* magazine article, notable popular accounts of trendspotting include Douglas Rushkoff's PBS *Frontline: The Merchants of Cool; Malcolm Gladwell, The Tipping Point* (Boston: Back Bay Books, 2002) and his "The Cool Hunt," *New Yorker*, March 17 1997, 78–88; Daniel Radosh, "The Trendspotting Generation," *GQ*, April 1998, 147–151; Lev Grossman, "The Quest for Cool," *Time*, September 8, 2003, 44–50. Peter Gloor and Scott Cooper, *Coolhunting: Chasing Down the Next Big Thing* (New York: AMACOM, 2007). Much of the journalistic writing on trendspotting is itself part of a genre of what Radosh calls "trend journalism," a notorious kind of journalistic trendspotting that follows the "rule of threes," the technique of using three examples of any particular practice as ground from which to grandly pronounce on some new cultural phenomenon. By far, the most insightful journalistic investigation of coolhunting can be found in Naomi Klein, *No Logo: 10th Anniversary Edition with a New Introduction by the Author* (New York: Picador, 2009).

Apart from the technical marketing literature, few academic critics have written directly about coolhunting, as opposed to writing generally on trends or the concept of cool. Fredric Jameson writes about "the relationship between fashion and high literature" in the "Sentences" chapter of *Postmodernism*, 131. In *The Laws of Cool*, Alan Liu discusses the concept of cool in relation to the history of information technology and knowledge work, but addresses contemporary subcultural cool in only a cursory manner. In *Hip Figures*, Michael Szalay alludes to coolhunting—and discusses branding—in the context of a larger investigation of how hipness was mobilized on behalf of the Democratic Party, largely repeating Naomi Klein's claims about the racial coding of cool.

3. See John E. Merriam and Joel Makower, *Trend Watching* (New York: Tilden Press, 1988). This book is a commercialization and popularization of Merriam's ideas, in the wake of the success of John Naisbitt's 1982 *Megatrends: Ten New Directions Transforming Our Lives* (New York: Warner Books, 1988). Merriam created an index of media trends for the bank and did not track street-level trends in fashion and taste. Still, these media-watching techniques respond to a similar sense, expressed famously by Alvin Toffler in *Future Shock*, that the present was changing faster than ever before.

4. Among the "trend shops" Edwards mentions, Promostyl was founded in 1966, Dominique Peclers in 1970, and Trend Union in 1975.

5. Janine Lopiano-Misdom and Joanne De Luca, *Street Trends: How Today's Alternative Youth Cultures Are Creating Tomorrow's Mainstream* (New York: Harper Paperbacks, 1998), xi.

6. Ibid.

7. Alan Farnham, "The Windfall Awaiting the New Inheritors," *Fortune*, May 7, 1990, http://money.cnn.com/magazines/fortune/fortune_archive/1990/05/07/73496/index.htm.

8. Faith Popcorn and Adam Hanft, *Dictionary of the Future: The Words, Terms and Trends That Define the Way We'll Live, Work and Talk* (New York: Hyperion, 2001), xiv.

9. Ibid.

10. Ibid., xv, xvii. Sir Thomas Elyot, *The Boke Named the Gouernour Deuised by Sir Thomas Elyot, Knight* (London: Thomæ Bertheleti, 1531). Popcorn and Hanft incorrectly attribute Elyot's English neologisms in this 1531 treatise to his Latin-English dictionary, *The Dictionary of Syr Thomas Eliot Knight* (London: Thomæ Bertheleti, 1538). For Elyot, a friend of Sir Thomas More pressed (possibly reluctantly) into King Henry VIII's service, and sent to sue for the annulment of the king's marriage before the Holy Roman Emperor Charles V, the nascent English Reformation might well have had the flavor of what Alvin Toffler would four-and-a-half centuries later call "future shock"—a turbulent time that, among other things, called for a reformation of the English language.

11. Popcorn and Hanft, *Dictionary of the Future*, xvii.

12. Andreas Huyssen, *After the Great Divide: Modernism, Mass Culture, Postmodernism* (Bloomington: Indiana University Press, 1986), 47.

13. David Ogilvy, *Ogilvy on Advertising* (New York: Vintage Books, 1985), 170. It might bear mentioning that Ogilvy himself wasn't a "moron" either. His claim is consistent with the findings of decades of consumer research indicating that the primary decision maker for household purchases and durable goods was often a woman. In 1959, Street & Street Publications released a massive study called "The American Woman," which systematically analyzed for the first time

the purchasing patterns of women as a group. For documentation of how marketers have tried to understand female consumers, see Cohen, *A Consumers' Republic*, 505.

14. In Gibson's novel, the male hacker "Case," the protagonist of *Neuromancer* (New York: Ace, 1986) transforms into the female coolhunter, "Cayce." Gibson has denied that he meant to allude to his previous novel, but it is hard to understand how he could have failed to notice such an obvious homonym. See Candas Jane Dorsey, "An Interview with William Gibson," *New York Review of Science Fiction* 15, no. 9 (2003): 10–11.

15. Many critics have noted that Michael Hardt and Antonio Negri have insufficiently analyzed the importance of affective work, and the sexual division of labor that undergirds such work, in their analysis of the more general category of "immaterial labor." On "immaterial labor," see Michael Hardt and Antonio Negri, *Empire* (Cambridge, MA: Harvard University Press, 2001). Here they analyze three aspects of immaterial labor, "the communicative labor of industrial production that has newly become linked in informational networks, the interactive labor of symbolic analysis and problem solving, and the labor of the production and manipulation of affects" (30). The category of immaterial labor also underestimates the continued importance of production, banished to zones geographically remote from the metropolis (or automated), but never eliminated, for capitalism's global empire. It also bears emphasizing that advanced industrial production remains incredibly important to allegedly postindustrial economies.

16. Sianne Ngai, *Our Aesthetic Categories: Zany, Cute, Interesting* (Cambridge, MA: Harvard University Press, 2012), 209.

17. Ibid., 188, 187.

18. Ibid., 208.

19. The trendspotter might be taken as a more critical variant of Alvin Toffler's (unfortunately named) "prosumer," especially if we see marketing and advertising as one important site where cultural production happens today. See Toffler, *The Third Wave* (New York: Bantam, 1984), 265–288.

20. A 2012 survey estimates that 71% of freelancers are women. Ed Gandia, *Freelance Industry Report: Data and Analysis of Freelancer Demographics, Earnings, Habits and Attitudes*, August 2012, 9, http://www.internationalfreelancersday .com/2012report/. MBO Partners, State of Independence Report, concludes: "Comparing independents to U.S. small business owners by gender presents a stark contrast: While women represent about half of all independent workers, they account for less than a third of small business owners in the US otherwise." MBO Partners, *Second Annual State of Independence in America Report*, September 2012, http://www.mbopartners.com/state-of-independence/docs/2012-MBO _Partners_State_of_Independence_Report.pdf.

21. Florida tries to reconfigure debates about the importance of "knowledge workers" and the "information economy" in ways that deemphasize "the fetish that was made of technology and virtual worlds," and wants us instead to examine "the ecosystems that harness human creativity and turn it into economic value." Although Florida, despite his claims to the contrary, paints a somewhat rosy picture of the new work situation certain Americans and other

global elites are facing—primarily by not discussing the political-economic context that makes the rise of a creative economy possible—he cannot deny that the rise of a community of hyperskilled creative workers is dialectically coupled to the strengthening of an almost completely Taylorized service sector, whose members Florida dub the "Service Class": "The growth of this Service Class is in large measure a response to the demands of the Creative Economy. Members of the Creative Class, because they are well compensated and work long and unpredictable hours, *require a growing pool of low-end service workers to take care of them and do their chores.* This class has thus been created *out of economic necessity* because of the way the Creative Economy operates." Florida, *The Rise of the Creative Class*, 71, my emphasis. It ought to go without saying that what Florida calls "economic necessity" is actually evidence of political choice.

22. Florida writes, "To some degree, these members of the Service Class have adopted many of the functions along with the tastes and values of the Creative Class, with which they see themselves sharing much in common. Both my hairdresser and housekeeper have taken up their lines of work to get away from the regimentation of large organizations; both of them relish creative pursuits. Service Class people such as these are close to the mainstream of the Creative Economy and prime candidates for reclassification" (77).

23. Luc Boltanski and Ève Chiapello, *The New Spirit of Capitalism*, 355–356.

24. How this imagined figure of the coolhunter relates to actual freelance workers is a question that goes beyond the scope of this chapter. It is true enough that discourses of "human capital" obscure the labor-capital relationship, preposterously claiming that all workers are now (and have always been) mini-capitalists. However, "human capital" might also name an idealized model of work that elites and policy planners are hellbent on making real. For example, U.S. Senator and former telecommunications venture capitalist Mark Warner advocates that the U.S. government formalize the labor practices of the so-called gig or sharing economy (terms used to describe firms such as Airbnb, Uber, and TaskRabbit) by creating a "third classification of employee." Doing so, he hopes, will "make capitalism work." Carmel DeAmicis, "U.S. Senator Mark Warner on Why We Need a New Class of Worker (Q&A)," *re/code*, July 15, 2015, https://recode.net/2015/07/15/u-s-senator-mark-warner-on-why-we-need-a -new-class-of-worker-qa/. For a discussion of the exploitation of freelancers, see Nicole S. Cohen, "Cultural Work as a Site of Struggle: Freelancers and Exploitation," *tripleC* 10, no. 2 (2012): 141–155. For a discussion of appropriations of socialist discourses of self-management, see Itzhak Revaz, "Deconstructing Management Science: Introducing the Self-Management Notes Project," *Viewpoint Magazine*, July 7, 2015, https://viewpointmag.com/2015/07/07/deconstructing -management-science-introducing-the-self-management-notes-project/.

25. I use "reification" in a broad sense to refer to "the moment that a process or relation is generalized into an abstraction, and thereby turned into a 'thing.'" Timothy Bewes, *Reification or the Anxiety of Late Capitalism* (London: Verso, 2002), 3.

26. Tom Vanderbilt, "The Advertised Life," in *Commodify Your Dissent:*

Salvos from the Baffler, ed. Thomas Frank and Matt Weiland (New York: W. W. Norton and Company, 1997), 128.

27. I appropriate this term from Jameson's *Archaeologies of the Future: The Desire Called Utopia and Other Science Fictions* (New York and London: Verso, 2005), xiv. In addition to Gibson's and Shakar's novels, this subgenre include novels such as Max Barry's *Jennifer Government* (London: Abacus, 2004), "An Orison of Sonmi~451" in David Mitchell's *Cloud Atlas* (New York: Ransom House, 2004), Colson Whitehead's *Apex Hides the Hurt* (New York: Doubleday, 2006), Othmer's *The Futurist* (New York: Anchor, 2007), and Gary Shteyngart's *Super Sad True Love Story* (New York: Random House, 2011).

28. I draw the term "novum" from Darko Suvin, "On the Poetics of the Science Fiction Genre," *College English* 34, no. 3 (1972): 373.

29. In *A Consumers' Republic*, Lizabeth Cohen discusses the transformation of the American consumer economy after the Second World War. In this account, Cohen argues that across-the-board economic growth caused U.S. economic inequality to flatten, threatening corporate profits. Planned obsolescence—the practice of building durable goods with expiration dates—was one solution to this crisis of profitability but came to be much criticized. In light of these criticisms, lifestyle- or identity-based market segmentation offered an alternative pathway toward corporate profitability. Wendell Smith and Pierre Martineau are credited with inventing market segmentation, although segmentation according to class (rather than lifestyle) started earlier. Pierre Martineau's breakthrough was to argue that, for the wealthy person, "what he buys will differ not only by economics but in symbolic value" (qtd. in Cohen 295). See the influential marketing essay of James H. Myers and Jonathan Gutman, "Life Style: The Essence of Social Class," *Life Style and Psychographics*, ed. William D. Wells (Chicago: American Marketing Association, 1974), 235–256.

The move from a form of market segmentation in the 1920s through the 1950s that depended on class to a form of market segmentation post-1950s based on lifestyle tracks the move from solidarity based on class to solidarity based on lifestyle or identity. Much marketing literature of this era concluded that actively excluding consumers from their marketing strategies would increase revenue. Corporations catered to "segments defined by age, affluence, and lifestyle, in the process drawing sharper distinctions between themselves and their competitors" (Cohen 297). Daniel Yankelovich's research divided wristwatch and automobile buyers into three "attitudinal groups": "those who bought the product for the lowest possible cost; those who bought for product quality, styling, and durability; and those who bought for prestige and out of other emotional needs" (299).

This technique has gotten so sophisticated that "modern-day marketers, equipped with advanced psychographic tactics, identify clusters of customers with distinctive ways of life and then set out to sell them idealized lifestyles constructed around commodities" (299). In this sort of economy, ironic resistance to marketing can be catered to as easily as anything else.

30. Hutcheon, *Irony's Edge*, 35.

31. Shakar seems to draw the idea of setting Middle City on the edge of a volcano from Thomas Frank's *One Market under God*, which uses the following

Carl Byoir quote as the epigraph of its first chapter: "American industry—the whole capitalist system—lives in the shadow of a volcano. The volcano is public opinion. It is in eruption. Within an incredibly short time it will destroy business or it will save it." Qtd. in Thomas Frank, *One Market under God: Extreme Capitalism, Market Populism, and the End of Economic Democracy* (New York: Anchor, 2001), 1.

32. Alex Shakar, *The Savage Girl* (New York: Harper Perennial, 2002), 23, 202. Subsequent references will be cited parenthetically.

33. Shakar cites Edwards's article in his novel's acknowledgements, but his debt to her article runs much deeper than mere inspiration. Shakar lifts whole situations and sentences from the *Spy* article, distributing them across his range of characters. In Edwards's article, for example, Marc Surrat, another French trendspotter from Éclat, relates the story of a young woman he once observed who was "crying as she wrote a letter" in a restaurant in Manhattan's financial district. "A young waiter started to approach her, hesitated, went back, gazed longingly. Finally the waiter walked away without speaking to the tearful woman . . ." Surrat diagnoses what went wrong: "The florescent lighting was ugly, and her sweater, the cut and color was all wrong . . . I went home and designed a sweater that would have stood up under that light. If she had worn it, the waiter would have stayed" (45).

In *The Savage Girl*, Javier spots "a dark-haired woman . . . sitting on her haunches peering down through a subway grate" where she has lost a pearl bead. A nearby bike messenger approaches her, slows down, observes her "plaintive look," but still chooses to pedal away. Javier explains to Ursula that the bike messenger did not stop because of the woman's lack of fashion sense: "The cream top was all wrong . . . with those jeans it made her look so stark and abject . . . If she'd been wearing this," he says, tapping the sketch with the red pencil, "he would've stopped. Anyone would've stopped. A whole crowd would have gathered" (24–25).

34. The phrase "name the nineties" appeared twice in *Spy* magazine: Jamie Malanowski, "Naked City," *Spy*, April 1988, 26; "The Spy 100," *Spy*, October 1988, 104. The phrase also appears in John Taylor, "Moral Cleansing," *New York Magazine*, February 4, 1991, 15. *Playboy* sponsored a "Name the Nineties Contest." See Tim Golden, "In, Out and Over; Trend Industry Looks Back at the 90's," *New York Times*, January 16, 1990, http://www.nytimes.com/1990/01/16/nyregion/in-out-and-over-trend-industry-looks-back-at-the-90-s.html.

35. Randall Rothenberg, "Proclaiming a Decade of Decency," *New York Times*, January 2, 1990, http://www.nytimes.com/1990/01/02/business/the-media-business-advertising-proclaiming-a-decade-of-decency.html. Tim Golden, "In, Out, and Over; Trend Industry Looks Back at the 90's," *New York Times*, January 16, 1990, http://www.nytimes.com/1990/01/16/nyregion/in-out-and-over-trend-industry-looks-back-at-the-90-s.html.

36. Paul Rudnick and Kurt Andersen, "The Irony Epidemic," 92. *Spy* also published an article in 1988 on the "Rise and Fall of a Great American Buzzword"—that is, "postmodernism." After a lengthy survey of postmodernism across different disciplines, the article concludes, "Someday, probably not too far in the future—April 30, 1989, just to be daringly specific about it—your

mother will mention the cute postmodern ottoman she's thinking about buying for the den, thereby providing the coda to *postmodern*'s reign as the lexicographic hot young thing." Bruce Handy, "Post-Postmodernism," *Spy*, April 1988, 108.

37. Wallace, "E Unibus Pluram: Television and U.S. Fiction," 59. In his interview with McCaffery, Wallace suggests that "it's a kind of black cynicism about today's world that Ellis and certain others depend on for their readership," and that (speaking against Ellis's practice) "in dark times, the definition of good art would seem to be art that locates and applies CPR to those elements of what's human and magical that still live and glow despite the times' darkness." Burn, *Conversations with David Foster Wallace*, 26. See Chapter 3 for a full discussion of Wallace's relationship to irony.

38. Young and Vanderbilt, "The End of Irony? The Tragedy of the Post-Ironic Condition," 6.

39. The term *Generation X* derived from Douglas Coupland, *Generation X: Tales for an Accelerated Culture* (New York: St. Martin's Griffin, 1991), 56.

40. Vanderbilt, "The Advertised Life," 132.

41. Upon encountering Young and Vanderbilt's *Modern Review* feature shortly before the publication of *Irony's Edge*, Linda Hutcheon wondered whether her recently completed manuscript might be "utterly out of date before it was even published." See her "Irony, Nostalgia, and the Postmodern," in *Methods for the Study of Literature as Cultural Memory*, ed. Raymond Vervliet (Atlanta, GA: Rodopi, 2000), 189.

42. Frank, *The Conquest of Cool*, 7.

43. Ibid.

44. Hebdige, *Subculture*, 3.

45. Ross, *No Respect*, 4, 8.

46. Ibid., 10.

47. Vanderbilt, "The Advertised Life," 132.

48. See Paul de Man, "The Rhetoric of Temporality," in *Blindness and Insight: Essays in the Rhetoric of Contemporary Criticism*, intro. Wlad Godzich (Minneapolis: University of Minnesota Press, 1983), 187–228, and "The Concept of Irony," in *Aesthetic Ideology*, 163–184.

49. Young and Vanderbilt, "The End of Irony? The Tragedy of the Post-Ironic Condition," 6.

50. Carrie McLaren, "Love for Sale," *Time Out New York*, October 4–11, 2001, 64.

51. Huyssen, *After the Great Divide*, 53. Note that Huyssen does not reject the "co-optation theory"; that is, he does not see any problem with the modernist's "desire to differentiate between forms of high art and depraved forms of mass culture and its co-options," but rather only objects to the pejorative figuration of mass culture as a woman.

52. Clune, *Writing against Time*, 60.

53. Frank, *The Conquest of Cool*, 25–26.

54. Lisa Duggan criticizes Frank in *The Twilight of Equality? Neoliberalism, Cultural Politics, and the Attack on Democracy* (Boston: Beacon Press, 2004), 75. Discussing his *One Market under God*, she summarizes Frank's "logic" as assuming, "If corporations can make profitable use of an idea, it is a bad idea."

She then notes the irony that a corporate publisher is "making very profitable use of Frank's ideas." Duggan is correct to reject this "logic," but is wrong to attribute it to Frank. This is, in fact, the logic that Frank is arguing against. By his account in *The Conquest of Cool*, corporations did not transform "good" countercultural ideas into "bad" ideas by using them (that is, by co-opting them). Instead, countercultural ideas about stylistic rebellion resembled entrepreneurial ideas. Both groups independently held similar "bad" ideas. If countercultural rebels truly understood their own "bad" ideas, on Frank's view, they would either be forced to reject their avowed ideas or be forced to accept that their nominal enemies have "good" ideas. The real questions are whether Frank accurately characterizes countercultural and corporate ideas and, if he is accurate, how we should judge these shared ideas.

55. McLaren, "Love for Sale," 64.

56. Here Shakar has Chas paraphrase, almost verbatim, consumer psychologist Ernest Dichter: "Trend spotting is the study of surfaces . . . Surfaces are important because surfaces are all most people will ever have . . . If you want to know the way the world is going, you must learn to read its affectations" (qtd. in Edwards 45).

57. See Grant McCracken, "Advertising: Meaning versus Information," in *Culture and Consumption II* (Bloomington: Indiana University Press, 2005), 162–170.

58. Likewise, much antibranding literature focuses on the effect of consumerism on children. See Alissa Quart, *Branded: The Buying and Selling of Teenagers* (New York: Basic Books, 2004).

59. Steven Shaviro, "Prophecies of the Present," *Socialism and Democracy* 20, no. 3 (2006): 11.

60. McLaren, "Love for Sale," 64.

61. Colebrook, *Irony*, 119.

62. Ron Hogan, "Interview with Alex Shakar," *Beatrice Interview*, May 19, 2007, http://www.beatrice.com/interviews/shaker/.

63. Ibid.

64. Alex Shakar, "The Savage Girl" (PhD diss., University of Illinois at Chicago, 2002), v. As far as I can tell, the two texts are identical.

65. McGurl, *The Program Era*, 405.

66. Alex Shakar, e-mail message to the author, October 18, 2006.

67. Many previous novels have incorporated poststructuralist language, of course. In my view, the more important development is the institutional and ideological commixture.

68. I draw the phrase "salaried mental workers" from Barbara and John Ehrenreich, "The Professional-Managerial Class," in *Between Labor and Capital*, ed. Pat Walker (Boston: South End Press, 1979), 12.

69. For an analysis of the promise and perils of this style, see Lee Konstantinou, "Periodizing the Present," *Contemporary Literature* 54, no. 2 (2013): 411–423.

70. I have in mind the proliferation of semiacademic publications such as *n+1*, *The New Inquiry*, *The Point*, the *Los Angeles Review of Books*, and the Post45 group's non-peer-reviewed journal, *Contemporaries*. The grim truth might be

that no sooner will the creative writer of fiction acquire her fiction-writing doctorate, thinking it will offer her a ticket into the PMC, than she will find herself, with the rest of the professoriat, thrown back into the contingency of (usually unpaid) freelance work and the temporary contract.

71. William Gibson, *Pattern Recognition* (New York: Berkeley Books, 2003), 97. Subsequent references will be cited parenthetically.

72. James Surowiecki, "The Decline of Brands," *Wired*, November 2004, 205.

73. The December 5, 2004, issue of the *New York Times Magazine* features an article on what William Gibson calls "guerilla marketing" in *Pattern Recognition*. In "The Hidden (in Plain Sight) Persuaders," an article about guerilla marketing, Rob Walker calls *Pattern Recognition* a "paranoid science-fiction novel about a future in which corporations have become so powerful they can bribe flunkies to infiltrate your life and talk up products," completely missing that the novel takes place in 2002 (130). I will have more to say on *Pattern Recognition* as SF later in this chapter.

74. Surowiecki, "The Decline of Brands," 206, 209.

75. Lauren Berlant, *Cruel Optimism* (Durham, NC: Duke University Press, 2011), 63–69.

76. Fredric Jameson, *Archaeologies of the Future*, 386.

77. Parkaboy's description of how he and Musashi transformed Judy into "Keiko" using Photoshop indirectly elaborates on this understanding of Cayce's cool-module:

> What we did was up the wattage for Taki, aiming to maximize libidinal disturbance, we shot this long tall Judy then reduced her by at least a third, in Photoshop. Cut'n'pasted her into Musashi's kid sister's dorm room at Cal. Darryl did the costuming himself, and then we decided to try enlarging her eyes a few clicks. That made all the difference. Judy's epicanthic folds are long gone, the way of the modest bust nature intended for her . . . and the resulting big round eyes are pure Anime Magic. This is the girl Taki's been looking for all his life, even though nature's never made one, and he'll know that as soon as he lays eyes on this image (129).

Sexual fetishes like Taki's, which Cayce can recognize across cultures and sexual orientations, are part of the mind's "culture module," whose parameters get set in the particular cultural environment one happens to grow up in. Those who understand the "salient parameters" that "maximize libidinal disturbance" can subsequently manipulate a "native speaker" of this particular culture. Parkaboy's version of pattern recognition is only incidentally a collective activity—we learn English rather than French as a result of where we grow up, but any notion of "public meanings" is basically incoherent under this model. Like Nora, Parkaboy and Musashi cut and paste the raw information of Judy's body and create Keiko from it, mixing it into a new constructed persona, but this mixture's success depends crucially on Taki's biologically grounded (though culturally specific) sexual fetishes.

78. It also might explain why Gibson's characters all seem so stereotyped. Japanese characters, at least those from Japan, behave like obsessive otaku types.

Cayce's therapist attributes her sensitivity to relations among the English, compared in stereotypical terms to equally stereotyped gun-toting Americans, to the fact that "it was such a highly codified behavior, as were all the areas of human activity around which Cayce suffered such remarkable sensitivity" (248).

79. At one point in the novel, Cayce sees herself in the mirror as "a black-legged, disjointed puppet," not unlike Dorotea's "puppet-head" and the "decidedly female crash-test dummies" that populate her friend Damien's apartment, an invocation of Pynchon's dummies in *V.* (*PR* 3, 5). For Pynchon's "Frankenstein's-monsterlike" SHROUD ("synthetic human, radiation output determined") and SHOCK (synthetic human object, casualty kinematics"), see *V.* 302, 303.

80. Marshall McLuhan and Quentin Fiore, *The Medium Is the Massage* (New York: Random House, 1967), 63, emphasis mine.

81. See Alvin Toffler, *Future Shock* (New York: Bantam, 1984). Toffler wrote in 1970 that "[t]oday the network of social ties is so tightly woven that the consequences of contemporary events radiate instantaneously around the world" (15).

82. Niklas Luhmann, *Observations on Modernity*, trans. William Whobrey (Stanford: Stanford University Press, 1998), 70–71.

83. For more on the concept of "total flow," see the "Video" chapter of Jameson's *Postmodernism*, esp. 76–78.

84. John Clute, "The Case of the World," *SCI FI Weekly*, February 24, 2003, http://www.scifi.com/sfw/issue305/excess.html (no longer available at this address).

85. Jameson, *Archaeologies of the Future*, 384.

86. Jaak Tomberg, "On the 'Double Vision' of Realism and SF Estrangement in William Gibson's *BIGEND TRILOGY*," *Science Fiction Studies* 40, no. 2 (2013), 263.

87. Jameson, *Archaeologies of the Future*, 384.

88. Ibid., 387, 388.

89. Ibid., 385.

90. William Gibson, "God's Little Toys," *Wired*, July 2005, http://www.wired.com/wired/archive/13.07/Gibson.html.

91. Pynchon, *The Crying of Lot 49*, 94–95.

92. Ibid., 96.

93. Fredric Jameson, "Totality as Conspiracy," in *The Geopolitical Aesthetic: Cinema and Space in the World System* (Bloomington: Indiana University Press, 1995), 10.

94. Compare this to Gibson's earlier description of cyberspace ("bright lattices of logic unfolding across that colorless void" [5]) in *Neuromancer*: "A graphic representation of data abstracted from the banks of every computer in the human system. Unthinkable complexity. Lines of light ranged in the nonspace of the mind, clusters and constellations of data. Like city lights, receding" (51). Also: "Program a map to display frequency of data exchange, every thousand megabytes a single pixel on a very large screen. Manhattan and Atlanta burn solid white. Then they start to pulse, the rate of traffic threatening to overload your simulation. Your map is about to go nova. Cool it down. Up your

scale. Each pixel a million megabytes. At a hundred million megabytes per second, you begin to make out certain blocks in midtown Manhattan, outlines of hundred-year-old industrial parks ringing the old core of Atlanta" (43). Finally, compare Cayce's sensitivity to the semiotics of the marketplace with Colin Laney's unusual ability to see "nodal points in history" in *All Tomorrow's Parties* (New York: Berkeley, 2003), 5. These descriptions can be understood in terms of Jameson's version of the "technological sublime" or as allegories in which new technologies are figures for an expanding multinational "space," the space of globalization. This is all largely in accord with Gibson's own professed sense that SF is always about the present. But what changes when Gibson turns to the present itself, stripping himself of many (although not all) of the figural potentials of SF?

95. That the brand might itself be thought of as a real commodity (rather than a mere advertisement for a commodity) should not, I hope, be controversial. Marx writes, "The commodity is, first of all, an external object, a thing which through its qualities satisfies human needs *of whatever kind.* The nature of these needs, whether they arise, for example, from the stomach, *or the imagination,* makes no difference." Karl Marx, *Capital: A Critique of Political Economy,* Volume 1, Intro. Ernest Mandel, Trans. Ben Fowkes (New York: Penguin, 1982), 125, my emphasis.

96. Bruce Robbins, "The Sweatshop Sublime," in *The Public Intellectual,* ed. Helen Small (Oxford: Blackwell, 2002), 179.

97. Ibid., 181.

98. Ibid., 187.

99. Jameson, *Postmodernism,* 314.

100. Ibid., 315.

101. Robbins, "The Sweatshop Sublime," 197.

102. Benjamin Kunkel, *Indecision* (New York: Random House, 2006), 216.

103. Ibid., 216.

104. See John Tomlinson, *Globalization and Culture* (Chicago: University of Chicago Press, 1999).

105. Of course, there's nothing intrinsically wrong with graduate school or humanistic education—and much to recommend it—but the undergraduate advised in this way might make something politically very different of her education than her recommender would imagine or prefer. Joshua Landy makes a similar point in his criticism of Martha Nussbaum's ethical understanding of the work literature does (or ought to do). See Landy, *How to Do Things with Fiction,* 33–34.

106. See Mary Jo Hatch and James Rubin, "The Hermeneutics of Branding," *Journal of Brand Management* 14, no. 1/2 (2006): 40–59.

107. Douglas Atkin, *The Culting of Brands: When Customers Become True Believers* (New York: Penguin Group, 2004), xiii. See also Matthew W. Ragas and B. J. Bueno, *The Power of Cult Branding* (Roseville, CA: Prima Publishing, 2002); Patrick Hanlon, *Primalbranding: Create Zealots for Your Brand, Your Company, and Your Future* (New York: Free Press, 2006).

108. Atkin, *The Culting of Brands,* xiii.

109. On the decline of civil society, see Robert D. Putnam, *Bowling Alone: The Collapse and Revival of American Community* (New York: Simon & Schuster, 2001).

110. Ronnie Ballantyne, Anne Warren, and Karinna Nobbs, "The Evolution of Brand Choice," *Journal of Brand Management* 13, no. 4–5 (2006): 339. See also Douglas G. Holt, *How Brands Become Icons* (Cambridge, MA: Harvard Business School Press, 2004). Holt supplements the common claim that "[l]oyalty is produced by the customer's relationship with the brand" with his assertion that "iconic brands" must symbolically resolve "acute contradictions in society" and that "[c]ustomers of iconic brands are loyal because they're locked into a social network . . . [t]o decommission an iconic brand is a collective decision" (150).

111. Gibson did not read *No Logo*, but was inspired by its title. Mark Flanagan, "William Gibson Interview," About.com Contemporary Literature, January 2003, http://contemporarylit.about.com/cs/authorinterviews/a/gibsonInterview _2.htm.

112. Robbins, "The Sweatshop Sublime," 193.

113. Timothy Bewes, *Reification*, 259.

114. Klein, *No Logo*, 21. Klein writes that "[t]he old paradigm had it that all marketing was selling a product. In the new model, however, the product always takes a back seat to the real product, the brand, and the selling of the brand acquired an extra component that can only be described as spiritual" (21).

115. This is also a point made by the libertarian author Virginia Postrel, *The Substance of Style: How Aesthetic Value Is Remaking Commerce, Culture, and Consciousness* (New York: Perennial, 2004), 45. I would emphasize, however, that the brand as commodity is not substantively different from other commodities. Its main difference resides in its use value.

116. Brands and trademarks have a long and complicated history, which I will not deal with at length in this space. For my purposes, it suffices to say that modern branding has had three major paradigms: first as a means of physically marking one's property; next as a way of guaranteeing the quality and authenticity of one's products; and finally as a form of intellectual property and an asset in its own right. "Branding" emerged in the early nineteenth century as a means of tracking cattle. (As Alex Frankel points out in *Wordcraft: The Art of Turning Little Words into Big Business* [New York: Three Rivers Press, 2004], the term "maverick" was used initially to denote the practice of Texas cattleman Samuel Maverick, who let his herd roam "unbranded.") In the consumer goods market, a brand was meant (perhaps surprisingly, from a contemporary perspective) to be a mark of authenticity, a guarantee of product quality and reliability. As production costs decreased during the 1990s, the brand in and of itself became a valuable asset. The academic marketing literature agrees that brands have become more or less "liberated" from the products whose authenticity they were once assumed to confer, which is not the same as saying in any simple-minded way that production no longer matters.

117. Klein writes, "It must be said that no one is more surprised by the power and appeal of brand-based activism than those who have spearheaded the campaigns. Many of the people leading the anti-sweatshop movement are longtime advocates on behalf of the Third World's poor and marginalized" (348).

118. Ibid., 134.

119. Maktoba Omar and Robert L. Williams Jr., "Managing and Maintaining Corporate Reputation and Brand Identity: Haier Group Logo," *Journal of Brand Management* 13, no. 4–5 (2006): 268.

120. Jameson, *Postmodernism*, 54.

121. Ibid.

122. For a fascinating discussion of what it might mean to think of capitalist logistics (and the global system of capitalist circulation) as susceptible to cognitive mapping and a discussion of Richard Sennett's "reconfiguration thesis," see Jasper Bernes, "Logistics, Counterlogistics, and the Communist Prospect," *Endnotes* 3 (2013), http://endnotes.org.uk/en/jasper-bernes-logistics-counterlogistics-and-the-communist-prospect.

123. The point of building brand-based cognitive mapping is not to create newer, better brands or to "uncool" existing brands, as if the core problem with capitalism were deceptive marketing or advertising, but rather to come to understand the brand as a real part of a global network of production, circulation, and consumption. On "subvertising," see Kalle Lasn, *Culture Jam: How to Reverse America's Suicidal Consumer Binge—and Why We Must* (New York: William Morrow, 2000).

124. See Patrick Jagoda, "Wired," *Critical Inquiry* 38, no. 1 (2011): 189–199; Jagoda, "Terror Networks and the Aesthetics of Interconnection," *Social Text* 28, no. 4 (2010): 65–89; Sianne Ngai, "Network Aesthetics: Julianna Spahr's *The Transformation* and Bruno Latour's *Reassembling the Social*," in *American Literature's Aesthetic Dimensions*, ed. Cindy Weinstein and Christopher Looby (New York: Columbia University Press, 2012), 367–392.

125. Michael Szalay, "The Incorporation Artist." Szalay, "Writer as Producer, or the Hip Figure after HBO," in *Mad Men, Mad World: Sex, Politics, Style and the 1960s*, ed. Lauren M. E. Goodlad, Lilya Kaganovsky, and Robert A. Rushing (Durham, NC: Duke University Press, 2013), 111–129.

126. John B. Thompson, *Merchants of Culture: The Publishing Business in the Twenty-First Century* (New York: Plume, 2012).

127. Szalay, "The Incorporation Artist."

128. Frederick Seidel, "'This Book Has Heat,'" *New York Review of Books*, July 11, 2013, http://www.nybooks.com/articles/archives/2013/jul/11/Rachel-kushner-book-has-heat/.

129. Bewes, *Reification*, xi.

130. Nealon, *Post-Postmodernism*, 50.

131. Ibid., 53.

132. Jennifer Egan, *A Visit from the Goon Squad* (New York: Anchor Books, 2011), 253. Subsequent references will be cited parenthetically.

133. Edward R. Tufte, *The Cognitive Style of PowerPoint: Pitching Out Corrupts Within*, Second Edition (Cheshire, CT: Graphics Press, 2006), 4.

134. Ibid.

135. One also wonders how Egan would write about orange sellers and appliance repairmen rather than punk CEOs.

136. Stephen Brown, "The Savage Girl," *Journal of the Academy of Marketing Science* 31, no. 1 (2003): 91.

137. Stephen Brown, "I can read you like a book! Novel thoughts on con-

sumer behavior," *Qualitative Market Research: An International Journal* 8, no. 2 (2005): 233.

138. William Gibson, "Buzz in Black," *William Gibson—Official Website*, December 31, 2005, http://www.williamgibsonbooks.com/blog/2005_12_01 _archive.asp.

139. Tom Peters, *The Brand You 50: Fifty Ways to Transform Yourself from an 'Employee' into a Brand That Shouts Distinction, Commitment, and Passion!* (New York: Knopf, 1999).

Conclusion

1. "About," *OccupyWallStreet*, http://occupywallst.org/about/.

2. "The Ballerina and the Bull" is an interesting image in its own right. The black-and-white image features a ballerina posed in arabesque atop *Charging Bull*. A cloud of tear gas envelopes the street behind the dancer, and gas-mask-clad protesters, who may be meant to represent black bloc anarchists, are rushing toward the camera. At the top of the poster, in red letters, is written the question, "What is our one demand?" Below, we find text reading, "#OccupyWallStreet. September 17th. Bring tent." The image notably figures the revolutionary subject, the figure of the occupier, as an artist. The white female ballerina's revolutionary creativity, we are meant to understand, thwarts the aggressive (presumably non-creative) world of Wall Street. On the one hand, her revolutionary creative performance seems to inspire the masked protesters behind her to continue fighting. In this sense, she resembles William S. Burroughs's wild boys: she is a media figure that is designed to inspire spontaneous revolutionary action. On the other hand, her guerrilla dance performance comes to seem like a weapon (and an end) in itself. Her goal is not to achieve objective silence, as it was for Burroughs, but expressive subjectivity. That is, in this poster the "one demand" of Wall Street's hashtag-armed occupiers seems to be nothing other than the demand to be allowed to be creative artists or, at the very least, free subjects modeled on the artist. Borrowing terms from Scott Cutler Shershow's critique of Autonomist Marxism, we might say that the ballerina "affirms and celebrates a Subject defined by its productivity and *constituted in and as a Work*" (she is a subject constituted in and as her art). Scott Cutler Shershow, *The Work and the Gift* (Chicago: University of Chicago Press, 2005), 76. Alternately, we might note the ahistorical character of this artist figure. In *Literature and the Creative Economy*, Sarah Brouillette discusses similarities between Autonomist theory and Richard Florida's analysis of the creative class. Contemporary Autonomists, she charges, have transformed workerism's theoretical insights into "a transhistorical framework that understands all work to be resistance to itself and, ideally, overcoming of itself." Brouillette, *Literature and the Creative Economy*, 47. At a post-Fordist moment, when affect has been increasingly integrated into the labor process, when capital has attempted to use information technologies to disempower workers, contemporary Autonomist Marxists nonetheless declare that "liberation from capitalism is actually more possible than ever before," putting their faith in the revolutionary redevelopment of communications technology (48). Versions of this view can be detected

in *Adbusters'* celebration of "meme warfare." Kalle Lasn has declared that "[w]hoever has the memes has the power" and that the next world war will be, as Marshall McLuhan once put it, a "guerilla war of information" Lasn, *Culture Jam*, 123. We might regard "The Ballerina and the Bull" as expressing something like a pop-Autonomism and therefore interpret the subsequent fight to control the meaning of the image as symptomatic of the failure of the theory of power that the image itself encodes. One need not dismiss the importance of political propaganda or reject the political desirability of some sort of expressive subjectivity to suspect that seizing and retaining power might require more than a good meme.

Yet I do not wish to criticize the figuration of the occupier in "The Ballerina and the Bull." Rather, I want to note what the ballerina herself overlooks: that *Charging Bull* is itself a work of "guerilla art." The sculpture was the work of the Italian-American artist Arturo Di Modica, who moved from Italy to SoHo in 1973. After Black Monday in 1987, Modica spend $360,000 to construct the 3½ ton sculpture in order to affirm the "strength and power of the American people." In December of 1989, he illegally placed the huge bronze sculpture in front of the New York Stock Exchange on Broad Street. When police were forced to take away the traffic obstruction, some Wall Street workers were understandably disappointed. One analyst with Goldman Sachs complained: "It's a tragedy that artists aren't allowed to express themselves in the spirit of Christmas and friendship." Robert D. McFadden, "SoHo Gift to Wall St.: A 3½-Ton Bronze Bull," *New York Times*, December 16, 1989, http://www.nytimes.com/1989/12/16/nyregion/soho-gift-to-wall-st-a-3-1-2-ton-bronze-bull.html. Police ultimately relocated the statue to Bowling Green Park, where it has become a big hit with tourists. Our temptation will be to conclude, as Rob Horning does in his astute analysis of the contradictions that Occupy Wall Street faced, that because "consumerist capitalism hijacks our will to be autonomous" we should therefore "usher the personal brand off the stage and supplant it with . . . a collective, civic subjectivity." Rob Horning, "Hipsterizing #OWS," *Jacobin*, no. 5 (2011): 42, 43. But the story of *Charging Bull* might lead us to conclude something different. The problem is not that we need to cultivate civic-minded public subjectivity apart from private consumerist individualism nor even that the bull has hijacked the ballerina's will to be autonomous. What matters isn't whether you have the will to be autonomous but whether you have the power to be autonomous. The artist who made *Charging Bull* enjoys such autonomy. As a figure for the 99%, the ballerina does not. If what the ballerina wants is autonomy, she will have to win it through political struggle, but her considerable talents *as* a ballerina will not necessarily be of much help in the fight.

3. This Twitter conflict has been reconstructed at *Adbusters* magazine, "Merchandising #occupy?" accessed May 4, 2014, https://storify.com/adbusters/stop-selling-occupy.

4. OWStreetnet, "Occupy Irony," OccupyWallStreet.net, http://occupywallstreet.net/story/occupy-irony.

5. "Statement of Autonomy," *#Occupy Wall Street NYC General Assembly*, http://www.nycga.net/resources/documents/statement-of-autonomy/.

6. OWStreetnet, "Occupy Irony."

7. *Adbusters* charges reprint fees for "original *Adbusters*' designs," but the fight over "The Ballerina and the Bull" did not invoke intellectual property questions. "Adbusters Reprints FAQ," *Adbusters*, https://www.adbusters.org /about/reprints (accessed August, 16, 2015).

8. Jodi Dean, "Occupy Wall Street: After the Anarchist Movement," *Socialist Register* 49 (2013): 56.

9. Mark Bray, *Translating Anarchy: The Anarchism of Occupy Wall Street* (Winchester, UK: Zero Books, 2013), 155.

10. Ibid., 158.

11. On the development of these principles, see David Graeber, *Direct Action: An Ethnography* (Oakland, CA: AK Press, 2009). Luis A. Fernandez, *Policing Dissent: Social Control and the Anti-globalization Movement* (New Brunswick, NJ: Rutgers University Press, 2008). Bray notes that, among those he interviewed, "72% of OWS organizers had explicitly anarchist or implicitly anarchistic politics." Bray, *Translating Anarchy*, 4. The validity of this claim is an open question, but even critics of Occupy, such as Dean, tend to associate the movement with the governing structures of the general assembly, spokescouncils, and working groups.

12. For overviews of Occupy's institutional form, see Bray, *Translating Anarchy*. See also James Miller, "Is Democracy Still in the Streets?" in *The Occupy Handbook*, ed. Janet Byrne (New York: Back Bay Books, 2012), 173–183.

13. The Occupy Wall Street library is cataloged at LibraryThing, http:// www.librarything.com/catalog/OWSLibrary.

14. Dean, "Occupy Wall Street," 59, my emphasis. Dean argues against some of the anarchist assumptions governing Occupy, but is hopeful that the collective sense of self-understanding Occupy awakened might lead to the formation of "a new communist party" (61). Given the anarchist political lineage of Occupy, I do not see how those who participated in the Occupy movement would find this proposal appealing.

15. Ibid., 53.

16. Linton Weeks, "The Hipsterfication of America," *NPR*, November 17, 2011, http://www.npr.org/2011/11/16/142387490/the-hipsterfication-of-america.

17. There are a handful of journalistic defenses of the contemporary hipster, though many of these are more opportunistic than serious. See Luke O'Neil, "It's Hip to Be Hip, Too," *Slate*, September 23, 2013, http://www.slate. com/articles/life/culturebox/2013/09/proud_of_being_a_hipster_one _bearded_indie_rock_loving_contrarian_article.html.

18. Mark Greif, "What Was the Hipster?" *New York Magazine*, October 24, 2010, http://nymag.com/news/features/69129/#.

19. Ibid.

20. Ibid.

21. Christian Lorentzen, "Why the Hipster Must Die," *Time Out New York*, May 30, 2007, http://www.timeout.com/newyork/things-to-do/why-the-hipster-must-die.

22. Douglas Haddow, "Hipsters: The Dead End of Western Civilization," *Adbusters*, July 29, 2008, https://www.adbusters.org/magazine/79/hipster.html.

23. Ibid.

24. Christie Wampole, "How to Live without Irony."

25. Alexandra Petri, "The Irony of Occupy Wall Street," *ComPost*, October 13, 2011, http://www.washingtonpost.com/blogs/compost/post/the-irony-of-occupy-wall-street/2011/10/12/gIQAhafdhL_blog.html.

26. Michael Taussig, "I'm So Angry I Made a Sign," in W. J. T. Mitchell, Bernard E. Harcourt, and Michael Taussig, *Occupy: Three Inquiries in Disobedience* (Chicago: University of Chicago Press, 2013), 11.

27. Horning, "Hipsterizing #OWS," 39.

28. Ibid.

29. Hayden White, "Auerbach's Literary History," in *Figural Realism: Studies in the Mimesis Effect* (Baltimore, MD: Johns Hopkins University Press, 2000), 91.

30. Bray claims that prefiguration partly derives from the German Autonomen's definition of "autonomy" as a demand to "practice different forms of life in the here and now." Bray, *Translating Anarchy*, 235. Bray cites Geronimo, *Fire and Flames: A History of the German Autonomist Movement* (Oakland, CA: PM Press, 2012), 103.

31. Rachel Kushner, *The Flamethrowers* (New York: Scribner, 2014), 8. Subsequent references will be cited parenthetically.

32. James Wood writes that *The Flamethrowers* is "nominally a historical novel (it's set in the mid-seventies), and, I suppose, also a realist one (it works within the traditional grammar of verisimilitude). But it manifests itself as a pure explosion of now." James Wood, "Youth in Revolt," *New Yorker*, April 8, 2013, http://www.newyorker.com/magazine/2013/04/08/youth-in-revolt. For a criticism of Wood's interpretation of the book, see Rachel Greenwald Smith, "Six Propositions on Compromise Aesthetics," *The Account*, no. 3 (2014), http://theaccountmagazine.com/?article=six-propositions-on-compromise-aesthetics.

33. I take "historical peculiarity" from Georg Lukács, *The Historical Novel* (Lincoln: University of Nebraska Press, 1983), 19. The phrase "forgotten how to think historically" is, of course, from Jameson, *Postmodernism*, 3.

34. Amy Elias, *Sublime Desire: History and Post-1960s Fiction* (Baltimore, MD: Johns Hopkins University Press, 2001), xvii, 187.

35. I would not categorize Elias's description of the "posthistorical romance" as postironic because those who write in this mode view history as, finally, irrecoverable. The desire to move beyond irony is necessary but not sufficient to be postironic—one must also deploy artistic forms that make the attempt with some hope of success.

36. Rachel Kushner, "Curated," *Paris Review*, no. 203 (2012), http://www.theparisreview.org/art-photography/6197/curated-by-rachel-kushner-the-flamethrowers. Subsequent references Ibid.

37. Lucio Castellano et al., "Do You Remember Revolution?" in *Radical Thought in Italy: A Potential Politics*, ed. Paolo Virno and Michael Hardt (Minneapolis: University of Minnesota Press, 2006), 226.

38. Nathan C. Martin, Interview with Rachel Kushner, *New Orleans Review*, http://www.neworleansreview.org/Rachel-kushner-im-not-sure-there-is-a-clear-distinction-between-to-communicate-and-to-monologue/.

39. Sasha Frere-Jones, "I Am a Camera: An Interview with Rachel Kushner,"

New Yorker, June 11, 2013, http://www.newyorker.com/online/blogs/books/2013/06/i-am-a-camera-an-interview-with-rachel-kushner.html.

40. Michael Hardt and Antonio Negri, *Multitude: War and Democracy in the Age of Empire* (New York: Penguin, 2005), xvii.

41. Ibid., 83.

42. Ibid., xiii–xiv.

43. Ibid., xviii.

44. Jonathan Lethem, *Dissident Gardens* (New York: Vintage, 2014), 38. Subsequent references will be cited parenthetically.

45. For a further discussion of this scene, see Lee Konstantinou, "Outborough Destiny," *Los Angeles Review of Books*, September 8, 2013, http://lareviewofbooks.org/review/outborough-destiny-jonathan-lethems-dissident-gardens.

46. Nathan Rabin, "The Bataan Death March of Whimsy Case File #1: Elizabethtown," *A.V. Club*, January 25, 2007, http://www.avclub.com/article/the-bataan-death-march-of-whimsy-case-file-1-emeli-15577.

47. William Gibson, *All Tomorrow's Parties* (New York: Berkeley, 2003), 210. My guess is that Gibson derived this idea from Jerrold Seigel, *Bohemian Paris: Culture, Politics, and the Boundaries of Bourgeois Life, 1830-1930* (Baltimore: Johns Hopkins University Press, 1999). Seigel writes, "Bohemia grew up where the borders of bourgeois existence were murky and uncertain," and it "probed and tested" the frontiers of the bourgeois world (11).

Acknowledgments

COOL CHARACTERS BEGAN LIFE at Stanford University. It started to become something like a book while I was an ACLS New Faculty Fellow in the English Department at Princeton. And I completed it as an Assistant Professor in the English Department at the University of Maryland, College Park. I can only thinly sketch the intellectual debts I've accumulated along the way. At Stanford, Ramón Saldívar, Ursula Heise, and Sianne Ngai supported my project at every stage in its long development, each providing a powerful characterological model of what the literary critic should aspire to be. Phil Ford, meanwhile, played a pivotal role in helping me formulate my prospectus, introducing me to the endless wonders of midcentury hip culture. Andrea Lunsford, Gavin Jones, Nicholas Jenkins, Joshua Landy, Jenna Lay, Jolene Hubbs, Mark Vega, Claire Bowen, Michael Benveniste, Joel Burges, Heather Houser, Harris Feinsod, Ed Finn, Parween Ebrahim, and Ema Vyroubalova offered me intellectual support and friendship. At Princeton, I am grateful to Bill Gleason, Anne Cheng, Diana Fuss, Sarah Rivett, and Joshua Kotin for their warm conversation. At UMD, Linda Kauffman, Peter Mallios, Edlie Wong, Scott Trudell, Matt Kirschenbaum, Brian Richardson, Sharada Balachandran Orihuela, Christina Walter, Martha Nell Smith, Orrin Wang, Michael Israel, Scott Wible, Kent Cartwright, and Bill Cohen saw this project to completion. Along the way, I have also received support from Tore Rye Andersen, Paul Bové, Matt Bucher, Samuel Cohen, Natalia Cecire, Michael Clune, Amy Elias, Andrew Goldstone, Andrew Hoberek, Linda Hutcheon, Adam Kelly, Mark McGurl, Bruce Robbins, Michael Szalay, Steven Shaviro, Leif Sorensen, Christian Thorne, Sarah Brouillette, Min Hyoung Song,

361

Patricia Stuelke, Joseph Jeon, Matt Tierney, Angela S. Allan, Sean Grattan, and Rachel Greenwald Smith. My brilliant Facebook and Twitter networks have become so extensive that it is impossible to individually thank everyone who deserves my gratitude. If anyone ever commented on one of my cryptic status updates, thank you. I benefited greatly from research trips to the Harry Ransom Center, the Berg Collection of English and American Literature at the New York Public Library, the David M. Rubenstein Rare Book and Manuscript Library at Duke, and the Library of Congress. At Harvard University Press, Lindsay Waters and Amanda Peery improved this book, which builds upon and expands ideas first explored in "The Brand as Cognitive Map in William Gibson's *Pattern Recognition*" in 2009 in *boundary 2* and "No Bull: David Foster Wallace and Postironic Belief" in *The Legacy of David Foster Wallace*, which I co-edited with Samuel Cohen and is published by the University of Iowa Press. My parents and sister have been unwaveringly caring during my long journey through academia. And Julie Prieto, meanwhile, has been a companion whose rich sense of irony deserves to be the subject of its own study. This book is dedicated to her.

Index

363